STATE RESPONSIBILITY FOR NON-STATE ACTORS

This book investigates how state responsibility can be determined for the wrongdoing of non-state actors. Every day, people, businesses and societies around the world pay a price arising from interactions between states and non-state actors. From insurrections that attempt to create new governments, to states arming belligerent proxies operating overseas, to companies damaging natural environments or providing suspect services, the impact of such situations are felt in numerous ways. They also raise many questions relating to responsibility. In answering these, *State Responsibility for Non-State Actors* provides a picture of what the law governing this area is, what it could be, and what it should be in light of past histories, present realities and future prospects.

Volume 87 in the series Studies in International Law

Studies in International Law

Recent titles in this series

The Responsibility to Protect and the Failures of the United Nations Security Council
P M Butchard

The Role of Multilateral Environmental Agreements: A Reconciliatory Approach to Environmental Protection in Armed Conflict
Britta Sjostedt

Prosecutorial Discretion at the International Criminal Court
Anni Pues

Judicial Deference in International Adjudication: A Comparative Analysis
Johannes Hendrik Fahner

Human Rights Commitments of Islamic States: Sharia, Treaties and Consensus
Paul McDonough

Intervention in Civil Wars: Effectiveness, Legitimacy, and Human Rights
Chiara Redaelli

General Principles as a Source of International Law: Art 38(1)(c) of the Statute of the International Court of Justice
Imogen Saunders

The Law of Humanity Project: A Story of International Law Reform and State-making
Ukri Soirila

Extraterritoriality and Climate Change Jurisdiction: Exploring EU Climate Protection under International Law
Natalie L Dobson

International Law and the War with Islamic State: Challenges for Jus ad Bellum and Jus in Bello
Saeed Bagheri

Private Actors as Participants in International Law: A Critical Analysis of Membership under the Law of the Sea
Armando Rocha

Truth and Transitional Justice: Localising the International Legal Framework in Muslim Majority Legal Systems
Alice Panepinto

For a complete list of titles in this series
see www.bloomsbury.com/uk/series/studies-in-international-law/

State Responsibility for Non-State Actors

Past, Present and Prospects for the Future

Richard Mackenzie-Gray Scott

•HART•
OXFORD • LONDON • NEW YORK • NEW DELHI • SYDNEY

HART PUBLISHING

Bloomsbury Publishing Plc

Kemp House, Chawley Park, Cumnor Hill, Oxford, OX2 9PH, UK

1385 Broadway, New York, NY 10018, USA

29 Earlsfort Terrace, Dublin 2, Ireland

HART PUBLISHING, the Hart/Stag logo, BLOOMSBURY and the Diana logo are trademarks of Bloomsbury Publishing Plc

First published in Great Britain 2022

A catalogue record for this book is available from the British Library.

A catalogue record for this book is available from the Library of Congress.

Library of Congress Control Number: 2022936765

ISBN: HB: 978-1-50995-154-3
ePDF: 978-1-50995-156-7
ePub: 978-1-50995-155-0

Typeset by Compuscript Ltd, Shannon

Foreword

THE RESPONSIBILITY OF states for internationally wrongful acts is one of the cornerstones of international law. It is foundational for the international legal order. Together with the sources of international law, it is one of those areas that every international lawyer must know, be they an academic or practitioner, a generalist or a specialist.

In the years since it was adopted, the International Law Commission's Articles on the Responsibility of States for Internationally Wrongful Acts has come to dominate the field. It is widely referenced and is even the subject of compilations of international decisions that refer to it. It is the starting point for any consideration of state responsibility and, for some, also the end point. It has been the model for other important statements.

Various aspects of the Articles have been interrogated. This has not been limited to questions of substance but extends to matters of form and influence. Whether to convene a diplomatic conference to consider a convention on state responsibility, based on the Articles, is a recurring question. Yet, despite the influence and authority of the Articles, questions and gaps remain.

In this timely and measured work, Dr Richard Mackenzie-Gray Scott considers the specific issue of state responsibility for the wrongdoings of non-state actors. With detailed analysis of the work of the successive ILC special rapporteurs, the debates at the ILC and the UN General Assembly Sixth Committee, as well as the jurisprudence of international courts and tribunals, it contains a close reading of the ILC articles on attribution. The work is at once rigorous and insightful.

More than simply an analysis of the tests for attribution in the law of state responsibility, Dr Mackenzie-Gray Scott takes a step back and considers the impact of globalization, neoliberalism, and shifting power balances on the state responsibility framework. In doing so, he identifies certain 'responsibility gaps' insofar as state responsibility for the wrongdoings of non-state actors are concerned. He invites us to consider whether the Articles are a product of its time and what the future for state responsibility for the wrongdoing of non-state actors might look like.

The work contains much food for thought for the academic and practitioner alike. The concrete proposals for the future warrant particularly careful reading.

Sandesh Sivakumaran
Cambridge, March 2022

Acknowledgements

I am grateful for all those who have helped me to write this book. Most of the research that underpins it was completed under the supervision of Sandesh Sivakumaran. Sandy began to guide me at a time when I was starting to find my feet as someone who likes doing research. He encouraged me to read widely, challenged me to improve how I convey findings, whilst always giving me the space to fully explain my ideas and the time to realise their strengths and weaknesses. Our discussions taught me so much and I feel immensely fortunate for his continued support. I also owe many thanks to Monica Hakimi for her constructive feedback on my work and providing words of encouragement every time we communicate. The same goes for Nigel White, even when we argue over the best place to get a chippy. I also wish to thank the examiners who were called upon to assess my grasp of the overall subject contained in these pages. Dapo Akande and Marko Milanovic provided what I recall to be a challenging and forgiving experience, one filled with helpful insights and a backing to 'Go full Scottish' afterwards on the bottle of impending fun. The publishing team at Bloomsbury also made the writing process enjoyable, and I thank them all. My colleagues, family and friends were also instrumental in maintaining my motivation while I wrote, and I am indebted in particular to Daniele Nunes, Ronan Cormacain and Sara Razai for reviewing parts of the manuscript. Lastly, to Maya and Mash, for being a constant reminder of how much more I still have to learn from other animals in addition to humans. The pair of you epitomise all that is good.

RMGS
Oxford, April 2022

Table of Contents

Table of Cases

Introduction

INTERNATIONAL LAW IS a funny field. Not funny so much in the sense of rib-tickling amusement, but more in the sense that by engaging with its content it can become a struggle to make any sense of it. The subject generally understood as 'international law', or perhaps more accurately 'international' 'law', appears to favour a logic comfortable with contradiction. States are sovereign and equal, but they are also not.[1] International law is international and is law, except when it is neither.[2] International law can be a force for good, yet it contributes to the immiseration of societies and of those who do not overcome the birth lottery (no matter their efforts).[3] International law creates and enables conflict, in addition to helping settle such disputes and advance cooperation.[4] This field is also fixated with fiction.[5] As does it fetishise certain inventions, such as states. For whatever reasons, much attention focuses on these abstract human creations.[6] However, other actors, some of which are also the product of effective storytelling, influence much of the many matters with which international law is concerned.[7] This book makes an attempt to address a related topic that touches the very heart of the weird and sometimes wonderful world of the international legal order – state responsibility, in particular the questions that arise when actors other than states undertake conduct that is contrary to international law and with which states are somehow connected.

[1] N MacCormick, 'Sovereignty: Myth and Reality' (1995) 11 *Scottish Affairs* 1; H Kelsen, 'The Principle of Sovereign Equality of States as a Basis for International Organization' (1944) 53 *Yale Law Journal* 207.

[2] A Roberts, *Is International Law International?* (Oxford, Oxford University Press, 2017); KT Gaubatz and M MacArthur, 'How International Is "International" Law?' (2001) 22 *Michigan Journal of International Law* 239; A D'Amato, 'Is International Law Really "Law"?' (1985) 79 *Northwestern University Law Review* 1293.

[3] K Pistor, *The Code of Capital: How the Law Creates Wealth and Inequality* (Princeton, NJ, Princeton University Press, 2019); J Linarelli, ME Salomon and M Sornarajah, *The Misery of International Law: Confrontations with Injustice in the Global Economy* (Oxford, Oxford University Press, 2018); B Milanovic, *The Haves and the Have-Nots: A Brief and Idiosyncratic History of Global Inequality* (New York, Basic Books, 2011); T Pogge, 'Recognized and Violated by International Law: The Human Rights of the Global Poor' (2005) 19 *Leiden Journal of International Law* 717.

[4] M Hakimi, 'The Work of International Law' (2017) 58 *Harvard International Law Journal* 1; M Hakimi, 'Constructing an International Community' (2017) 111 *American Journal of International Law* 317.

[5] R Lewis, *Legal Fictions in International Law* (Cheltenham, Edward Elgar, 2021).

[6] But not all attention. See, for example, A van Aaken and T Broude, 'The Psychology of International Law: An Introduction' (2019) 30 *European Journal of International Law* 1225; T Broude, 'Behavioral International Law' (2015) 163 *Pennsylvania Law Review* 1099; A van Aaken, 'Behavioral International Law and Economics' (2014) 55 *Harvard International Law Journal* 421.

[7] I Bremmer, 'Big Tech Can See a Future Where the Nation State Is No Longer the Master' *The Times* (19 November 2021) www.thetimes.co.uk/article/big-tech-can-see-a-future-where-the-nation-state-is-no-longer-the-master-ndt7cqzxf.

Those who choose to engage with such questions of international responsibility are often confronted with two overarching themes. The first is the current regulatory focus of international law being largely aimed at states. The second is the interactions that occur between states and other actors, which have become so common to everyday life that they can go unnoticed. Yet the roles and impacts of these other actors across this world and beyond remain significant. When combined with the involvement of states, intricate problems are presented when conduct occurs that is wrongful. Individuals, communities, businesses and societies more generally suffer in such situations. Whether it is a hacker flush with fresh finances from a state wanting them to shutdown a power grid located elsewhere, a private military cohort continuing an age-old imperialist campaign, a government relying on the services of a technology company to track the location of people, or neglecting the regulation of another company that damages the natural environment, state responsibility is an ever-present consideration when states act in consort with, use, enable or allow non-state actors to undertake wrongful conduct. This book thus explores one main question: how can the international responsibility of a state be determined for the conduct of a non-state actor?

The further into the weeds research goes in engaging with this question the more questions are revealed, in particular those that centre on why the applicable legal framework is the way it is at present, and what are the consequences of this in various domains. Probing these questions demonstrates the challenges and opportunities to be found in applying the law of state responsibility to matters involving non-state actors. There is a wealth of work that can be brought to bear on these matters, which this book brings together. It provides an exposition of the bases for determining state responsibility for the conduct of non-state actors, the respective requirements of each base, their history, their value, their gibberish, all whilst offering insights into how the law in this area might develop. Through this investigation certain features of the international law applicable to determining state responsibility for non-state actors become clearer, including with respect to their application in practice. While the potential of the state responsibility framework is substantial in terms of addressing the problems put before it involving non-state actors, there is also room for improvement. But before delving into the details, it is first worth clarifying the methodology underpinning the subject matter contained in these pages and the structure that the book follows.

1. METHODOLOGY

The research in this book takes a predominantly doctrinal approach, which can also be described as expository or the examination of black-letter law.[8] In answering the principal research question through the initial use of a doctrinal methodology, further space opens up to adopt other methods in addressing issues ranging from whether

[8] T Hutchinson, 'The Doctrinal Method: Incorporating Interdisciplinary Methods in Reforming the Law' (2015) 3 *Erasmus Law Review* 130.

states are the actors that actually make international law, to what is the value behind a particular approach to determining the international responsibility of a state. While open to debate, there is sometimes no clear dividing line between doctrinal research methods and others, in which each one can be a component of the other.[9] That said, other research methods are present here, in particular comparative, contextual and theoretical, all of which help highlight the promise of developing the law in this area with respect to being in a better position to address the challenges it faces now and will likely face in the future.[10] A number of ideas are advanced that may better align the law of state responsibility with the current and likely future realities involving the interactions between states and non-state actors. These in part come about as a result of adopting the methodologies of analogy and extrapolation.[11] Both are used in lawmaking in order to supplement a particular body of law.[12] There is not so much an issue of whether the law can be developed in such ways, but 'rather, in what circumstances it is appropriate to do so'.[13] As this appropriateness rests on a number of grounds, the use of analogy and extrapolation is limited to where there are at least similarities present in terms of subject matter, context and applicable norms.[14] This doctrinal but no less mixed-methods approach may also be construed as 'reform-oriented'.[15] Research can be considered to fall within this category of methodological approaches if it challenges the boundaries of the law in a particular area.[16] The extent of the challenge towards the law of state responsibility in its engagement and lack thereof with non-state actors varies throughout the book, but remains a constant theme. There are also points in which arguments for change are presented. So too are reasons offered regarding why some changes are undesirable in addition to not being necessary at this time.

Although it can take a bit of bashing, and rightly so, a doctrinal methodology serves a number of purposes and has further benefits relevant within the context of this research. One is that such a method can provide coherence within an area where there exists incoherence.[17] With respect to the law applicable to determining the international responsibility of states for the conduct of non-state actors that is contrary to international rules, the extent of incoherence can be considerable, signalling the significance of doctrinal approaches to this subject. Employing this method

[9] Debating methodological choices and the significance of these choices is discussed in E Fisher, B Lange, E Scotford and C Carlarne, 'Maturity and Methodology: Starting a Debate about Environmental Law Scholarship' (2009) 21 *Journal of Environmental Law* 213.

[10] P Roberts, 'Interdisciplinarity in Legal Research' in M McConville and WH Chui (eds), *Research Methods for Law*, 2nd edn (Edinburgh, Edinburgh University Press, 2017) 90.

[11] See S Sivakumaran, 'Techniques in International Law-Making: Extrapolation, Analogy, Form and the Emergence of an International Law of Disaster Relief' (2017) 28 *European Journal of International Law* 1097.

[12] ibid 1117; see also 1116–1122.

[13] ibid 1118–1119.

[14] ibid 1131.

[15] T Hutchinson, 'Developing Legal Research Skills: Expanding the Paradigm' (2008) 32 *Melbourne University Law Review* 1065, 1068.

[16] ibid 1084.

[17] T Hutchinson, 'Doctrinal Research: Researching the Jury' in D Watkins and M Burton (eds), *Research Methods in Law* (Abingdon, Routledge, 2013) 7, 10.

also allows works to be used as a reference point for those involved in legal practice and policymaking. By offering guidance on how the rules in this area can and do apply, those presented with issues concerning state responsibility for the conduct of non-state actors can examine past precedents and key developments pertinent to the respective problems they are tasked with solving. Legal doctrine can also give the law 'precision, coherence, and a transparent structure',[18] in addition to offering a measure of stability in a world where many things are influenced by political dynamics that are sometimes everything but stable.[19] With law being separate from and an extension of politics, a key feature of coupling a doctrinal method with at least one other is that legal questions are answered by reference to the law and those answers are not automatically accepted merely because they correspond to what the law says. There is an added layer of importance to this in the context of the law relating to the international responsibility of states, because what the law is can be conflated with what the law is thought to be, or ought to be.

Sticking to doctrinal analysis alone has intrinsic limitations in terms of offering meaningful insights into the difficulties posed by the multifaceted relationships between states and non-state actors that lead to occurrences of wrongful conduct. But by examining the sources that make up the international law is this area, including the practice of states, state-empowered entities, non-state actors, the decisions of domestic, regional and international courts and tribunals, in addition to related commentary, richer and more nuanced understandings of the law are uncovered. Teasing out common themes, points of tension and key issues across these materials makes it possible to clarify, critique and show where alterations would not go amiss in this area. The methodological combination used for this book essentially results in the examination of what the applicable international law says about questions concerning state responsibility for non-state actors, whilst situating the answers to these questions in their societal context, comparing them to answers in other areas, and critiquing them from different normative standpoints. The book therefore attempts to encapsulate a balance between what the law is, what it could be and what it should be.

2. STRUCTURE

The structure of this book follows a progression that ties together the histories behind the legal framework of state responsibility as it applies to non-state actors, its present application and its development. Chapter 1 serves three main functions. First, it shows how non-state actors interface with the current law on international responsibility. Second, it provides some scene setting and context to the book, helping underscore its relevance, including regarding the occurrence of responsibility gaps and the associated issue of avoidance. Third, it sets the parameters for what

[18] A Peczenik, 'Scientia Juris: Legal Doctrine as Knowledge of Law and as a Source of Law' in E Pattaro (ed), *A Treatise of Legal Philosophy and General Jurisprudence*, vol 4 (Dordrecht, Springer, 2005) 6.
[19] ibid; see also 7–14.

is addressed in the book and offers crucial definitions, such as what constitutes a 'non-state actor'. Chapter 2 looks into non-state actors that exercise governmental authority. It scrutinises four separate bases for determining state responsibility for the conduct of these types of non-state actors, continuing a discussion about the forms and functions of attribution under international law. The place of domestic law in such settings also becomes apparent, calling into question the reasoning followed by those that created the four bases.

Chapter 3 addresses questions of attribution that centre on perceived state control over non-state actors. It analyses the creation, development and scope of application of the law on this matter. The chapter also draws attention to the role and influence of the International Law Commission (ILC) and the International Court of Justice (ICJ), in particular the relationship between the two institutions and how it has shaped narratives and perceptions on state responsibility for non-state actors. The involvement of states in international lawmaking is also cast into further doubt, at least in so far as the law of state responsibility applicable to the conduct of non-state actors is concerned. Chapter 4 focuses on how to determine state responsibility for conduct that occurred when states were previously non-state actors. This matter of retroactivity features the practice of non-state actor movements that attempt to create new governments within states, or entirely new states. The challenges in these situations due to factors such as peacebuilding, political stability, statehood and recognition are also reflected upon.

Chapter 5 engages with the matter of non-state actors' conduct being acknowledged and adopted by states. In addition to covering the relevant practice, it puts forward some thoughts on moral responsibility from the perspective of answerability and how these understandings offer a way to recalibrate approaches to state responsibility concerning the conduct of non-state actors. The potential and value to be found in basing international responsibility on state choice is also considered in light of the normative outlook that is portrayed. Chapter 6 explores the concept of complicity and its application to situations where states provide aid or assistance to non-state actors that carry out conduct that is contrary to international rules. It confronts the conventional approach to complicity in international law, whilst setting out the requirements pertinent to tackling cases of possible state complicity in non-state actor wrongdoing and showing why a test for determining international responsibility on this basis would make inroads in supplementing this legal framework. The chapter also provides an argument about the operation of complicity, forming part of the debate surrounding whether a general international rule on complicity should take the form of an attribution test or as a distinct basis for determining indirect state responsibility.

Chapter 7 sinks its teeth into the prevalent application of due diligence across domestic, regional and international law. In learning from these fields, an alternative approach to the concept is proposed, one that formulates and applies due diligence as a general rule, which if implemented would be used to assess the failings of states that contribute to non-state actors' wrongdoing and the subsequent apportionment of international responsibility. This analysis presents a possibility in which the omissions of states would be accounted for through the existence of a new basis for determining indirect state responsibility for the conduct of non-state actors. Chapter 8 is devoted to that which is currently dormant in discourses on the international responsibility of states for the conduct of non-state actors. It uncovers a default approach towards non-state actors that has remained a missing part of the law of state responsibility for too long. In constructing an argument for bringing this part back into practice, lucidity is found when contemplating three seemingly unrelated subjects: legislative drafting; making international law more international; and the non-exceptional nature of non-state actors being involved in state affairs. This last chapter also inspects two further tests that can be used to determine state responsibility for non-state actors, which relate to instigation and coercion, respectively.

These chapters coalesce the content of practice and literature to help grasp the creation, development, application, substance and scope of the law applicable to determining the international responsibility of states for the conduct of non-state actors that is contrary to international rules. By looking to the past to gain an appreciation for the framework that exists today, this book showcases histories that need not repeat themselves. By focusing on the present to show how this framework plays out right now, it emphasises the consequences that accompany solidity and shortcomings in the law. And by conceiving what may come to pass based on these perceptions of past and present, this book hopefully makes it slightly easier to see some prospects for the future.

1

Non-state Actors and the Applicable International Law on Responsibility

EVEN IN LIGHT of developments that illustrate the prominence of non-state actors in shaping events that concern international law, this field continues to focus much of its attention on states. International responsibility is an example of one area of international law that currently focuses predominantly on states. At present, 'the law' on responsibility at the international level is for the most part limited to states and intergovernmental organisations.[1] This approach to international responsibility means difficult questions arise when non-state actors interact with states, and, in the course of these interactions, conduct occurs that is contrary to international rules. This chapter focuses on the means by which the international law on state responsibility developed in order to address questions regarding the interactions between states and non-state actors, and what impact this development has had. It begins with a look at the history of the attribution provisions that were created by the ILC to form part of its Articles on Responsibility of States for Internationally Wrongful Acts (ARSIWA), which, even before completion,[2] became a point of reference for determining state responsibility for non-state actor conduct. 'Non-state actors' are also defined for the purposes of this book and reflections are offered on some of the issues that arise when matters centre on attempting to determine non-state actor responsibility under international law. The ever-present term of 'responsibility gaps' in international law is also engaged with by offering a definition of the term and analysing the factors that lead to their creation when states interact with non-state actors. Some reasons are then offered as to why the international law applicable to determining state responsibility for non-state actor conduct is important in light of the manner in which international law currently functions, and attempts are made to illustrate why this area can offer opportunities and solutions to contemporary problems. This first chapter aims to provide a better understanding

[1] Articles on Responsibility of States for Internationally Wrongful Acts, adopted by the International Law Commission at its Fifty-Third Session (2001), UN Doc A/56/10, 43, UN Doc A/RES/56/83, Annex, UN Doc A/CN.4/L.602/Rev.1, GAOR 56th Session Supp No 10, 43; Articles on the Responsibility of International Organizations, adopted by the International Law Commission at its Sixty-Third Session (2011), UN Doc A/66/10, UN GAOR, 66th Session Supp No 10.

[2] See, for example, *Kenneth P Yeager v The Islamic Republic of Iran* (1987) Iran–US CTR, vol 17, 92, 101–02.

of how the features of the state responsibility framework that can apply to non-state actors came into formation, and why state responsibility is an important area of international law with respect to addressing the conduct of non-state actors.

1. A VIEW ON THE HISTORY OF ATTRIBUTION IN THE WORK OF THE ILC

The ILC began its study on state responsibility in 1955.[3] The fruits of this study culminated in 2001, when the ARSIWA were declared finalised. This document is part of a toolkit for taking a legal approach to assessing situations where states have been involved in conduct that is contrary to international rules. As will become clear, although the final version of the ARSIWA is not exhaustive of the international law that can be applied to determining state responsibility for non-state actor conduct, this document forms a starting point for much analysis, in particular with respect to the concept of attribution. Attribution is particularly important in the context of an international legal order that currently focuses much of its attention on attempting to regulate the conduct of states. These abstract actors cannot do anything without the involvement of a physical actor, such as a human or an autonomous robot.[4] Attribution therefore exists as the mechanism by which international law determines whether conduct of a physical being can be 'attached' to an abstract state.[5] The provisions contained in the ARSIWA that focused on attribution were created to determine when this attachment should take place. This section examines how these provisions developed, providing a peek at the work of the ILC, in particular the efforts of its special rapporteurs. This approach highlights the key junctures in the preparatory work of the ARSIWA which shaped the attribution provisions that ultimately made the final cut in 2001.

1.1. The Formulation of Attribution by the ILC

The work of the ILC on attribution resulted in the creation of Articles 4–11 of the ARSIWA. These provisions were what the ILC ultimately decided should be the determinants for when conduct should be attributed to a state for the purpose of assessing its international responsibility. More or less in line with decisions from international courts and tribunals over the period spanning the 1930s to the 1980s,[6] attribution was

[3] ILC Report, Seventh Session, 2 May–8 July 1955, UNGA, Tenth Session, Supp 9 (A/2934), YBILC (1955) vol II, 42.

[4] E Hart, 'We're Teaching Robots to Evolve Autonomously – So They Can Adapt to Life Alone on Distant Planets' *The Conversation* (1 February 2021) https://theconversation.com/were-teaching-robots-to-evolve-autonomously-so-they-can-adapt-to-life-alone-on-distant-planets-153159.

[5] J Crawford, *State Responsibility: The General Part* (Cambridge, Cambridge University Press, 2013) 113.

[6] *Phosphates in Morocco*, Judgment, 1938, PCIJ, Series A/B, No 74, 10; *Dickson Car Wheel Company (USA) v United Mexican States* (1931), UNRIAA, vol IV (Sales No 1951.V.1) 669, 678; *United States Diplomatic and Consular Staff in Tehran (United States of America v Iran)*, Judgment, 24 May 1980, ICJ Rep 1980, 3, para 56.

embraced by the ILC as one of the necessary components of the international law on state responsibility.[7] Although the ILC can claim it was the author of the ARSIWA provisions on attribution, five special rapporteurs influenced their construction: Francisco Garcia-Amador, Roberto Ago, Willem Riphagen, Gaetano Arangio-Ruiz and James Crawford. These individuals brought unique and impactful perspectives that shaped the formulation of the various provisions. Yet the weight afforded to the work of each one varied.

1.1.1. Francisco Garcia-Amador

Garcia-Amador examined state responsibility from the perspective of the individual person,[8] including with respect to litigation.[9] His contributions to the ILC effort show that he did not take a state-centric approach to international responsibility. His works outside the role of special rapporteur spoke to an understanding of international law in which 'all legitimate interests' merited 'adequate protection under such a proposed legal order'.[10] His work on state responsibility was based on these perspectives,[11] championing individuals as subjects of international law.[12] Yet attaching international legal personality to non-state actors resulted in criticism.[13] By going beyond the perceived bounds of mainstream international law at that time, Garcia-Amador viewed non-state actors as a significant part of international law and relations. However, the manner in which attribution was approached during the drafting of the ARSIWA does not echo such a train of thought, beginning with the shelving of Garcia-Amador's ideas by the ILC.[14] The formation of attribution through the work of the ILC thus began with sidelining an underlying notion that the international law applicable to state responsibility should expand past the abstract state. That said, attribution maintained its presence in the foreground of the ILC's work.

1.1.2. Roberto Ago

The next special rapporteur, Roberto Ago, viewed attribution as an essential element of state responsibility early in his work.[15] He reasoned that the operation

[7] ARSIWA, Art 2, Commentary, para 6.

[8] Report, International Responsibility, FV Garcia-Amador, A/CN.4/96, YBILC (1956) vol II; Second Report, International Responsibility, FV Garcia-Amador, A/CN.4/106 (1957); Third Report, International Responsibility, FV Garcia-Amador, A/CN.4/111, YBILC (1958) vol II; Fourth Report, State Responsibility, FV Garcia-Amador, A/CN.4/119, YBILC (1959) vol II; Fifth Report, International Responsibility, FV Garcia-Amador, A/CN.4/125 and Corr 1, YBILC (1960) vol II; Sixth Report, International Responsibility, FV Garcia Amador, A/CN.4/134 and Add 1, YBILC (1961) vol II.

[9] Report, Garcia-Amador (1956) 197–99.

[10] FV Garcia-Amador, *The Changing Law of International Claims* (New York, Oceana, 1984) 754.

[11] For further insight into Garcia-Amador's approach to state responsibility, see FO Vicuna, 'Francisco V Garcia-Amador' (1993) 25 *Inter-American Law Review* 5.

[12] Report, Garcia-Amador (1956) 197.

[13] For a summary, see D Muller, 'The Work of Garcia Amador on State Responsibility for Injuries Caused to Aliens' in J Crawford, A Pellet and S Olleson (eds), *The Law of International Responsibility* (Oxford, Oxford University Press, 2010) 69, 72.

[14] ibid.

[15] Second Report, State Responsibility, Roberto Ago, A/CN.4/233, YBILC (1970) vol II, 187.

of attribution consists 'of conduct which must be attributable, not to the individual or group of individuals which has actually engaged in it, but to a State as a subject of international law'.[16] There were those who questioned whether attribution should be an element of determining state responsibility.[17] Yet with Ago steering the ILC project, it became clear that attribution was not only a necessary element of determining state responsibility, but also that assessments concerning attribution should operate independently of the legal obligation(s) at issue. This was a significant development at the time, as without the concept of attribution being part of international law there would be less guidance on how and when conduct can be attached to an abstract actor, such as a state. However, in accepting that attribution should form part of the international law applicable to state responsibility, the question became what conduct should be attributed to states when determining their responsibility. Engaging with this question went to the heart of the ILC's work, in which the answers provided were based on insights from a selection of sources.

Ago undertook a detailed analysis of the conditions in which international law appeared to permit conduct of an actor being attributed to a state.[18] His work led him to understand attribution as an indispensable part of the international law on responsibility.[19] He then began separating attribution into different forms.[20] The common denominator of this task was ascertaining the conditions surrounding conduct of corporeal actors, and how this affected attaching that conduct to a state.[21] The forms of attribution were split into a number of categories.[22] This work was well-received by the ILC.[23] Consequently, the ILC provisionally adopted the following articles in 1975:

Article 5

Attribution to the State of the conduct of its organs

Article 6

Irrelevance of the position of the organ in the organization of the State

Article 7

Attribution to the State of the conduct of other entities empowered to exercise elements of the governmental authority

Article 8

Attribution to the State of the conduct of persons acting in fact on behalf of the State

[16] ibid.

[17] A Soldati, *La responsabilité des Etats dans le droit international* (Paris, Librairie de jurisprudence ancienne et moderne, 1934) 75 et seq; see also I Brownlie, *Principles of Public International Law* (Oxford, Clarendon Press, 1966), 356.

[18] Second Report, Ago (1970) 185–96; Third Report, State Responsibility, Roberto Ago, A/CN.4/246 and Add 1–3, YBILC (1971) vol II(1), 233–74.

[19] Third Report, Ago (1971) 215.

[20] Ibid; Fourth report, State Responsibility, Roberto Ago, A/CN.4/264 and Add 1, YBILC (1972) vol II.

[21] Ibid; Third Report, Ago (1971) 233.

[22] Fourth Report, Ago (1972) 71.

[23] ILC Report, Twenty-Fifth Session, 7 May–13 July 1973, UNGA, Twenty-Eighth Session, Supp 10 (A/9010/Rev.1), YBILC (1973) vol II, 168.

Article 9

Attribution to the State of the conduct of organs placed at its disposal by another State or by an international organization

Article 10

Attribution to the State of conduct of organs acting outside their competence or contrary to instructions concerning their activity

Article 11

Conduct of persons not acting on behalf of the State

Article 12

Conduct of organs of another State

Article 13

Conduct of organs of an international organization

Article 14

Conduct of organs of an insurrectional movement

Article 15

Attribution to the State of the act of an insurrectional movement which becomes the new government of a state or which results in the formation of a new state[24]

By the time these had been produced, the ILC noted that it had 'completed' its work on attribution.[25] This was not the case, but these provisions did not resurface until four years later in 1979, when the ILC reaffirmed its commitment to them without making any amendments.[26]

1.1.3. Willem Riphagen and Gaetano Arangio-Ruiz

In 1980 attribution was scrutinised by Willem Riphagen, but formed a comparatively small portion of his work.[27] After this time the ILC received some comments from states.[28] Although provisional, these comments provide an insight on what the ILC chose to develop further.[29] The successor to Riphagen, Gaetano Arangio-Ruiz, also dealt with attribution, but primarily in relation to reparation. However, he did make what was to some a controversial insight: 'attribution does not really seem to be an

[24] ILC Report, Twenty-Seventh Session, 5 May–25 July 1975, UNGA, Thirtieth Session, Supp 10 (A/10010/Rev.1), YBILC (1975) vol II, 60.

[25] ILC Report, Twenty-Sixth Session, 6 May–26 July 1974, UNGA, Twenty-Ninth Session, Supp 10 (A/9610/Rev.1), YBILC (1974) vol II(1) 275.

[26] ILC Report, Thirty-First Session, 14 May–3 August 1979, UNGA, Thirty-First Session, Supp 10 (A/34/10), YBILC (1979) vol II, 240–42.

[27] Preliminary Report, Content, Forms and Degrees of International Responsibility (Part 2 of the Draft Articles on State Responsibility), Willem Riphagen, A/CN.4/330 and Corr 1, 2 (French only) and 3, YBILC (1980) vol II(1), 111–12.

[28] Seventh Report, State Responsibility, Willem Riphagen, A/CN.4/397 and Corr 1 & 2 and Add 1 & Corr 1, YBILC (1986) vol II(1) 6–18.

[29] For example, states suggesting the deletion of Draft Article 6 ('Irrelevance of the position of the organ in the organization of the State'): Seventh Report, Riphagen (1986) 9. A similar response was given towards Draft Articles 12 and 13, which were also subsequently deleted: Seventh Report, Riphagen, ibid 12.

operation carried out by legal rules'.[30] He appeared to view attribution as a process that hinged on something more than legal criteria. What he was perhaps getting at was basing attribution provisions on factual occurrences, in addition to, or instead of, them being based on perceived legal rules. If the ILC had adopted this approach when creating the attribution provisions under the ARSIWA, then this would have been an example of operationalising the principle that specified legal consequences attach to particular facts. For example, if the ILC had created provisions based on attribution taking place depending on whether a particular fact occurred, such as a provision stipulating that conduct would be attributed to a state if a state provided the funding for that conduct to take place.[31] However, the ILC did not follow this line of thinking, continuing with its formulation of the attribution provisions based on what it decided were accurate reflections of international law.[32] By the time the 1990s came around, a position within the ILC had aligned favouring the draft provisions submitted by Ago in 1975, which formed part of the draft articles adopted by the ILC on their first reading in 1996.[33] The draft attribution provisions thus remained unchanged for over twenty years. In 1997 the work was then taken forward by the ILC, with states being invited to provide further feedback.[34]

1.1.4. James Crawford

In working through the responses from states, James Crawford assessed attribution systematically.[35] He also reiterated the view of the other rapporteurs and the ILC that attribution was 'plainly central to the definition of state responsibility'.[36] The first of Crawford's contributions was splitting the attribution provisions into three groups, a step that made it easier for the ILC to assess each provision going forward:

1. Draft Articles that specify the circumstances in which conduct is attributable to the state (5, 7, 8, 9 and 15).[37]
2. Draft Articles that provide clarification of this first group (6 and 10).

[30] Second Report, State Responsibility, Gaetano Arangio-Ruiz, A/CN.4/425 & Corr 1 and Add 1 & Corr 1, YBILC (1989) vol II(1) 51; see also 50–53.

[31] An example in which international law bases legal consequences on the occurrence of particular facts are the criteria for statehood enshrined in the Montevideo Convention on the Rights and Duties of States (signed 26 December 1933, entered into force 26 December 1934) 165 UNTS 3802, Art 1.

[32] A point on which Arangio-Ruiz was in harmony with these reflections was with respect to the view that attribution should be unrestricted for state organs acting in their official capacity. See Second Report, Arangio-Ruiz (1989) 51.

[33] ILC Report, Forty-Eighth Session, 6 May–26 July 1996, UNGA, Fifty-First Session, Supp 10 (A/51/10), YBILC (1996) vol II(2), 58–60; For further insights, see J Crawford, J Peel and S Olleson, 'The ILC's Articles on Responsibility of States for Internationally Wrongful Acts: Completion of Second Reading' (2001) 12 *European Journal of International Law* 963, 964, 965, 966, 969, 976 (n 50), 981, 983 and 985.

[34] ILC Report, Forty-Ninth Session, 12 May–18 July 1997, UNGA, Fifty-Second Session, Supp 10 (A/52/10), YBILC (1997) vol II(1), 8.

[35] First Report, State Responsibility, James Crawford, A/CN.4/490 and Add 1–7 (1998) 32–55.

[36] ibid 32.

[37] It should be noted that the numbers of the articles referred to here are those that were provisionally adopted by the ILC in 1975 (set out above), which remained unchanged beyond the adoption of the draft articles on first reading in 1996.

3. Draft Articles that elaborate upon the circumstances in which conduct is not attributable to the state (11, 12, 13 and 14).[38]

With respect to the latter group, Crawford held the view that it was not necessary to pronounce on when conduct is not attributable to a state.[39] The United States and Switzerland also took a similar stance, expressing doubts of the 'wisdom' behind this approach.[40]

Another aspect of Crawford's work was his rollout of the 'basic principles underlying the notion of attribution':

1. The limited responsibility of the state.
2. The distinction between state and non-state sectors.
3. The 'unity of the state'.
4. *Lex specialis* rules.
5. The distinction between attribution and breach of obligation.[41]

The first principle is based on the premise that if an event occurs within a location over which a state exercises power and authority, this alone is not sufficient to attribute that event to the state. In order for a state to be internationally responsible for a particular event, the related conduct of the event must be attributable to it.[42] The second principle is that attribution exists to separate the public and private spheres of societies. Crawford did not elaborate as to the significance of such a distinction, but acknowledged the difficulties attached to such an understanding.[43] The third principle is that all components of the state should be indistinguishable for attribution purposes. This was argued to be the case even if a state has domestic laws that treat its officials as distinct legal persons. The fourth principle is that attribution under the international law on state responsibility is not absolute, meaning attribution rules from other areas of international law can be applied depending on the circumstances.[44] The fifth principle is that attribution does not speak to the lawfulness/unlawfulness of the conduct linked to the state, in that attribution determines whether conduct can be attributed to a state without assessing whether that conduct may have breached a legal obligation.

The first report of the ILC after Crawford began his work addressed questions on attribution that he and a number of states brought to light.[45] The comments of states also revealed issues such as whether the attribution provisions adequately dealt with matters such as private actors exercising governmental functions.[46] In terms of the scope of the draft articles at the time of 1998, the ILC noted that there needed to

[38] First Report, Crawford (1998) 32.
[39] ibid.
[40] ibid 33.
[41] ibid 33–34.
[42] ARSIWA, Art 2 and Commentary.
[43] First Report, Crawford (1998) 34.
[44] This matter will be examined further in chapter 6.
[45] ILC Report, Fiftieth Session, 20 April–12 June 1998 and 27 July–14 August 1998, UNGA, Fifty-Third Session, Supp 10 (A/53/10), YBILC (1998) vol II(2).
[46] ibid 9.

be a 'pruning' of the 'unduly detailed Part One, especially the "negative" articles on attribution' (i.e. those that addressed conduct not attributable to states).[47] In 1999 the ILC completed its review of Part One of the draft articles on its second reading, encompassing draft provisions 1–35.[48] By 2000 the ILC was nearly finished its work, with the Drafting Committee provisionally adopting the draft provisions on attribution.[49] The 2001 report of the ILC, before it formally adopted the ARSIWA on second reading,[50] tweaked some of the wording for the final version and rearranged the order of provisions that reflect the structure known today.[51]

1.2. Significance of this Work

The attribution provisions of the ARSIWA were shaped over years. The work as a whole reflects a process that strived for simplicity – a goal established from the outset.[52] Yet whether the attribution provisions embody this ethos is another question. The work of the ILC also reflects an approach to the international law on state responsibility as it appeared to stand around the time of the mid-twentieth century.[53] Although not finalised until 2001, a number of the attribution provisions did not significantly change from those that were created by Roberto Ago in the 1970s, which were based on sources from before this period. The following chapters will show that where such alterations did take place, they were of a nature that pushed considerations regarding non-state actors further outside the scope of the ARSIWA.[54]

Inter- and intra-state relations during the period of time in which the ILC was working on the ARSIWA involved non-state actors perhaps to a lesser extent than today.[55] But during the time it created the ARSIWA, the ILC may not have foreseen the future role non-state actors would play in contexts concerning international responsibility. This understanding is arguably reflected in the general stance of the ILC towards attribution concerning the conduct of non-state actors, viewing it as 'a point of departure' from the international law applicable to state responsibility.[56] What factors led to this viewpoint? Why is attribution for non-state actor conduct limited to 'exceptional circumstances'?[57] What are these circumstances? And who decided what these circumstances should be?

[47] ibid 114.

[48] Third Report, State Responsibility, James Crawford, A/CN.4/507 (2000) 3.

[49] ILC Report, Fifty-Second Session, 1 May–9 June 2000 and 10 July–18 August 2000, UNGA, Fifty-Fifth Session, Supp 10 (A/55/10), YBILC (2000) vol II(2) 124–26.

[50] Text of the ARSIWA adopted by the ILC at its Fifty-Third Session, in 2001, and submitted to the UNGA as a part of the Commission's report covering the work of that session (A/56/10). The report, which also contains commentaries on the draft articles, appears in (2001) YBILC, vol II, Part Two, as corrected.

[51] ILC Report, Fifty-Third Session, 23 April–1 June 2001 and 2 July–10 August 2001, UNGA, Fifty-Sixth Session, Supp 10 (A56/10), YBILC (2001) vol II(2), 80–120.

[52] See ILC Report, Twenty-Fifth Session, 7 May–13 July 1973, UNGA, Twenty-Eighth session, Supp 10 (A/9010/Rev.1), YBILC (1973) vol II, 173.

[53] Report, Garcia-Amador (1956) 174.

[54] This process with respect to each specific attribution provision is examined in chapters 2–5.

[55] R Baumann and FA Stengel, 'Foreign Policy Analysis, Globalisation and Non-state Actors: State-centric After All?' (2014) 17 *Journal of International Relations and Development* 489.

[56] ARSIWA, Art 4, Commentary, para 2.

[57] Crawford (n 5) 125.

1.2.1. The Impact of Draft Article 11

The ILC adopted a doctrinal methodology in its work on attribution, analysing judicial and state practice, in addition to academic works. This approach solidified a general understanding that states could not and should not be held responsible for conduct that was undertaken by non-state actors. According to Roberto Ago:

> State practice [from before 1971 shows] that the State is not responsible for acts committed by persons whom that State's system of municipal law does not consider as part of the State machinery.[58]

The idea that conduct of a non-state actor could be attributed to a state was surrounded with scepticism during the preparatory work of the ARSIWA. This was conceivably why the draft articles originally had a provision stipulating that conduct of non-state actors could not be attributed to states, in order to be unambiguous on the matter.[59] The commentary to this provision gave examples of non-state actor conduct that should not be considered attributable to states,[60] including conduct undertaken in a 'private capacity'.[61] This provision highlighted that attribution under international law only concerned conduct contrary to an obligation 'on the part of organs of the State or organs of another entity exercising elements of the governmental authority'.[62] The commentary to Draft Article 11 stated that it would be 'inadvisable to introduce an exception to this rule', which 'fully meets the needs of contemporary international life and does not require to be altered'.[63] The commentary also stressed that attribution should not extend to quasi-public actors.[64] The provision was aimed at excluding conduct, of any actor, from being attributed to a state, so long as the actor was not a state organ or official wielding governmental authority. The ILC expressed the view that conduct of private actors 'are in no circumstances attributable to the state'.[65]

1.2.2. The Influence of the Past on the Present

The position of the ILC that non-state actor conduct should not be attributable to states was informed by state practice. At The Hague Conference in 1930 every participating state was of the view that 'acts of private individuals could never be attributed to the State as a source of international responsibility'.[66] In another setting, the United States expressed that: '[A] state can only incur international responsibility in connexion with the acts of individuals if it has failed to fulfil its international obligations to provide protection.'[67] Italy made it 'clear' that 'only actions or omissions on the part

[58] Third Report, Ago (1971) 234.
[59] ILC Report, Twenty-Seventh Session, 5 May–25 July 1975, UNGA, Thirtieth Session, Supp 10 (A/10010/Rev.1), YBILC (1975) vol II, 70.
[60] ibid 70–83.
[61] ibid 71.
[62] ibid.
[63] ibid 82.
[64] ibid 71.
[65] ibid; see also 82.
[66] ibid 76.
[67] ibid 77.

of the official authorities of the State could be attributed to the latter as international wrongful acts involving its international responsibility'.[68] The former Soviet Union and Switzerland also held the view that 'in the case of injurious actions committed by individuals in law, only the conduct of the organs of the State with regard to such actions may be invoked as a source of state responsibility'.[69]

In 1975 the ILC noted that the idea of non-state actor conduct being attributed to states 'regardless of the attitude which organs of the State may take towards those acts' had 'tempted some modern writers' but had 'no true adherents at present'.[70] The approach of the ILC towards non-state actors was grounded in the views of some states and some writers from a particular period in history, in which the mainstream position appeared to be that 'the acts of private persons acting as such were never taken into account in determining the international responsibility of the State'.[71] The ILC made no indication that this position could change. For example, it was believed that state responsibility for non-state actor conduct could not be 'indirect' or 'vicarious',[72] which at the time around the 1970s were considered 'irregular' approaches to determining state responsibility.[73]

Although the underlying approach to formulating the provisions on attribution speaks to a now-dated understanding of the interactions that can occur between states and non-state actors, the ILC did not have a crystal ball, relying instead on what was certain from past practice and writings. Judicial decisions helped uphold this belief that non-state actor conduct could not and should not be attributed to states. In the *Poggioli* case four individuals attempted to murder another.[74] It was questioned whether their acts were attributable to the state,[75] in which the decision, as read by the ILC, 'in no way intended to accept the idea that the actions of individuals could as such be attributed to the State'.[76] The ILC examined a number of other cases that took similar positions on non-state actors, in that their conduct could not be attributed to states.[77] States also advocated in favour of solidifying this position. For example, Canada expressed 'that responsibility in respect of the conduct of an entity which is not part of the formal structure of the State must be more restrictively delineated'.[78] A continuous general theme of the preparatory work of the ARSIWA was that non-state actor conduct could not and should not be attributed to states.[79]

The approach to attribution under the ARSIWA reflects a viewpoint focused on state officials, and not actors that can form relationships with states without the use of domestic law to stipulate that they are officially acting on the behalf of a state. Yet

[68] ibid.
[69] ibid 79.
[70] ibid 80.
[71] ibid 72.
[72] ibid 73.
[73] ibid.
[74] UNRIAA, Mixed Claims Commission (Italy–Venezuela), 13 February and 7 May 1903, vol X, 477–692.
[75] ibid; see also 689.
[76] ILC Report, Twenty-Seventh Session, 5 May–25 July 1975, UNGA, Thirtieth Session, Supp No 10 (A/10010/Rev.1), YBILC (1975) vol II, 74.
[77] ibid 75–77.
[78] Seventh Report, Riphagen (1986) 10.
[79] See also Third Report, Ago (1971); Fourth Report, Ago (1972) 204.

there is evidence that shows the ILC did not have to take this approach. Although the reliance on state practice was important for what the ILC saw as clarifying the positive law from that moment in time, the preparatory work shows that the ILC was selective in what practice was incorporated into its final product. For example, Germany doubted the reach and utility of the attribution provisions, precisely because of the general focus on state officials: 'States increasingly entrust persons outside the structure of State organs with activities normally attributable to a State.'[80] Germany also spearheaded the doubts of other states by raising a prescient concern: 'The concept lying at the basis of chapter II [attribution of conduct] seems to be rooted more in the past than in present conditions.'[81] Mongolia expressed several 'doubts as to the coverage of acts of natural persons, who, at the time of committing a violation of international law, do not act as State representatives but nevertheless act under the authority and control of the State'.[82] In the connection between the state and the actor carrying out its decisions, Mongolia believed that 'mention should be made of the trend towards [a] broader understanding that … a State is responsible for its own activities and for those of persons, whether they be individuals, [or] private or public corporations'.[83] Switzerland also disapproved of the approach taken by the ILC towards attribution regarding the conduct of non-state actors.[84] France and the United Kingdom voiced concerns that the attribution provisions were unclear with respect to how far they extended to non-state actors.[85] France went further in its assessment, taking the position that limiting much of the content on the attribution provisions to state officials raised difficulties.[86] The United States criticised the draft provisions on attribution for their contradictory statements on non-state actors.[87] Other states went into further details on what they saw as issues with the specific attribution provisions.[88]

Some states were apprehensive about the position that the ILC adopted on attribution, arguing that the provisions 'should be sufficiently broad to ensure that States could not escape responsibility based on formal definitions of their constitutive organs, particularly in view of the recent developments concerning the increasing delegation of public functions to the private sector'.[89] Although it can be argued either way whether the ILC ultimately created attribution provisions that are 'sufficiently broad' enough to capture conduct from actors that are not state officials but nevertheless act on the behalf of states, it is understandable that some states considered the ARSIWA to reflect dated practice and sources. In the final

[80] First Report, Crawford (1998) 33 (emphasis added).

[81] State Responsibility, 50th Session of the ILC (1998), Agenda Item 2, Comments and observations received by Governments, A/CN.4/488 and Add 1–3, 105.

[82] First Report, Crawford (1998) 33.

[83] ibid.

[84] State Responsibility, 50th Session of the ILC (1998) 105 and 106.

[85] ibid 106 and 107.

[86] ibid 105, 106, 108, 109.

[87] ibid 108.

[88] These responses are addressed in chapters 2–5.

[89] ILC Report, Fiftieth Session, 20 April–12 June 1998 and 27 July–14 August 1998, UNGA, Fifty-Third Session, Supp 10 (A/53/10), YBILC (1998) vol II(2), 153.

commentaries that supplement the ARSIWA, the sources used to support the formulation of Articles 4–11 can be broken down into distinct periods of time.[90]

Article 4

Period of time	Number of sources	% of total sources
1850–1900	5	8.3
1900–1950	33	55
1950–1990	16	26.7
1990–2001	6	10

Article 5

Period of time	Number of sources	% of total sources
1850–1900	0	0
1900–1950	1	50
1950–1990	1	50
1990–2001	0	0

Article 6

Period of time	Number of sources	% of total sources
1850–1900	0	0
1900–1950	1	10
1950–1990	3	30
1990–2001	6	60

Article 7

Period of time	Number of sources	% of total sources
1850–1900	10	32.3
1900–1950	13	41.9
1950–1990	6	19.4
1990–2001	2	6.4

Article 8

Period of time	Number of sources	% of total sources
1850–1900	0	0
1900–1950	4	13.8
1950–1990	18	62.1
1990–2001	7	24.1

[90] See all the sources for these provisions in ILC Report, Fifty-Third Session, 23 April–1 June 2001 and 2 July–10 August 2001, UNGA, Fifty-Sixth Session, Supp 10 (A56/10), YBILC (2001) vol II(2), 40–54.

Article 9

Period of time	Number of sources	% of total sources
1850–1900	1	14.3
1900–1950	4	57.1
1950–1990	2	28.6
1990–2001	0	0

Article 10

Period of time	Number of sources	% of total sources
1850–1900	4	18.2
1900–1950	13	59.1
1950–1990	2	9.1
1990–2001	3	13.6

Article 11

Period of time	Number of sources	% of total sources
1850–1900	0	0
1900–1950	0	0
1950–1990	4	100
1990–2001	0	0

There are different points that can be drawn from these findings. For example, that Articles 6 and 11 are the most 'modern' of all the attribution provisions in the ARSIWA. Or that Articles 7, 9 and 10 are the most dated. Further points can be made when seeing the total number of sources used to support the formulation of Articles 4–11, which can be broken down into the following:

Period of time	Number of sources	% of total sources
1850–1900	20	12.1
1900–1950	69	41.8
1950–1990	52	31.5
1990–2001	24	14.6

The concerns and critiques of states that the attribution provisions were dated are therefore understandable. The majority of the sources referred to in the final commentaries are from before 1950 (53.9 per cent). In light of the numbers, the comment of Germany in particular, which was made in 1998,[91] that the ILC approach to attribution was based more in the past than the (then) present, is not only accurate, but raises

[91] State Responsibility, 50th Session of the ILC (1998) 105.

the question of why the ILC should base the content of provisions by predominantly, if not exclusively, considering situations that have happened in the past, instead of, or at least in addition to, considering situations that could happen in the future. Where codifying international law is not possible, the ILC has the mandate to promote the progressive development of international law, 'meaning the preparation of draft conventions on subjects which have not yet been regulated by international law or in regard to which the law has not yet been sufficiently developed in the practice of States'.[92] The ILC has room to use some imagination when drafting provisions for outputs such as the ARSIWA. That said, the UN in general is founded on an approach to international law that can be resistant to change, especially if such change risks being at the expense of stability:

> The drafters of article 13(1)(a) of the Charter of the United Nations, at the San Francisco Conference, in 1945, considered a proposal to make an explicit reference to 'revision' of existing international rules, but opted for the words 'progressive development' since 'juxtaposed as they were with codification, they implied modifications of as well as additions to existing rules' so as to 'establish a nice balance between stability and change, whereas "revision" would lay too much emphasis on change'.[93]

With respect to the drafting process of the ARSIWA, after their provisional adoption in the mid-1970s, the ILC did note the importance of ensuring that the attribution provisions reflected developments in international law.[94] And to an extent this was achieved: there are almost as many selected sources from after 1950 (46.1 per cent) than date before this period (53.9 per cent). However, the ILC approach to attribution when drafting the ARSIWA was centred on an idea that viewed non-state actors as some sort of externality, which has resulted in critique.[95] Although the ILC cannot be faulted too heavily for this state-centric focus, in particular because selected sources highlighted this viewpoint, and this is easy to say in hindsight, it did lack imagination by consistently looking to the past when creating 'law' that was intended to form part of the future. Perhaps this is one reason for such drafting processes not to be dominated by a doctrinal methodology. Looking to the past is important, but failing to consider the future can result in problems. Better balances can be struck between these positions. International law need not be a field in which creativity is crushed under the guise of pragmatism.

Whether, and the extent to which, non-state actors should be considered as an exception with respect to the operation of attribution remains debatable. Do state organs undertake more functions on the behalf of states than non-state actors do today? There are trends showing the extent to which the public sector is

[92] Statute of the ILC (1947), UNGA Res. 174(II) [21 November 1947], Arts 1 and 15; See also UN, *The Work of the International Law Commission*, vol 1 (8th edn, 2012) 46.

[93] ibid. See also Document 848; II/2/46, *The United Nations Conference on International Organization*, [1945], vol 9, 177–78.

[94] ILC Report, Fiftieth Session, 20 April–12 June 1998 and 27 July–14 August 1998, UNGA, Fifty-Third Session, Supp 10 (A/53/10), YBILC (1998) vol II(2), 52.

[95] RP Mazzeschi, 'The Marginal Role of the Individual in the ILC's Articles on State Responsibility' (2004) 15 *Italian Yearbook of International Law* 39.

being privatised across states, such as is the case with healthcare, immigration and policing.[96] States are constantly forming formal and informal relationships with non-state actors. Attribution is a key mechanism by which international law attempts to address these relationships, including when conduct occurs that is contrary to an international rule. The abstract state requires physical beings for it to function. Whether the actor in question happens to have been provided a piece of paper (such as a contract) stipulating that from the perspective of domestic law it is a state official does not matter all that much. What matters is whether the conduct in question was undertaken on behalf of the state; hence why even the conduct of state organs must be undertaken in their official capacity for that conduct to be attributable to the state for which they work.[97] By maintaining a default collective mindset stipulating that conduct by an actor in the 'private sphere' cannot be attributed to states, the ILC contributed to restraining the international law applicable to determining state responsibility from developing in a manner that could perhaps have attempted to keep close to the pace of developments involving the interactions between states and non-state actors that have occurred since the completion of the ARSIWA, and even before then.[98] This limitation placed on the state responsibility framework in its engagement, or lack thereof, with non-state actors is important for another reason: although there are limited exceptions, international law currently remains in a place in which determining the international responsibility of non-state actors is not possible.

2. CURRENT DIFFICULTIES WITH DETERMINING NON-STATE ACTOR RESPONSIBILITY

As the term suggests, 'non-state actor' 'includes all actors that do not fall within the category of States'.[99] Philip Alston proposes that 'anything that is not a state, whether it be me, IBM, the IMF, Shell, Sendero Luminoso, or Amnesty International, is conceptualized as a "not-a-state"'.[100] From this view, there are states and there are 'the rest'.[101] Non-state actors can thus be defined in the negative, in that they encompass actors that cannot be regarded as a state. There is an exception of intergovernmental organisations, which can be regarded as 'state-empowered entities', meaning

[96] See respectively as examples on these topics B Dixon-Warren, 'Privatization of Health Care' (2009) 180 *Canadian Medical Association Journal* 429; JM Chacón, 'Privatized Immigration Enforcement' (2017) 52 *Harvard Civil Rights-Civil Liberties Law Review* 1; B Forst and PK Manning, *The Privatization of Policing: Two Views* (Washington, DC, Georgetown University Press, 1999).

[97] ARSIWA, Art 4, Commentary, paras 1–13.

[98] C Chinkin 'A Critique of the Public/Private Dimension' (1999) 10 *European Journal of International Law* 387, 395; see also BS Chimni, 'The Articles on State Responsibility and the Guiding Principles of Shared Responsibility: A TWAIL Perspective' (2020) 31 *European Journal of International Law* 1211.

[99] S Sivakumaran, 'Beyond States and Non-state Actors: The Role of State-Empowered Entities in the Making and Shaping of International Law' (2017) 55 *Columbia Journal of Transnational Law* 343, 350.

[100] P Alston, 'The 'Not-a-Cat' Syndrome: Can the International Human Rights Regime Accommodate Non-state Actors?' in P Alston (ed), *Non-state Actors and Human Rights* (Oxford, Oxford University Press, 2005) 3, 4.

[101] ibid 19.

actors that states empower to carry out particular functions and can include state representatives.[102] The apparent dichotomy between states and non-state actors is not so neat, and the influence of state-empowered entities, in particular the ILC and the ICJ, in creating the law of state responsibility becomes clearer the further this area is scrutinised. Although intergovernmental organisations have separate legal personality from states, act in a separate capacity and are regarded as separate for the purposes of international responsibility,[103] they are composed of states among other things. The likes of the UN and so forth would not be able to do all that much without contributions from states. State representatives and support are crucial to the functioning of intergovernmental organisations. When intergovernmental organisations undertake conduct, states can be part of acting for and/or through them, albeit under the auspices of a varied role. Should conduct occur during the course of these relationships that is contrary to international rules, consideration can be given to whether any subsequent international responsibility is that of the state, the intergovernmental organisation, or should be shared between these actors.[104] As a result of intergovernmental organisations conducting their work with and sometimes through the medium of state organs, despite their actual and potential differing agendas, and being able to distinguish them from their members, these actors do not fit neatly into the definitional division of state and non-state actor. They are neither states nor non-state actors. For these reasons, intergovernmental organisations fall outside the scope of this book, considering its focus on the international law applicable to determining state responsibility for the conduct of non-state actors. Yet before turning further to this matter, it is helpful to examine the difficulties with determining the responsibility of non-state actors themselves. In doing so, this section highlights three overarching factors that prevent the international responsibility of non-state actors from being determined, which draws attention to some of the current limitations of international law.

2.1. Lack of International Legal Obligations

Determining state responsibility can be a relatively straightforward process. While assessments on this matter depend on applicable facts, which can often be what make such determinations difficult, all that is required from the perspective of international law is clarifying whether the state in question had a legal obligation, and whether the conduct that breached this obligation was attributable to that state, which are the requirements of an internationally wrongful act.[105] Determining whether a non-state

[102] See Sivakumaran (n 99).

[103] See the Articles on the Responsibility of International Organizations, adopted by the International Law Commission at its Sixty-Third Session (2011), UN GAOR, 66th session Supp No 10, UN Doc A/66/10.

[104] Considerable work has been undertaken on the topic of shared responsibility in international law. See, for example, A Nollkaemper, J d'Aspremont, C Ahlborn, B Boutin, N Nedeski, I Plakokefalos and D Jacobs, 'Guiding Principles on Shared Responsibility in International Law' (2020) 31 *European Journal of International Law* 15; A Nollkaemper and I Plakokefalos (eds), *Principles of Shared Responsibility in International Law: An Appraisal of the State of the Art* (Cambridge, Cambridge University Press, 2014).

[105] ARSIWA, Art 2, Commentary, paras 1–13.

actor is internationally responsible for something is not so straightforward.[106] A key reason for this is the limitation placed on international legal personality, which determines whether an actor can be bound by an international obligation. For the purposes of establishing international responsibility, legal personality is a threshold requirement, meaning if it is not met, the actor in question cannot have its international responsibility established, even when the factual conduct in question was contrary to an international rule.

From a mainstream viewpoint, entities are either 'subjects' or 'objects' of international law. Subjects can be the bearer of legal obligations and rights, and objects are actors that cannot.[107] States are the principal subjects of international law. Through their acceptance they allow for the incorporation of other actors onto this plane. Non-state actors can therefore become subjects. Examples include belligerent groups and movements aiming for self-determination.[108] Yet the capacity of international law to engage with non-state actors has changed, in part making the idea of subjects and objects less helpful.[109] Rosalyn Higgins also argues that international law is 'held captive' by the subject/object doctrine, and proposes that actors should be considered as 'participants' in the international legal order.[110] Categorising actors as 'subject' or 'object' may well stem from hesitation about granting more power to non-state actors. Veronika Bilkova points out that states are fearful of 'enhancing the legitimacy' of certain types of non-state actors, such as armed groups.[111] Even the development of instruments that confer legal obligations on non-state actors point toward this stance, as they explicitly state that such instruments cannot be construed in a way that would afford legal status to non-state actors, or 'legitimise' or 'recognise' them in any way.[112]

In terms of enforcing rights, determining legal personality is crucial in establishing whether the conduct of an actor that was arguably contrary to the right(s) of another, actually held a legal obligation.[113] The legal personality approach towards international responsibility prevents non-state actors that have undertaken conduct

[106] L Lane, 'The Horizontal Effect of International Human Rights Law' *GroJIL-blog* (1 August 2018) https://grojil.org/2018/08/01/the-horizontal-effect-of-international-human-rights-law/.

[107] R Higgins, *Problems and Process: International Law and How We Use It* (Oxford, Oxford University Press, 1994) 49.

[108] A Clapham, *Human Rights Obligations of Non-state Actors* (Oxford, Oxford University Press, 2006) 59.

[109] A Weenink, 'The Relevance of Being Important or the Importance of Being Relevant? Non-state Actors in International Relations Theory' in B Arts, M Noortmann and B Reinalda (eds), *Non-state Actors in International Relations* (Farnham, Ashgate, 2001) 59; R Wedgwood, 'Legal Personality and the Role of Non-governmental Organizations and Non-state Political Entities in the United Nations System' in R Hofmann (ed), *Non-state Actors as New Subjects of International Law: International Law – From the Traditional State Order Towards the Law of the Global Community* (Berlin, Duncker & Humblot, 1999) 21.

[110] Higgins (n 107) 49–55.

[111] V Bilkova, 'Armed Opposition Groups and Shared Responsibility' (2015) 62 *Netherlands International Law Review* 69, 81.

[112] See, for example, African Union Convention for the Protection and Assistance of Internally Displaced Persons in Africa (Kampala Convention), Adopted by the Special Summit of the Union Held in Kampala, Uganda, 23 October 2009, Art 15, para 2 and Art 7, para 1.

[113] W. Hohfeld, 'Some Fundamental Legal Conceptions as Applied in Judicial Reasoning' (1913) 23 *Yale Law Journal* 16, in particular 28–59.

that is contrary to an international rule (for example, arbitrary deprivation of human life) from being held responsible under international law in circumstances where they do not hold an international legal obligation.[114] By taking a Hohfeldian perspective on the matter, the significance of non-state actors' lack of legal obligations at the international level becomes clearer.[115] Under this paradigm, rights only exist if there is a corresponding duty-bearer. This means that if an actor has no duties, then exposure exists for the recipient of conduct originating from that actor. The actor carrying out the conduct is placed in a position of privilege, thereby creating a setting in which the actor who is the recipient of that conduct has no rights. The following diagram provides an illustration of this understanding:

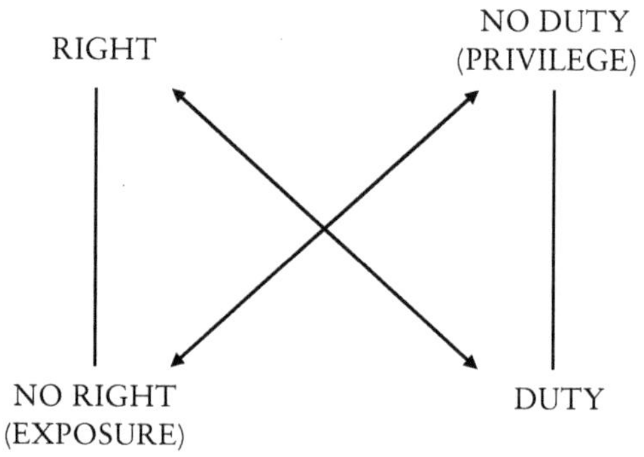

With limited exceptions, such as rules under international humanitarian law and (arguably) human rights law,[116] this is why non-state actors cannot commit internationally wrongful acts that would establish their international responsibility, because from the outset of their conduct they are not bound by international rules, and consequently have no international legal obligations. Under international investment law, the obligations contained in bilateral investment treaties can only be breached by states.[117] Claimants in such cases must establish that conduct extended beyond a contractual breach, in that there was 'sovereign power' exercised by the state in question.[118] Even if there has been a breach beyond a contractual obligation, unless the conduct in question can be attributed to the state, there is no way for an investor to enforce its rights. During his work on the ARSIWA, Ago

[114] For further insights, see E. Duruigbo, 'Corporate Accountability and Liability for International Human Rights Abuses: Recent Changes and Recurring Challenges' (2008) 6 *Northwestern Journal of International Human Rights* 222.

[115] Hohfeld (n 113).

[116] A Clapham, 'Human Rights Obligations of Non-state Actors in Conflict Situations' (2006) 88 *International Review of the Red Cross* 491.

[117] *Impregilo SpA v Islamic Republic of Pakistan*, Decision on Jurisdiction, ICSID Case No ARB/03/3 (22 April 2005) para 260.

[118] *Bayindir Insaat Turizm Ticaret VE Sanay AS v Islamic Republic of Pakistan*, Award, ICSID Case No ARB/03/29 (27 August 2009).

dedicated a portion of his attention to 'subjects which may commit internationally wrongful acts'.[119] This work also highlights that, although not always true, generally speaking, only states and intergovernmental organisations can commit internationally wrongful acts.

Some non-state actors can bear obligations. This is most notable in the case of non-state armed groups, which have obligations under international humanitarian law.[120] The *Urbaser v Argentina* case also highlights the possible existence of obligations being borne by non-state actors under investment law.[121] Here the Tribunal ruled favourably on the counterclaim of the host state that the investor had obligations to respect human rights.[122] The investor argued that it was not bound by human rights law – a contention rejected by the Tribunal.[123] The rationale behind this ruling was that because investors are the recipients of rights under bilateral investment treaties, they should also bear obligations.[124] Although these examples show there are exceptions, the current limitations of international law prevent many non-state actors from attaining legal personality and subsequently bearing legal obligations, making it 'unclear to what extent non-state actors bear obligations under international law'.[125]

Treaties do not typically include language that suggests they bind non-state actors. There are, however, limited exceptions. For example, Article 4(1) of the Optional Protocol to the Convention on the Rights of the Child on the involvement of children in armed conflict places an obligation on non-state armed groups not to recruit persons under the age of eighteen.[126] Article 2(e) of the Kampala Convention sets out an objective to: 'Provide for the respective obligations, responsibilities and roles of armed groups, non-state actors and other relevant actors.'[127] It also goes into further detail regarding the obligations of non-state actors, but in a self-contained manner that does not speak to any broader application.[128] Both

[119] Third Report, Ago (1971) 224–26; Second Report, Ago (1970) 195–97.

[120] For example, Common Article 3 to the Geneva Conventions. See also D Murray, 'How International Humanitarian Law Treaties Bind Non-state Armed Groups' (2015) 20 *Journal of Conflict & Security Law* 101; A Bellal, G Giacca and S Casey-Maslen, 'International Law and Armed Non-state Actors in Afghanistan' (2011) 93 *International Review of the Red Cross* 47.

[121] *Urbaser SA and Consorcio de Aguas Bilbao Bizkaia, Bilbao Biskaia Ur Partzuergoa v The Argentine Republic*, Award, ICSID Case No ARB/07/26 (8 December 2016).

[122] ibid paras 1182–21.

[123] ibid para 1194.

[124] For further insights into this case, see E Guntrip, '*Urbaser v Argentina*: The Origins of a Host State Human Rights Counterclaim in ICSID Arbitration?' *EJIL: Talk!* (10 February 2016) www.ejiltalk.org/urbaser-v-argentina-the-origins-of-a-host-state-human-rights-counterclaim-in-icsid-arbitration/.

[125] J D'Aspremont, A Nollkaemper, I Plakokefalos and C Ryngaert, 'Sharing Responsibility Between Non-state Actors and States in International Law: Introduction' (2015) 62 *Netherlands International Law Review* 49, 54.

[126] Optional Protocol to the Convention on the Rights of the Child on the involvement of children in armed conflict (adopted 25 May 2000, entered into force 12 February 2002) A/RES/54/263, 2173 UNTS 222.

[127] African Union Convention for the Protection and Assistance of Internally Displaced Persons in Africa (Kampala Convention), Adopted by the Special Summit of the Union Held in Kampala, Uganda, 23 October 2009.

[128] ibid Art 3, paras h and i, Art 7, paras 4 and 5.

states and non-state actors have expressed their opposition to creating international legal obligations for the latter.[129] It is also worth considering that if it is accepted that non-state actors have the requisite legal personality to bear international obligations, in practice it would fall to states with respect to enforcing those obligations.[130] Another factor to consider is that if international responsibility of non-state actors could be established irrespective of whether they are bound by international obligations, this could risk 'throwing open the floodgates to "buck-passing"' by states,[131] in addition to altering, or creating some exception to, the requirements of an internationally wrongful act.

2.2. Absence of International Law Governing Responsibility

It has been acknowledged that 'there is no express international law of responsibility applicable to non-state actors'.[132] It is clear that determining the international responsibility of a non-state actor can be a 'thorny' predicament.[133] This is not to say that doing so is impossible, just limited. For example, non-state actors in armed conflict 'are bound by international humanitarian law, yet international law seems to lack a conception of international responsibility of such groups for internationally wrongful acts'.[134] The creation of the Articles on the Responsibility of International Organizations (ARIO) was a step towards not limiting international responsibility to states.[135] However, the work undertaken on this project also highlights the interwoven problem of legal personality and international responsibility. In his work on the ARIO, Giorgio Gaja stated that the starting point for determining international

[129] 'Norms on the Responsibilities of Transnational Corporations and Other Business Enterprises with Regard to Human Rights' (2003) UN Doc E/CN.4/Sub.2/2003/12/Rev.2; 'The OECD Guidelines for Multinational Enterprises', *OECD Declaration and Decisions on International Investment and Multinational Enterprises: Basis Texts* (DAFFE/IME, 2000); 'Interim Report of the Special Representative of the Secretary-General on the Issue of Human Rights and Transnational Corporations and Other Business Enterprises' (2006) UN Doc E/CN.4/2006/97. See also, more recently, the developments on the 'Zero Draft' treaty: P Thielborger and T Manandhar, 'Bending the Knee or Extending the Hand to Industrial Nations? A Comment on the New Draft Treaty on Business and Human Rights' *EJIL: Talk!* (23 August 2019) www.ejiltalk.org/bending-the-knee-or-extending-the-hand-to-industrial-nations-a-comment-on-the-new-draft-treaty-on-business-and-human-rights/.

[130] UNSC Res 1373 (28 September 2001), UN Doc S/RES/1373; E Rosand, 'Security Council Resolution 1373, the Counter-terrorism Committee, and the Fight against Terrorism' (2003) 97 *American Journal of International Law* 333.

[131] M Karavias, 'Shared Responsibility and Multinational Enterprises' (2015) 62 *Netherlands International Law Review* 91, 97.

[132] BK Woodward, 'Non-state Actor Responsibilities: Obligations, Monitoring and Compliance' in N Gal-Or, C Ryngaert and M Noortmann (eds), *Responsibilities of the Non-State Actor in Armed Conflict and the Market Place* (Leiden, Brill, 2015) 29, 31.

[133] D'Aspremont et al (n 125).

[134] A Nollkaemper and D Jacobs, 'Shared Responsibility in International Law: A Conceptual Framework' (2013) 34 *Michigan Journal of International Law* 359, 369.

[135] Articles on the Responsibility of International Organizations, adopted by the International Law Commission at its Sixty-Third Session (2011), UN Doc A/66/10, UN GAOR, 66th session Supp No 10.

responsibility of a particular actor is examining whether it can and does hold an international obligation:

> When considering a definition of international organizations that is functional to the purposes of draft articles on responsibility of international organizations, one has to start from the premise that responsibility under international law may arise only for a subject of international law.[136]

This is a key reason behind why there is currently no international legal framework governing non-state actor responsibility. Such a framework would need to address non-state actors generally, which international law is not currently in a position to do. The international legal personality of non-state actors is relative, not generally unqualified. This may be why there are those 'sceptical of the prospects of transposing the state responsibility regime to non-state actors'.[137] Whether states would accept such a development is also a concern. In addition, in specific contexts, such as armed conflict, non-state actors exist temporarily. This limited time in existence serves as an additional, albeit less convincing, factor as to why an international responsibility framework for non-state actors does not currently exist.[138]

2.3. Forum Considerations

Another obstacle with respect to determining the international responsibility of non-state actors is the lack of legal fora at the international level. The international legal order does not presently function in a manner that allows non-state actors to be litigated against outside of international criminal law (which has its own set of problems),[139] or international investment law claims by states against investors (which is rare).[140] Although investment law can provide space for adjudicating claims against non-state actors, such claims are not typically brought by the state initially, but instead arise from counterclaims.[141] This is in part because international investment law is an area that was established with a view to protecting private investments

[136] ILC, First Report, Responsibility of International Organizations, UN Doc A/CN.4/532, 26 March 2003, para 15.

[137] D'Aspremont et al (n 125) 65.

[138] The temporary nature of non-state actors does not affect, for example, individual responsibility under international criminal law, which perhaps indicates that the limited time of existence is not such an important factor when considering a general framework of liability for a particular actor within an area of law. The responsibility here is not for the group as such, but its individual members.

[139] C Mylonopoulos, 'Contemporary Problems of International Criminal Law' (2015) 3 *Peking University Law Journal* 285; A Zidar and O Bekou (eds), *Contemporary Challenges for the International Criminal Court* (London, British Institute of International and Comparative Law, 2014).

[140] Few cases have been filed by a state against an investor before ICSID, for example: *Gabon v Société Serete SA* (ICSID Case No ARB/76/1), where the case was eventually settled, and *Spyridon Roussalis v Romania* (ICSID Case No ARB/06/1), which was admitted on the basis of an umbrella clause found in Art 2, para 6 of the Romania–Greece bilateral investment treaty (Award, 7 December 2011) para 781.

[141] Y Kryvoi, 'Counterclaims in Investor–State Arbitration', LSE Law, Society and Economy Working Papers 8/2011, http://eprints.lse.ac.uk/38469/1/WPS2011-08_Kryvoi.pdf.

situated abroad, meaning the system was set up such that the likelihood of an investor bringing a claim against a state is greater than the inverse.[142] The current functions of international dispute-settlement procedures '[do] not square with' the notion of the international responsibility of non-state actors.[143] For example, even where non-state actors are bound by international legal obligations, there 'is currently no international judicial or quasi-judicial organ with the competence to adjudicate complaints against' them.[144]

Domestic courts could potentially adjudicate cases involving non-state actors and questions of international responsibility, although they can be reluctant to treat non-state actors as international legal persons.[145] Domestic litigation is also not possible for other reasons. For example, in the context of armed conflict, there exists the issue of establishing (and then running) a court in a state where there is (or was) a conflict.[146] Even if a domestic court could be successfully formed in such settings, there would be the difficulty of maintaining independence and impartiality.[147] Domestic courts during peacetime can also struggle with questions of international law,[148] and are sometimes not able to scrutinise claims of an international nature.[149] Even in these relatively peaceful environments there exist barriers to pursuing cases through domestic legal machinery.[150] For example, in contexts concerning private military companies, there can be a lack of clarity between military and civilian tribunals, which means claims can become lost in the interface between the two.[151] Obstacles to determining non-state actor responsibility through judicial and quasi-judicial dispute-settlement mechanisms also stem from the 'limited jurisdictional

[142] See G Laborde, 'The Case for Host State Claims in Investment Arbitration' (2010) 1 *Journal of International Dispute Settlement* 97.

[143] Karavias (n 131) 105.

[144] V Bilkova, 'Establishing Direct Responsibility of Armed Opposition Groups for Violations of International Humanitarian Law' in Gal-Or et al (n 132) 263, 282.

[145] M Nowak and KM Januszewski, 'Non-state Actors and Human Rights' in M Noortmann, A Reinisch and C Ryngaert (eds), *Non-state Actors in International Law* (Oxford, Hart, 2015) 113, 119.

[146] AS Hansen, 'From Intervention to Local Ownership: Rebuilding a Just and Sustainable Rule of Law after Conflict' in C Stahn and JK Kleffner (eds), *Jus Post Bellum: Towards a Law of Transition from Conflict to Peace* (The Hague, Asser, 2008) 131.

[147] MS Ellis, *Sovereignty and Justice: Balancing the Principle of Complementarity between International and Domestic War Crimes Tribunals* (Cambridge, Cambridge Scholars, 2014) 126–51.

[148] See, for example, with respect to the courts of England and Wales, *Commissioner for Her Majesty's Revenue and Customs & Anor v Ben Nevis (Holdings) Limited & Ors* [2012] EWHC 1807 (Ch), where the Court struggled with the interpretation and application of the Vienna Convention on the Law of Treaties; *Serdar Mohammed v Ministry of Defence* [2014] EWHC 1369 (QB), where the Court misunderstood the relationship between different international legal regimes, in particular the conflict between a state's obligations under the UN Charter and those under the ECHR, in addition to IHL acting as the lex specialis that can prevail over rules under human rights law; *Smith & Ors v Ministry of Defence* [2013] UKSC 41, where the extent of extraterritorial jurisdiction was arguably incorrectly assessed by the Court.

[149] In the international investment law context, it has been pointed out that domestic courts have a limited capacity to properly address claims due to factors such as lack of expertise, person-power and time availability. See B Yimer, N Cisneros, L Bisiani and R Donde, 'Application of International Investment Agreements by Domestic Courts', *Trade Law Clinic* (E780), Geneva (10 June 2011).

[150] M Feit, 'Responsibility of the State under International Law for the Breach of Contract Committed by a State-Owned Entity' (2010) 28 *Berkeley Journal of International Law* 142, 164.

[151] For further insights on this issue, see DL Snyder, 'Civilian Military Contractors on Trial: The Case for Upholding the Amended Exceptional Jurisdiction Clause of the Uniform Code of Military Justice' (2008) 44 *Texas International Law Journal* 65.

remit' of these bodies.[152] International judicial and quasi-judicial bodies operate on the basis of state consent, meaning their respective jurisdiction does not currently extend to non-state actors.

2.4. A Revealing Equation

Choosing to focus on non-state actors in the context of determining international responsibility assumes that international law is in a position to provide for the functioning of such a framework, which is not the case at present. The lack of suitable forums for dispute settlement, in addition to most non-state actors currently lacking international legal personality, and therefore any subsequent international legal obligations, means that determining the international responsibility of non-state actors is not possible at present. There may come a day when an international responsibility framework for non-state actors comes into existence, but one does not exist right now. When this reality is coupled with that of the state-centric focus towards attribution in the development of the ARSIWA, a revealing equation starts to emerge. What happens when non-state actor responsibility cannot be determined under international law and the state responsibility framework accounts for non-state actors in a limited way? The next section provides an answer to this question, one that begins to show the difficulties that arise when applying the ARSIWA framework to interactions between states and non-state actors.

3. RESPONSIBILITY GAPS IN INTERNATIONAL LAW

Although 'the increasing expansion of the non-state sector into former state domains due to privatisation and delegation of state duties to private bodies' poses considerable concerns regarding international responsibility, 'there is thus far only very limited recognition' that non-state actors can have international legal rules applied directly to, and enforced against, them.[153] The unlikelihood of being able to determine non-state actor responsibility means that determining state responsibility can become the focus of claims where conduct occurred that was contrary to international rules. In the context of litigation, potential applicants 'will frequently have no option other than to bring an action against the state'.[154] Aoife Nolan emphasises that 'it is important not to underestimate' the importance of state responsibility 'as a legal tool for addressing' conduct committed by non-state actors that was contrary to international rules.[155] Yet what happens when the law of state responsibility cannot address such

[152] D'Aspremont et al (n 125) 55.

[153] A Nolan, 'Addressing Economic and Social Rights Violations by Non-state Actors through the Role of the State: A Comparison of Regional Approaches to the "Obligation to Protect"' (2009) 9 *Human Rights Law Review* 225, 229.

[154] ibid.

[155] ibid 230.

situations? Addressing this question raises the issue of responsibility gaps. The analysis below teases out a definition of the phenomenon. This approach also continues the conversation about the value of developing the state responsibility framework with respect to its engagement, or lack thereof, with non-state actors.

3.1. Defining Responsibility Gaps

'Responsibility gaps' has not yet developed into a term of art. Although commentators mention their existence, they do not define the concept.[156] In helping arrive at a definition, examining the facts of a notable case provides a starting point. In the *Nicaragua* case before the ICJ, the United States provided assistance to a paramilitary rebel group: the Contras.[157] The United States granted $27 million for 'humanitarian assistance' to this non-state actor, which was depicted as 'the provision of food, clothing, medicine, and other humanitarian assistance'.[158] Despite this assurance, the ICJ found that the United States 'was providing funds for military and paramilitary activities by the Contras in Nicaragua'.[159] The United States also provided military training to the Contras;[160] relayed intelligence information to the Contras;[161] and armed the Contras.[162] The United States also administered military recommendations to the Contras in the form of 'tactical directives'.[163] The Contras appeared to be acting as an unofficial proxy of the United States, and were recognised by the ICJ as being dependent on the state.[164] In sum, the United States enabled this non-state actor to carry out conduct such as kidnap, assassination, torture and rape.[165] In light of these factors the ICJ held:

> The Court does not consider that the assistance given by the United States to the *contras* warrants the conclusion that these forces are subject to the United States to such an extent that any acts they have committed are imputable to that State. It takes the view that the *contras* remain responsible for their acts, and that the United States is not responsible for the acts of the *contras*, but for its own conduct vis-à-vis Nicaragua.[166]

Later chapters will show how the ICJ essentially invented the law to arrive at this conclusion.[167] However, it should be noted that the overall result reached by the ICJ in

[156] N Tsgourias and M Farrell, 'Cyber Attribution: Technical and Legal Approaches and Challenges' (2020) 31 *European Journal of International Law* 941; P Webb and R Garciandia, 'State Responsibility for Modern Slavery: Uncovering and Bridging the Gap' (2019) 68 *International & Comparative Law Quarterly* 539; C Hoppe, 'Passing the Buck: State Responsibility for Private Military Companies' (2008) 19 *European Journal of International Law* 989.

[157] *Military and Paramilitary Activities in and against Nicaragua (Nicaragua v United States of America)*, Judgment, 27 June 1986, ICJ Rep [1986] 14.

[158] ibid para 97.

[159] ibid para 99.

[160] ibid paras 112, 115, 117, 120, 121, 228, 242.

[161] ibid paras 106, 110, 243.

[162] ibid paras 228, 242, 268.

[163] ibid paras 102–10.

[164] ibid para 112. The ICJ noted that the exact extent of this dependency could not be established.

[165] ibid paras. 20 and 113.

[166] ibid para. 116.

[167] In particular chapter 3.

this case did not result in a responsibility gap. The United States was held responsible for breaching its obligations not to interfere in the affairs of another state, not to use force against another state and not to infringe another state's sovereignty.[168] However, what would have been the outcome had the United States not been held responsible for these other breaches? It is worth reflecting on situations in which states share relationships with non-state actors to extents similar in the *Nicaragua* case. Proxy wars are one example, which entail a state delegating to a non-state actor to fight for its interests in a conflict, without that state being formally and optically involved.[169] Although the nature of the connection between states and non-state actors varies from case to case, states (sometimes significantly) enable non-state actors to carry out their conduct. Yet even significant state involvement in such conduct does not mean their international responsibility can be established. In the *Nicaragua* case the United States was not held responsible for the conduct of the Contras, despite participating in it to the degree that it did.

Responsibility gaps come into existence as a matter of international law when establishing non-state actor responsibility is not possible, and establishing state responsibility does not happen (despite it being possible), for conduct that is contrary to an international rule. For example, if a multinational clothing company housed its workers in factories in which the conditions amounted to degrading treatment, but the company does not have international legal personality, meaning it cannot bear international legal obligations, and state responsibility cannot be established under international law, then a responsibility gap will exist in international law. That said, a responsibility gap existing in international law does not mean a responsibility gap will necessarily exist in domestic law. Developments in domestic law are presenting new ways to establish non-state actor responsibility for conduct that is contrary to international rules.[170] This means that although a responsibility gap may exist when applying international law, a responsibility gap may not exist when applying domestic law.

A responsibility gap in international law is thus the outcome of a situation where an actor bearing a right prescribed by an international rule is subjected to conduct that is contrary to that rule, but those that physically undertook the conduct or contributed to its occurrence cannot have their international responsibility established. The factors that lead to this outcome in international law when states interact with non-state actors are twofold. First, the non-state actor that physically undertakes the conduct that is contrary to the applicable international rule is not bound by that rule. Lack of international legal personality contributes to this outcome. Second, although bound by the relevant international rule, there is no way to link the conduct of the non-state actor to the state for the purposes of establishing its

[168] *Nicaragua*, para 292.

[169] See A Mumford, 'Proxy Warfare and the Future of Conflict' (2013) 158 *Royal United Services Institute Journal* 40; Y Bar-Siman-Tov, 'The Strategy of War by Proxy' (1984) 19 *Cooperation and Conflict* 263.

[170] W Tiruneh, 'Holding the Parent Company Liable for Human Rights Abuses Committed Abroad: The Case of Four Nigerian Farmers and Milieudefensie v Shell' *EJIL: Talk!* (19 February 2021) www.ejiltalk.org/holding-the-parent-company-liable-for-human-rights-abuses-committed-abroad-the-case-of-the-four-nigerian-farmers-and-milieudefensie-v-shell/.

international responsibility. International law is not currently in a place to address the first matter. The limitations posed by international legal practice mean that non-state actors cannot be held internationally responsible for their conduct, except in the limited cases where they bear international obligations. However, there are ways to link the conduct of non-state actors to states for the purpose of establishing their international responsibility. International law is therefore not completely useless at addressing situations where responsibility gaps might occur through the combined conduct of states and non-state actors. The remainder of this book illustrates how, and the extent to which, the law of state responsibility can address this matter. Yet before moving on to examining the international law applicable to determining state responsibility for non-state actor conduct, there are further points to consider regarding why this component of international law deserves further attention, in particular with respect to responsibility gaps.

3.2. Avoidance as a Norm of State Practice?

States outsource to non-state actors across a range of sectors. This redistribution of who carries out what particular tasks has implications when determining the international responsibility of states. For example, states avoid officially involving themselves in particular situations by delegating to proxies that do not officially form part of the state structure.[171] Although the reasons for this practice are likely multiple, by delegating to non-state actor proxies, states increase the degrees of separation between themselves and any potential conduct that is contrary to international law, thus decreasing the likelihood that their international responsibility can be established. A concern in such situations is whether states outsource to non-state actors for the purpose of avoiding international responsibility. It is this practice where responsibility gaps can occur, potentially with great frequency, because (1) the non-state actors will not have international legal obligations, and (2) there is no way to link the conduct of the non-state actors to states. Where states outsource to non-state actor proxies in order to provide a loophole out of their international legal obligations, such conduct can be categorised as avoidance. Avoidance is thus a specific practice that can lead to responsibility gaps in settings where conduct of a non-state actor is contrary to an international rule.

To clarify, this understanding of avoidance is not the same as that with respect to the validity of international agreements or the nullification of awards.[172] Nor is it the same as avoidance in the context of the capability of domestic law to quash international rules.[173] It should also be noted that outsourcing itself is owed to a variety of

[171] American Bar Association, *The Legal Framework Regulating Proxy Warfare* (December 2019) www.americanbar.org/content/dam/aba/administrative/human_rights/chr-proxy-warfare-report-2019.pdf.

[172] AD McNair, *The Law of Treaties* (Oxford, Clarendon, 1961) 206–36; KS Carlston, *The Process of International Arbitration* (New York, Columbia University Press, 1946) 63–258.

[173] WF Fairey, 'The Helms–Burton Act: The Effect of International Law on Domestic Implementation' (1997) 46 *American University Law Review* 1289.

factors, such as states implementing neoliberal economic policies.[174] Therefore, not every instance of outsourcing denotes that a state is attempting to subvert international rules through formal or informal delegation to non-state actors. Avoidance is teleologically conditioned, meaning the concept taken within the parameters of state conduct refers to intended consequences, or lack thereof.[175] Although a potential hurdle exists in terms of determining the intentions of states, any such assessment will become less troublesome the further facts are established in a particular case.[176] Determining state intent also forms part of the current international law on state responsibility for complicity.[177] But in what settings are states likely to intentionally outsource to non-state actors in order to implement their policy choices without running the risk of having their international responsibility called into question?

One example where avoidance can arise is when states rely on non-state actors to conduct cyber operations against other states.[178] Another example is states delegating the management of their borders to private security services.[179] Yet a further example is the practice of states assigning involvement in armed combat operations to private military companies.[180] Simultaneously, this example provides further insight into responsibility gaps, in particular the potential frequency with which they can occur. The UN has focused on private military actors for many years, with state outsourcing becoming a focal point of discussions at the General Assembly.[181] The UN takes the view that private military companies operate 'without oversight and accountability'.[182] This could be owed to the arguably 'low level of ratification of and accession to the International Convention against the Recruitment, Use, Financing and Training of Mercenaries'.[183]

Perhaps states in today's world prefer to delegate their apparent 'monopoly on the use of force'.[184] Delegating shields states from their international responsibility being called into question should private contractors undertake conduct that is contrary to international rules, creating responsibility gaps where establishing the

[174] C Crouch, 'The Paradoxes of Privatisation and Public Service Outsourcing' (2015) 86 *Political Quarterly* 156.

[175] HW Baade, 'Nullity and Avoidance in Public International Law: A Preliminary Survey and a Theoretical Orientation' (1964) 39 *Indiana Law Journal* 497.

[176] See this in the context of complicity (chapter 6).

[177] See ARSIWA, Art 16 and Commentary.

[178] See T Maurer, *Cyber Mercenaries: The State, Hackers, and Power* (Cambridge, Cambridge University Press, 2018).

[179] UNGA, HRC, A/HRC/45/9 (9 July 2020).

[180] Nollkaemper and Jacobs (n 134) 375.

[181] UNGA, 'Use of mercenaries as a means of violating human rights and impeding the exercise of the right of peoples to self-determination' (24 August 2007), Report of the Working Group on the use of mercenaries as a means of violating human rights and impeding the exercise of the right of peoples to self-determination, UN Doc A/62/301, paras 68–72; UNGA, 'Use of mercenaries as a means of violating human rights and impeding the exercise of the right of peoples to self-determination' (13 September 2006), Report of the Working Group on the use of mercenaries as a means of violating human rights and impeding the exercise of the right of peoples to self-determination, UN Doc A/61/341, paras 34 and 69.

[182] ibid UN Doc A/62/301, para 72.

[183] ibid para 71; see International Convention against the Recruitment, Use, Financing and Training of Mercenaries (adopted 4 December 1989, entered into force 20 October 2011), 2163 UNTS 75.

[184] UNGA, 'Use of mercenaries as a means of violating human rights and impeding the exercise of the right of peoples to self-determination' (13 September 2006) (n 181) para 27 (emphasis added).

responsibility of these non-state actors does not occur.[185] It has been argued that the shortcomings in the applicable law on private military companies are so extensive that instead of preventing impunity, as laws focused on responsibility should, current rules actually enable it.[186] States can disguise their participation in armed hostilities by using the private sector to construct a form of plausible deniability.[187] This general practice of outsourcing has been summarised elsewhere as a state using a non-state actor 'as its "long arm" with a view to perpetrating a violation of its international law obligations'.[188] Yet in such situations, no breach of international law actually occurs because again (1) the non-state actor does not have international legal personality (meaning no subsequent international legal obligation to breach), and (2) the conduct of the non-state actor that was contrary to an international rule cannot be attached to the state.

The current limitations of the law on international responsibility create an environment in which the practice of avoidance can flourish. If states perceive that they need or want something done that risks breaching their international obligations, turning to non-state actors to undertake what is needed or wanted reduces (and in some cases eliminates) this risk. Avoidance can therefore result in states adopting particular courses of action in line with their policy choices that subvert international rules in the process. A consequence of not being able to establish international responsibility in situations in which conduct has occurred that is contrary to international rules is the vitiation of international legal obligations and corresponding rights. The efficacy of state responsibility is an important part of a well-functioning international legal order, even if the universality of this system remains debatable.[189] State outsourcing to non-state actor proxies challenges this efficacy, in which rules of international law are jeopardised. Some may accept such practices as part and parcel of everyday life. Yet doing so sends a message of being willing to tolerate impunity. Although it is unclear whether avoidance is a norm of state practice, it could become so, especially in a world in which states rely on non-state actors to carry out their policy choices.[190]

[185] A Tarzwell, 'In Search of Accountability: Attributing the Conduct of Private Security Contractors to the United States Under the Doctrine of State Responsibility' (2009) 11 *Oregon Review of International Law* 179, 181–89; JL Gómez del Prado, UN Working Group on the Use of Mercenaries, 'Private Military and Security Companies and Challenges to the UN Working Group on the Use of Mercenaries' (2008).

[186] HY Liu, *Law's Impunity: Responsibility and the Modern Private Military Company* (London, Bloomsbury, 2015).

[187] OR Jones, 'Implausible Deniability: State Responsibility for the Actions of Private Military Firms' (2009) 24 *Connecticut Journal of International Law* 239, 258.

[188] Karavias (n 131) 97.

[189] KT Gaubatz and M MacArthur, 'How International Is "International" Law?' (2001) 22 *Michigan Journal of International Law* 239; A Roberts, *Is International Law International?* (Oxford, Oxford University Press, 2017).

[190] For example, states' reliance on private technology companies to assist in their responses to public health emergencies. See A Zwitter and OJ Gstrein, 'Big Data, Privacy and COVID-19 – Learning from Humanitarian Expertise in Data Protection' (2020) 5 *Journal of International Humanitarian Action* 1.

4. WHY IS THIS AREA OF INTERNATIONAL LAW IMPORTANT?

Even in light of the reality that states can, and do, attempt to or successfully manipulate the international legal framework on responsibility to their advantage, there are reasons for challenging this dynamic. In reflecting on the issues addressed above, this section speaks a wee bit more to the question of why the international law applicable to determining state responsibility for the conduct of non-state actors is important in light of the manner in which international law currently functions. Although it can be improved, this body of law offers opportunities, and in some cases solutions, to the problems it is confronted with when states and non-state actors interact in ways resulting in conduct that is contrary to international rules.

4.1. International Law is Still a Predominantly State-Focused Legal Order

For better or worse, the international legal order continues to revolve around states. Understanding international law as a state-centric legal order may be viewed as a 'defunct' or 'old' notion.[191] To an extent it is not difficult to sympathise with such a line of argument. There are trends that highlight the proliferation of legal relationships among various actors, and a growing pool of the interests promoted and ostensibly protected by international law.[192] Yet the international law on responsibility barely extends its focus beyond states.[193] And developing an international responsibility framework for non-state actors is not feasible at this time. Right now:

> The practice of states delegating power to private entities ... raises questions as to the corresponding distribution of responsibility for damages caused ... [yet] as a matter of international law, only the delegating state (or organization) can be held responsible for harm resulting from the act of the private entity.[194]

There is also the point to consider that shifting scrutiny to assessing non-state actor responsibility means any state involvement in conduct that was contrary to international rules could be overlooked. Buck-passing by states is a real possibility in situations where the separate conduct of a state and a non-state actor combined to result in collective conduct that was contrary to an international rule. Responsibility can be apportioned proportionately in such situations, whilst being mindful about what can be achieved when applying the law of a particular legal system. Although the

[191] See the analysis and discussion in the following works: PB Stephan, 'Privatizing International Law' (2011) 97 *Virginia Law Review* 1573; DB Hollis, 'Why State Consent Still Matters: Non-state Actors, Treaties, and the Changing Sources of International Law' (2005) 23 *Berkeley Journal of International Law* 137, 173; PW Singer, 'War, Profits, and the Vacuum of Law: Private Military Firms and International Law' (2003) 42 *Columbia Journal of Transnational Law* 521.

[192] R McCorquodale, 'An Inclusive International Legal System' (2004) 17 *Leiden Journal of International Law* 477.

[193] D Momtaz, G Cahin and O Frouville, 'Attribution of Conduct to the State: State Organs and Entities Empowered to Exercise Elements of Governmental Authority' in Crawford et al (eds), *The Law of International Responsibility*, 261.

[194] Nollkaemper and Jacobs (n 134) 375.

law of state responsibility can fall short of dealing with the consequences attached to conduct of non-state actors that is contrary to international rules,[195] and these actors can lie 'beyond the purview of the ILC Articles on State responsibility',[196] there is as of yet an alternative framework within international law with respect to addressing conduct that involved a non-state actor and a state and was contrary to an international rule. But the law applicable to determining state responsibility for non-state actor conduct can develop, in addition to being interpreted in ways that allow it to effectively engage with state-to-non-state actor interactions.

4.2. Opportunities to Develop International Law

The plurality of actors in societies across the world is a matter with which international law is currently playing catch-up.[197] The law of international responsibility is learning this lesson, especially when non-state actors 'team up with states to bring about a prohibited or harmful outcome, either by taking joint action, or by one actor aiding and assisting the other'.[198] Examining the current legal framework applicable to these interactions helps assess the extent to which international law can and cannot address them. Hersch Lauterpacht believed that the international legal order should develop in ways that allow its body of law to meaningfully engage with factual realities.[199] Does the current state responsibility framework do so? There is plenty to suggest it is perhaps ill-equipped to do so.[200] States provide (sometimes extensive) support to non-state actors, as are they (sometimes heavily) involved in conduct contrary to international law. Yet, as will become clearer, it is not all that difficult for a state to circumvent the current legal framework governing international responsibility. In some cases this framework is exploited to the benefit of states and non-state actors alike. The efficacy of international law therefore becomes even more questionable in the absence of any international responsibility for conduct that is contrary to international rules. Alain Pellet considers it to be the case that with no international responsibility there is no international law, noting that responsibility is the 'necessary corollary of law'.[201]

A further reason for scrutinising the state responsibility framework with respect to its engagement and lack thereof with non-state actors can be appreciated by reflecting on a point made by Helmut Aust: 'There is no better recipe for disappointment than

[195] A Bellal, 'Establishing the Direct Responsibility of Non-state Armed Groups for Violations of International Norms: Issues of Attribution' in Gal-Or et al (n 132) 304, 304.

[196] G Nolte and HP Aust, 'Equivocal Helpers – Complicit States, Mixed Messages and International Law' (2009) 58 *International & Comparative Law Quarterly* 1, 7.

[197] Bilkova (n 111) 69.

[198] D'Aspremont et al (n 125) 65.

[199] H Lauterpacht, *The Function of Law in the International Community* (Oxford, Oxford University Press, 2011) 109 and 407–13.

[200] M Gibney, 'The Downing of MH17: Russian Responsibility?' (2015) 15 *Human Rights Law Review* 169, 174; See also S Macleod, 'Private Security Companies and Shared Responsibility: The Turn to Multistakeholder Standard-Setting and Monitoring through Self-regulation "Plus"' (2015) 62 *Netherlands International Law Review* 119.

[201] A Pellet, 'The Definition of Responsibility in International Law' in Crawford et al (n 13) 3, 4.

an immense development of international law in substantive terms which then falls foul of a lack of accompanying steps on the procedural level.'[202] The law on state responsibility that is applicable to non-state actor conduct is in some ways procedural, in that it determines whether other rules of international law can be applied to states.[203] The enforcement of primary rules is a value to protect. The extent to which the law of state responsibility can contribute to this protection hinges on the extent to which it can attach conduct undertaken by a physical actor to an abstract state. Safeguarding rights-holders requires examining the ways in which conduct can be attributed to states, determining whether different approaches from attribution are feasible, and analysing how these alternatives can be utilised. This undertaking concerns maintaining the links between states and the primary rules to which they have bound themselves, which aim to protect many values and interests.[204] State responsibility is an area that can spearhead the development of international law in this regard, especially because it consists of rules that have general applicability across different sub-fields of international law.

5. CONCLUSION

The international law applicable to determining state responsibility for the conduct of non-state actors is a part of society that plays a role in maintaining the efficacy of being able to enforce international rules. Responsibility gaps challenge this ability to adequately govern state conduct. States can subvert the current responsibility framework to their advantage. They are influential actors, meaning they can abuse such power to the detriment of others. By empowering non-state actors to take on more tasks, states increase the degrees of separation between themselves and conduct that is contrary to international rules. States can utilise non-state actors who may be held responsible for conduct contrary to international rules, without subjecting themselves to the same scrutiny. The ILC made a significant contribution to this area by completing the ARSIWA. Understanding and building on this advancement is important for the progression of international law in line with contemporary practice. There are many contexts in which states no longer take the primary role in particular courses of action. Non-state actors are frequently utilised to help fulfil state policy. Despite the existing problem of states not being held to account for their involvement in conduct that is contrary to international rules, there are approaches that have the potential to ensure that such conduct does not go unchecked. The following chapters examine the details of the law on state responsibility with respect to governing interactions between states and non-state actors, and consider how this framework might be developed.

[202] HP Aust, *Complicity and the Law of State Responsibility* (Cambridge, Cambridge University Press, 2011) 427.

[203] P-M Dupuy, 'The International Law of State Responsibility: Revolution or Evolution?' (1989) 11 *Michigan Journal of International Law* 105, 126.

[204] Whose values and interests are actually protected by international law is another question. See generally J Linarelli, M Salomon and M Sornarajah, *The Misery of International Law: Confrontations with Injustice in the Global Economy* (Oxford, Oxford University Press, 2018).

2

Non-state Actors that Exercise Governmental Authority

THE STANCE ADOPTED by the ILC towards non-state actors when drafting the ARSIWA, combined with the difficulties that come with attempting to determine non-state actor responsibility under international law, can create responsibility gaps when states and non-state actors form relationships that lead to conduct that is contrary to international rules. The possibility of state avoidance is also a product of this equation. Such outcomes question whether, and the extent to which, the law of state responsibility can address such issues. This chapter begins the scrutiny of the ARSIWA attribution provisions with respect to the extent to which they can, and cannot, address matters in which states act in consort with, use, enable or allow non-state actors to undertake conduct that is contrary to international rules. It focuses on conduct of non-state actors that may be attributed to states based on links showing that governmental authority has been exercised. Determining state responsibility based on this basis of attribution can take a number of forms.

The line between the public sector and the private sector is markedly blurry across many states today, making attribution based on a test of governmental authority particularly important because private actors carry out public functions. Whether it is governments utilising technology developed by companies to assist their responses to emergencies, militias policing entire communities, or airlines carrying out border security protocols, states change in terms of what roles are carried out by what actors at particular moments in time. Sometimes this means that public interests are ostensibly being advanced through private actors that are, in part, acting on the behalf of states. The structures of states across this world vary, with governmental authority being wielded by a variety of actors, signifying the value for the state responsibility framework of attempting to accommodate this reality. But to what extent does the ARSIWA do so?

The term 'governmental authority' is present in four of the attribution provisions in the ARSIWA: 5, 6, 7 and 9.

Article 5 reads:

> *Conduct of persons or entities exercising elements of governmental authority*
>
> The conduct of a person or entity which is not an organ of the State under article 4 but which is empowered by the law of that State to exercise elements of the governmental

authority shall be considered an act of the State under international law, provided the person or entity is acting in that capacity in the particular instance.[1]

Article 6:

Conduct of organs placed at the disposal of a State by another State

The conduct of an organ placed at the disposal of a State by another State shall be considered an act of the former State under international law if the organ is acting in the exercise of elements of the governmental authority of the State at whose disposal it is placed.[2]

Article 7:

Excess of authority or contravention of instructions

The conduct of an organ of a State or of a person or entity empowered to exercise elements of the governmental authority shall be considered an act of the State under international law if the organ, person or entity acts in that capacity, even if it exceeds its authority or contravenes instructions.[3]

Article 9:

Conduct carried out in the absence or default of the official authorities

The conduct of a person or group of persons shall be considered an act of a State under international law if the person or group of persons is in fact exercising elements of the governmental authority in the absence or default of the official authorities and in circumstances such as to call for the exercise of those elements of authority.[4]

The extent to which non-state actors can be engaged by these provisions hinges on what 'governmental authority' means. This consideration quickly meets a hurdle: the term holds different meanings across states – owing to the differences in domestic legal systems. On the one hand, therefore, the extent to which international law can provide interpretative guidance regarding the term 'governmental authority' is limited. On the other, by analysing 'governmental authority' as applied under Articles 5, 7 and 9, whilst taking into consideration the overall broader context of each respective provision, it will be possible to gauge the parameters of these tests, how this affects their applicable scope, and how these understandings impact assessments of state responsibility for non-state actor conduct. Readers may have noticed that Article 6 was left out in the previous sentence, and deliberately so. The reasons are twofold. First, Articles 5, 7 and 9 do not convey that they exclusively concern the conduct of states. In so far as Articles 5 and 9 are concerned, at face value these provisions apply to non-state actors exclusively. However, from reading Article 6 and its commentary, the provision has no applicability to non-state actors, only states. Any application of Article 6 to non-state actors thus relies on doing so by analogy, whereas the other three provisions can apply to non-state actors without any need for

[1] ARSIWA, Art 5.
[2] ARSIWA, Art 6.
[3] ARSIWA, Art 7.
[4] ARSIWA, Art 9.

analogy. Second, although the provision could be applied by analogy to non-state actors, this would make little sense. Such a test would actually depend more on assessing factors that are addressed under other bases of attribution (for example, a state issuing instructions or a state acknowledging and adopting the conduct in question as its own).[5] Before turning to how the concept of governmental authority developed with respect to attribution, it is perhaps worthwhile to provide some further clarity as to why extending the application of Article 6 by analogy to non-state actors would not add much, if anything, to the international law applicable to determining state responsibility for non-state actor conduct.

1. THE (IM)PRACTICALITIES OF ANALOGY: ARTICLE 6 AND NON-STATE ACTORS

The practice of states placing persons or other actors at the disposal of another state is not unknown. An example would be a state lending personnel of its armed forces to another state that is a military ally.[6] Article 6 concerns instances in which an organ of one state is placed at the disposal of another state. Attribution under this provision takes place when the organ that is placed at the disposal of the latter exercises elements of the governmental authority of that state. International responsibility thus falls on the state that is utilising the organ should it undertake conduct that is contrary to an international rule.

Although Article 6 explicitly refers to state organs, the language of the provision presents a paradox because the 'governmental authority' being exercised must be of the state utilising the actor lent to it and not the state to which the actor belongs. This calls into question why the actor being lent should be limited to state organs. Article 6 was constructed by the ILC to assist in allocating responsibility when states benefit from the conduct of other persons or entities lent to them by another state. Its existence is an attempt to address situations in which if an actor acting for the benefit of a state were to undertake conduct that was contrary to an international rule, that state would not be able to claim that the conduct in question could not be attributed to it because the actor was not one of its own organs, in that the actor did not form part of its official state structure. This understanding conveys a message that Article 6 perhaps should apply by analogy to non-state actors. However, the hesitancy towards this approach lies in the practical point of doing so in light of several factors. Would applying Article 6 by analogy to non-state actors bring anything new to the state responsibility framework? The answer to this question becomes clearer in light of (1) how Article 6 developed, (2) the limitations of this provision when applied in practice, and (3) when attempting to answer the following question: can non-state actors be placed at the disposal of a state? The remainder of this section engages with these points in turn.

[5] See respectively Arts 8 and 11, ARSIWA.

[6] For more examples, see the commentary to Art 6; See also R Kolb, *The International Law of State Responsibility: An Introduction* (Cheltenham, Edward Elgar, 2017) n 259.

1.1. A Short History of How the Provision Developed

The idea of attributing conduct to a state for the conduct of actors placed at its disposal by another state first arose in Ago's third report to the ILC.[7] Article 6 was created out of a perceived need to address situations in which a state was using actors that were not part of its official machinery to perform certain tasks or functions. The provision that became Article 6 was based on some international practice.[8] Examination of these sources at the time led to an understanding that conduct of an actor lent by one state to another state could be attributed to the latter if the actor had been 'placed at the disposal of' that state, 'that is to say, if it is acting under the authority and in accordance with the instructions of the "beneficiary" State'.[9] Article 6 during its drafting was originally intended to apply across a spectrum of actors so long as they had international legal personality and the beneficiary state used the actor loaned to it.[10] The premise of the draft provision not being limited to state organs was based on the stance that what really appeared to matter was the beneficiary entity being a state.[11] The status of the actor being lent was a matter that was not examined in any detail.[12]

Both Ago and the ILC envisaged the inclusion of intergovernmental organisations in Article 6.[13] The draft provision that became Article 6 viewed these entities as having the potential to play roles in which their organs were placed at the disposal of states.[14] The trigger for attribution purposes was thus understood as the beneficiary state's use of whatever actor had been lent to it and whether that actor had exercised governmental authority of the state to whose benefit it was ostensibly acting. Attribution under this provision was envisaged as relating to assistance that may be given in situations such as suppressing an insurrectional movement or responding to a disaster.[15] As Ago himself put it

> Obviously, assistance of this nature may be provided not by another State but by an international organization or institution; and it goes without saying that situations of this kind are likely to become increasingly frequent in the widening framework of bilateral or multilateral assistance programmes.[16]

[7] Third Report, State Responsibility, Roberto Ago, A/CN.4/246 and Add 1–3, YBILC (1971) vol II(1), 267.

[8] United Nations Reports of International Arbitral Awards, vol II (United Nations publication, Sales No 1949.V.I) 1115–16; *Mr Anfora to Mr Arbiju*, 14 November 1872 (Archivio del Ministero degli Affari Esteri italiano, serie Politica A, No 1244); ACh Kiss, *Répertoire de la pratique française en matière de droit international public* (Paris, CNRS, 1965) vol III, no 898, 524.

[9] Third Report, Ago (1971) 272.

[10] ibid 268–73.

[11] ibid 268.

[12] The status of the 'beneficiary' may also not need to be a state, as alluded to by the ICJ in the *Bosnia Genocide* case (see discussion below).

[13] Third Report, Ago (1971) 274; ILC Report, Twenty-Third Session, 26 April–30 July 1971, UNGA, Twenty-Sixth Session, Supp No 10, A/8410/Rev.1, YBILC (1971) vol. II(1), 346.

[14] ibid.

[15] Third Report, Ago (1971) 267.

[16] ibid.

A significant change that took place during the creation of what became Article 6 was the deletion of references to the provision's application to actors in addition to state organs. Draft Article 9, which eventually became Article 6, was provisionally adopted by the ILC in 1974,[17] and then upon first reading in 1996.[18] It read:

> *Attribution to the State of the conduct of organs placed at its disposal by another State or by an international organization*
>
> The conduct of an organ which has been placed at the disposal of a State by another State or by an international organization shall be considered as an act of the former State under international law, if that organ was acting in the exercise of elements of the governmental authority of the State at whose disposal it has been placed.[19]

The first report of James Crawford contributed to altering the ILC's position on this provision.[20] It got the ball rolling towards the perspective that the provision should only apply to state organs, opposing outlooks that it should apply to other actors, in particular intergovernmental organisations.[21] The ILC adopted this recommendation, concluding that what became Article 6 was a 'limited but useful provision [and] should be retained so far as it related to the organs of States'.[22]

1.2. Limitations of the Provision

The reaction of states towards the initial inclusion of actors that were not state organs was mixed.[23] There were states that opposed the provision only applying to state organs. For example, France argued that the use of '"state organ" is too restrictive. It would be better to use the expression "any State organ or agent".'[24] The discussions in the drafting committee were similarly filled with uncertainties regarding how far the intended scope of application should extend.[25] What became Article 6 also received relatively little attention when compared with the comments received from states regarding the other attribution provisions. It has, however, received some attention since the ARSIWA was finalised.[26]

[17] ILC Report, Twenty-Sixth Session, 6 May–26 July 1974, A/9610/Rev.1, UNGA, Twenty-Ninth Session, Supp No 10, YBILC (1974), vol II(1), 277.

[18] ILC Report, Forty-Eighth Session, 6 May–26 July 1996, A/51/10, UNGA, Fifty-First Session, Supp No10, YBILC (1996) vol. II(2), 59.

[19] ibid.

[20] First Report, State Responsibility by James Crawford, A/CN.4/490 and Add 1–7 (1998) 44–46.

[21] ibid 46.

[22] ILC Report, Fiftieth Session, 20 April–12 June and 27 July–14 August 1998, A/53/10, UNGA, Fifty-Third Session, Supp No 10, YBILC (1998) vol II(2), 84.

[23] For example, Chile was in favour of the provision as it stood originally. Yugoslavia wanted to extend its application to ultra vires acts of the organ placed at the disposal of the beneficiary: Observations and comments of Governments on chapters I, II and III of Part I of the draft articles on State responsibility for internationally wrongful acts, A/CN.4/328 and Add 1–4, YBILC (1980) vol II(1), 97 and 105, respectively.

[24] State Responsibility, 50th Session of the ILC (1998), Agenda Item 2, Comments and observations received by Governments, A/CN.4/488 and Add 1–3, 108.

[25] Draft articles on State responsibility: texts adopted by the Drafting Committee – title of chap II and articles 7–9, A/CN.4/L.207, YBILC (1974) vol I, 153–54.

[26] Constance Regional Court (27 July 2006), case no 4 O 234/05 H; *Catan and Others v Moldova and Russia*, App Nos 43370/04, 8252/05 and 18454/06 (ECtHR, Judgment, 19 October 2012) para 74; *Electrabel*

The ICJ in the *Bosnia Genocide* judgment offers some insights into the applicable scope of Article 6. The provision arose in this case with respect to the Court's approach to the 'Scorpions' – not the rock band,[27] but the paramilitary group.[28] Their actions were prominent in the Srebrenica massacre, meaning it was necessary to establish whether this conduct was attributable to the state for the purpose of determining its international responsibility.[29] Marko Milanovic notes that during this case it 'was not conclusively established before any court … [what] was the exact position of the Scorpions in relation to Serbia'.[30] It was unclear whether the Scorpions were functioning as part of the wider (non-official) state machinery. The ICJ ruled that the evidence available before the Court was not sufficient to establish that the Scorpions were a state organ.[31] Article 6 was considered in these circumstances because the Scorpions were alleged to have been 'incorporated into Croatian Serb armed forces which were put at the disposal of the Bosnian Serbs'.[32] The response of the ICJ to this dynamic resulted in the following statement:

> [T]he act of an organ placed by a State at the disposal of another public authority shall not be considered an act of that State if the organ was acting on behalf of the public authority at whose disposal it had been placed.[33]

This stance of the ICJ is important for a few reasons with respect to the scope of Article 6. First, the state providing the actor in question appears to have attribution precluded if that actor was acting on behalf of another state to which it was placed. This component of preclusion is also mentioned in the commentary to the provision,[34] as well as being noted by the ECtHR.[35] Second, the ICJ implied that Article 6 might also apply to non-state actors by the use of the term 'public authorities' instead of 'state organs'. Whether this particular aspect of the judgment opens the door for the application of Article 6 to non-state actors will be dealt with below. Overall, the Court's rationale in the *Bosnia Genocide* case led it to taking the view that the conduct of the Scorpions was not attributable to the state under Article 6.[36]

SA v Hungary, ICSID, Case No ARB/07/19, Decision on Jurisdiction, Applicable Law and Liability (30 November 2012) para. 6.74; *Jaloud v The Netherlands*, App No 47708/08 (ECtHR, Judgment, 20 November 2014) paras 98 and 151; *Big Brother Watch and others v United Kingdom*, App Nos 58170/13, 62322/14 and 24960/15 (ECtHR, Judgment, 13 September 2018) para 420.

[27] See, for example, 'Rock You Like a Hurricane' (1984).

[28] *Application of the Convention on the Prevention and Punishment of the Crime of Genocide (Bosnia and Herzegovina v Serbia and Montenegro)*, Judgment of 26 February 2007, ICJ Rep [2007] 43, paras 289, 389, 390–95, 413.

[29] For more details on the conduct of the Scorpions in this case, see M Milanovic, 'State Responsibility for Genocide: A Follow-up' (2007) 18 *European Journal of International Law* 669, 674.

[30] ibid.

[31] *Application of the Convention on the Prevention and Punishment of the Crime of Genocide (Bosnia and Herzegovina v Serbia and Montenegro)*, Judgment of 26 February 2007, ICJ Rep [2007] 43, para 389.

[32] Milanovic (n 29) 674.

[33] *Application of the Convention on the Prevention and Punishment of the Crime of Genocide (Bosnia and Herzegovina v Serbia and Montenegro)*, Judgment of 26 February 2007, ICJ Rep [2007] 43, para 389.

[34] ARSIWA, Art 6, Commentary, para 1.

[35] *Behrami and Saramati v France, Germany and Norway* App Nos 71412/01 and 78166/01 (ECtHR, 2 May 2007) para 34.

[36] *Application of the Convention on the Prevention and Punishment of the Crime of Genocide (Bosnia and Herzegovina v Serbia and Montenegro)*, Judgment of 26 February 2007, ICJ Rep [2007] 43, para 414.

Another factor that relates to the applicable scope of Article 6 is that the term 'governmental authority' is not synonymous with 'control'. Yet the use of the term under Article 6 is linked to the type of 'control' that is perceived from the perspective of attribution considerations because determining whether a state has 'control' over the actor in question, for example if it issued instructions to it, assists in indicating whether the loaned actor was in fact acting on behalf of the beneficiary state. This understanding was also emphasised in the preparatory stages of what became Article 6, but is absent from the final commentaries:

> The condition that the organ in question shall have been 'placed at the disposal' of a State does not mean only that the organ must be appointed to perform functions appertaining to the State at whose disposal it is placed. It also requires that, in performing the functions entrusted to it by the beneficiary State, the organ shall act in conjunction with the machinery of that State and under its exclusive direction and control, not on instructions from the sending State.[37]

A crucial question when applying Article 6 is thus whether a beneficiary state has exercised the requisite level of 'control' that could be indicative of governmental authority being exercised through the loaned actor. Yet this approach to determining the exercise of governmental authority brings with it the matter of whether this attribution provision should extend its applicable scope to non-state actors.

1.2.1. *Why Article 6 Could Apply by Analogy to Non-state Actors*

The attribution test of 'acting in the exercise of elements of the governmental authority' under Article 6 rests on facts pointing to an actor being lent by one state to another, and then being used by the latter state. Whether the actor in question happens to be a state organ or not is arbitrary for attribution purposes for several reasons. First, there is no domestic law nexus under Article 6. The exercise of 'governmental authority' under this provision refers to that of the beneficiary state, meaning the domestic law that makes a particular actor a state organ in its 'home' state is irrelevant for attribution under this provision. Second, the role or mission that the actor undertakes for the beneficiary state may not necessarily be analogous to that 'normally' filled by an organ of that state or the one lending it, which again means the status of the actor under domestic law of the lending state is of no relevance. Third, the status of the actor is also irrelevant because under international law the loaned actor would essentially be acting as a de facto organ of the beneficiary state, and, in order to fulfil the 'governmental authority' requirement, a form of 'control' will likely have to be exercised over it for the lent period in order to satisfy the attribution threshold of the provision.[38] Fourth, there is a wonky logic in arguing that situations in which a state loans a non-state actor to a beneficiary state where the non-state actor then exercises governmental authority of the beneficiary is not attributable to that state, but an

[37] ILC Report, Twenty-Sixth Session, 6 May–26 July 1974, A/9610/Rev.1, UNGA, Twenty-Ninth Session, Supp No 10, YBILC (1974) vol II(1), 287.

[38] ARSIWA, Art 6, Commentary, para 4.

organ of the lending state – even though it is not acting in that official capacity – would be attributable to the beneficiary, especially if the beneficiary state utilised the two separate actors in the same way and their roles and conduct were factually identical.

So long as governmental authority has been exercised, why should it matter what status the actor has in another role as part, or not, of its lending state's organisational structure, especially considering that any loaned actor will likely be acting as a de facto state organ of the beneficiary state for a limited period? The ultimate decision of the ILC to exclude non-state actors from the scope of Article 6, a position that some states opposed,[39] is at odds with the above points. Although the ILC initially accepted that the provision should extend beyond state organs,[40] it becomes clear that the remarks of James Crawford that favoured limiting attribution under Article 6 to state organs were prescient. Before clarifying this point, it is first necessary to address the following question: so long as a state utilises an actor lent to it, what is the significance as a matter of international law whether the actor in question happens to be categorised as a state organ or not, which, it should be recalled, is determined by domestic law?

1.2.2. *How Article 6 Could Apply by Analogy to Non-state Actors*

There are some considerations to take into account if Article 6 were to be applied by analogy to non-state actors. The first is whether non-state actors could be the actor lending one of its own 'organs' to a state.[41] The second is whether non-state actors could be the actor that has been lent by a state. The last is whether a non-state actor could be a 'beneficiary' instead of a state. The first consideration is unlikely to be addressed by the international legal framework in the area of state responsibility because of the current doctrinal and arguably predominant approach taken towards the law in this field. For those who believe the law in this area should stick to what states do and do not do, and states alone, for the purposes of Article 6, it would be difficult to reconcile any other position than that which the actor lending one of its organs was a state.[42] The second consideration is perhaps more likely to be accepted in light of current understandings regarding attribution, in that this consideration is more in conformity with the traditional and (sometimes) fundamentalist approach to state responsibility, because it focuses on states interacting with one another, albeit

[39] State Responsibility, 50th Session of the ILC (1998), Agenda Item 2, Comments and observations received by Governments, A/CN.4/488 and Add 1–3, 108.

[40] ILC Report, Twenty-Sixth Session, 6 May–26 July 1974, A/9610/Rev.1, UNGA, Twenty-Ninth Session, Supp No 10, YBILC (1974), vol II(1), 277; ILC Report, Forty-Eighth Session, 6 May–26 July 1996, A/51/10, UNGA, Fifty-First Session, Supp No 10, YBILC (1996) vol II(2), 59.

[41] This is a similar understanding to how the role of intergovernmental organisations was envisaged in the original draft of the provision that became Art 6: ILC Report, Twenty-Sixth Session, 6 May–26 July 1974, A/9610/Rev.1, UNGA, Twenty-Ninth Session, Supp No 10, YBILC (1974) vol II(1) 277.

[42] J Crawford, 'The System of International Responsibility' in J Crawford, A Pellet and S Olleson (eds), *The Law of International Responsibility* (Oxford, Oxford University Press, 2010) 17; see also J Crawford and S Olleson, 'The Nature and Forms of International Responsibility' in M Evans (ed), *International Law*, 2nd edn (Oxford, Oxford University Press, 2006) 451.

by utilising the services of non-state actors. The last consideration may be viewed as inappropriate as the first, albeit for different reasons, as it concerns the international responsibility of non-state actors themselves. This consideration also falls within the scope of settings in which states provide assistance to non-state actors, and thereby relates to assessments focusing on potential state complicity in non-state actor conduct, which is a separate consideration from attribution.[43]

In light of the above, the ruling of the ICJ in the *Bosnia Genocide* judgment becomes all the more confusing, which is worth requoting:

> [T]he act of an organ placed by a State at the disposal of another public authority shall not be considered an act of that State if the organ was acting on behalf of the public authority at whose disposal it had been placed.[44]

This understanding of the Court implies that a non-state actor could be the beneficiary of a loaned organ, so long as it was a 'public authority'. Yet it 'is doubtful that the rule in Article 6 can truly be expanded to cover non-state actors in such an off-hand way as the Court did in paragraph 389 of its judgment'.[45] That said, when could Article 6 apply by analogy to non-state actors, not when these actors are the beneficiaries, as the ICJ implies, but when they are the actor being lent by one state to another?

1.2.3. *When Article 6 Could Apply by Analogy to Non-state Actors*

Situations where one state could place a non-state actor at the disposal of another state are not unfathomable, but illusive. An example would be where a state has lent a health agency to help another state in aid efforts during a public health emergency. The commentary to Article 6 mentions the use of health services for this purpose, but does not mention that not all health services in every state will be state organs.[46] For example, during the 2014–2016 Ebola outbreak a number of states offered the services of their healthcare agencies to the affected states in western Africa to assist in their response efforts.[47] Guinea, Liberia and Sierra Leone coordinated the administration of these agencies to work alongside their own state organs in response to the outbreak by, among other things, implementing public health emergency protocols and quarantining neighbourhoods within each respective state.[48] The foreign health agents working in these states could have been exercising elements of the governmental authority of these beneficiary states. Of the actors involved in responding to the Ebola outbreak, it is apparent that some were state organs, such as the health

[43] See chapter 6.

[44] *Application of the Convention on the Prevention and Punishment of the Crime of Genocide* (*Bosnia and Herzegovina v Serbia and Montenegro*), Judgment of 26 February 2007, ICJ Rep [2007] 43, para 389.

[45] Milanovic (n 29) 676.

[46] ARSIWA, Art 6, Commentary, para 3. Under domestic law, not all health units will be state organs. This will change from state to state. For example, in the United States the healthcare system is largely privatised, whereas in Belgium it is public.

[47] T Salaam-Blyther, 'US and International Health Responses to the Ebola Outbreak in West Africa', Congressional Research Service Report (29 October 2014).

[48] ibid 5.

ministries of Guinea and Liberia.[49] What is uncertain is whether other actors involved in the response, especially those loaned by foreign states, were de facto state organs of the lending state, other types of non-state actors or quasi-public entities that provide healthcare in their home state and perhaps exercise elements of governmental authority in doing so. For example, the United States Agency for International Development was involved in assisting with the Ebola outbreak. Although it is a government agency, it is unclear whether some of its branches can be considered as state organs under US domestic law because they are listed as 'independent' of the organisation itself.[50]

As mentioned above, one method of determining whether the attribution threshold under Article 6 has been satisfied is showing that the beneficiary state issued some form of instructions to the non-state actor lent to it.[51] Yet this is the point at which the practicality of attempting to apply Article 6 by analogy to non-state actors begins to fall apart. If a finding of instructions being issued by a state to a non-state actor were established, then, regardless of whether a lending state had placed the non-state actor at the disposal of a beneficiary state, attribution based on different tests would become a more relevant consideration. This raises the question whether it is possible for a beneficiary state to regulate such non-state actors without issuing instructions in some form.

Perhaps the last nail in the coffin of thoughts aimed at applying Article 6 by analogy to non-state actors arrives when attempting to discern the meaning of 'placed at the disposal'. Clarifying what this phrase means highlights that applying Article 6 by analogy to non-state actors becomes superfluous in light of other applicable attribution tests, in particular that under Article 8. This point is based on several factors. The first is the 'establishment of a functional link' between the actor that has been loaned and the receiving state.[52] This means that the receiving state must actually use the actor placed at its disposal. How can a state use a non-state actor without issuing a form of instructions or empowering it to exercise governmental authority (which would be addressed by applying Articles 8 and 5, respectively)? The second factor is that in order for conduct to be attributed to a state under Article 6 the loaned actor being used cannot retain autonomy; it must act in conjunction with the beneficiary's state machinery and be directed by it.[53] The loaned actor must not be acting for the lending state, at least officially. If an actor does not retain autonomy when carrying out its conduct, then it can be inferred that is has been issued some form of instructions, which again points to the appropriateness of applying alternative attribution tests.

A similar issue occurs when attempting to understand what 'acting in the exercise of elements of the governmental authority of the receiving State' means.[54] In light of the limited commentary and practice surrounding the provision, determining whether

[49] ibid 17.

[50] For more information, visit www.usaid.gov/who-we-are.

[51] ILC Report, Twenty-Sixth Session, 6 May–26 July 1974, A/9610/Rev.1, UNGA, Twenty-Ninth Session, Supp No 10, Yearbook of the ILC (1974) vol II(1), 287.

[52] ARSIWA, Art 6, Commentary, para 4.

[53] ibid.

[54] ibid para 5.

'governmental authority' has been exercised for the purposes of attribution under Article 6 may well be a non-starter. The analysis above is based on the premise that if states have the power to place their organs at the disposal of one another, they can also place non-state actors at the disposal of one another, with the additional benefit of increasing the degrees of separation between the lending state and any repercussions that could fall on the loaned actor if it were to undertake conduct contrary to international rules. The example of the Ebola outbreak squares with at least some of the logic behind the formation of Article 6, if not its current language. However, attribution assessments in such settings are more likely to fall within the ambit of other tests that need not be extended by analogy to non-state actors.

1.3. Can Non-state Actors Be Placed at the Disposal of a State?

Although the short answer to the above question is yes, the longer answer explored above is revealing. Attempting to address questions of state responsibility in settings where non-state actors may have been placed at the disposal of states is somewhat of a redundant exercise if done through the application of Article 6 by analogy. If this provision were to be applied by analogy to non-state actors, attribution would likely hinge on whether the beneficiary state issued some form of instructions or authority to the non-state actor in question, which would be covered by other attribution tests, for example, Articles 8 and 5, respectively. Further, if the non-state actor happened to be the beneficiary of a state organ being lent to it, and that organ undertook conduct contrary to an international rule, such a situation could be addressed by examining it from the perspective of state complicity in non-state actor wrongdoing. Perhaps what is most revealing about attempting to ascertain whether Article 6 could be applied by analogy to non-state actors is that the term 'governmental authority' appears to have little or no bearing on whether the attribution threshold under this provision would be satisfied. Is this any different with respect to the use of this term under the other attribution provisions of the ARSIWA? Answering this question requires looking at how the ARSIWA provisions that concern governmental authority came to be.

2. ORIGINS AND DEVELOPMENT OF THE TERM 'GOVERNMENTAL AUTHORITY'

Before the idea of 'governmental authority' arose in the work of the ILC, analysis focused on situations where non-state actors performed functions 'normally' undertaken by state organs.[55] The term 'exercising elements of the governmental authority'

[55] ILC Report, Fourteenth Session, 24 April–29 June 1962, UNGA, Seventeenth Session, Supp 9 (A/5209), YBILC (1962) vol II, 91; ILC Report, Twenty-Second Session, 4 May–10 July 1970, UNGA, Twenty-Fifth Session, Supp 10 (A/8010/Rev.1), YBILC (1970) vol II, 305–09; see also the work of Garcia-Amador: Report, Garcia-Amador (1956); Second Report, Garcia Amador (1957); Third Report, Garcia-Amador (1958); Fourth Report, Garcia-Amador (1959); Fifth Report, Garcia-Amador (1960); Sixth Report, Garcia-Amador (1961).

was born out of a rationale that situations could present themselves in which non-state actors undertook 'state-like' roles.[56] There was a perceived need to create an attribution test that addressed conduct of private persons used by states as their auxiliaries, sometimes without any official acknowledgement of states. Such themes were present in legal practice during the beginning of the twentieth century.[57] Ago considered that states should bear responsibility when acts of non-state actors related 'to one of the functions, tasks or missions [of the state] resulted in a breach of an international obligation'.[58] A key proposition that shaped the 'governmental authority' criterion was that state responsibility for private persons undertaking conduct that would traditionally lie with the state should be analysed on the basis of a yardstick examining

> the public character of the function or mission in the performance of which the act or omission contrary to international law was committed, rather than the formal link between the State organization and the person whose conduct is in question.[59]

This standpoint was to an extent embedded in Draft Article 7, which was provisionally adopted in 1974:

> *Attribution to the State of the conduct of other entities empowered to exercise elements of the governmental authority*
>
> 1. The conduct of an organ of a territorial governmental entity within a State shall also be considered as an act of that State under international law, provided that organ was acting in that capacity in the case in question.
> 2. The conduct of an organ of an entity which is not a part of the formal structure of the State or of a territorial governmental entity, but which is empowered by the internal law of that State to exercise elements of the governmental authority, shall also be considered as an act of the State under international law, provided that organ was acting in that capacity in the case in question.[60]

The actors referred to in this provision are those that are apparently separate from the state, but empowered by the same domestic laws as state organs. Crawford expressed doubts regarding whether such actors could actually be viewed as separate from the state.[61] These doubts were, and still are, pertinent because despite Ago framing the creation of this provision as extending attribution beyond state organs, a formal link in the form of domestic law was, and still is, required between states and non-state actors that exercise governmental authority. Yet the ILC wanted to attempt guarding against states avoiding responsibility because of the involvement of actors whose classification under domestic law was unclear.[62] This is because private entities have

[56] Third Report, Ago (1971) 262.

[57] Mexico–United States of America General Claims Commission, 15 July 1927, UNRIAA, vol IV, 267.

[58] Third Report, Ago (1971) 264.

[59] ibid.

[60] ILC Report, Twenty-Sixth Session, 6 May–26 July 1974, UNGA, Twenty-Ninth Session, Supp 10 (A/9610/Rev.1), YBILC (1974) vol II(1), 277.

[61] First Report, Crawford (1998) 33. This doubt also applied to Draft Articles 6, 7, 9, 10, 12 and 13.

[62] ILC Report, Twenty-Sixth Session, 6 May–26 July 1974, UNGA, Twenty-Ninth Session, Supp 10 (A/9610/Rev.1), YBILC (1974) vol II(1), 278.

separate legal personality to the state under domestic law, meaning their agents are not considered to be state organs under national legal systems. But for the purposes of international law, they can be empowered by the domestic laws of states to officially act for them.

During the drafting of the ARSIWA there were indications that states were establishing entities to undertake tasks that were in their interests, but in a way so as to ensure those actors had separate organisational structures from states. Among these entities lay those that exercised public-like authority 'usually of a regulatory or executive nature'.[63] In formulating the test under Article 5, the ILC considered one provision would adequately govern the types of state activity envisaged at the time.[64] What was viewed as a determinative factor affecting attribution based on a test of governmental authority were indications that pointed to non-state actors carrying out specified functions that were 'akin to those normally exercised by organs of the state'.[65] Yet the ILC went a step further, adopting the idea that a formal link existing in domestic law was necessary for the purposes of determining whether public functions had been delegated to non-state actors. It can thus be questioned what the practical difference is between Article 5 and Article 4 for attribution purposes. Recall that Article 4 defines state organs as 'any person or entity which has that status in accordance with the internal law of the State' to act for the state.[66] And Article 5 concerns actors that are apparently not state organs, but which are 'empowered by the law of that State' to act for the state. One provision appears to say tomato and the other appears to say tomato, albeit in two different ways. Agree or disagree, the existence of domestic law is the kicker under both provisions.

Yet it is questionable why the domestic law requirement exists for the purposes of attribution under Article 5, as this position was met with pushback during the drafting of this provision. There were 'a number of Governments that had suggested deleting the reference to internal law to avoid creating the impression that it was necessarily the decisive criterion',[67] which will be shown became the case when Article 5 began applying in practice. The term 'governmental authority' was also debated. Views were expressed that 'it would be preferable to use the term "functions", which was broader than the term "governmental authority"'.[68] Comments from states also reveal that although the ILC discussed the test enshrined in Article 5 at length, ambiguity remained. The UK requested 'clearer guidance' on what entities would fall within the scope of this test, and called for 'clarification of the notion "governmental authority"'.[69] As with the domestic law requirement, which makes it difficult to distinguish between state organs and non-state actors that exercise governmental authority, what is the difference between such actors from the perspective of

[63] ibid 281.
[64] ibid 282–83.
[65] First Report, Crawford (1998) 38.
[66] Art 4(2), ARSIWA.
[67] ILC Report, Fiftieth Session, 20 April–12 June 1998 and 27 July–14 August 1998, UNGA, Fifty-Third Session, Supp 10 (A/53/10), YBILC (1998) vol II(2), 154.
[68] ibid 159.
[69] First Report, Crawford (1998) 38.

international law if both types officially conduct their duties on the behalf of states, as prescribed by domestic law?

Germany considered that the test 'might not sufficiently take into account the fact that States increasingly entrust persons outside the structure of State organs with activities normally attributable to a State'.[70] In assessing this feedback, Crawford argued that treating actors that could fall within the scope of Article 5 as 'separate from the State machinery proper' was 'an error'.[71] Again this raises the question: if actors are part of the official state structure, in that domestic law stipulates they are part of a state, what is the difference between a 'state organ' and another actor that exercises state authority? Although this problem is in part a definitional one for domestic law, under international law it bears directly on what conduct can and cannot be attributed to states. Yet this does not mean that a definition of 'governmental authority' could not have been provided by the ILC.

However, Crawford believed that the ILC should not have attempted to define 'governmental authority'.[72] The ILC followed Crawford's assessment, which is why the commentary to Article 5 specifically states that it does 'not attempt to identify precisely the scope of "governmental authority" for the purpose of attribution'.[73] This is because '[b]eyond a certain limit, what is regarded as "governmental" depends on the particular society, its history and traditions'.[74] That said, when applying this test, elements that consistently arise through its interpretation become clearer, which in turn help explain what governmental authority actually is for the purposes of attribution. This application also points to a finding that the functions of state organs are only slightly, if at all, different from the functions of non-state actors that exercise governmental authority, especially in states where parts of the public sector are, or are being, privatised. To give an illustration of this, a police officer is understood to be a state organ under domestic law, meaning they are understood as such for the purposes of international law, and a community support officer is understood not to be a state organ under domestic law, meaning they are understood as such for the purposes of international law. Both actors officially act on the behalf of the state and both exercise state authority prescribed by domestic laws. What is the difference between such actors for the purposes of attribution under international law?

3. WHAT *IS* 'GOVERNMENTAL AUTHORITY' FOR THE PURPOSES OF ATTRIBUTION?

Governmental authority 'has increased in relevance as the modern state has outsourced increasing numbers of what would classically have been considered "government" functions'.[75] The entities envisaged by the ILC falling within this category of actors

[70] ibid.
[71] ibid.
[72] ibid 39.
[73] ARSIWA, Art 5, Commentary, para 6.
[74] First Report, Crawford (1998) 39. This sentence is used verbatim in para 6 of the final commentary to Art 5.
[75] Crawford, *State Responsibility: The General Part*, 127.

are those entrusted by states with the provision of general services or the performance of specific missions. The range of possible actors is wide. They can include 'public corporations, semi-public entities, public agencies of various kinds and even, in special cases, private companies'.[76] Examples of general service entities are state-owned oil companies, prisons, public transport providers, healthcare units, policing services, armed services and immigration bodies. Examples of entities undertaking specific missions are security services employed to guard mining sites, or a private military company being 'secretly appointed … to help an insurrectional movement in a neighbouring country'.[77] Many questions arise regarding attribution and non-state actor conduct in light of Articles 5, 7 and 9: what are public functions? What is conduct of a 'public character'? What functions of a state can we assume to be public, especially in light of the modern practices of states and their outsourcing to the private sphere? And how are any of these functions different from what state organs do in their official capacity? A common feature of Articles 5, 7 and 9 is that their creation was based on an intention to expand the reach of attribution under the ARSIWA to situations where state organs are not present. Was this intention achieved? The following analysis helps provide answers to these questions, drawing on developments in practice that also help determine the applicable scope of each provision.

3.1. The Article 5 Version of Governmental Authority

In the *Moses* case the arbitrator overseeing proceedings had the idea that 'a functionary or a person vested with authority represents *pro tanto* [to that extent] his government which, from an international point of view is the ensemble of all the functionaries and of all persons vested with authority'.[78] A similar stance was taken in the *German Settlers* case.[79] Commentators working in the same period as these cases also helped entrench this view.[80] In a more recent case, two related points were made.[81] First, construction work aimed at developing public infrastructure, such as roads and bridges, is a 'core function' of a state, meaning if work of this nature is outsourced to private contractors, then their conduct can be attributed to the state that hired them.[82] Second, it was held that: 'Any entity empowered by a State to exercise elements of governmental authority is for that purpose acting as an organ of State.'[83] Although Article 5 gives the appearance that it extends attribution under the ARSIWA beyond state organs, it is restricted to actors that can be officially considered as part of the state machinery as determined by domestic law, which encompasses

[76] ARSIWA, Art 5, Commentary, para 2; see also Communication No 120/1998 (25 May 1999), UN Doc CAT/C/22/D/120/1998.

[77] Third Report, Ago (1971) 263.

[78] JB Moore, *International Arbitrations*, vol III (Washington, 1871) 3127.

[79] *Certain questions relating to settlers of German origin in the territory ceded by Germany to Poland*, Advisory Opinion, 10 September 1923, PCIJ, Series B, No 6, 22.

[80] D Anzilotti, *Cours de droit international* [1929] (Paris, 1999) 469.

[81] *Garanti Koza LLP v Turkmenistan*, ICSID Case No ARB/11/20, Award (19 December 2016).

[82] ibid para 335.

[83] ibid.

state organs and actors that officially act on the behalf of a state – whatever the actual differences are between these two types of actors.

Based on the commentary to the ARSIWA it is hard to picture the difference. For example, the police are given as an example of entities that should be classified as state organs, even if domestic law does not make reference to this status.[84] This is why the word 'includes' is used in paragraph 2 of Article 4 ('An organ includes any person or entity which has that status in accordance with the internal law of the State'[85]), to convey a message that a state 'cannot avoid responsibility for the conduct of a body which does in truth act as one of its organs merely by denying it that status under its own law'.[86] According to the ILC, 'state organ' is a term that is supposed to be broadly read for the purposes of Article 4,[87] making it hard to grasp in what ways such actors are any different from those that have also been empowered by the applicable domestic law to act for the state, which appear to fall under Article 5. An official link between an actor and a state comes about via domestic law stipulating as much.[88] Domestic law determines whether a connection between an actor and a state is official or not. Yet Article 5 implies that governmental authority can extend beyond the public sector as there are instances in which there appears to be a separation between non-state actors that have been empowered to act for states, and state organs that have also been empowered to do so.[89] But is this a distinction without a difference?

One possible answer in the negative to this question can be seen in export credit agencies. These agencies appear not to fall into the category of state organs, despite being empowered by domestic law to officially act on the behalf of states.[90] They are regulated under domestic laws, regulations or charters, all of which empower them to exercise governmental authority.[91] Another example of the potential difference between Articles 4 and 5 becomes apparent when reflecting on a case brought against

[84] ARSIWA, Art 4, Commentary, para 11.

[85] This provision reads:

Conduct of organs of a State

1. The conduct of any State organ shall be considered an act of that State under international law, whether the organ exercises legislative, executive, judicial or any other functions, whatever position it holds in the organization of the State, and whatever its character as an organ of the central Government or of a territorial unit of the State.
2. An organ includes any person or entity which has that status in accordance with the internal law of the State.

[86] ARSIWA, Art 4, Commentary, para 11.

[87] ibid.

[88] For example, in the *Flemingo* case, statutory provisions showed that public functions relating to transport had been delegated to a non-state actor: *Flemingo DutyFree Shop Private Limited v Poland*, PCA, Award, IIC 883 (2016), 12 August 2016, para 439.

[89] *Saint-Gobain Performance Plastics Europe v Venezuela*, ICSID Case No ARB/12/13, Decision on Liability and the Principles of Quantum (30 December 2016) paras 457–58; *Women Victims of Sexual Torture in Atenco v Mexico*, Preliminary Objection, Merits, Reparations and Costs, Series C No 371 (IAtCHR, Judgment, 28 November 2018) para 205 and n 303.

[90] For example, the Export Credit Agencies in the United Kingdom and the United States are separate divisions of the government, but in Canada and Australia they are corporations that are owned by the state. See O Can and SL Seck, 'The Legal Obligations with Respect to Human Rights and Export Credit Agencies' ECA-Watch, Halifax Initiative Coalition and ESCR-Net, Final Discussion Paper (4 June 2006), in particular at 6–10, where attribution is discussed.

[91] ibid 5.

Oman, where it was held that Article 5 'provides a useful guide as to the dividing line between sovereign and commercial acts'.[92] Yet the commentary to Article 4 states: 'It is irrelevant for the purposes of attribution that the conduct of a State organ may be classified as "commercial".'[93] Whether commercial conduct is attributable to a state may therefore indicate whether an actor in a particular case should be classified as a state organ or a non-state actor that has been empowered to exercise governmental authority. It should be recalled that in some domestic legal systems

> the status and functions of various entities are determined not only by law but also by practice, and reference exclusively to internal law would be misleading. The internal law of a State may not classify, exhaustively or at all, which entities have the status of 'organs'.[94]

This may well be one difference between Articles 4 and 5, in that state organs can undertake commercial conduct in their official capacity, and that conduct will likely still be attributable to the state, and non-state actors that are empowered to exercise governmental authority can also undertake commercial conduct, but that conduct will be less likely to be attributed to the state.

In the *Eureko* case it was noted that attribution under Article 5 encompasses conduct undertaken for the benefit of a state.[95] Here it was ambiguous what status the Polish Treasury held under domestic law.[96] Yet because the conduct of the actor in question was contrary to the applicable treaty and that actor had been empowered to exercise governmental authority, Poland was held responsible 'whatever may be the status of the State treasury in Polish law'.[97] The *Nobel Ventures* arbitration also highlights that a finding of 'governmental authority' being exercised by an actor means that for the purposes of attribution it does not matter all that much whether an actor is perceived to be part of the public or private sphere of society.[98] In this case the respondent state argued that distinctions have to be drawn between governmental and commercial conduct when determining state responsibility.[99] This may be true in the general sense. However, the Tribunal noted that the conduct of a non-state actor that is not a state organ could be attributed to a state in specific situations if it exercised 'elements of governmental authority'.[100] It was thus held that the acts of a private company were attributable to the state.[101] A similar stance was taken in the *Ximenez-Lopes* case.[102] Affirming that 'governmental authority' has been exercised is unaffected by the sphere to which an actor belongs under international or domestic law, whether public, private or somewhere quasi in nature.[103] This answers the

[92] *Adel A Hamadi Al Tamimi v Oman*, ICSID, Case No ARB/11/33, Award (3 November 2015) para 324.
[93] ARSIWA, Art 4, Commentary, para 6.
[94] ibid para 11.
[95] *Eureko BV v Republic of Poland*, Partial Award (19 August 2005) para 132.
[96] ibid paras 115–34.
[97] ibid para 134.
[98] *Noble Ventures, Inc. v Romania* (ICSID Case No ARB/01/11), Award (12 October 2005).
[99] ibid para 67.
[100] ibid para 70.
[101] ibid para 80.
[102] *Ximenes-Lopes v Brazil*, Merits, Reparations and Costs, I-ACHR, Series A, No 149, Judgment (4 July 2006) paras 84–87.
[103] A point made by Sudan suggests this is not the case: 'With regard to article 5, entitled "Conduct of persons or entities exercising elements of governmental authority", the conduct of persons or entities that

question of what actors can wield governmental authority, in that, theoretically at least, anyone and anything can. Yet this does little to answer the question of what governmental authority is, and overlooks the domestic law requirement and what are considered to be, for the time being at least, public functions.

3.1.1. Domestic Law Requirement

Under Article 5, elements of governmental authority being exercised must be 'empowered by the law' of the state with which there is a link.[104] If attribution is to take place, governmental authority must come about by domestic law pointing towards such empowerment. The commentary and preparatory work of the ARSIWA provide little indication as to what type of domestic law is needed, which again makes it difficult to determine what the difference is for the purposes of international law between a state organ and an actor exercising governmental authority.[105] Legislation seems appropriate. Whether a contract would also suffice is uncertain. The importance of contracts governing the relationships between states and non-state actors should not be understated. In certain fields in particular, such as the employment of private companies to act for the state, a contract will predicate the mandate prescribed by the state.[106] On the uncertainty of whether contracts would suffice as domestic law for the purposes of Article 5, it is worth noting that contracts are not law in and of themselves; it depends on what the contract stipulates and the law governing the particular contract, both of which determine whether it is or is not a contract in the eyes of the law. Some commentators have mentioned that contracts may qualify as domestic law for attribution purposes under Article 5.[107] Yet if contracts between states and non-state actors were to satisfy the element of 'empowered by the law', this would depend on being able to access and review those contracts.

Here exists a catch-22. Whether a contract is domestic law for the purposes of Article 5 can only be determined by examining such a document. But if there is no way to view it, such a determination cannot be made.[108] Logic suggests that there will be domestic laws within government contracts with private actors in order to

do not belong to State organs is a matter of internal law. To attribute such conduct to the State and hold the latter responsible for it would undermine the principle that international law and the national law of the State are complementary' (UNGA, Responsibility of States for internationally wrongful acts, Comments and information received from Governments, Report of the Secretary-General (12 July 2019), A/74/156, The Sudan, 6, para 2).

[104] ARSIWA, Art 5.

[105] ibid, Commentary, paras 1–7; ILC Report, Twenty-Sixth Session, 6 May–26 July 1974, UNGA, Twenty-Ninth Session, Supp 10 (A/9610/Rev.1), YBILC (1974) vol II(1), 277–83.

[106] See UK Ministry of Defence, 'Military Interaction with Private Military and Security Companies', Joint Doctrine Note 1/08 (Development, Concepts and Doctrine Centre) 2–5.

[107] S Taylor, 'Australian Funded Care and Maintenance of Asylum Seekers in Indonesia and Papua New Guinea: All Care but No Responsibility' (2010) 33 *University of New South Wales Law Journal* 337, 345; OR Jones, 'Implausible Deniability: State Responsibility for the Actions of Private Military Firms' (2009) 24 *Connecticut Journal of International* 239, 267–68.

[108] Depending on the powers of a particular court or tribunal, it could compel a party to a dispute to reveal the contents of the contract. In settings involving national security matters, this possibility may become more unlikely the more classified a matter becomes.

protect and balance the interests of both parties.[109] This cannot be assumed, however. Some commentators have focused on the term 'governmental authority' as though it were the principal consideration under Article 5.[110] This is understandable, as, at face value, Article 5 attempts to indicate as much. However, the term is secondary to the requirement of existing domestic law indicating that a non-state actor has been empowered to exercise governmental authority.[111] The commentary to Article 5 reveals that the use of the term 'governmental authority' and the provision overall was not intended to have a scope of application beyond a point in which the existence of domestic law is not necessary:

> The formulation of article 5 *clearly limits it to entities which are empowered by internal law to exercise governmental authority*. … The internal law in question must *specifically authorize* the conduct as involving the exercise of public authority; it is not enough that it permits activity as part of the general regulation of the affairs of the community. *It is accordingly a narrow category*.[112]

It is therefore not really through international law that an attributable link is established between non-state actor and state under this provision. Article 5 is instead just a reflection of what some people think the international law should be, in that international law requires a nexus to exist under domestic law if conduct is to be attributable to states, just as international law requires the same for actors to be deemed state organs. But why does the domestic law requirement exist?

In the comments received by governments during drafting of the ARSIWA, Japan argued that the 'empowered by the law' requirement refined the scope of attribution too far.[113] The consequence of restraining on what at first sight looks like a flexible attribution provision is states hiding behind domestic law when questions regarding their responsibility arise. The ILC noted that states avoiding responsibility 'by relying on their internal legal structures' was a matter that needed further attention.[114] Avoidance by domestic law remains a pertinent issue. The *Helnan* case provides insights as to how the 'empowered by the law' element can be approached to address this concern.[115] The claimant to this dispute argued that conduct of a non-state actor, EGOTH, was attributable to Egypt under either Article 4 or 5.[116] Egypt's counter-arguments were based on the non-state actor having separate legal personality and

[109] HLA Hart, 'The Ascription of Responsibility and Rights' (1949) 49 *Proceedings of the Aristotelian Society* 171, 175.

[110] DD Caron, 'The ILC Articles on State Responsibility: The Paradoxical Relationship between Form and Authority' (2002) 96 *American Journal of International Law* 857, 861; R McCorquodale and P Simons, 'Responsibility Beyond Borders: State Responsibility for Extraterritorial Violations by Corporations of International Human Rights Law' (2007) 70 *Modern Law Review* 598, 606–24.

[111] Crawford, *State Responsibility: The General Part*, 132.

[112] ARSIWA, Art 5, Commentary, para 7 (emphasis added).

[113] State Responsibility, Fifty-Third Session of the ILC (2001), Comments and Observations received from Governments, A/CN.4/515 and Add 1–3, 48–49.

[114] ILC Report, Fiftieth Session, 20 April–12 June 1998 and 27 July–14 August 1998, UNGA, Fifty-Third Session, Supp 10 (A/53/10), YBILC (1998) vol II(2), 158–59.

[115] *Helnan International Hotels A/S v Republic of Egypt* (ICSID Case No ARB/05/19), Decision on Objection to Jurisdiction (17 October 2006).

[116] ibid paras 84–90.

that none of its contracts were linked to the state through domestic law.[117] In answering whether EGOTH's conduct was attributable to Egypt, the Tribunal held:

> Even if EGOTH has not been officially empowered by law to exercise elements of the governmental authority, its actions within the privatisation process are attributable to the Egyptian State.[118]

This ruling contradicts the element of 'empowered by law'. The ruling can thus be read in two ways. First, the Tribunal mistakenly applied Article 5. Second, the Tribunal was attempting to alter the application of Article 5 by consciously reading out the 'empowered by the law' requirement.

Despite this decision, Article 5 is thought of as requiring two elements to be satisfied. The first, despite being disputed by states, is that there must be evidence of some form of domestic law that appears to empower an actor to undertake a particular role on the behalf of the state in question. The second is that in the course of this role, it must be shown that the entity has been empowered by this domestic law to exercise elements of governmental authority.[119] Taken in combination, application of these elements results in an obscure attribution threshold that appears to be not so different to that under Article 4; and, when taken separately, these elements are difficult to prove. The first because of the possible difficulties in obtaining the domestic law needed if it is not publicly available. The second because the term 'governmental authority' is contextual and means different things in different settings.[120] Therefore, showing whether elements of governmental authority have actually been exercised by non-state actors rests on what can be characterised as 'public functions'.[121]

3.1.2. The Public Function Element

The commentary to Article 5 suggests the 'public character' of functions being exercised are those that would be 'normally exercised by State organs'.[122] The problem with this perspective in today's world is that because states can frequently rely on non-state actors to carry out their work, gauging what functions state organs 'normally' exercise today is not straightforward. Functions that are 'public in character' has become a diluted concept. For example, states rely on private military companies to participate on their behalf in armed combat operations, which are arguably settings in which state organs would 'normally' exercise the associated combat functions. The use of force by states is perhaps one of the starkest examples of functions that are public in character,[123] and yet this can no longer be said to be absolute, owing to the modern-day practices of states.[124]

[117] ibid paras 82–83.

[118] ibid para 93.

[119] ARSIWA, Art 5, Commentary, para 5.

[120] ibid para 6.

[121] ibid para 2.

[122] ibid.

[123] The Court in *Transaero, Inc v La Fuerza Aerea Boliviana*, Judgment (29 July 1994), 30 F 3d 148, 153 (DC Cir 1994) made such a point when it stated that the 'core functions' of an air force were 'predominantly governmental'.

[124] The decision of a US court asserts the contrary: *Al-Quraishi and 71 additional unidentified plaintiffs v Nakhla and L-3 Services Inc (formerly Titan Corporation)*, Decision on motion to dismiss (29 July 2010),

However, outsourcing does not necessarily negate the overall sense of what functions conventionally fall to state organs, for the time being at least. Certain functions are arguably public in character, meaning if they were to be undertaken by a non-state actor, such instances would point towards the potential for elements of governmental authority to be exercised. Domestic law thus becomes a helpful point of reference for establishing what can be viewed as functions normally undertaken by state organs.[125] One role is policing.[126] This raises important questions in many contexts. For example, states employ private companies to police their borders and patrol their streets.[127] When such actors are implicated in conduct that is contrary to their employer state's international legal obligations, it is likely that the governmental authority test would be met. Another example is private airlines that have powers conferred upon them by states that allow them to control immigration functions by, for example, quarantining people.[128] Other traditionally public roles can be deduced from drawing inferences from their attachment to different branches of the state structure.[129] An example from the executive branch is detention, where states incarcerate inmates in private prisons. This practice raises numerous concerns, including state responsibility.[130] If the international responsibility of a state were to be called into question in such a setting, it would be likely that both elements under Article 5 would be satisfied because domestic law is often publicly available by way of legislation.[131] Those employed by private prisons during their working hours, and these prisons as collective entities, are therefore arguably exercising elements of governmental authority by assuming a function that is 'normally' undertaken by state organs. Yet what is 'normal' in this sense can be hard to gauge.

Even dispute settlement is not a function of society that is purely public in character. This matter appeared before the ILC when drafting the ARSIWA. Concerns relating to state responsibility for private means of dispute settlement were raised at a number of junctures.[132] These revolved around religious institutions: 'In some situations, for example, religious bodies may exercise a degree of authority, perhaps including the power to punish persons for breaches of religious laws, but may not formally be a part

728 F Supp 2d 702 (District of Maryland) para 116: 'Operation of a military force is one of the most basic governmental functions, and one for which there is no privatized equivalent.'

[125] ARSIWA, Chapter II, Commentary, para 6.

[126] ibid.

[127] K Côté-Boucher, F Infantino and MB Salter, 'Border Security as Practice: An Agenda for Research' (2014) 45 *Security Dialogue* 195; See also T Hesson, '15 Companies That Profit From Border Security' *ABC News* (15 April 2013) http://abcnews.go.com/ABC_Univision/Politics/15-companies-profit-border-security/story?id=18957304.

[128] ARSIWA, Art 5, Commentary, para 2.

[129] ARSIWA, Art 4, Commentary, para 6.

[130] See B Obama, 'The President's Role in Advancing Criminal Justice Reform' (2017) 123 *Harvard Law Review* 811, 819–31.

[131] ibid 831; see also SQ Yates, 'Phasing Out Our Use of Private Prisons', US Department of Justice (18 August 2016) www.justice.gov/archives/opa/blog/phasing-out-our-use-private-prisons; Office of the Inspector General, US Department of Justice, 'Review of the Federal Bureau of Prisons' Monitoring of Contract Prisons' (August 2016) https://oig.justice.gov/reports/2016/e1606.pdf.

[132] First Report, Crawford (1998) 33; State Responsibility, 50th Session of the ILC (1998), Agenda Item 2, Comments and observations received by Governments, A/CN.4/488 and Add 1–3, 106; State Responsibility, Fifty-Third Session of the ILC (2001), Comments and Observations received from Governments, A/CN.4/515 and Add 1–3, 49.

of the governmental structure of the State.'[133] Religious dispute-settlement bodies are in place to govern matters that arise with respect to, for example, Islamic law,[134] the Catholic Church[135] or arbitration by a Beth Din.[136] As bodies governing religious disputes exercise a judicial role, their functioning calls into question whether their conduct could be viewed as satisfying the governmental authority test under Article 5. The United Kingdom saw this as a matter that required attention.[137] This enquiry was never clarified by the ILC, and remains a point of uncertainty. In deciding whether non-state actors were part of the wider instrumentalities of the state, the Tribunal in the *Hyatt* case stated that 'under the regime established by the Constitution an exercise of "religious" authority may also constitute an exercise of "governmental" authority'.[138] Here Iran argued that an agent of the state had acted 'not in his governmental capacity but in his capacity as a religious leader'.[139] It appears as though alternative dispute-settlement bodies in their role do not exercise governmental authority for the purposes of Article 5. Their functions relate to a compartment of life within a state, but which remain part of a society's private sphere at present.[140]

Other settings where the threshold of governmental authority is not likely to be met, even if there is existence of domestic law pointing toward the empowerment of non-state actors, are those relating to commercial activities.[141] If a non-state actor undertakes commercial activity, it is doubtful that governmental authority would be exercised.[142] In the view of the ILC, state ownership of an entity is therefore not sufficient for satisfying the attribution threshold under Article 5.[143] This applies 'even where such [a] corporation is wholly owned by the state or the state has a controlling interest in it'.[144] Commercial activity cannot be contorted to mean that functions of a public character are present regarding the role or the conduct of a non-state actor, unless there is some indication that the business enterprise is somehow in the public interest, thereby indicating it may be acting on behalf of the state. The Tribunal in the *United Parcel Services* case upheld this standpoint.[145] The ruling highlighted that even if a non-state actor is empowered to exercise elements of governmental authority, it

[133] State Responsibility, Fiftieth Session of the ILC (1998), Agenda Item 2, Comments and observations received by Governments, A/CN.4/488 and Add 1–3, 106.

[134] See generally MM Keshavjee, *Islam, Sharia & Alternative Dispute Resolution* (Basingstoke, Palgrave, 2013).

[135] I.M Ellman, 'Driven from the Tribunal: Judicial Resolution of Internal Church Disputes' (1981) 69 *California Law Review* 1378.

[136] G Fried, 'The Collision of Church and State: A Primer to *Beth Din* Arbitration and the New York Secular Courts' (2004) 31 *Fordham Urban Law Journal* 633.

[137] State Responsibility, Fifty-Third Session of the ILC (2001), Comments and Observations received from Governments, A/CN.4/515 and Add 1–3, 49.

[138] *Hyatt International Corporation v Iran* (1985) 9 Iran–US Claims Tribunal 72, 94.

[139] ibid 93.

[140] See C Chinkin, 'A Critique of the Public/Private Dimension' (1999) 10 *European Journal of International Law* 387, 391–92.

[141] Yet this rule is not absolute: ARSIWA, Art 4, Commentary, para 6.

[142] That said, conduct of such a non-state actor could still be attributed to a state under alternative attribution tests.

[143] ARSIWA, Art 5, Commentary, para 3.

[144] McCorquodale and Simons (n 110) 606.

[145] *United Parcel Services, Inc v Canada*, UNCITRAL, Award (11 June 2007) paras 76–78.

must actually be doing so at the time of the infringement, and not merely carrying out commercial activity. Korea took a similar stance in the *Measures Affecting Trade in Commercial Vessels* case.[146] This position is, however, not undisputed. In the context of trade and economic governance, Christine Chinkin contends that the 'argument that state responsibility is not applicable to commercial acts that constitute international wrongs committed by the state seems illogical'.[147] Within certain facets of commercial conduct, decisions are made by states, for example, regulating financial markets, or choosing not to, which is an ostensible expression of public preference.[148]

The granting of immunity can be a helpful indicator as to whether governmental authority has been exercised. Such an approach to assessing governmental authority is 'useful, and achieves consistency between these different areas of international law'.[149] Instances where sovereign authority is being wielded may also shed light on whether governmental authority has been exercised.[150] Governmental authority could exist in a case when a court/tribunal makes a finding of immunity.[151] The case of *DRC v Hemisphere Associates* provides guidance on this point.[152] Here the Court acknowledged that immunity is granted to acts that are 'governmental' in nature.[153] It went on to rule that negative pronouncements of sovereign, governmental acts begin to manifest themselves once state officials begin to engage in activities that are private in nature.[154] In examining whether immunity should be granted, focus falls on the 'nature of the act' in order to separate 'the public and private spheres of state action'.[155] The Court held that immunity does not protect defendants in cases where the actor being sued has 'not performed any activities connected with the exercise of governmental authority'.[156] A positive finding of state immunity thus points to non-state actor conduct being state-like for the purposes of attribution under Article 5.

The 'functions of a public character' element relates to the role held by a non-state actor that serves a public function (ie that which would 'normally' be assumed by a state organ).[157] It is not sufficient to satisfy the attribution threshold under Article 5 that a non-state actor merely wields governmental authority – it must exercise it. Assessing whether a non-state actor has done so depends on the role that the actor had at the time of the conduct that was contrary to an international rule. This is a

[146] *Korea: Measures Affecting Trade in Commercial Vessels*, Report of the Panel (7 March 2005), WTO Doc WT/DS273/R, para 7.39.

[147] Chinkin (n 140) 392.

[148] ibid.

[149] Crawford, *State Responsibility: The General Part*, 130.

[150] *Luigiterzo Bosca v Lithuania*, UNCITRAL, PCA Case No 2011-05, Award, 17 May 2013, paras 123–28.

[151] See, for example, *Ungar v Palestine Liberation Organization [PLO] and Palestinian Authority*, Appeal Judgment (2005), Docket No 04-2079, 402 F.3d 274 (1st Circuit).

[152] *Democratic Republic of the Congo and Ors v FG Hemisphere Associates LLC*, [2011] Final appeal (Provisional Judgment) 4 HKC 151.

[153] ibid para 66.

[154] ibid para 74.

[155] H. Tonkin, *State Control over Private Military and Security Companies in Armed Conflict* (Cambridge, Cambridge University Press, 2011) 105.

[156] *DRC v Hemisphere Associates*, para 134.

[157] See ARSIWA, Art 5, Commentary, para 2: 'and the conduct of the entity relates to the exercise of the governmental authority concerned'.

two-pronged approach to the public function element.[158] Whether a particular role of a non-state actor is actually public in character can also be determined by it performing services that are intended for the community of the state as a whole.[159] The Court in the *Compagnie Noga D'Importation* case made a similar point when stating that certain types of financing were 'governmental' in nature because they helped improve the state overall.[160] This rationale can also apply in instances where a non-state actor has assisted a state in expropriating property. In the *Hyatt* case the Tribunal attributed conduct of a charity to Iran for expropriating contractual rights.[161] National interest expropriation would thereby be indicative of exercising governmental authority. The Court in the *La Générale des Carrières* case also points toward an understanding that exercising governmental authority is part of a wider pool of 'sovereign acts' serving 'the purposes of the state'.[162]

Although it is hard to tell what the practical distinction is between state organs and non-state actors that exercise governmental authority for the purposes of attribution, there may be the odd subtle differences in situations that mean the attribution threshold under Article 5 is satisfied where the threshold under Article 4 is not. Yet it is hard to say in the abstract what these differences are considering that both provisions hinge on whether a link exists under domestic law between the abstract state and a particular actor that acts on its behalf in a particular role. The public function element of Article 5 provides some insight into what governmental authority means, in that if a non-state actor undertakes conduct that could be undertaken by the executive branch of a state, then that actor will likely be exercising governmental authority. And this point perhaps reveals the true distinction between state organs and non-state actors that exercise governmental authority – the key is in the name: governmental. The legislative and judicial branches of a state are state organs, and actors that fall into the executive branch (government) are also state organs, but their role can be undertaken by non-state actors empowered to exercise similar if not the same authority of the state. But what happens when such actors undertake conduct that was not prescribed by domestic law as part of their role? In other words, what happens when the practices of non-state actors extend beyond the authority granted to them by states?

3.2. The Article 7 Version of Governmental Authority

Article 7 can apply to settings in which an actor conducted itself in a manner that a state did not authorise.[163] The provision is an apparent 'expression of accepted principles

[158] ARSIWA, Art 5, Commentary, para 2.

[159] Observations and comments of Governments on chapters I, II and III of Part I of the draft articles on State responsibility for internationally wrongful acts, A/CN.4/328 and Add 1–4, YBILC (1980) vol II(1), 96.

[160] *Compagnie Noga D'Importation et D'Exportation SA v Russian Federation*, United States, Appeal Judgment (16 March 2004), 361 F.3d 676 (2nd Circuit) para 28.

[161] *Hyatt International Corporation v Iran* (1985) 9 Iran–US Claims Tribunal 72, 94.

[162] *La Générale des Carrières et des Mines v FG Hemisphere Associates LLC*, Appeal Judgment [2012] UKPC 27, para 46.

[163] ARSIWA, Art 7, Commentary, para 1.

of international law',[164] and began to be applied in practice before the ARSIWA was finalised.[165] The HRC, ECtHR and the House of Lords have also restated the value of the provision.[166] Of the states choosing to comment on the draft ARSIWA, they all scrutinised Article 7 in so far as it applied to state organs.[167] The extent to which this provision can apply to non-state actors depends on what 'governmental authority' means in the context of conduct that goes beyond the official mandate provided by a state. The first question is whether 'governmental authority' under Article 7 is similar in scope to 'governmental authority' under Article 5. From an initial reading, the omission of the 'empowered by the law' requirement in the text of the provision would suggest that the applicable scope is different. If no nexus is needed in domestic law, then this provision can be applied to a wider pool of non-state actors that are clearly distinct from state organs. Non-state actors in this category could have no legal ties with states, meaning their conduct could be attributed to states regardless of whether there were links between the two under domestic law, so long as there existed factual links.

However, this interpretation of Article 7 is out of sync with its commentary: 'As formulated, article 7 only applies to the conduct of an organ of a State or of an entity empowered to exercise elements of the governmental authority, i.e. only to those cases of attribution covered by articles 4, 5 and 6.'[168] It thus becomes clearer that the attribution threshold in instances where a non-state actor is linked to a state is governmental authority provided by domestic law. Although absent from the text of Article 7, the term 'empowered by the law' appears to apply. It is difficult to envisage how non-state actors can be empowered by a state to exercise governmental authority without a state officially mandating it through domestic law, even though non-state actors can be empowered in the more literal sense to undertake particular forms of conduct without any need for domestic law stipulating as much.

The ruling in the *Yeager* case also stipulates that governmental authority should be conferred by domestic law when applying Article 7.[169] This understanding helps distinguish between ultra vires conduct of an actor in its official capacity and conduct that is purely private.[170] In order to satisfy the attribution threshold under Article 7,

[164] *Amco Asia Corporation and Others v Republic of Indonesia* (ICSID Case No ARB/81/1) Award (31 May 1990) para 172; See also *Metalclad Corporation v United Mexican States*, NAFTA (ICSID Additional Facility), Award (30 August 2000) para 73.

[165] See, for example, *Prosecutor v Dusko Tadić*, Appeal Judgment, Case No IT-94-1-A, 15 July 1999, paras 121–23.

[166] Views of the HRC under the Optional Protocol to the International Covenant on Civil and Political Rights (*Sarma v Sri Lanka*), Communication No 950/2000: Sri Lanka, CCPR/C/78/D/950/2000, 31 July 2003, para 9.2; *Ilaşcu and Others v Moldova and Russia* App No 48787/99 (ECtHR, 8 July 2004), para 319; *Jones, Redress (intervening) and Ors (intervening) v Ministry of the Interior of Saudi Arabia and Lieutenant Colonel Abdul Aziz* [2006] UKHL 26, para 77.

[167] Observations and comments of Governments on chapters I, II and III of Part I of the draft articles on State responsibility for internationally wrongful acts, A/CN.4/328 and Add 1–4, YBILC (1980) vol II(1), 97 and 102 (Chile and the Netherlands, respectively); Comments and observations of Governments on part one of the draft articles on State responsibility for internationally wrongful acts, A/CN.4/414, YBILC (1988) vol II(1), 3 (Germany).

[168] ARSIWA, Art 7, Commentary, para 9.

[169] *Yeager v Islamic Republic of Iran* (1987), Iran–US CTR, vol 17, 111, para 65.

[170] ARSIWA, Art 7, Commentary, para 7.

the non-state actor must have undertaken conduct during a period where it was acting in its official capacity. As summarised by the Iran–US Claims Tribunal, attributable conduct under Article 7 is that 'carried out by persons cloaked with governmental authority'.[171] States in such situations can incur international responsibility even if non-state actors exceed their authority.[172] Having held the conduct of a non-state 'institution of public interest' was attributable to Romania, the Tribunal in the *Nobel Ventures* case stated this conclusion would have been identical even if the conduct at issue were to be considered ultra vires.[173] The Tribunal explicitly referred to Article 7 as applying equally to state organs and non-state actors acting in an official capacity on behalf of states. The ECtHR supports this view that a state can be held responsible for any of its 'agents' where their conduct exceeds their authority.[174]

The difficulty with applying Article 7 to attribute conduct of non-state actors to states is distinguishing between unauthorised but still 'official' conduct undertaken during a role that is designed to act on behalf of a state and private conduct that is not undertaken in that capacity.[175] In the *ADF* case the Tribunal upheld the official capacity element of Article 7: 'An unauthorized or *ultra vires* act of a governmental entity of course remains, in international law, the act of the State of which the acting entity is part, if that entity acted in its official capacity.'[176] If a non-state actor was present in its state-appointed role, even if acting beyond its authority or contrary to instructions, then its conduct can be attributed to a state.[177] The key element is whether a non-state actor was exercising elements of apparent state authority at the time when the conduct contrary to an international rule occurred.[178] A non-state actor conducting itself in excess of its competence does not prevent that conduct from being attributed to a state that prescribed the competence to undertake conduct on its behalf, even if that conduct is unlawful under the domestic law of the state with which the non-state actor shares a link.[179] The practice applying Article 7 suggests that domestic law is also the link that is needed between non-state actor and state if the provision's attribution threshold is to be satisfied. In terms of recognising whether

[171] *Petrolane, Inc v Iran* (1991), Iran–US CTR, vol 27, 64, 92.

[172] McCorquodale and Simons (n 110) 608.

[173] *Noble Ventures, Inc v Romania* (ICSID Case No ARB/01/11), Award (12 October 2005) para 81.

[174] *Ilaşcu and Others v Moldova and Russia*, App No 48787/99 (ECtHR, 8 July 2004) para 319.

[175] The ICJ grappled with this question in *Armed Activities on the Territory of the Congo (Democratic Republic of the Congo v Uganda)*, Judgment, 19 December 2005, ICJ Rep [2005] 168, paras 213, 214 and 243. See, in particular, Dissenting Opinion of Judge ad hoc Kateka, para 54.

[176] *ADF Group Inc v United States of America* (ICSID Additional Facility Case No ARB(AF)/00/1), Award (9 January 2003) para 190 (including n 184).

[177] See the discussion on Art 7 in *Jones, Redress (intervening) and Ors (intervening) v Ministry of the Interior of Saudi Arabia and Lieutenant Colonel Abdul Aziz* [2006] UKHL 26, paras 12–14 and 77–85; see also the ECtHR's approach in *Jones and Others v United Kingdom*, App Nos 34356/06 and 40528/06 (ECtHR, 14 January 2014) para 108.

[178] ARSIWA, Art 7, Commentary, para 8. See also *Sarma v Sri Lanka* (Communication No 950/2000), 31 July 2003, UN Doc CCPR/C/78/D/950/2000, para 9.2.

[179] *Ioannis Kardassopoulos and Ron Fuchs v Georgia*, ICSID, Case Nos ARB/05/18 and ARB/07/15, Award, 3 March 2010, para 273; Court of Justice of the European Union, Case C-334/08, Opinion of Advocate General Kokott (15 April 2010) paras 29 and 30, and n 11; *United States – Anti-Dumping and Countervailing Measures on Certain Coated Paper from Indonesia*, WTO, Report of the Panel, WT/DS491/R (6 December 2017) para 7.179.

governmental authority exists for the purpose of ultra vires non-state actor conduct, the attribution threshold of this provision is thus similar to Article 5, with a safeguard that unauthorised conduct is still attributable to states that delegate to non-state actors through domestic law to undertake conduct on their behalf. The key difficulty with determining attribution considerations under Article 7 is identifying whether governmental authority has been exercised in the course of conduct that conflicts with that very same authority.

3.3. The Article 9 Version of Governmental Authority

This chapter has shown that governmental authority can be granted by a state to a non-state actor, signifying that such an actor is officially acting on behalf of the state. Domestic law is the crucial component in this process, which determines whether a non-state actor is a state organ or a non-state actor wielding governmental authority for the purposes of attribution. Both types of actor wield the authority of a state, as prescribed by domestic law. Domestic law can thus show whether governmental authority has been explicitly exercised, either by a state organ or a non-state actor officially acting on behalf of a state. But what about cases where governmental authority is implicitly exercised by a non-state actor, where conduct is undertaken on behalf of a state, but unofficially?

Article 9 is particularly distinct from Articles 5 and 7 in its treatment of the governmental authority concept. Although practice relating to this provision is sparse, what does exist shows that conduct of a non-state can be attributed to a state based on a test of governmental authority without a nexus existing under domestic law between these entities.[180] In the *Yeager* case the Tribunal examined whether conduct of persons part of a revolutionary movement were attributable to Iran.[181] In doing so it referenced the part of the draft article that became Article 9:

> An act is attributable [to a state] even if a person or group of persons was in fact merely exercising elements of governmental authority in the absence of the official authorities and in circumstances which justified the exercise of those elements of authority.[182]

The applicability of Article 9 rests on two considerations. First, whether a state organ was absent in a particular setting where one should have been present. Second, whether a non-state actor stepped into a particular role out of necessity, due to the absence of a state organ that should have been undertaking that same role. During the drafting of this provision, Chile highlighted that it concerned 'the conduct of persons who, as individuals, were acting in fact on behalf of the state – that is to say, without having been formally appointed as organs of the State system'.[183] Attribution

[180] ARSIWA, Art 9, Commentary, para 1.
[181] *Yeager v Islamic Republic of Iran* (1987), Iran–US CTR, vol 17, 103.
[182] ibid para 42.
[183] Observations and comments of Governments on chapters I, II and III of Part I of the draft articles on State responsibility for internationally wrongful acts, A/CN.4/328 and Add 1–4, YBILC (1980) vol II(1), 96.

under Article 9 thus applies to non-state actors that exercise governmental authority 'without any actual authority to do so'.[184] The performance of tasks associated with a non-state actor stepping into the role of a state organ means that non-state actors can be 'transformed, at least temporarily, into interpreters of the will and action of the State' without domestic law stipulating such a mandate.[185] The attribution threshold of this provision may therefore be satisfied in cases where non-state actors justifiably exercise state authority, especially if there is an absence of state organs that are vital to the stability or public order of a state.[186]

The ILC provides some illustrative examples of situations where Article 9 could become a pertinent consideration: 'revolution, armed conflict or foreign occupation, where the regular authorities dissolve, are disintegrating, have been suppressed or are for the time being inoperative. They may also cover cases where lawful authority is being gradually restored, e.g. after foreign occupation.'[187] Although it has been scarcely applied or referred to in practice, there are examples of situations that highlight the relevance of the provision. One such setting is where a state loses power and authority over its territory.[188] In the *Yeager* case members of the Revolutionary Guard were treated as non-state actors whose conduct was attributable to Iran under Article 9.[189] Here guards undertook roles related to immigration control and overseeing customs operations at Tehran airport. It was held that conduct was attributable to Iran, even if not authorised by the state, because the guards 'exercised elements of governmental authority in the absence of official authorities, in operations of which the new Government must have had knowledge and to which it did not specifically object'.[190] In the aftermath of such uprisings, and before the creation of a new or restored, fully functioning government, there may well be non-state actors assuming roles to which state officials are temporarily absent, meaning attributing their conduct to the state is possible.[191]

Another example of when Article 9 could apply is in settings of 'failed states'.[192] These exist when there is internal disruption leading to disintegration of public power structures and a collapse of law and order.[193] This setting means that non-state actors may assume governmental roles in an attempt to, for example, protect citizens or restore peace. This type of action can arise from within the state itself and by way of external intervention. Such settings pose complex questions with respect to attribution, in particular if non-state actors act as a temporary administration. Some insights can be drawn from the *Da Costa* case, even though it involved an

[184] ARSIWA, Art 9, Commentary, para 1.
[185] Observations and comments of Governments, A/CN.4/328 (1980) 97.
[186] ibid.
[187] ARSIWA, Art 9, Commentary, para 1.
[188] ARSIWA, Art 9, Commentary, para 4.
[189] *Yeager v Islamic Republic of Iran* (1987), Iran–US CTR, vol 17, 111, para 43.
[190] ibid.
[191] In such settings a link between Arts 9 and 10 also exists, which is addressed in chapter 4.
[192] V Cojanu and AI Popescu, 'Analysis of Failed States: Some Problems of Definition and Measurement' (2007) 25 *Romanian Economic Journal* 113.
[193] D Thürer, 'The "Failed State" and International Law' (1999) 81 *International Review of the Red Cross* 731.

intergovernmental organisation and not a non-state actor.[194] The Court here pointed out that the UN Transitional Administration in East Timor 'was established to act as the temporary governmental authority'.[195] The key issue central to this case was not attribution, but what laws were applicable with respect to the enforcement of a prison sentence. Nonetheless, the case highlights that intergovernmental organisations can and do exercise elements of governmental authority in situations in which Article 9 could be applied – in this case, a territorial administration. If non-state actors were to undertake the same or similar roles, this would suggest that their conduct could be attributed to the applicable state.[196]

The tricky aspect of assessing whether the attribution threshold of Article 9 can be satisfied is the absence of domestic law that points towards the potential for non-state actors to exercise governmental authority. Instead, this authority needs to be inferred from the role a non-state actor undertakes that is to the benefit of the state whose responsibility is under question.[197] Governmental authority arises from the role in which a non-state actor undertakes public functions because the state is not undertaking, or cannot undertake, what would normally be undertaken by the relevant public authority, meaning if a non-state actor fills that role, its conduct is aimed at being for the sake of that state.

There is an overarching component of necessity in Article 9 cases. Satisfying the attribution threshold of this provision depends on the existence of circumstances calling for the exercise of governmental authority by a non-state actor. There are three elements that must be satisfied. First, the non-state actor 'must be performing governmental function' on their own initiative.[198] No mandate from the state exists. The 'nature of the activity performed is given more weight than the existence of a formal link between the actor(s) and the organisation of the State'.[199] Article 9 applies to conduct attached to a role assumed by a non-state actor that is public in character. Second, there must be an absence of a state organ, or a state organ not conducting its activities, in order to justify the non-state actor exercising those functions.[200] Where there has been a 'total collapse of the State apparatus', or where state organs do not carry out their functions, non-state actors can be justified in exercising the absent authority.[201] Third, circumstances must call for a non-state actor to exercise elements of governmental authority.[202] This means that the role assumed by a non-state actor was necessary in maintaining a part of the society within the state in question, but the specific conduct undertaken by the non-state actor in such a role need not necessarily be essential for the public interest in order to attribute that conduct to the state.[203]

[194] *Da Costa v Timor-Leste*, Appeal Judgment, Case No 03/02, ILDC 1971 (TL 2003), 18 July 2003, Timor-Leste [tl].

[195] ibid para 23.

[196] It appears there has been no application of Art 9 in such a setting to show how this would work specifically in practice.

[197] Observations and comments of Governments, A/CN.4/328 (1980) 97.

[198] ARSIWA, Art 9, Commentary, para 4.

[199] ibid.

[200] ibid para 5.

[201] ibid.

[202] ibid para 6.

[203] ibid; see also *Velásquez-Rodríguez v Honduras* (IACtHR, 29 July 1988), in particular paras 148–76.

In comparison with Articles 5 and 7, Article 9 is exceptional in its treatment of governmental authority because it is not limited by the element of being empowered by domestic law, as indicated by the words 'in fact' within the text.[204] The nexus between non-state actor and state instead exists through material conduct, showing elements that are in some sense state-like in nature.[205] The provision can apply to any actors that assume roles that typically lie with state organs or non-state actors empowered by domestic law to exercise state authority, but out of need are filled by non-state actors that empower themselves to exercise elements of governmental authority. The notion of 'state official' is thus absent. Non-state actors in settings where Article 9 could apply are not officially acting on behalf of their respective states. Such actors are in a state of temporary limbo in terms of where they sit in the not so neat distinction between the public and private spheres of society – for a time they belong to both and neither all at the same time. They cannot be assumed to be public officials, but are private entities attempting to act in an official public capacity, where the state alternative is inexistent or dysfunctional. When doing so, governmental authority can exist by default, depending on what the actor does and how it links to a role normally/traditionally filled by a public official. Yet this understanding of 'traditional' and 'normal' in this context is becoming harder to grasp in an era where privatisation is widespread.

Another dissimilarity between Article 9 and Articles 5 and 7 is that these latter two provisions treat governmental authority as it links to a non-state actor's role of a 'public character or function'. Domestic law under these two provisions will show that governmental authority has been bestowed on a non-state actor. This element is absent from Article 9, meaning governmental authority needs to be determined by examining both the role and the conduct of the non-state actor in question, where inferences need to be drawn from its conduct to help determine its role. For example, if a non-state actor were to police borders in an ungoverned part of a state, its conduct would logically point to its role as acting border security. Yet if attribution considerations under Article 9 were to be evaluated on conduct alone, without reflecting on what role such conduct would 'normally' fit into within the state structure, pronouncements on such conduct could stretch the applicable scope of the provision to a point where there is no end. To take the same example, if a non-state actor were to stop a person from coming into the ungoverned territory, but was not acting in a role as part of a wider border security effort, then Article 9 could not be construed to mean that governmental authority had been exercised in that one-off instance. There is an element of systematic action on the part of the non-state actor in such instances. Isolated or random conduct of non-state actors is unlikely to show that governmental authority has been exercised, even if these actors appear to be 'traditionally'/'normally' 'state-like'/'public' in character.

[204] ARSIWA, Art 9.

[205] See comments by the US in State Responsibility, Fifty-Third Session of the ILC (2001), Comments and Observations received from Governments, A/CN.4/515 and Add 1–3, 50.

4. CONCLUSION

Governmental authority denotes the existence of state power. It can be granted by a state to a non-state actor, or assumed by a non-state actor without a state according it where there is an absence of state authority. Articles 5 and 7 fall into the former category and Article 9 into the latter. The key factor impacting the establishment of an attributable link between non-state actor conduct and a state under Articles 5 and 7 is the existence of domestic law showing that a non-state actor has been empowered to exercise governmental authority and has actually done so. This limits the applicable scope of these provisions when considering the likelihood of accessing domestic law aside from legislation. Whether other forms of domestic law would qualify as such for the purposes of these provisions is also uncertain. States can therefore lawfully empower non-state actors to act on their behalf through their domestic laws, whilst relying on those same laws to shield them from having conduct from these actors attributed to them. Despite the concerns that were raised in the ILC about domestic law shielding states from having their international responsibility called into question, Articles 5 and 7 alleviate these concerns only to the extent that the domestic law is accessible. It is therefore understandable that some states disputed the ILC's creation of the domestic law requirement.

The key factor impacting attribution under Article 9 is the existence of circumstances necessitating that a non-state actor fill a role that a state has neglected, and when acting in this capacity thereby exercises elements of governmental authority by default. There need be no domestic legal nexus between state and non-state actor here. At first glance, this may suggest that the applicable scope of this provision can perhaps extend further than its comparators. Theoretically maybe, but the use of Article 9 in practice is unlikely. This is not surprising, as the ILC intended it to apply only in rare cases, presenting a kind of fait accompli. Due to the lack of practice surrounding the provision, much of its potential applicability remains theoretical. What is clear is that in cases where it could be applicable, non-state actors would not be acting on behalf of states, but acting in spite of states' failure to act. The term 'governmental authority' for the purposes of Article 9 thus refers to instances in which non-state actors assume roles of conventionally public bodies out of some form of necessity. Yet this provision also rests on a general assumption about what state officials should be doing in their day-to-day activities. And this is not so easy to understand in a world of delegated public authority. What should state officials be doing in a world where much is delegated to the private sector? While the understanding of functions of a public character may be clear with an eye on the past, with an eye in the present, it is not always clear what matters states actually govern, and what they should and should not do in terms of exercising their power and authority. And if current trends are anything to go by, future practice could mean that the very distinction between public and private roles becomes non-existent in some sectors.

Yet even if it is possible to determine what a state official should have been doing, and a non-state actor did undertake a 'public' role for the 'benefit' of a state, meaning the attribution threshold under Article 9 were satisfied, this would not automatically mean the international responsibility of the state in question could be established. There may exist settings where the state will not have power and authority over the area where the non-state actor is operating, meaning the state may have no legal obligations under primary rules. The difficulty then becomes how Article 9 can be of value if attribution through its application is triggered, but because of the very nature of the circumstances in which this provision would be applicable, the state, whose responsibility is being questioned, does not hold any legal obligations in the circumstances, owing to facts that may prevent it from exercising any power and authority over an area.

The value of Articles 5 and 7 rests on different foundations: their unclear, or perhaps even non-existent, separation of non-state actors that exercise governmental authority from state organs, both of which are created via domestic law and undertake roles that are officially on the behalf of states. James Crawford made it plainly clear that non-state actors that exercise governmental authority are not separate from the official state structure. The domestic law requirement also raises a wider matter regarding international law-making and the authority afforded to particular sources. Recall that a number of states were unambiguously against the application of this requirement. Yet today it appears as though the ILC has successfully created a perception that this requirement, and the attribution provisions on governmental authority more broadly, are international rules. Courts and tribunals have declared that these three provisions and their requirements reflect customary international law. But if there is an apparent lack of, and even contradictory, state practice and opinio juris, why does this occur? Is the creation of international law really the exclusive purview of states? The next chapter suggests some answers to these questions, whilst examining the ties between states and non-state actors that extend beyond those formalised through domestic law.

3

Attribution Based on Perceived State Control Over Non-state Actors

THE PREVIOUS CHAPTER showed how attributable links between non-state actors and states can be established based on governmental authority being exercised by non-state actors. State responsibility for non-state actor conduct can therefore be addressed in two ways by attribution based on applying the concept of governmental authority. First, where there exists a legal nexus in domestic law between a state and a non-state actor. This extends to instances where a non-state actor acts beyond the authority mandated to it by a state. Second, where non-state actors empower themselves to exercise elements of governmental authority. This shows that there need not be a nexus in domestic law between a state and a non-state actor in order to attribute non-state actor conduct to a state. Yet attribution under this strand of the governmental authority test occurs only in exceptional circumstances, where non-state actors act out of necessity and not necessarily on the behalf of states. What about circumstances where non-state actors are not acting out of necessity but in fact on the behalf of states? How does the ARSIWA attribution framework account for such instances? This chapter addresses these questions by examining attribution based on factual links existing between states and non-state actors.

Article 8 concerns attributing conduct of an entity to a state where it has directed, controlled or instructed the non-state actor in carrying out specific activities:

> The conduct of a person or group of persons shall be considered an act of a State under international law if the person or group of persons is in fact acting on the instructions of, or under the direction or control of, that State in carrying out the conduct.[1]

In coming to include these three criteria, the ILC addressed attribution in the negative – in that it focused on exceptions to the general position that non-state actor conduct is not attributable to states.[2] The perceived need for such a provision was to account for situations in which non-state actors became 'the extended arm' of

[1] ARSIWA, Art 8.
[2] ibid Commentary, para 1.

state organs.[3] If the ARSIWA framework did not account for circumstances in which non-state actors were not exercising governmental authority, but were still acting for a state, then states could 'easily' avoid responsibility by way of 'private delegation'.[4] The ILC therefore developed an attribution provision intended to address the types of situations in which non-state actors act on the behalf of states without there necessarily being any official links between them, such as those provided by domestic law. This chapter analyses the provision that the ILC ultimately settled on to apply in such settings: Article 8. The creation of this provision will be examined, before turning to its application in practice, including the impact its use has had, all of which highlight why it is a significant component of the state responsibility framework applicable to non-state actors.

1. THE DEVELOPMENT OF ARTICLE 8

The inclusion of an attribution provision within the ARSIWA intended to address non-state actors acting in fact on the behalf of states was proposed in the 1970s.[5] The proposition was born out of a rationale considering that there could be situations in which non-state actors were not formally appointed to act for states but could still perform functions for them. The roots of Article 8 are based on the premise that depending on what states need doing, 'private natural or legal persons – while definitely remaining such – are entrusted by the public authorities with the provision of a service or the performance of a specific task'.[6] The ILC saw non-state actors acting in this capacity when 'prompted to do so by organs of the state or of one of the other entities' that are empowered by domestic law to exercise state authority.[7] Draft Article 8 was thus provisionally adopted in 1974:

> *Attribution to the State of the conduct of persons acting in fact on behalf of the State*
>
> The conduct of a person or group of persons shall also be considered as an act of the State under international law if
>
> (a) it is established that such person or group of persons was in fact acting on behalf of that State; or
>
> (b) such person or group of persons was in fact exercising elements of the governmental authority in the absence of the official authorities and in circumstances which justified the exercise of those elements of authority.[8]

Paragraph (a) addressed attribution for non-state actors that states use to act for them. The ILC viewed the reasons behind states conducting their activities without

[3] R Wolfrum, 'State Responsibility for Private Actors: An Old Problem of Renewed Relevance' in M Ragazzi (ed), *International Responsibility Today: Essays in Memory of Oscar Schachter* (Leiden, Nijhoff, 2005) 423, 427.

[4] J Crawford, *State Responsibility: The General Part* (Cambridge, Cambridge University Press, 2013) 141.

[5] Third Report, Ago (1971) 262.

[6] ibid 263.

[7] ILC Report, Twenty-Sixth Session, 6 May–26 July 1974, UNGA, Twenty-Ninth Session, Supp 10 (A/9610/Rev.1), YBILC (1974) vol II(1), 283.

[8] ibid.

the involvement of state officials as 'self-evident'.[9] By delegating to non-state actors, states 'make use of persons who are not formally part of the State machinery'.[10] The following passage shows how the ILC viewed such state conduct, and why it was important that attribution addressed it:

> [States] call upon private individuals or groups of private individuals to take on the duties and tasks in question, although here again these individuals or groups are not thereby formally attached to the structures in question and do not, in other words, thereby become *de jure* organs of the State or of the other entities mentioned. The Commission, also bearing in mind the important role played by the principle of effectiveness in the international legal order, considered that that order must of necessity take into account, in the cases contemplated, the existence of a real link between the person performing the act and the State machinery rather than the lack of a formal legal nexus between them. The conduct in which the persons or groups in question thus engage in fact on behalf of the State should therefore be regarded under international law as acts of the State.[11]

The ILC provided few details of what a 'real link' was vis-à-vis defining conduct undertaken on behalf of a state.[12] The ILC referenced a number of scholars who at the time 'unanimously upheld' the standpoint that attribution could be based on a non-state actor acting in fact on behalf of a state.[13] Courts and tribunals also adopted this understanding that conduct of a non-state actor could be attributed to a state when acting on its behalf.[14] In the *Zafiro* case a Tribunal held that conduct of a crew aboard a US merchant ship was attributable to the United States.[15] Here it was established that the ship was in fact acting on behalf of the United States because it was supporting US naval operations by providing supplies.[16] In *Stephens*, a group of guards who were not state organs could not be determined as 'auxiliaries' to the Mexican Army, yet their conduct was attributable to Mexico because they 'acted for' the state.[17] The Claims Commission concluded that the acts of a person who was part of the guards as a group triggered Mexico's responsibility because it had employed that group.[18] The principle at the heart of the draft provision was that attribution should occur if a non-state actor was 'actually appointed by organs of the State to discharge a particular function or to carry out a particular duty, [and] that they performed a given task at the instigation of those organs'.[19] This understanding also encompassed non-state actors acting 'in concert with and at the instigation of the organs of a State', meaning

[9] ibid.
[10] ibid.
[11] ibid.
[12] OD Frouville, 'Attribution of Conduct to the State: Private Individuals' in J Crawford, A Pellet and S Olleson (eds), *The Law of International Responsibility* (Oxford, Oxford University Press, 2010) 257, 266.
[13] ILC Report, Twenty-Sixth Session, 6 May–26 July 1974, UNGA, Twenty-Ninth Session, Supp 10 (A/9610/Rev.1), YBILC (1974) vol II(1), 283 (n 592).
[14] For some examples, see ibid 284–86.
[15] UNRIAA, vol VI (United Nations publication, Sales No 1955.V.3) 160.
[16] ibid.
[17] UNRIAA, vol VI (United Nations publications, Sales No 1951.V.1) 267.
[18] ibid.
[19] ILC Report, Twenty-Sixth Session, 6 May–26 July 1974, UNGA, Twenty-Ninth Session, Supp 10 (A/9610/Rev.1), YBILC (1974) vol II(1), 285. See chapter 8 for attribution based on instigation.

related actions 'must be regarded as an act of that State'.[20] The sources examined by the ILC at the time showed that paragraph (a) of the original provision was based on legal practice and literature.

However, a concern remained: paragraph (b). It is clear that this paragraph contained elements of what is now Article 9.[21] It is true that Articles 8 and 9 share the commonality that they both relate to non-state actors that have not been formally appointed through domestic law to act for states. But separating the two paragraphs was welcome for the reason that they address different issues. What was not separated from what became Article 8 was a draft provision that was merged with it. Draft Article 11 – encompassing the general stance that conduct of non-state actors cannot be attributed to states – was worked into what became Article 8. Prompted by a comment from Germany, whose 'importance' was emphasised by Riphagen,[22] what exists now as an attribution test that sets out when non-state actor conduct can be attributed to states, contains an underlying general premise that such conduct should not be attributed to states.

1.1. Key Cases that Influenced the Drafting of the Provision

The comments received by states were welcoming of Draft Article 8 in its form applying to non-state actors 'in fact acting on behalf of' states:

> The inclusion of subparagraph (a) is therefore fully justified, since the performance of such work means that the private entities are transformed, at least temporarily, into interpreters of the will and action of the State.[23]

This position was soon to change. Arguably the most influential component in shaping the criteria behind what became Article 8 was the *Nicaragua* case.[24] This case created two attribution tests: 'complete dependence'[25] and 'effective control'.[26] The ICJ's understanding was that non-state actors transform into de facto state organs if their 'complete dependence' on the state is demonstrated by the facts in a given case.[27] The ICJ decided that the threshold of this test had not been met, meaning the conduct of the Contras could not be attributed to the United States generally, as conduct of an established state organ would be.[28] The Court then examined whether there could be an additional basis for attribution.

[20] ibid 284.
[21] Examination of the preparatory work to Art 8 reaffirms that Art 9 became what was Draft Article 8(b).
[22] Seventh Report, Riphagen (1986) 12.
[23] Observations and comments of Governments on chapters I, II and III of Part I of the draft articles on State responsibility for internationally wrongful acts, A/CN.4/328 and Add 1–4, YBILC (1980) vol II(1), 97.
[24] *Military and Paramilitary Activities in and against Nicaragua (Nicaragua v United States of America)*, Judgment, 27 June 1986, ICJ Rep [1986] 14.
[25] ibid paras 109 and 110.
[26] ibid para 115.
[27] ibid paras 109–10.
[28] ibid paras 111–12.

The creation of the 'effective control' test remains a controversial assertion of the ICJ. This part of the judgment has been criticised.[29] It was also crucial in shaping the approach of the ILC towards attribution under Article 8. The key paragraph reads:

> All the forms of United States participation mentioned above, and even the general control by the respondent State over a force with a high degree of dependency on it, would not in themselves mean, without further evidence, that the United States directed or enforced the perpetration of the acts contrary to human rights and humanitarian law alleged by the applicant State. Such acts could well be committed by members of the contras without the control of the United States. For this conduct to give rise to legal responsibility of the United States, it would in principle have to be proved that that State had effective control of the military or paramilitary operations in the course of which the alleged violations were committed.[30]

From reading this passage with the Court's ruling regarding dependency, it is clear that the effective control test was intended by the ICJ to be a subsidiary test for attribution. Milanovic describes this approach:

> According to the Court, *general* control, or a *high* degree of dependency are insufficient to impute *all* of the acts of the *contras* to the US – that control would have to be complete, and the dependency total for such kind of attribution to occur. However, this also means that at least *some* of the acts of the group could be attributed to the state, if the state had *effective control* over the particular operation in the course of which violations of international human rights or humanitarian law have been committed.[31]

Consequently, the ICJ found that the conduct of the Contras could not be attributed to the United States.[32] The major debates concerning this position stem from the following question: what *is* 'effective control'? Nicaragua's argument in the case gives a clearer picture of what this test could mean:

> It is contended by Nicaragua that the United States Government is effectively in control of the contras, that it devised their strategy and directed their tactics, and that the purpose of that Government was, from the beginning, to overthrow the Government of Nicaragua.[33]

The ICJ took inspiration from this argument. Nicaragua contended that the United States was 'effectively in control' of the Contras, whereas the Court created and applied an attribution test and decided to label it 'effective control' to determine

[29] See, for example, *Armed Activities on the Territory of the Congo (Democratic Republic of the Congo v Uganda)*, Judgment, 19 December 2005, ICJ Rep [2005] 168, Separate Opinions of Judge Simma, para 8 and Judge Kooijmans, para 25; M Gibney, K Tomasevski and J Vedsted-Hansen, 'Transnational State Responsibility for Violations of Human Rights' (1999) 12 *Harvard Human Rights Journal* 267, 283–88; M Gibney, 'The Downing of MH17: Russian Responsibility?' (2015) 15 *Human Rights Law Review* 169, 170–71; A Cassese, 'The Nicaragua and Tadić Tests Revisited in Light of the ICJ Judgment on Genocide in Bosnia' (2007) 18 *European Journal of International Law* 649; T Meron, 'Classification of Armed Conflict in the Former Yugoslavia: Nicaragua's Fallout' (1998) 92 *American Journal of International Law* 236; AE Chase, 'Legal Mechanisms of the International Community and the United States Concerning State Sponsorship of Terrorism' (2004) 45 *Virginia Journal of International Law* 41.

[30] *Nicaragua*, Judgment, 27 June 1986, para 115.

[31] M Milanovic, 'State Responsibility for Genocide' (2006) 17 *European Journal of International Law* 553, 577 (emphasis original).

[32] *Nicaragua*, Judgment, 27 June 1986, para 116.

[33] ibid para 20.

whether the interactions between the United States and the Contras were sufficient to attribute the conduct of the non-state actor to the state.[34] Nicaragua's written arguments also use the word 'effectively' in the context of alleged US 'control' over, and 'support' given to, 'mercenary forces'.[35] Before these arguments of Nicaragua were made, there had been no mention of control being linked with any variation or denomination of the word 'effective'. Additionally, Nicaragua used the exact phrase 'direction and control' to emphasise that state responsibility should be borne for the conduct of non-state actors in specific settings.[36] This was the first time 'direction and control' was mentioned in the context of attributing non-state actor conduct to a state.[37] It also perhaps explains the original proposal of Crawford that used 'and' instead of 'or' between the two words.[38] This argument of state 'direction and control' was, according to Nicaragua, 'fully supported by international law authorities'.[39] However, the only authority cited by Nicaragua was four pages (263–66) of Ago's Third Report,[40] where he writes on attribution relating to private persons performing 'public functions' or 'in fact acting on behalf of the state'.[41] In these pages of this report (in particular 264) the words 'control' and 'direct' are used in the context of attribution based on the 'public purpose' of an actor.[42] In an example analysed by Ago using the words 'control' and 'direct', a naval officer (a state organ) exercised 'command' over a merchant vessel, which led to a Tribunal holding that: '[T]he liability of the State ... must depend on the nature of the service in which ... the vessel is engaged and the purpose for which she is employed.'[43] Conduct of the

[34] See also the statement in the oral proceedings made on behalf of Nicaragua in *ICJ Pleadings, Oral Arguments, Documents: Militarily and Paramilitary Activities in and against Nicaragua (Nicaragua v United States of America)* vol V, 181: 'Attention then turned to the rag-tag groups of ex-National Guardsmen operating on the northern borders of Nicaragua. As you heard yesterday, they were turned into a fighting force of 3,500 and then 7,000, and now perhaps 10,000 to 11,000 men – an effective military instrument. ... And that instrument, through the financial, strategic, logistic and operational controls exercised by the United States, was at the service of United States purposes towards Nicaragua. That is why it was created'; see also the overarching link to Nicaragua's main argument at 229.

[35] Written proceedings, Memorial of Nicaragua (30 April 1985), *ICJ Pleadings, Oral Arguments, Documents: Militarily and Paramilitary Activities in and against Nicaragua (Nicaragua v United States of America)* vol IV, para 253. It should be noted that the argument at this paragraph is a direct quote from I Brownlie, *International Law and the Use of Force by States* (Oxford, Clarendon Press, 1963) 370, 371–72. The point made by Brownlie here relates to state responsibility by drawing inferences, as he analyses indirect state uses of force through relationships with non-state actors, which is a matter that concerns primary rules of international law.

[36] Written proceedings, Memorial of Nicaragua (30 April 1985), *ICJ Pleadings, Oral Arguments, Documents: Militarily and Paramilitary Activities in and against Nicaragua (Nicaragua v United States of America)* vol IV, para 252.

[37] See the full argument of Nicaragua in this regard: Written proceedings, Memorial of Nicaragua (30 April 1985), *ICJ Pleadings, Oral Arguments, Documents: Militarily and Paramilitary Activities in and against Nicaragua (Nicaragua v United States of America)* vol IV, paras 252–62.

[38] See analysis below.

[39] Written proceedings, Memorial of Nicaragua (30 April 1985), *ICJ Pleadings, Oral Arguments, Documents: Militarily and Paramilitary Activities in and against Nicaragua (Nicaragua v United States of America)* vol IV, para 252.

[40] ibid.

[41] Third Report, Ago (1971) 262–67.

[42] ibid 264.

[43] ibid, citing the Tribunal in the *Zafiro* case (United Nations, *Reports of International Arbitral Awards*, vol VI (United Nations publication, Sales No 1955.V.3) 160 et seq).

vessel's crew was therefore viewed as attributable to the state.[44] The 'control' spoken of in this case was that which could be arguably inherent in an employer–employee relationship, which is more akin to attribution based on a non-state actor exercising elements of governmental authority prescribed by domestic law. The phrase 'direction and control' is not mentioned in Ago's Third Report. Even if one adopts an expansive reading of Ago's work here, the idea of attribution being based on state 'direction and control' is not present.[45] Nicaragua's assertion of 'fully supported by international law authorities' was thus overstated. This would not be such a major concern, save that the ICJ (and ultimately the ILC) cherry-picked this rationale to create a new attribution test that to this day is portrayed as an international rule.

From the reasoning of the ICJ it is clear that devising strategy, directing tactics and aiming to overthrow the Nicaraguan government did not equate to the United States exercising 'effective control' over the Contras.[46] The ICJ chose not to elaborate upon this stance, making it difficult to assess what effective control means for the purposes of attribution.[47] More confusing is that the Court simultaneously implied that the United States did have control to some degree, yet the extent of it could not be established.[48] Further, the Court, in creating the effective control test, arguably went beyond its mandate. The role of the ICJ is to interpret what the law *is* in a particular situation, and apply it accordingly in coming to its conclusions. It is not for the Court to create law. This is made clear in its statute and supplementary commentary.[49] The Court can influence the development of international law, but not because it creates new law.[50] Although judicial discretion is inherent in judicial decision-making, the test of effective control did not fall under one of the sources of international law at the time in which the ICJ came to its decision. Before the *Nicaragua* case, in so far as attribution of conduct and non-state actors is concerned, there is no mention of an 'effective control' test in the context of determining state responsibility. Even 'control' generally for the purposes of attribution was not apparent in the ILC's work before this case was heard. Research outside the ARSIWA's preparatory work also makes no

[44] ibid.

[45] The only other related authority provided by Nicaragua (para 253, Written Memorial of 1985) was G Piotrowski, 'Où en sommes-nous sur le problème de l'agression' (1957) 35 *Revue de droit international* (Sottile) 415. However, this work relates to state aggression under international law, affirming that Nicaragua conflated concepts linked to this area with the law of state responsibility, in particular attribution.

[46] *Nicaragua*, Judgment, 27 June 1986, paras 75, 97, 104, 112.

[47] Despite the criticisms of overall control, which will be discussed shortly, it should be noted that the ICTY in *Tadić* actually provided discussion on the concept of 'overall control' and what it means in the context of attribution (see *Prosecutor v Dusko Tadić*, Appeal Judgment, Case No IT-94-1-A, 15 July 1999, paras 120–38), as opposed to the ICJ's lack of discussion relating to 'effective control' in *Nicaragua* – only once was effective control mentioned in the judgment (para 115).

[48] *Nicaragua*, Judgment, 27 June 1986, paras 110–12.

[49] A Pellet, 'Article 38' in A Zimmermann, C Tomuschat, K Oellers-Frahm and CJ Tams (eds), *The Statute of the International Court of Justice: A Commentary*, 2nd edn (Oxford, Oxford University Press, 2012) 731, 748–870.

[50] Indeed, with respect to the creation of Art 8 of the ARSIWA, the ICJ's ruling in *Nicaragua* was particularly influential. See ARSIWA, Art 8, Commentary, paras 4 and 5; see also J Crawford, 'The International Court of Justice and the Law of State Responsibility' in CJ Tams and J Sloan (eds), *The Development of International Law by the International Court of Justice* (Oxford, Oxford University Press, 2013) 71, 78–85.

mention of control being applied for such usage. None of the Special Rapporteur's reports before Crawford refer to control as a distinct attribution test. The same applies with respect to the reports of the ILC, discussions at the Commission, and the comments and observations made by states.

The commentary to Article 8 (paragraph 5, note 160) indicates that there apparently was a matter before the *Nicaragua* case that dealt with attribution based on perceived state control of non-state actor conduct: the *Starrett* case.[51] However, upon examination of the case, it does not discuss attribution based on state control being exercised over a non-state actor.[52] The page of this case (143) cited in the ARSIWA commentary as reference to state control being apparently 'necessary for the purposes of attribution of conduct to the State'[53] makes no mention of control, even generally. In the *Starrett* case, control was not necessary for attributing conduct of a non-state actor to a state. The case discusses ownership as a potential basis of attribution, by examining state shareholder percentages held in a company.[54] The Tribunal also made several pronouncements indicating control cannot be used as a sole basis of attribution, ruling that 'government control' over a company 'does not amount to dominion over' it.[55] In assessing whether the state had unlawfully expropriated property, the Tribunal held:

> It has, however, to be borne in mind that assumption of control over property by a government does not automatically and immediately justify a conclusion that the property has been taken by the government, thus requiring compensation under international law.[56]

These findings show that the ICJ invented the effective control test. This so-called rule was not based on customary international law, or even signs of state practice. It was not enshrined in an international legal instrument. It was not a general principle of law,[57] nor was it mentioned (at the time) in previous judicial decisions or by 'highly qualified publicists'. For the purposes of highlighting the development of what became Article 8, this analysis is crucial for showing that an invention part of an international case, which became the centrepiece of Article 8, was not based on positive law. Antonio Cassese was right to say that effective control 'was not based on any judicial or state practice'.[58] It has been pointed out that in adopting concepts and definitions, legal bodies 'should not adopt either an expansive or a restrictive … [approach] but the *legally correct* one'.[59] With respect to the formation of 'effective control' by the ICJ, the Court did none of these, but instead created a fiction, one that the ILC ultimately based an attribution provision on.

[51] *Starrett Housing Corporation v Iran* (1983) Iran–US CTR, vol 4, 122.

[52] ibid. Pages 130, 144, 145, 146, 151, 154, 155, 156 of the case mention the *word* 'control', but not in the context of attribution of conduct.

[53] ARSIWA, Art 8, Commentary, para 5, n 160.

[54] *Starrett Housing Corporation v Iran* (1983) Iran–US CTR, vol 4, 122, see 136 and 146.

[55] ibid 154.

[56] ibid 155.

[57] See the criteria necessary for a concept to be considered a general principle in O Schachter, *International Law in Theory and Practice* (Leiden, Nijhoff, 1991) 50.

[58] Cassese (n 29) 654.

[59] Milanovic (n 31), 558 (emphasis in original).

The next noteworthy matter in the process that created Article 8 is the *Yeager* case.[60] In addressing the issue whether the acts of members of the Revolutionary Guard were attributable to Iran under international law, the Tribunal referred to Draft Article 8(a): 'It is generally accepted that a State is also responsible for acts of persons, if it is established that those persons were in fact acting on behalf of the State.'[61] This ruling is important because it came after the *Nicaragua* judgment. The Tribunal ruled that the international practice and academic work researched by the ILC made it clear that conduct of a non-state actor could be attributed to a state so long as it was acting in fact on the behalf of that state.[62] The ICTY later reaffirmed the stance of the Iran–US Claims Tribunal, holding in the *Rajić* case that conduct of a non-state actor 'shall "be considered as an act of the State under international law" if "it is established that such person or group of persons was in fact acting on behalf of that State"'.[63]

A turning point in the application of a control-based attribution test for determining state responsibility was the *Loizidou* case, which focused on extraterritoriality.[64] Here it needed to be determined whether Turkey had exercised its jurisdiction extraterritorially for the purposes of establishing its responsibility. The ECtHR stressed that jurisdiction extends beyond national territory, meaning the obligations of states also extend extraterritorially if a jurisdictional threshold is met.[65] In the Court's view, this threshold was the 'effective control' of a state over an area outside its national territory.[66] This test relates to whether substantive human rights law can apply in a particular case. The test is an element of determining state responsibility, but with respect to determining legal obligations. The attribution of conduct necessary for the same purpose of determining state responsibility is a separate issue, one that the Court did not deal with. Attribution of conduct was not connected to the ECtHR's ruling, which relates to a different understanding and test of 'effective control'. The ILC mistakenly read this case as evidencing a test of state control over a non-state actor conduct for the purpose of satisfying the attribution threshold of Article 8, and features in the provision's commentary as support for this test existing in practice.[67]

Another key case impacting what became Article 8 was *Tadić*.[68] The reason for the *Tadić* case making pronouncements on questions of attribution was because the ICTY had to ascertain whether the conflict at issue was international or non-international.[69] In the Appeals Chamber it was argued that state responsibility was not relevant for

[60] *Yeager v Iran* (1987), Iran–US CTR, vol 17, 103.

[61] ibid para 42.

[62] ibid.

[63] *Prosecutor v Ivica Rajić*, Trial Chamber, Case No IT-95-12-R61, 13 September 1996, para 24, citing the ILC's Draft Article 8.

[64] *Loizidou v Turkey*, App No 15318/89 (ECtHR, 18 December 1996).

[65] ibid para 52.

[66] ibid.

[67] ARSIWA, Art 8, Commentary, para 5.

[68] *Prosecutor v Dusko Tadić*, Appeal Judgment, Case No IT-94-1-A, 15 July 1999.

[69] See further issues with having to examine matters of state responsibility in the context of international criminal law in D Akande and A Tzanakopoulos, 'The Crime of Aggression in the ICC and State Responsibility' (2017) 58 *Harvard International Law Journal* 33.

this purpose.[70] The Tribunal disagreed, deeming it necessary to examine the question of whether a non-international armed conflict transformed into an international armed conflict through a relationship based on state control over a non-state actor.[71] The related analysis led to the 'overall control' test's creation. The ICTY looked unfavourably on the effective control test.[72] The first of two overarching reasons that the test was viewed as 'unconvincing' by the ICTY was because it ran contrary to the 'very logic of the entire system of international law on State responsibility'.[73] The ICTY advanced this argument on a number of grounds.[74] First, every circumstance where a non-state actor acts on a state's behalf does not require a high attribution threshold.[75] Second, 'effective control' can only be satisfied when specific instructions have been issued by a state, meaning it is limited to a small number of possible scenarios in which a non-state actor could be acting on behalf of a state.[76] Third, 'effective control' does not take into consideration the abundance of other possible scenarios in which a non-state actor has acted on a state's behalf.[77] Fourth, distinctions need to be drawn between individuals acting on the behalf of a state, and groups that are 'hierarchically structured' (eg military units, corporations or rebel groups), meaning 'control' is not an appropriate indicator for assessing attribution in such circumstances.[78] Fifth, the 'whole body of international law on State responsibility is based on a realistic concept of accountability, which disregards legal formalities and aims at ensuring that States entrusting some functions to individuals or groups must answer for their actions', which effective control undermines.[79] Sixth, the ICTY stated that international law should possess the capacity to hold any state responsible for acts in breach of its international legal obligations – whether through actors that have a de jure or de facto connection to a state – and should do so

> regardless of whether or not the State has issued *specific instructions*. … Clearly, the rationale behind this legal regulation is that otherwise, States might easily shelter behind, or use as a pretext, their internal legal system or the lack of any specific instructions in order to disclaim international responsibility.[80]

The second overarching reason that the ICTY denounced the effective control test, as clarified above, is that the ICJ invented it.[81] The Appeals Chamber highlighted that in order to attribute conduct of a non-state military/paramilitary group to a state 'it must be proved that the State wields overall control over the group'.[82] The underlying rationale of the *Tadić* judgment regarding attribution is that the extent

[70] ibid paras 83–89.
[71] ibid para 97.
[72] ibid para 115.
[73] ibid para 116.
[74] ibid paras 117–23.
[75] ibid para 117.
[76] ibid para 118.
[77] ibid para 119.
[78] ibid paras 120.
[79] ibid paras 121 and 122.
[80] ibid para 123 (emphasis in original).
[81] ibid paras 124–45.
[82] ibid para 131.

of the requisite state control will always vary.[83] The overall control test was intended to apply only in settings in which a non-state military/paramilitary group was potentially acting on behalf of a state. It is unclear whether the test of 'overall control' was part of state practice or case-law. The analysis of the ICTY points to hints of the test being present in international law, but it appears that this test too was invented by a judicial body. The test tangentially relates to state responsibility, but in a forum limited to international criminal law.[84]

Tadić featured substantially in the discussions surrounding Article 8 and forms part of the provision's final commentary.[85] However, the overall control test also has no neat place in the law governing state responsibility for non-state actors. The ICJ and a number of people have argued that the ICTY had no mandate to rule on questions of state responsibility.[86] It is therefore questionable whether the test it constructed has a place within this area of international law. What is more plausible is that the test is only relevant where a relationship between a state and a non-state actor has the potential to impact whether an armed conflict becomes 'internationalised'.[87] In such cases it may be appropriate to apply it. Cases that do not concern armed conflict *and* whether the relationship between a state and a non-state actor can change what rules of international humanitarian law apply may lie outside the applicable scope of this test.[88] Although it can, the overall control test need not extend to non-state actors for the primary purpose of determining state responsibility, but concerns situations where a state wielding authority over a non-state actor can influence what rules of international humanitarian law are to apply when determining the guilt of a person under international criminal law, or for international humanitarian law in and of itself for determining the character of an armed conflict.[89] The ILC understanding mixes 'attribution of acts of an individual to a state for the purposes of generating state responsibility, with attribution for determining whether individuals were acting as *de facto* state officials thereby rendering [a] conflict international'.[90] Despite the similarities between this test created by the ICTY and those created by the ICJ, overall control appears to be a primary rule-specific test, in that it forms part of

[83] ibid para 137.

[84] The ICJ noted this point in the *Bosnia Genocide* case (para 403); but see the point that the test may have needed to be discussed because it was necessary for determining the character of an armed conflict: Cassese (n 29) 651–56.

[85] ARSIWA, Art 8, Commentary, para 5.

[86] *Application of the Convention on the Prevention and Punishment of the Crime of Genocide* (*Bosnia and Herzegovina v Serbia and Montenegro*), Judgment, 26 February 2007, ICJ Rep [2007] 43, paras 403–07; M Lehto, *Indirect Responsibility for Terrorist Attacks: Redefinition of the Concept of Terrorism Beyond Violent Acts* (Leiden, Nijhoff, 2009) 215; B Simma, 'Universality of International Law from the Perspective of a Practitioner' in HR Fabri, R Wolfrum and J Gogolin (eds), *Select Proceedings of the European Society of International Law*, vol II (Oxford, Hart, 2008) 1, 23.

[87] *Prosecutor v Dusko Tadić*, Appeal Judgment, Case No IT-94-1-A, 15 July 1999, paras 160–62.

[88] D Carron, 'When Is a Conflict International? Time for New Control Tests in IHL' (2016) 98 *International Review of the Red Cross* 1019, 1026–31.

[89] See generally K Macak, *Internationalized Armed Conflicts in International Law* (Oxford, Oxford University Press, 2018).

[90] S Sivakumaran, 'Application of the Convention on the Prevention and Punishment of the Crime of Genocide' (2007) 56 *ICLQ* 695, 702.

international humanitarian law, and is thus separate from attribution considerations under the law of state responsibility, even though it can be considered to apply as such and could continue to apply in this way.[91] It is understandable that the ILC included insights brought by the ICTY in the *Tadić* case regarding attribution. Yet from the moment of the switch away from the 'acting in fact on behalf of' test towards that of an attribution test based on state 'control', the ILC appeared to be grasping at straws to find and present examples that dealt with any type of perceived state control over a non-state actor, regardless of whether those examples related to state responsibility or attribution of conduct.

1.2. The Significance of Crawford's Perspective in Shaping Article 8

It has been argued that when Crawford started working on Draft Article 8 he had more material to work with than Ago.[92] This may be true. But whether this material actually pointed towards the inclusion of criteria that are now part of Article 8 is another question. Crawford's first report for the ILC indicates a potential misreading of the previous work on Draft Article 8.[93] Part of the commentary to the draft read:

> [I]n each specific case in which international responsibility of the State has to be established, it must be genuinely proved that the person or group of persons were actually appointed by organs of the State to discharge a particular function or to carry out a particular duty, that they performed a given task at the instigation of those organs.[94]

Crawford saw this as meaning the following: 'In the passage just cited, the phrases "actually appointed" and "performed ... at the instigation of" together imply that article 8(a) is limited to cases of actual direction or instruction, that is, to cases of actual agency.'[95] These phrases combined may implicitly highlight that state control, direction or instruction could point to a non-state actor being 'appointed' to act for a state. Yet state 'control', 'direction' and/or 'instruction' appear to instead be *indicators* of non-state actors acting in fact on behalf of states. There are many other indicators that could also show 'appointment' or 'instigation', such as financing, dependency, ownership or the existence of a contract to carry out a 'given task'.

Crawford took this part of the commentary as a starting point to construct an argument that 'control' played a crucial role for attribution purposes.[96] His perspective also came from a piece of commentary to a different draft article (the draft provision stipulating that non-state actor conduct cannot be attributed to states):

> Where that Government is known to encourage and even promote the organization of such groups, to provide them with financial assistance, training and weapons, and to co-ordinate

[91] See ICRC, Convention (I) for the Amelioration of the Condition of the Wounded and Sick in Armed Forces in the Field, Commentary (2016), paras 268–71.

[92] O De Frouville, 'Attribution of Conduct to the State: Private Individuals' in Crawford et al (n 12) 257, 266.

[93] First Report, Crawford (1998) 40.

[94] ILC Report, Twenty-Sixth Session, 6 May–26 July 1974, UNGA, Twenty-Ninth Session, Supp 10 (A/9610/Rev.1), YBILC (1974) vol II(1), 284–85.

[95] First Report, Crawford (1998) 40.

[96] ibid 40–43.

> their activities with those of its own forces for the purpose of possible operations, and so on, the groups in question cease to be individuals from the standpoint of international law. They become formations which act in concert with, and at the instigation of, the State, and perform missions authorized by or even entrusted to them by that State. They then fall into the category of persons or groups which are linked, in fact if not formally, with the State machinery and are frequently called '*de facto* organs', and which were dealt with in article 8(a) of this draft.[97]

His reading of this material led to the following analysis and question:

> The language of 'promotion' and 'coordination' is less emphatic than that of 'appointment' or 'instigation', and it raises the question whether the de facto control of a State over a person or group should be treated as a distinct basis for attribution. If not, then the language of article 8(a) may need reconsideration. As a matter of ordinary language, a person may be said to act 'on behalf of' another person without any actual instruction or mandate from that other person. The question is not simply one of drafting, it is one of substance. To what extent should de facto agency be limited to cases of express agency?[98]

Crawford acknowledged that a non-state actor could act on behalf of a state without the presence of any 'actual instruction or mandate'. Yet he saw it necessary to limit factual links between non-state actors and states to 'express agency'.[99] The language of 'promotion' and 'coordination' appear to be further examples of indicators that a non-state actor could have been acting on behalf of a state. Such language does not allude to a requirement of control being necessary for attribution.

With the aim of altering the draft attribution provision, despite some states being in favour of the test under the original provision,[100] Crawford sought out rulings of courts and tribunals that had applied control tests.[101] As seen in the cases analysed above, which were used by Crawford to show the apparent existence of an attribution test based on state 'control' over non-state actor conduct, they *do not* show state control being a basis for attribution under the law of state responsibility. The exception is the effective control test created by the ICJ, which was not based on positive law. Crawford also pointed out that (then Judge) Ago in the *Nicaragua* case had criticised the Court for its use of the term 'control' in its assessments.[102] The other, related exception of the overall control test applies for the purposes of determining whether an armed conflict can be internationalised, even though it can apply as part of the law governing international responsibility. The other cases used as authority by Crawford either reaffirmed the existence of the 'acting in fact on behalf of a state' test,[103] or related to matters separate from attribution of conduct.[104]

[97] ILC Report, Twenty-Seventh Session, 5 May–25 July 1975, UNGA, Thirtieth Session, Supp 10 (A/10010/Rev.1), YBILC (1975) vol II, 80.

[98] First Report, Crawford (1998) 40.

[99] There are important implications tied to this position of 'express' versus 'implied' agency relationships, which are analysed below.

[100] Observations and comments of Governments on chapters I, II and III of Part I of the draft articles on State responsibility for internationally wrongful acts, A/CN.4/328 and Add 1–4, YBILC (1980) vol II(1), 97.

[101] First Report, Crawford (1998) 40–43.

[102] ibid 40.

[103] The question as to whether this test exists today is explored in chapter 8.

[104] It is clear that some states conflated attribution of conduct with responsibility when giving their comments on Draft Article 8. Mongolia, for example, stated: 'Although they seem to be skilfully drafted, Mongolia has some doubts as to the coverage of acts of natural persons, who, at the time of committing

The inferences drawn from incoherent case-law led the ILC to changing the apparently 'less than clear' attribution test of a non-state actor 'acting in fact on behalf of a state'.[105] When making his recommendation to the ILC, Crawford relied heavily on the *Nicaragua* judgment:

> It can be argued that the issue presented in *Military and Paramilitary Activities in and against Nicaragua* related specifically to the extent of the obligation of a State to control irregular forces or auxiliaries acting under its auspices, and that this is either a question of the content of the relevant primary rule, or alternatively a customary *lex specialis* in that specific context. However that may be, the issue of the direction and control of a State as a basis for attribution does arise in a general way, and in the above-mentioned case the Court appears to have been treating this issue as one of general principle. Moreover it is not clear why conduct of auxiliary armed forces in operations under the specific direction and control of a State should be attributable to the State, but not analogous conduct under State direction and control in other spheres. The position taken by the majority of the Court in *Military and Paramilitary Activities in and against Nicaragua* was not the subject of any specific dissent in that case, nor has it been criticized as overbroad in later decisions or in the literature. For all of these reasons, the Special Rapporteur is provisionally of the view that article 8(a) should be clarified, that it is desirable to attribute to the State specific conduct carried out under its direction and control, and that appropriate language to that effect should be added. The text and commentary should make it clear that it is only if the State directed and controlled the specific operation and the conduct complained of was a necessary, integral or intended part of that operation, that the conduct should be attributable to the State. The principle should not extend to conduct which was only incidentally or peripherally associated with an operation, or which escaped from the State's direction and control.[106]

Crawford considered this practice to indicate that conduct of a non-state actor could only be attributed to a state when there was a form of explicit authorisation given by a state to undertake a particular course of conduct, in the form of 'instructions' or 'directions', which was a position that needed to be 'broadened' – and, according to Crawford, was by the ICJ in *Nicaragua* – by allowing for attribution to be triggered if it could be proven that a state had exercised 'control' over a non-state actor in specific instances where the conduct in question was contrary to an international rule. For this reason, Crawford proposed a new version of Draft Article 8:

> *Attribution to the State of conduct in fact carried out on its instructions or under its direction and control*
>
> The conduct of a person or group of persons shall also be considered as an act of the State under international law if:
>
> (a) The person or group of persons was in fact acting on the instructions of, or under the direction and control of, that State in carrying out the conduct; or

a violation of international law, do not act as State representatives but nevertheless act under the authority and control of the State. In this connection mention should be made of the trend towards [a] broader understanding that under customary international law, as applied to environmental protection, a State is responsible for its own activities and for those of persons, whether they be individuals, private or public corporations, as long as their activities are under the State's jurisdiction or control' (State Responsibility, Fiftieth Session of the ILC (1998), Agenda Item 2, Comments and observations received by Governments, A/CN.4/488 and Add 1–3, 107).

[105] First Report, Crawford (1998) 43.

[106] ibid.

(b) The person or group of persons was in fact exercising elements of the governmental authority in the absence of the official authorities and in circumstances which called for the exercise of those elements of authority.[107]

In his explanatory notes, Crawford states that state 'authorization', 'instruction', 'mandate' or 'direction' are examples of a non-state actor acting on behalf of a state.[108] This fits with the argument that these terms are merely indicators of a non-state actor acting on a state's behalf, or, to put it another way, a state 'appointing' a non-state actor to act for it. Ultimately, Crawford saw Draft Article 8 as a provision that should only cover forms of non-state actor conduct that were perceived to have been 'controlled' by a state.[109]

1.3. The ILC Endorsement of Crawford's Perspective

The response of the ILC to the proposed changes was approval. It first remarked that when a non-state actor acts on behalf of a state 'pursuant to express instructions' its actions would be 'clearly' attributable to the state.[110] It then noted that a question arose whether conduct should also be attributed to a state when a non-state actor has acted under its 'direction and control'.[111] This stance of the ILC is perplexing for two reasons. First, the previous international practice analysed by Ago shows that a non-state actor 'acting in fact on behalf of' a state could be indicated by a state exercising direction and control over it. Second, at no point in any of the case-law or literature cited by Crawford was a two-pronged test of direction *and* control present.[112] The only exception is the use of the exact phrase 'direction and control' by Nicaragua in its arguments before the ICJ. Yet the ILC ignored the fact that no rule had developed altering the 'acting in fact on behalf of' test, which was based on the practice and literature brought to light by Ago.

There was no positive law justifying the transformation of this draft provision to being based on a different test stipulating that state instructions need to be issued in some form. Despite the previous endorsement of Ago's findings by the ILC and states, the ILC appeared to forget that no material had been put forward to suggest that change in the law had occurred to indicate that express state authorisation was the threshold for attribution concerning factual links between states and non-state actors. The ILC stated: 'The subsequent jurisprudence provided some support for replacing the express authorization test by a broader effective control test.'[113] This

[107] ibid 56.

[108] ibid.

[109] ibid.

[110] ILC Report, Fiftieth Session, 20 April–12 June 1998 and 27 July–14 August 1998, UNGA, Fifty-Third Session, Supp 10 (A/53/10), YBILC (1998) vol II(2), 81.

[111] ibid.

[112] It should be noted that this was later changed, which is why the final Art 8 has the word 'or' between 'direction' and 'control'.

[113] ILC Report, Fiftieth Session (A/53/10), YBILC (1998) vol II(2), 81.

'subsequent jurisprudence' is *one case* where the ICJ invented a new test. And yet these factors went unchallenged:

> The Special Rapporteur recommended clarifying the paragraph to cover both situations of actual instructions and cases of direct and effective control where there was a nexus to the act in question. On the other hand, the provision should not be so widely drafted as to risk covering the activities of State-owned corporations, whose activities were not, in fact, directed or controlled by the State.[114]

The ILC leaned heavily on Crawford's perspective and took on board ideas that were not clear. For example, in the very same paragraph of the ILC's report the word 'and' is replaced with 'or' between 'directed' and 'controlled'. It appears the ILC itself was not sure what the new test was, but what was likely certain in the collective mind of the ILC was that the test of 'acting in fact on behalf of a state' had been replaced with a test of state authorisation based on state 'instructions', 'direction' or 'control'.

This ultimate end point is an aspect of the ARSIWA that is flawed. There was weird reasoning behind the shift. The problem is not so much that the ICJ invented the 'effective control' test, but that the ILC appeared to mistake this invention as evidence of a new international rule, which then ostensibly justified replacing the original attribution test that was based on evidence and approved by states. It is true that other cases were analysed aside from *Nicaragua* in attempting to show that perceived state control over non-state actor conduct was necessary in order for attribution to occur, but mistakenly so. Another point was made during drafting, which expressed concern that 'contrary to the underlying intentions behind the proposal' to apparently 'broaden' attribution under Draft Article 8, such a stance could 'result in a narrower and more rigid rule of attribution which would make it more difficult to determine responsibility'.[115] However, this concern remained unaddressed. It may be that the original test unearthed by Ago did need to be refined further. Nevertheless, proposing indicators of a potential test does not mean that those indicators become the new test because of a perceived need for precision. Yet this is, at least in part, why the insertion of the three criteria came about.

There is a perplexity to Article 8 when examining its drafting history. The crucial problems it poses are twofold. First, it is not based on positive law, but instead work that relied heavily on an invention in one case, yet this was sufficient to replace an alternative test that was based on more sources and seemingly approved by states. Secondly, the ILC framed this development in a manner that attempted to make it appear as though it was somehow broadening the attribution threshold under the draft provision. Up until the 1980s the formulation of Draft Article 8 was based on international practice addressing matters of attribution for the purposes of determining state responsibility. After this point in time, work on the draft provision became disjointed, primarily due to substantial reliance on, and misinterpretation of, ambiguous and contradictory rulings from courts and tribunals. Perhaps what occurred

[114] ibid.
[115] ibid 83.

during these later stages in its drafting history is a deeper-rooted reason behind why Article 8 has been critiqued so much since the ARSIWA was adopted.[116]

It is difficult to grasp what states thought of the changes made to the original provision. Only eight made comments.[117] Those that did appeared to be welcoming of the proposed changes, which cemented the retention of the instructions, direction and control criteria. The silence of states perhaps points toward their implied acceptance of the change, which is not surprising.[118] The original test ('acting in fact on behalf of') is less precise than the final test ('in fact acting on the instructions of, or under the direction or control of'). Such a shift towards refining the possible establishment of state responsibility in instances where a non-state actor has acted for a state is helpful for states wishing to practice avoidance. Article 8 provides states plenty of wiggle room in this regard, as there are many ways in which a non-state actor can act for a state without it being under its 'direction or control' or taking 'instructions' from it. The comments from the Netherlands in particular show its acceptance of the final provision, whilst also shedding light on the effectiveness of the ILC's rhetoric in framing the final provision as 'broadening' attribution:

> The Netherlands is pleased to note that the words 'direction or control' allow for the application of both a strict standard of 'effective control', as used by the ICJ in the *Military and Paramilitary Activities in and against Nicaragua* case, and a more flexible standard as applied by the Appeals Chamber of the International Tribunal for the Former Yugoslavia in the *Tadić* case. This inbuilt ambiguity is a positive element and offers scope for progressive development of the legal rules on State responsibility.[119]

It is clear that Article 8's formulation was a product of the ILC favouring the effective control test invented by the ICJ.[120] According to the ILC, the change to Draft Article 8 was intended 'as an amplification, not a narrowing, of the previous formulation, having regard in particular to the discussion of issues in the case concerning *Military and Paramilitary Activities in and against Nicaragua*. The Drafting Committee could, however, discuss whether some other formulation was to be preferred.'[121] Yet it appears no such discourse took place, resulting in a proposal from one person, based on a test invented in one case, becoming part of the state responsibility framework and in the process supplanting a previous test that rested on more stable foundations.

[116] See, for example, *Armed Activities*, Judgment, 19 December 2005, Separate Opinions of Judge Simma, para 8 and Judge Kooijmans, para 25; C Ryngaert, 'State Responsibility and Non-state Actors' in M Noortmann, A Reinisch and C Ryngaert (eds), *Non-state Actors in International Law* (Oxford, Hart, 2015) 163, 168–74; Cassese (n 29); G Nolte and HP Aust, 'Equivocal Helpers – Complicit States, Mixed Messages and International Law' (2009) 58 *ICLQ* 1; E Roucounas, 'Non-state Actors: Areas of International Responsibility in Need of Further Exploration' in M Ragazzi (ed), *International Responsibility Today: Essays in Memory of Oscar Schachter* (Leiden, Nijhoff, 2005) 391.

[117] State Responsibility, Fifty-Third Session of the ILC (2001), Comments and Observations received from Governments, A/CN.4/515 and Add 1–3, 49.

[118] This becomes more plausible when considering the fact that there were no public objections to the ARSIWA in 2001.

[119] State Responsibility, Fifty-Third Session of the ILC (2001), Comments and Observations received from Governments, A/CN.4/515 and Add 1–3, 49.

[120] ARSIWA, Art 8, Commentary, paras 4 and 5.

[121] ILC Report, Fiftieth Session, 20 April–12 June 1998 and 27 July–14 August 1998, UNGA, Fifty-Third Session, Supp.10 (A/53/10), YBILC (1998) vol II(2), 84.

2. APPLICATION OF CONTROL-BASED ATTRIBUTION IN PRACTICE

The history surrounding Article 8 calls into question developments since its adoption, in particular whether more recent practice can provide clarity on its contents. There have been a number of cases that have referred to (but not applied) Article 8, or applied it without analysis.[122] The ICJ became a key contributor to assessing the provision's application in practice through the *Bosnia Genocide* case.[123] Prior to this judgment, where the ICJ ruled against the overall control test of the ICTY, the Court had the opportunity to rule on an appropriate test for attribution in the contexts envisaged by Article 8, as in the *Armed Activities* case, matters of non-state actors, state responsibility and perceived state control were before the Court.[124] Yet the ICJ did not provide an opinion on the issue. There are also a number of domestic cases that add further insights into debates regarding control-based attribution.[125] The uncertainty regarding what attribution test is most suitable for application in practice manifests itself in the fact that a host of distinct insights into control-based attribution have been proposed.[126] Developing alongside these understandings have been critiques of the effective control test, which focus on its apparently restrictive character,[127] particularly in contributing to the creation of a state responsibility framework that can discount the participation of non-state actors in state activity.[128]

[122] WTO Appellate Body Report, *United States – Countervailing Duty Investigation on Dynamic Random Access Memory Semiconductors (DRAMS) from Korea*, WT/DS296/AB/R (27 June 2005), para 69; Arbitral tribunal (under UNCITRAL arbitration rules), *Encana Corporation v Republic of Ecuador*, London Court of International Arbitration, Case No UN3481, Award of 3 February 2006, para 154; *Armed Activities*, Judgment, 19 December 2005, paras 155–60; *Consorzio Groupement LESI-DIPENTA v People's Democratic Republic of Algeria* (ICSID Case No ARB/03/08), Award (10 January 2005) s II, para 19; *LES. SpA and Astaldi SpA v People's Democratic Republic of Algeria* (ICSID Case No ARB/05/3), Decision (11 July 2006) paras 78 and 79; *Saipem SpA v People's Republic of Bangladesh* (ICSID Case No ARB/05/07), Decision on Jurisdiction and Recommendation on Provisional Measures (21 March 2007) para 148; *EnCana Corporation v Republic of Ecuador* (LCIA Case No UN3481), Award (3 February 2006) para 154; *Waste Management, Inc v United Mexican States* (ICSID Additional Facility Case No ARB(AF)/00/3) ('Waste Management II'), Award (30 April 2004) para 75; *EDF (Services) Ltd v Romania* (ICSID Case No ARB/05/13), Award (8 October 2009) para 201.

[123] *Bosnia Genocide*, Judgment, 26 February 2007.

[124] *Armed Activities*, Judgment, 19 December 2005, paras 155–60.

[125] These are analysed below.

[126] See, for example, S Talmon, 'The Responsibility of Outside Powers for Acts of Secessionist Entities' (2009) 58 *ICLQ* 493; DD Caron, 'The Basis of Responsibility: Attribution and Other Trans-substantive Rules' in RB Lillich and DB Magraw (eds), *The Iran–United States Claims Tribunal: Its Contributions to the Law of State Responsibility* (New York, Transnational, 1998) 109; JA Hessbreugge, 'The Historical Development of the Doctrines of Attribution and Due Diligence in International Law' (2004) 36 *Journal of International Law and Politics* 265.

[127] *Armed Activities*, Judgment, 19 December 2005, Separate Opinions of Judge Simma, para 8 and Judge Kooijmans, para 25; Ryngaert (n 116) 168–74; Cassese (n 29). Those who reached the final decision in *Nicaragua* also appear to illustrate that this present approach to attribution is too precise (see *Nicaragua*, Separate Opinion of Judge Ago, para 16: 'Only in cases where certain members of those forces happened to have been specifically charged by United States authorities to commit a particular act, or carry out a particular task of some kind on behalf of the United States, would it be possible so to regard them').

[128] EB Weiss, 'Invoking State Responsibility in the Twenty-First Century' (2002) 96 *American Journal of International Law* 799; Nolte and Aust (n 116); Roucounas (n 116) 391; P Allott, 'State Responsibility and the Unmaking of International Law' (1988) 29 *Harvard International Law Journal* 1; A Bellal, 'Establishing the Direct Responsibility of Non-state Armed Groups for Violations of International Norms: Issues of Attribution' in N Gal-Or, C Ryngaert and M Noortmann (eds), *Responsibilities of the Non-state Actor in Armed Conflict and the Market Place* (Leiden, Brill, 2015) 304.

2.1. The ICJ Standing its Ground

Support has been expressed for Article 8.[129] Despite the diverse criticisms, the ICJ has opined that the effective control test forms part of customary international law.[130] State control is also viewed as a cornerstone requirement of attribution.[131] The *Bosnia Genocide* case before the ICJ was crucial in shaping such perceptions. Having held that organs of the state did not perpetrate the Srebrenica massacres, the ICJ examined whether a non-state actor acting on behalf of the state had done so. The Court noted that the applicable rule in such an instance was Article 8.[132] It first pointed out that in order to attribute conduct of a non-state actor to a state that was not based on a relationship of 'complete dependence', it must be proven that the non-state actor 'acted in accordance with that State's instructions or under its "effective control"'.[133] Further, the 'effective control' must be exercised over every 'operation' of the non-state actor where conduct that is contrary to international law has occurred.[134] The Court held the same requirement also applies to a state giving instructions.[135] This requirement is mentioned in Article 8's commentary.[136] According to the ICJ, it is not enough to show that a state was instructing, directing or controlling a non-state actor in a general sense.[137] The only exception would be if the non-state actor were 'completely dependent' on the state, meaning its general activities would be attributed to the state as though it were a de facto state organ.[138]

So when does the general input of a state become specific enough for the purposes of satisfying the attribution threshold under the effective control test? One instance would be if a state owned a non-state actor, thereby being in a general position to control it, but the conduct of the non-state actor could not be attributed to the state under Article 8 unless it directed or instructed it to carry out a specific course of conduct.[139] The Applicants questioned this rationale, arguing that the effective control test had been challenged by the ICTY's overall control test.[140] The ICJ advanced several arguments as to why it found the effective control test to be more appropriate. First, the ICTY was not 'called upon' to rule on questions of state responsibility.[141] Second, overall control was employed for determining whether an armed conflict could be internationalised.[142] Third, the Court rejected the conceptual parameters of

[129] Crawford (n 4) 156.
[130] *Bosnia Genocide*, Judgment, 26 February 2007, paras 401 and 414.
[131] J Crawford and J Watkins, 'International Responsibility' in S Besson and J Tasioulas (eds), *The Philosophy of International Law* (Oxford, Oxford University Press, 2010) 283, 295; V Lanovoy, 'The Use of Force by Non-state Actors and the Limits of Attribution of Conduct' (2017) 28 *European Journal of International Law* 563, 573–79.
[132] *Bosnia Genocide*, Judgment, 26 February 2007, para 398.
[133] ibid para 400.
[134] ibid.
[135] ibid.
[136] ARSIWA, Art 8, Commentary, paras 7 and 8.
[137] *Bosnia Genocide*, Judgment, 26 February 2007, para 400.
[138] ibid paras 399–400.
[139] ARSIWA, Art 8, Commentary, para 6.
[140] *Bosnia Genocide*, Judgment, 26 February 2007, para 402.
[141] ibid para 403.
[142] ibid para 404.

overall control for apparently being too expansive, in that it had the 'major drawback of broadening the scope of State responsibility' because it 'stretches too far, almost to breaking point' the link between a state and its international responsibility.[143] In other words, attribution under Article 8 should not expand beyond conduct where a state has not issued specific instructions to a non-state actor.

There are several inconsistencies in the Court's reasoning. The ICJ acknowledged 'acting on behalf of a state' is the key consideration for attribution purposes between any actor and a state, yet it somewhat contradicts this stance by arguing this consideration should be limited to a state issuing instructions to a non-state actor. It is clear that a non-state actor 'acting, on whatever basis, on its behalf' is still crucial for assessing attribution of conduct to a state. The question remains why proof of such a finding is not enough for attribution purposes. The ICJ provided no insight as to *why* it chose not to elaborate on this point. Yet it is at the very least arguable that the reason is in part because the Court treated Article 8 as 'holy scripture'.[144] It is also arguable that the 'acting in fact on behalf of' test might have been considered too imprecise a test, and thus the ICJ felt it appropriate to refine it by interpreting it through the lens ultimately settled on by the ILC. That said, there was little scrutiny of Article 8 as a whole. It is questionable whether the provision is customary international law, certainly with respect to the time of drafting until finalised.[145] Yet the ICJ declared it so without evidence.

There is another problem with the mainstream position on Article 8 created by the ICJ and the ILC. State control, direction or instructions being separate indicators of a single attribution test becomes a more reasonable argument when further scrutinising the ruling of the ICJ. Article 8 puts forward three distinct, non-cumulative thresholds: direction, control and instructions. This points towards the understanding that if one of these elements were satisfied then conduct of a non-state actor could be attributed to a state. On closer inspection, however, these seemingly separate requirements appear to be applied as one by the ICJ, where they are intertwined, and all of which must be satisfied as a collective in order to satisfy the attribution threshold under Article 8 – thereby reflecting that the state had final say over the specific conduct of the non-state actor in question. The issuance of specific instructions may be separate from control in the mind of the ILC, yet from the standpoint of the ICJ the yardstick of control is stretched 'too far' – 'almost to breaking point' – if it does not include the issuance of instructions or direction by a state.[146] It is also highly unlikely that evidence of 'direction' can be recognised without the presence of instructions in some form, regardless of how widely the term is interpreted.[147] A fusion of control,

[143] ibid para 406.

[144] M Milanovic, 'State Responsibility for Genocide: A Follow-Up' (2007) 18 *European Journal of International Law* 669, 693.

[145] Whether the provision has become a customary rule since the adoption of the ARSIWA is dealt with below.

[146] *Bosnia Genocide*, Judgment, 26 February 2007, para 406.

[147] The *Oxford English Dictionary* defines direction as '[t]he management or guidance of someone or something' (https://en.oxforddictionaries.com/definition/direction).

direction and instruction could have possibly been the ICJ's underlying (and unmentioned) reading in the *Nicaragua* case of what encapsulates 'effective control', which has since been extracted and then dismantled by the ILC, before being transposed into Article 8. From the perspective of the ICJ, 'effective control' and Article 8 are synonymous.

However, what satisfies the attribution threshold of this test remains unclear. Based on the reasoning of the ICJ in the *Bosnia Genocide* and *Nicaragua* cases, combined with the preparatory work, commentary and final creation of the ILC, several observations can be drawn regarding the scope of Article 8. For clarity, it is worth addressing these in the negative. If a state were to arm a non-state actor this would not satisfy the test under Article 8. If a state were to fund or financially sustain a non-state actor this conduct would be insufficient to satisfy this provision's attribution threshold.[148] If a state were to provide logistical support to a non-state actor, for example, in the form of transporting supplies or fixing faulty weaponry, the test would not be met. If a state were to gather intelligence for a non-state actor and disseminate such information, the subsequent conduct of the non-state actor based on that information would not be attributable to the state. If a state were to train a non-state actor the threshold of this test would not be met. If a state were to authorise particular conduct of a non-state actor, that conduct may not be attributable to the former. This last issue is unclear, as from the understanding of the ILC, 'authorisation' can be equated with instruction,[149] thus addressing an explicit form of authorisation, but remaining silent on implicit forms. Conversely, when reflecting on the *Behrami/Saramati* decision of the ECtHR and applying it by analogy to non-state actors, it highlights that authority over a particular actor will likely result in the conduct of that actor being attributed to a state, but only if supplemented by an indication of simultaneous 'control'.[150] It can be deduced that even if all these facts were present in a case, it is doubtful that such cumulative state conduct would satisfy the attribution threshold under Article 8. What can be taken from this breakdown is that the scope of attribution under Article 8 does not encompass many types of state conduct that could occur as part of a relationship with a non-state actor.

Judge Al-Khasawneh voiced several concerns regarding the majority ruling on attribution in the *Bosnia Genocide* case.[151] He argued that the Court erred in applying the effective control test, which 'followed Article 8', as the situation in the *Bosnia Genocide* case was different from that in the *Nicaragua* case.[152] As there was 'a unity of goals, unity of ethnicity and a common ideology', the application of the effective control test was 'not necessary' in proving the link between non-state actor and

[148] This is not the same standard as a state owning a non-state actor, where satisfying the threshold would depend on whether the non-state actor was exercising elements of governmental authority. See ARSIWA, Art 8, Commentary, para 6 and ARSIWA, Art 5.

[149] ARSIWA, Art 8, Commentary, para 8.

[150] *Behrami and Saramati v France, Germany and Norway* App Nos 71412/01 and 78166/01 (ECtHR, 2 May 2007) paras 132–41.

[151] *Application of the Convention on the Prevention and Punishment of the Crime of Genocide* (*Bosnia and Herzegovina v Serbia and Montenegro*), Dissenting Opinion, Vice-President Al-Khasawneh.

[152] ibid para 36.

state.[153] He argued that 'a strong case can be made for the proposition that the test of control is a variable one'.[154] In his view, attribution tests based on perceived state control over non-state actors do not have a fixed pattern of conduct that would trigger them because they are predisposed to change. It was emphasised that 'some ILC members drew attention to the fact of there being varying degrees of sufficient control required in specific legal contexts'.[155] Citing *Tadic* and more recent case-law of the ICTY, Al-Khasawneh emphasised that the overall control test provides more flexibility in its application.[156] The then Vice-President of the ICJ was sceptical of Article 8, in particular regarding the inadequacy of the ILC's explanation as to why effective control should be preferred to overall control.[157] In Al-Khasawneh's view, the ICJ's rationale and rejection of the test applied in *Tadić* failed to address the issue of different types of activities where a non-state actor was acting on behalf of a state, which 'call[s] for subtle variations in the rules of attribution'.[158] The final passage of the dissent points towards a key 'danger' of Article 8's application: allowing criminal-like policies of states to continue without any possibility of international responsibility ensuing because of the utilisation of a non-state actor.[159] The dissent suggests that a more comprehensive approach to attribution should be taken in such cases where a non-state actor appears to have acted in fact on the behalf of a state.

Another aspect of the *Bosnia Genocide* case that has yet to be clarified is the link between 'control' and 'dependence'. The two concepts have been read to mean the same thing.[160] They *are* related, but distinct. This point is not one of semantics, but substance. 'Complete dependence' reaffirms the same test applied in *Nicaragua*.[161] It is an attribution test for determining whether a non-state actor is or was in fact indistinguishable from a de jure state organ. A finding of a non-state actor being 'completely dependent' on a state thus transforms that actor into being viewed as a de facto state organ. The test has also been labelled 'complete control'.[162] However, at no point in the *Nicaragua* or *Bosnia Genocide* cases does the ICJ refer to 'complete control'. It has been highlighted that '[t]he ILC does not discuss the issue of control required under Article 4, though it seems to favour a more restrictive approach, such as the one in the first *Nicaragua* test of complete control'.[163] The issue of control is not discussed in the preparatory work or commentary to this provision because the adopted test is that of complete dependence.

It is helpful to separate these two concepts when addressing questions concerning attribution of conduct. If this is not done, there is no way to distinguish between

[153] ibid.
[154] ibid para 37.
[155] ibid.
[156] ibid.
[157] ibid para 38.
[158] ibid para 39.
[159] ibid.
[160] Milanovic (n 31) 581.
[161] *Nicaragua*, Judgment, 27 June 1986, para 110; see also the ICJ's analysis leading up to the use of this test at para 109.
[162] Milanovic (n 31) 576.
[163] ibid 583.

'control' within the meaning under Article 8, and 'control' for the purposes of establishing a relationship of dependence sufficient to show that a non-state actor is or was a de facto state organ. For instance, what is the difference between 'complete control', and 'control' being exercised, for example, by way of direction or instruction? The two concepts can show that a non-state actor has acted on a state's behalf, yet it would be an error to interpret 'dependence' and 'control' as one. Such problems of interpretation need not arise. A non-state actor can be dependent on a state without a state directing or instructing it. This is not the same for control. In order to demonstrate state control over a non-state actor, directions or instructions need to be given by a state, or perhaps the state must be perceived to be in a position where it had the power and authority to prevent the non-state actor's conduct.[164] In order to show dependence, an established predominant reliance on a state by a non-state actor may need to be demonstrated.[165]

Paragraphs 109 and 110 of the *Nicaragua* case need not be read in a vacuum, as the discussion relating to control was a precursor for the effective control test's creation.[166] Some of the factors that the ICJ examined for the purposes of attribution are more akin to suggesting a relationship of dependence: whether a non-state actor was created by a state;[167] whether a state selected, installed or paid leaders part of a non-state actor;[168] whether a state provided financial support to a non-state actor;[169] whether a state trained a non-state actor;[170] whether a state provided intelligence information;[171] whether a state armed a non-state actor.[172] The same can be said for factors pointing more towards a relationship based on state control: giving specific instructions regarding the course of a specific mission. The approach of the ICJ to the issue infers that state control is the result of non-state actor dependence, which is misleading. More accurately, 'dependence creates the *potential* for control'.[173] Control and dependence may sometimes be interrelated in cases where a state and a non-state actor share links, but, in general, the two concepts are distinct.

2.2. Analogising Insights from Domestic Cases

Domestic cases add further insight into understandings of 'effective control' in the context of attribution. Their rulings emphasise that there remain alternative ways

[164] See the analysis below regarding the application of effective control in domestic cases.

[165] *Jorgic* (Oberlandesgericht, Düsseldorf), Decision, 26 September 1997 (unreported) – see *Tadić*, para 129; Macak (n 89) 46 (n 128).

[166] This is evident from the placing in which the Court first referred to 'effective control' (para 115), as it logically follows on from the discussion in paras 109–14. It also helps explain why the ICJ only mentions 'effective control' once in the entire judgment.

[167] *Nicaragua*, Judgment, 27 June 1986, paras 93 and 94.

[168] ibid para 112.

[169] ibid para 97.

[170] ibid paras 112, 115, 117, 120, 121, 228, 242.

[171] ibid paras 106, 110, 243.

[172] ibid paras 228, 242, 268.

[173] Talmon (n 126) 497 (emphasis in original).

in which such a test can be interpreted. However, the insights examined here require being applied by analogy to non-state actors. This is because the cases below concern attribution in the context of state organs that are placed at the disposal of intergovernmental organisations, which is a separate issue from assessing attribution in the context of determining state responsibility for non-state actor conduct. That said, these cases provide further insight into how the concept of control factors into attribution considerations.

2.2.1. Nuhanović *and* Mustafić

These cases were litigated in a number of steps. The analysis here predominantly relates to the Dutch Court of Appeal's ruling,[174] which reversed the District Court ruling.[175] The District Court took the view that the conduct of Dutchbat (the Netherlands branch of the UN peacekeeping force UNPROFOR) was only attributable to the UN because of its 'operational command and control',[176] meaning the Netherlands was not held responsible for Dutchbat's eviction of Bosnian nationals from a compound under its charge that led to multiple killings. The Court of Appeal overturned this ruling,[177] whilst giving insights into the application of 'effective control'.[178]

It was agreed that Dutchbat was 'placed under the command of' the UN. But whether this implied actual 'command and control' being transferred to the UN was questioned.[179] In the Court's view, the important consideration is 'who actually was in possession of "effective control"'.[180] The Court held:

> The question whether the State had 'effective control' over the conduct of Dutchbat … must be answered in view of the circumstances of the case. This does not only imply that significance should be given to the question whether that conduct constituted the execution of a specific instruction, issued by the UN or the State, *but also* to the question whether, *if there was no such specific instruction*, the UN or *the State had the power to prevent the conduct concerned*. Moreover, the Court adopts as a starting point that the possibility that more than one party has 'effective control' is generally accepted, which means that it cannot be ruled out that the application of this criterion results in the possibility of attribution to more than one party. For this reason the Court will only examine if the State exercised 'effective control' over the alleged conduct and will not answer the question whether the UN also had 'effective control'.[181]

[174] *Hasan Nuhanović v the Netherlands*, Court of Appeal in The Hague, Civil Law Section (5 July 2011) LJN: BR5388; 200.020.174/01; *Mustafić et al v the Netherlands*, Court of Appeal in The Hague, Civil Law Section (5 July 2011) LJN: BR5386; 200.020.173/01.

[175] *Hasan Nuhanović v the Netherlands*, District Court in The Hague, Civil Law Section (10 September 2008) LJN: BF0181; 265615/HA ZA 06-1671; *Mustafić et al v the Netherlands*, District Court in The Hague, Civil Law Section (10 September 2008) LJN: BF0182; 265618/HA ZA 06-1672.

[176] ibid paras 4.8–4.14.5.

[177] *Hasan Nuhanović* (5 July 2011); *Mustafić et al* (5 July 2011).

[178] It should also be noted that unlike the ECtHR in *Al-Jedda*, the Dutch Court of Appeal categorically affirmed 'effective control' (as opposed to 'ultimate authority and control') as the applicable attribution test in situations where states have participated in peacekeeping missions.

[179] *Hasan Nuhanović* (5 July 2011) para. 5.7.

[180] ibid.

[181] ibid para 5.9 (emphasis added).

Two points can be drawn here. First, an attribution of conduct test based on 'effective control' is contextual and need not be applied rigidly. In light of the overall finding of the Court, in addition to the rationale leading there, it is clear that 'effective control' can be adapted to mean different things depending on the circumstances. Second, state instructions are arguably not necessary for satisfying the attribution threshold of such a test. Applying these insights by analogy to questions of attribution based on effective control in the context of determining state responsibility for non-state actor conduct helps show that, so long as an actor was undertaking a role on the behalf of a state, then if the state had the means to prevent that actor from carrying out the conduct that was contrary to an international rule, such conduct can be attributed to the state.[182] This reading is significant. Incorporating it into applications of Article 8 would mean that so long as a state were deemed to be in a position of authority where it was able to change the course of a non-state actor's conduct, attributing that conduct to the state would be appropriate. Effective control of a state over non-state actor conduct could thus be understood as a state's actual 'power to prevent' non-state actor conduct, in addition to viewing this test as one stipulating that state instructions need be issued with respect to the specific conduct of the non-state actor in question.[183]

It has been stressed that with respect to the potential broader scope of 'effective control', the Court's 'interpretation acknowledges the limitations of relying on direct orders',[184] which is important, not least because 'in many cases, human rights abuses occur at the foot-soldier level, having been ordered neither by the United Nations nor by the relevant state'.[185] This is similar for relationships between states and non-state actors in settings of conflict. Such an approach to attribution makes sense, as states do wield the power to exercise authority and influence over many types of field operations, meaning they are 'in the position to ensure that no wrongful conduct is committed' by non-state actors.[186] Rather 'than applying a default attribution [test] when the conduct does not occur pursuant to direct orders … [the Court's] interpretation of the ['effective control'] standard requires a deeper analysis as to the different forms of control' that can be exercised by a state.[187] Being able to apply all the details of the relationships states have with non-state actors is important when assessing state responsibility. Attribution under Article 8 could also take into account the extent to which a state relies on a non-state actor to get something done in a particular context, even in the absence of evidence pointing to a state issuing instructions.

[182] There is a link between such readings of 'effective control' for the purposes of attribution of conduct and due diligence, which is examined in chapter 7.

[183] T Dannenbaum, 'Killings at Srebrenica, Effective Control, and the Power to Prevent Unlawful Conduct' (2012) 61 *ICLQ* 713, 726.

[184] B. Boutin, 'Responsibility of the Netherlands for the Acts of Dutchbat in Nuhanovic and Mustafic: The Continuous Quest for a Tangible Meaning for "Effective Control" in the Context of Peacekeeping' (2012) 25 *Leiden Journal of International Law* 521, 529.

[185] T Dannenbaum, 'Translating the Standard of Effective Control into a System of Effective Accountability: How Liability Should be Apportioned for Violations of Human Rights by Member State Troop Contingents Serving as United Nations Peacekeepers' (2010) 51 *Harvard International Law Journal* 113, 156.

[186] Boutin (n 184) 529.

[187] Dannenbaum (n 183) 722.

A crucial point to be taken away from the Court's approach to attribution and control is that the mere presumption of state control being present in a particular setting is not sufficient to satisfy an 'effective control' attribution test.[188] What is necessary is the state being able to lawfully make use of its position in such a context, but not doing so. This reading is closely related to that of Tom Dannenbaum, in which 'effective control' can be 'held by the entity that is best positioned to act effectively and within the law to prevent the abuse in question'.[189] If such interpretations were to become part of the practice of applying Article 8, then care would need to be exercised to ensure that such a step did not conflate attribution with due diligence considerations. This is particularly important if due diligence is ever to apply as a secondary rule of international law. The insights on attribution taken from the *Nuhanović* and *Mustafić* cases being analogised to apply to relationships between states and non-state actors means that attribution of conduct could take place if it were deemed that a state could have prevented the conduct of a non-state actor that was contrary to an international rule.[190] This closely relates to how state responsibility is determined based on a failure of a state to exercise due diligence in a particular case.[191] That said, attribution of conduct and due diligence need not be conflated, even if Article 8 were to be read in a way that incorporates a prevention assessment. For example, if it were considered that a state did not *attempt to prevent* conduct of a non-state actor that was reasonably foreseeable, then its international responsibility could be established for a failure to exercise due diligence.[192] In contrast, if it were considered that a state exercised effective control over a non-state actor, meaning it was established that the state was in a position so that it could have actually prevented the conduct of the non-state actor from taking place, then that conduct could be attributed to the state. The importance of this approach to attribution is that it extends the potential scope of Article 8 to instances where non-state actors may have acted in fact on the behalf of states, but in the absence of state instructions, which under the current approach to applying Article 8 prevents non-state actor conduct from being attributed to states. Courts and other bodies faced with questions of state responsibility for non-state actor conduct in the future may 'be inspired to take into account' the decisions in the *Nuhanović* and *Mustafić* cases.[193]

2.2.2. Mothers of Srebrenica

This case was based on a claim that Dutchbat had failed to prevent genocide and, consequently, the state should be held responsible.[194] The Hague District Court

[188] For the Court's insights on this point, see paras 5.18–5.20.
[189] Dannenbaum (n 185) 157.
[190] A related point is made in A Nollkaemper, 'Dual Attribution: Liability of the Netherlands for Conduct of Dutchbat in Srebrenica' (2011) 9 *Journal of International Criminal Justice* 1143, 1148.
[191] See chapter 7, which addresses concerns with respect to conflating attribution of conduct with due diligence assessments.
[192] See conclusion in R Mackenzie-Gray Scott, 'Due Diligence as a Secondary Rule of General International Law' (2021) 34 *Leiden Journal of International Law* 343.
[193] Boutin (n 184) 535.
[194] *Mothers of Srebrenica v The Netherlands*, Judgment (16 July 2014), The Hague District Court, Case No C/09/295247, para 3.1.

was faced with the issue of whether Dutchbat's conduct could be attributed to the Netherlands. In interpreting effective control, the Court reasoned: '*effective control* means the actual say or "*factual control*" of the State over the Dutchbat's specific actions'.[195] Although the rulings of the ICJ and supplementary academic commentary has clarified that 'effective control' is an attribution test for examining state responsibility for non-state actors' specific undertakings, the Dutch Court read the test as 'effective control of Dutchbat's actions *in general* by the State'.[196] The Court also departed from the ICJ approach, in which 'effective control' entails the issuance of instructions, ruling that: '[I]n order to accept *effective control* there would be no requirement for the State in giving instructions to Dutchbat to have broken the structure of the chain of command at the UN or exercised independent operational authority to give orders.'[197] In clarifying this previous point, it was held:

> [Attribution] comes down to the actual say over specific actions whereby all of the actual circumstances and the particular context of the case must be examined. … not only is the question significant as to whether the actions constituted implementation of a specific instruction the State had given but also whether in the absence of any such specific instruction the State had it in its powers to prevent the actions concerned.[198]

The Court determined that 'effective control' is based on a state's potential power and authority over a non-state actor. In the Court's view, even if 'command' over a non-state actor is not present, 'effective control' can still be exercised, meaning 'there is room' for attribution to take place.[199] These insights of The Hague District Court point towards 'effective control' meaning a state wielding the *potential* to exercise factual control over a non-state actor through its normative power.[200] Analogising this understanding to applications of Article 8 would mean that the attribution threshold of this provision could be met in the absence of instructions for a specific undertaking.[201]

A further insight that was provided in this case can also be analogised to determine state responsibility for ultra vires conduct of a non-state actor whose conduct

[195] ibid para 4.34 (emphasis original).
[196] ibid para (c) (emphasis added).
[197] ibid para 4.46 (emphasis original).
[198] ibid.
[199] ibid para 4.47.
[200] It should be noted that The Hague Court of Appeal later ruled that Dutchbat performed the disputed acts without 'factual control' of the state 'over specific acts' and that these acts were 'within "the official capacity" and "within the overall functions"' of the UN operation, meaning Dutchbat's conduct was held to be not attributable to The Netherlands (*Mothers of Srebrenica v The Netherlands*, Judgment (27 June 2017), The Hague Court of Appeal, Case Nos 200.158.313/01 and 200.160.317/01, para 32.1). The Supreme Court of The Netherlands then ruled: 'The wrongful conduct of Dutchbat facilitated the serious violation of fundamental rights. That justifies a judicial declaration entailing wrongful conduct, despite the fact that causality has not been established' (para 2.2.4). Further, some acts of Dutchbat were 'performed under the command and control of the UN, without the State exercising effective control in that regard. Those acts cannot be attributed to the State for that reason' (para 5.1). However, 'the State did have effective control of Dutchbat's conduct' on a specific occasion, and that conduct was attributed to The Netherlands (*Mothers of Srebrenica v The Netherlands*, Judgment (19 July 2019), Supreme Court of The Netherlands, Case No 17/04567, para 5.1). For further analysis, see T. Dannenbaum, 'A Disappointing End of the Road for the Mothers of Srebrenica Litigation in the Netherlands' *EJIL: Talk!* (23 July 2019) www.ejiltalk.org/a-disappointing-end-of-the-road-for-the-mothers-of-srebrenica-litigation-in-the-netherlands/.
[201] See also *Mothers of Srebrenica*, paras 4.48 and 4.53.

could be attributed to the state under Article 8. In other words, circumstances in which a state and a non-state actor share a connection, the state exercises 'effective control', and the non-state actor undertakes conduct contrary to the instructions of the state.[202] In the present case the actor in question was a state organ transferred to an intergovernmental organisation to act in a different capacity for a prescribed period.[203] Should the actors in other cases be states and non-state actors, attribution could account for scenarios in which a non-state actor is acting in fact on behalf of a state, but where both entities have contrary objectives. This would mean that the effective control test would address non-state actor conduct that was contrary to state instructions, in that if the state issued instructions to do X but the non-state actor did Y, the Y would still be attributable to the state, so long as the non-state actor was part of a wider operation that was being undertaken on the behalf of that state. Ultra vires attribution based on factual relations between states and non-state actors, where a non-state actor *was not* exercising governmental authority, could therefore apply alongside Article 7. Attribution for ultra vires conduct of non-state actors would thus not just be addressed in settings where non-state actors were officially acting on the behalf of states, but where they unofficially do so as well.

2.3. Moving Past the Mainstream Understanding of Article 8

What can be taken from the above cases is that they do not align to produce a clear picture of what 'effective control' means. The final version of Article 8 embodies this attribution test invented by the ICJ. In taking this test forward in the *Bosnia Genocide* case, the Court certainly showed its support for it, yet did not provide clarity on its applicable scope. Therefore:

> One should … accept the Court's conclusion with utmost caution, not only because the Court provided no reasoning for its position, but also because it exposes a hole in the ILC Articles on State Responsibility, which, comprehensive though they may be, still do not provide all the answers to questions of state responsibility for acts of non-state actors.[204]

The final product of the ILC and rulings of the ICJ appears to have boxed many into thinking that state control is needed to establish an attributable link between a state and a non-state actor that share factual ties. The conflicting opinions in related literature, combined with the insights gained from examining other cases that addressed effective control in the context of attribution of conduct, speak to an understanding that attribution under Article 8 remains an unresolved subject,[205] despite those who

[202] A similar reading can also be envisaged when applying the complete dependence test.

[203] *Mothers of Srebrenica v The Netherlands*, Judgment (16 July 2014), The Hague District Court, Case No C/09/295247, para 4.58 (emphasis original).

[204] Milanovic (n 144) 676. The quote cited refers to the ICJ's application of Art 6 ARSIWA by analogy. However, its words also hold true with respect to the Court's application of Art 8/effective control.

[205] See, for example, *Adel A Hamadi Al Tamimi v Sultanate of Oman* (ICSID Case No ARB/11/33), Award (3 November 2015) para 320, where the Tribunal rules that the parameters of attribution under Art 8 'remain the subject of debate'.

contend it is settled. At present, a circle of incoherence exists, which starts with the premise of state control being necessary to attribute non-state actor conduct to states that share relationships based on factual connections, and ending in the question of what is control for this purpose. There exists indecision and hesitation regarding what is the most appropriate attribution test to apply when state responsibility is being considered because of a factual relationship shared with a non-state actor. Although the test under Article 8 could continue to be applied in practice and interpreted in multiple ways, should it? Are courts and tribunals that apply this test really relying on positive law to resolve disputes, or are they relying on opinions that claim as much?

3. ARTICLE 8 AND INTERNATIONAL CUSTOM

Has Article 8 become a customary rule since the ARSIWA was officially completed in 2001? The analysis of the preparatory history of the provision and application in practice cast doubt over its perceived status as a customary rule during drafting up until completion. Of contemporary relevance is whether it is customary today, especially given the many unproven assertions that it is customary international law.[206] This matter has in part been obscured by the ARSIWA enjoying 'the veneer of a multilateral treaty',[207] meaning those applying the provisions within the ARSIWA often do so without scrutiny, which is particularly fitting to Article 8.[208] The work of the ILC also took half a century, which can add to a sense of grandeur surrounding the ARSIWA. Yet this does not prevent the provisions of this document from being challenged. Despite the authority that comes hand-in-hand with the ARSIWA, this section raises a question regarding whether the predominant view on Article 8 is overstated, if not baseless.

Before examining state practice it is worth considering the perspective of whether reputed opinions that are not from states can be treated as evidence of a customary rule. If this question is answered in the negative, then proof of Article 8 being a customary rule must be found in state practice, away from judicial pronouncements and the work of selected commentators. Yet if this question is answered in

[206] For example, the ICJ (*Bosnia Genocide*, paras 385 and 398; *Armed Activities*, para 160) and ICSID Tribunals (*Saipem SpA v Bangladesh* (ICSID Case No ARB/05/07), Decision on Jurisdiction and Recommendation on Provisional Measures (21 March 2007) para 148; *Noble Ventures, Inc v Romania* (ICSID Case No ARB/01/11), Award (12 October 2005) para 69); Crawford, *State Responsibility: The General Part*, 146 and 148; Talmon (n 126) 495; V Lanovoy, *Complicity and its Limits in the Law of International Responsibility* (Oxford, Hart, 2016) 312; Lanovoy (n 131) 574; K Macak, 'Decoding Article 8 of the International Law Commission's Articles on State Responsibility: Attribution of Cyber Operations by Non-state Actors' (2016) 21 *Journal of Conflict & Security Law* 405, 407; R Jorritsma, 'Emerging Voices: The Role of Attribution Rules Under the Law of State Responsibility in Classifying Situations of Armed Conflict' *Opinio Juris* (17 August 2015) http://opiniojuris.org/2015/08/17/emerging-voices-the-role-of-attribution-rules-under-the-law-of-state-responsibility-in-classifying-situations-of-armed-conflict/.

[207] RD Sloane, 'On the Use and Abuse of Necessity in the Law of State Responsibility' (2012) 106 *American Journal of International Law* 447, 450.

[208] D Bodansky and JR Crook, 'Symposium: The ILC's State Responsibility Articles: Introduction and Overview' (2002) 96 *American Journal of International Law* 773, 775.

the affirmative, then the mere critique of these authorities casts doubt, albeit minimally, on the dominant assumption that Article 8 embodies customary international law. This is not an abnormal theme in international law. Kevin Jon Heller has noted the 'bore' of apparent custom being created without evidence of state practice and opinio juris.[209] Such an outcome becomes more likely when prominent individuals and institutions, for whatever reasons in line with fulfilling whatever agendas, assert that a particular concept forms part of customary international law. Concepts can be perceived to be customary international rules so long as the 'right' actors say so. And who are these actors? In the area of state responsibility, the ILC and the ICJ certainly appear to be. But these actors are not states. Neither are the commentators that align their own views with the outputs of these bodies, who can support, and in some instances help create and maintain, the perceptions afforded to such outputs. This practice appears to be especially prevalent in the context of the ILC and its special rapporteurs, as an 'aura surrounds the remarkable scholarly work of the Commission's special rapporteurs'.[210] More generally, this may be why the 'comprehensive scope and authoritative tone' of the ARSIWA might have resulted in 'more deference than is warranted'.[211]

3.1. State Practice

For argument's sake, it can be assumed that state practice and opinio juris matters in assessing whether Article 8 is a rule of customary international law. So what story does this practice tell since this provision was finalised in 2001? A convenient place to begin the answer to this question is examining the arguments made by states during proceedings where Article 8 has been cited. In the *Armed Activities* case there was minimal reference to Article 8 by the parties. Uganda referred to 'command and control' in a number of submissions, but there was no mention of Article 8.[212] The only mention of the provision by Uganda was to point out that it is not related to self-defence.[213] In response, the Democratic Republic of the Congo (DRC) referred to Article 8.[214] In a rejoinder it comments that it 'is *possible* to take into account Article 8'.[215] Note the DRC did not think it is necessary to take Article 8 into account.

[209] KJ Heller, 'The Seemingly Inexorable March of "Unwilling or Unable" Through the Academy' *Opinio Juris* (6 March 2015) http://opiniojuris.org/2015/03/06/the-seemingly-inexorable-march-of-unwilling-or-unable-through-the-academy/.

[210] Allott, 'State Responsibility and the Unmaking of International Law', 11.

[211] L Chircop, 'A Due Diligence Standard of Attribution in Cyberspace' (2018) 67 *ICLQ* 643, 659.

[212] *Armed Activities on the Territory of the Congo*, Counter-Memorial Submitted by Uganda (21 April 2001) vol I, 37; *Armed Activities on the Territory of the Congo*, Written Observations of the Republic of Uganda on the Question of the Admissibility of the Counter-Claims Made in the Counter-Memorial of the Republic of Uganda of 21 April 2001 (15 August 2001) 15–16.

[213] *Armed Activities on the Territory of the Congo*, Rejoinder Submitted by Uganda (6 December 2002) vol I, para 272.

[214] *Armed Activities on the Territory of the Congo*, Reply of the DRC (May 2011) vol I, paras 3.131 and 3.132.

[215] ibid para 3.131 (emphasis added).

'Control' is mentioned by the DRC, but in the context of who would benefit from a state's 'support', 'control', 'authority' or 'influence'.[216] The DRC also denounced the 'command and control' argument advanced by Uganda.[217] During the proceedings, the DRC and Uganda referred to Article 8 eight times.[218] In the *Bosnia Genocide* case the first reference to Article 8 was in its draft form by Bosnia and Herzegovina, stating that the provision 'must be interpreted widely'.[219] In the same submission, mention was also made of 'command and control'.[220] Due to the period of time in which these arguments were advanced, the reference to Draft Article 8 was to the test of a non-state actor 'acting in fact on behalf of the State', not the final version of Article 8 that embodies the effective control test.[221] And there was no further reference to Article 8 in written submissions by the states party to the dispute after 1998. During oral arguments in 2006, the final version of Article 8 was referred to thirty-three times by the parties.[222]

Although the insights need to be applied by analogy to Article 8, the cases in the Dutch courts examined above point towards the use of an 'effective control' test as being part of state practice.[223] As do similar cases before Belgian, German and UK courts.[224] The Federal Constitutional Court of Germany has also held that 'private individuals' acts can be attributed to a State if, for instance, such acts are controlled by that State'.[225] Effective control was also referred to by a Canadian court, being cited as one of a number of means for determining whether an individual was responsible for participating in crimes against humanity.[226] On this point it was

[216] *Armed Activities on the Territory of the Congo*, Demande en indication de mesures conservatoires République Démocratique du Congo contre la République de L'Ouganda (19 June 2000) 3.

[217] *Armed Activities on the Territory of the Congo*, Observations écrites additionnelles sur les demandes reconventionnelles présentées par L'Ouganda (February 2003) paras 1.25 and 1.42.

[218] Oral Proceedings, Verbatim record 2005/5, 50; Oral Proceedings, Verbatim record 2005/7, 25 and 30; Oral Proceedings, Verbatim record 2005/11, 22; Oral Proceedings, Verbatim record 2005/14, 34.

[219] *Application of the Convention on the Prevention and Punishment of the Crime of Genocide*, Memorial of the Republic of Bosnia and Herzegovina (15 April 1994) para 6.3.1.1.

[220] ibid paras 2.1.0.6 and 3.2.0.3.

[221] *Application of the Convention on the Prevention and Punishment of the Crime of Genocide*, Reply of the Government of Bosnia and Herzegovina (23 April 1998) 760.

[222] Oral Proceedings, Verbatim record 2006/8, 29 and 33; Oral Proceedings, Verbatim record 2006/9, 51, 52, 55; Oral Proceedings, Verbatim record 2006/8, 28, 30, 38, 39, 44, 47; Oral Proceedings, Verbatim record 2006/16, 35, 36; Oral Proceedings, Verbatim record 2006/17, 44; Oral Proceedings, Verbatim record 2006/21, 16; Oral Proceedings, Verbatim record 2006/31, 34, 37, 43; Oral Proceedings, Verbatim record 2006/35, 38, 47; Oral Proceedings, Verbatim record 2006/40, 49, 51, 52.

[223] See above analysis on *Nuhanović*, *Mustafić* and *Mothers of Srebrenica*.

[224] *Mukeshimana-Ngulinzira and ors v Belgium and ors*, First instance judgment, RG No 04/4807/A, 07/15547/A, 8 December 2010, Brussels (Court of First Instance); *Anonymous v German Federal Government*, First instance judgment, 26 K 5534/10, 9 February 2012, North Rhine-Westphalia, Cologne [VG]; *Arrest of Somali Pirate Suspects Case, Anonymous v Federal Government*, Appeal judgment, 4 A 2948/11, Deutsches Verwaltungsblatt 375, 18 September 2014, North Rhine-Westphalia; Higher Administrative Court [OVG]; *R (on the application of Al-Jedda) v Secretary of State for Defence* [2007] UKHL 58.

[225] UNGA, 62nd Session, Comments and information received from Governments, A/62/63 (9 March 2007) 13, para 25.

[226] *Minister of Citizenship and Immigration v Ezokola*, Appeal judgment, 2011 FCA 224, 15 July 2011, Federal Court.

held that effective control over the offences at issue was not necessary to establish responsibility.[227] The Dutch courts in assessing superior responsibility for international law violations during armed conflict have also applied a test based on effective control.[228] Aside from those mentioned, there appear to be no other domestic courts or tribunals that have applied or referred to Article 8 or the term 'effective control' as it is understood with respect to attribution of conduct.

There are, however, further pronouncements of states relating to Article 8 and effective control present in other arenas. In the *Catan* case before the ECtHR, Russia contended that 'the Court could only find that Russia was in effective control if it found that the "Government" of the "MRT" could be regarded as an organ of the Russian State in accordance with the approach of the [ICJ]' in the *Bosnia Genocide* case.[229] This argument appears to conflate the Article 8/effective control test with the complete dependence test, which is confirmed by examining Russia's reasoning in an earlier decision:

> The Russian Government emphasised that one of the necessary conditions for State responsibility under international law was the possibility of attributing the conduct in question to the State. They referred to Chapter II of the ILC's Draft Articles and the case-law of the ICJ to the effect that the conduct of persons other than the State's own governmental authorities could be considered the acts of that State only if they acted on the State's instructions or under its direction and control, to the extent that there was a relationship of 'complete dependence' between the State authorities and the persons in question and control in respect of each operation in which the alleged violations occurred.[230]

Russia also made a similar argument in another ECtHR case.[231] A common theme in these cases was that Russia, as pointed out by the ECtHR, mistakenly cited the effective control test for attribution purposes where the term was being referred to in the context of whether extraterritorial jurisdiction could be established.

South Korea, before the WTO Appellate Body, referred to Article 8 in 2005:

> Korea explains that article 8, which is entitled 'Conduct directed or controlled by a State', provides that private conduct shall be attributed to a State only 'if the person or group of persons is in fact acting on the instructions of, or under the direction or control of, that State in carrying out the conduct.' Korea finds 'striking' the similarity of wording in the reference to 'carrying out' a conduct and submits that the requirement of conduct taking place in order to establish State responsibility is a matter of 'common sense'.[232]

[227] ibid.

[228] *Public Prosecutor v F*, First instance, Criminal procedure, LJN: BA9575, 09/750001-06, 25 June 2007, The Hague District Court; *H v Public Prosecutor*, Appeal Judgment, Case No 22-006131-05, Decision No LJN: AZ7143, 29 January 2007, The Hague Court of Appeal.

[229] *Catan and Others v Moldova and Russia*, App Nos 43370/04, 8252/05 and 18454/06 (ECtHR, Judgment, 19 October 2012) para 115.

[230] *Catan and Others v Moldova and Russia*, App Nos 43370/04, 8252/05 and 18454/06 (ECtHR, Decision, 15 June 2010) para 87.

[231] *Mozer v Moldova and Russia*, App No 11138/10 (ECtHR, Judgment, 23 February 2016) para 102.

[232] WTO Appellate Body Report, *United States – Countervailing Duty Investigation on Dynamic Random Access Memory Semiconductors (DRAMS) from Korea*, WT/DS296/AB/R, 27 June 2005, para 69.

Argentina relied on Article 8 in its arguments before an ICSID tribunal,[233] as did Latvia[234] and Croatia,[235] as well as India in an UNCITRAL arbitration.[236] In a different arbitration, Argentina agreed that a question concerning attribution was 'subject to the principles contained in' Article 8, and 'that the appropriate test is "effective control"'.[237] Turkey has also submitted that one of the means for attributing non-state actor conduct to a state is based on 'effective control'.[238] The Czech Republic has argued that Article 8 'sets a demanding threshold', yet, similar to Russia before the ECtHR, conflated complete dependence and effective control, arguing that satisfying both tests is required to attribute conduct of a non-state actor to a state.[239] Zimbabwe argued in an ICSID case that conduct of a non-state actor was not attributable to it because there was 'nothing to show' that these actors 'were acting as instruments of the State in complete dependence on the State, or that they were acting on the instructions or under the direction or control of the State'.[240]

In its Request for Bifurcation, Canada in the *Mesa Power Group* case argued that it did 'not dispute that in certain instances the OPA [a non-state actor] exercises governmental authority or acts directly upon the instructions of Ontario, such that its actions are attributable to Canada'.[241] In its Counter-Memorial, Canada infers that it views Article 8 as customary international law,[242] and refers to the provision an additional two times,[243] in addition to citing it as an authority a further three times in its Post-Hearing Submission.[244] In the *MNSS* case, Montenegro argued that it was

> not responsible for Prva Banka's conduct; a private company's acts may be attributed to the State only if the State uses it as a vehicle to commit acts in breach of international law. The Central Bank never exercised control of Prva Bank that would justify the attribution of the Prva Banka's acts to the Respondent.[245]

[233] *Teinver SA, Transportes de Cercanías SA and Autobuses Urbanos del Sur SA v The Argentine Republic* (ICSID Case No ARB/09/1), Decision on Jurisdiction (21 December 2012) paras 264 and 275 and the same paragraphs in the Award of 21 July 2017.

[234] *UAB E energija (Lithuania) v Republic of Latvia* (ICSID Case No ARB/12/33), Award (22 December 2017) paras 815.

[235] *Georg Gavrilović and Gavrilović d.o.o. v Republic of Croatia* (ICSID Case No ARB/12/39), Award (26 July 2018) para 771.

[236] *White Industries Australia Limited v The Republic of India*, UNCITRAL, Final Award, 30 November 2011, paras 8.1.1–8.1.21.

[237] *Teinver SA, Transportes de Cercanías SA and Autobuses Urbanos del Sur SA v The Argentine Republic* (ICSID Case No ARB/09/1), Award (21 July 2017) paras 721 and 722.

[238] *Tulip Real Estate and Development Netherlands BV v Republic of Turkey* (ICSID Case No ARB/11/28), Award (10 March 2014) para 304.

[239] *InterTrade Holding GmbH v The Czech Republic*, UNCITRAL, PCA Case No 2009-12, Final Award, 29 May 2012, para 162.

[240] *Bernhard von Pezold and Others v Republic of Zimbabwe* (ICSID Case No ARB/10/15), Award (28 July 2015) para 438.

[241] *Mesa Power Group, LLC v Canada*, UNCITRAL, PCA Case No 2012-17, Request for Bifurcation (3 December 2012) para 10.

[242] *Mesa Power Group, LLC v Canada*, UNCITRAL, PCA Case No 2012-17, Government of Canada Counter-Memorial and Reply on Jurisdiction (28 February 2014) para 293.

[243] ibid para 304.

[244] *Mesa Power Group, LLC v Canada*, UNCITRAL, PCA Case No 2012-17, Post-Hearing Submission (18 December 2014) paras 12 and 13.

[245] *MNSS BV and Recupero Credito Acciaio NV v Montenegro* (ICSID Case No ARB(AF)/12/8), Award (4 May 2016) para 262.

Poland used Article 8 in a case before the PCA.[246] In the *Saint-Gobain* case Venezuela submitted that:

> CVG Bauxilum did not act on the instructions, or under the direction or control, of Respondent within the meaning of Article 8 of the ILC Draft Articles; even though CVG Bauxilum is ultimately subject to the administrative oversight ('tutela') of MIBAM, this is not sufficient for establishing direct State control within the meaning of Article 8 of the ILC Draft Articles.[247]

Further:

> CVG Bauxilum's conduct cannot be attributed to [the] Respondent under Article 8 of the ILC Draft Articles because [the] Claimant cannot show a particular act that was internationally wrongful [was] the result of the State's 'instructions, directions or control'.[248]

In a separate matter, Venezuela contended that conduct of a company should not have been attributed to the state because it was not acting 'under the effective control of' Venezuela.[249] Pakistan has stated that one way in which non-state actor conduct can be attributed to a state is if the conduct in question was 'specifically and individually directed, instructed or controlled by the State'.[250] Egypt has also applied Article 8 in attempts to disprove claims that a non-state actor's conduct was attributable to it on two separate occasions,[251] where in the more recent instance the state saw the provision as 'being declaratory of customary international law'.[252]

These findings reflect the instances of state practice concerning Article 8 since 2001. There appear to be no other examples at this time. Aside from those cited above, there are further examples of courts and tribunals referring to Article 8 and/or effective control applied in the context of attribution of conduct.[253] In these instances it appears as though it was the dispute-settlement body ruling on the case that refers to the test and not the states party to the respective disputes. The instances of state practice found also do not extend beyond the arena of litigation. There appears to be no evident state practice concerning Article 8 beyond the proceedings of courts and tribunals. It is clear that twenty-three states have made reference to Article 8 or the term effective control applied in the context of attribution of conduct.[254] There

[246] *Mr Kristian Almås and Mr Geir Almås v The Republic of Poland*, UNCITRAL, PCA Case No 2015-13, Award (27 June 2016) paras 102 and 103.

[247] *Saint-Gobain Performance Plastics Europe v Bolivarian Republic of Venezuela* (ICSID Case No ARB/12/13), Decision on Liability and the Principles of Quantum (30 December 2016) para. 365.

[248] ibid para 522.

[249] *Koch Minerals Sàrl and Koch Nitrogen International Sàrl v Bolivarian Republic of Venezuela* (ICSID Case No ARB/11/19), Award (30 October 2017) para 7.15.

[250] *Karkey Karadeniz Elektrik Uretim AS v Islamic Republic of Pakistan* (ICSID Case No ARB/13/1), Award (22 August 2017) para 354; see also para 355.

[251] *Ampal-American Israel Corporation and others v Arab Republic of Egypt* (ICSID Case No ARB/12/11), Decision on Liability and Heads of Loss (21 February 2017) para 124; *Unión Fenosa Gas, SA v Arab Republic of Egypt* (ICSID Case No ARB/14/4), Award (31 August 2018) para 9.45.

[252] ibid para 9.49.

[253] See UNGA, 74th Session, Compilation of decisions of international courts, tribunals and other bodies, A/74/83 (23 April 2019) 19–22; UNGA, 71st Session, A/71/80 (21 April 2016) 19–21; UNGA, 68th session, A/68/72 (30 April 2013) 18–20; UNGA, 62nd Session, A/62/63 (9 March 2007) 20–22; UNGA, 62nd Session, A/62/62 (1 February 2007) 40.

[254] See other uses of the term 'effective control': Belgian Letter to UNSC, UN Doc S/2016/523 (7 June 2016); German Letter to UNSC, UN Doc. S/2015/946 (10 December 2015).

is state practice regarding Article 8. Whether what does exist is sufficient to fulfil the customary international law threshold is at the very least questionable. The conventional position is that custom finds its source in the widespread and consistent practice of states.[255] Although this conventional position could also be inaccurate today, it is said that international custom cannot be established if state practice is sparse and/or contradictory,[256] which appears to be the case with the Article 8/effective control test.

3.2. Opinio Juris

The final consideration is the opinio juris requirement, which indicates *why* Article 8 has been referred to by states. From the state practice found, there are mixed indications as to whether the states referring to Article 8 did so because they saw themselves as legally bound by this test. One state (Egypt) clearly views the provision as declaratory of custom, whereas another (Canada) infers it. An argument could be made that the mere reference to Article 8 by the parties in the disputes examined above means that an inference can be drawn to suggest that such use equates to those states feeling legally required to abide by the content of the provision. However, even if such an approach were stretched to its limits, the language used by these states that could be suggestive of them viewing Article 8 as a binding rule is scant – save those of Canada (in the *Mesa Power Group* case) and Egypt (in the *Unión Fenosa Gas* case). The ARSIWA is not a treaty. If it were, this would aid the search for opinio juris suggestive of Article 8 being positive law. In this respect, not being a treaty is the downfall of the ARSIWA. Yet the fact that it is not a treaty was, and perhaps still is, because of insufficient consensus amongst states regarding the content within the provisions, which points back to the practice of states not being consistent.

It is also worth noting that the UNGA resolution that included the final version of the ARSIWA was adopted without a vote.[257] There may be those who argue that Article 8 forms part of international custom because it was cited by the UNGA, thereby reflecting the opinio juris of all UN Member States and their tacit consent through acceptance by acquiescence of all the provisions in the ARSIWA. However, this would be inaccurate for three reasons. First, to say that adoption by the UNGA of all the provisions within the ARSIWA reflects their customary status would render the ILC's mandate of contributing to the progressive development of international law moot. Accepting that UNGA Resolution 56/83 renders all of the ARSIWA as customary means that there is no provision within this instrument that embodies 'progressive development', as all the provisions would be codifying custom. Second, if taking this first position to its logical conclusion is a step too far, in that the adoption of the ARSIWA by the UNGA does not necessarily mean that certain of its provisions cannot be progressive development, then it would be difficult to tell from this UNGA

[255] Statute of the ICJ, Art 38(1)(b); Pellet (n 49) 731.
[256] *Delimitation of the Maritime Boundary in the Gulf of Maine Area* (Canada/United States of America), Judgment, 12 October 1984, ICJ Rep [1984] 246, para 81.
[257] UNGA Res 56/83, UN Doc A/RES/56/83 (12 December 2001).

resolution alone what provision belonged to either one of the two categorizations of progressive development or codification. Third, the language of the resolution states that the UNGA 'takes note of' the ARSIWA,[258] which is not a case for adopting its content as such.

These findings raise fundamental questions about international law-making. The role of the ILC and the ICJ appears to be significant in determining what is perceived as international custom, at least in the area of state responsibility as it applies to non-state actors. An argument could be made that Article 8 reflects custom if no states have expressly objected to it. But why would they? Diplomacy thrives off dubiety. The current formulation of this provision benefits states that use non-state actors to act in fact on their behalf without risking any conduct that is contrary to international rules being attributed to them. Even if Article 8 is custom due to state silence, what does this say about *who* creates international law? Is it really states? If certain people and/or institutions that have the 'right' brand say a rule has customary status and others (including maybe states) jump on the bandwagon, then it is not states creating the law. States would merely be accrediting the arguments or assertions of others by approving of what the law is said to be. Their stamp of approval makes law. Their involvement in the process need not be extensive. Encroachment of the ILC and ICJ into the realm of international law-making that is, according to some, reserved to states, opens a Pandora's box. Whose words are the authority on a subject? And what reach is accorded to the worth of such authorities? Is an academic more influential than a state diplomat in creating custom? Do states rubber-stamp the work of the 'right' people because they assume their work to be an accurate representation of the positive law on a subject? Is state practice and opinio juris really a 'primary' source of international law that takes precedence over the opinions of institutions such as the ILC and the ICJ? With respect to the law on attribution governing factual ties between states and non-state actors, it does not appear to be.

4. CONCLUSION

Whether Article 8 has become a customary rule since adoption is at the very least dubious. That is if the understanding is being adhered to that international law is created by states. There is state practice and some indications that states have referred to the provision out of a sense of legal obligation. The claims of Article 8 being part of international custom from courts, tribunals and commentators are therefore somewhat understandable, even though they are strained, given the available evidence. It could be argued that lack of mention of Article 8 by states is somehow negative custom, in that their acquiescence implicitly proves acceptance and adherence to the provision. But how can the rigour and robustness of such an argument be measured if it is based on something that does not exist? The ICJ has emphasised that a concept cannot become customary if its scope of application proves to be uncertain,[259] which

[258] ibid.

[259] *North Sea Continental Shelf* (Germany/Denmark; Germany/Netherlands), Judgment, 20 February 1969, ICJ Rep [1969] 3, para 72.

is yet another reason why Article 8/effective control is likely not customary, recalling: '[T]he very considerable, still unresolved controversies as to the exact meaning and scope of this notion, must raise further doubts as to the potentially norm-creating character of the rule.'[260]

Even if Article 8 is customary international law today, this does not negate there being apparently no evidence in state practice of the effective control test that formed the basis for changing Draft Article 8 in 1998 to the provision we have today. The issuance of instructions may now be considered necessary for attributing non-state actor conduct to states, but this criterion appeared not to be part of positive law at the time when it was incorporated into the drafting of the ARSIWA. With respect to the mandate of the ILC, Article 8 must have therefore been 'progressive development'. Should it be seen as a progressive development of international law, in particular considering the practice that formed the basis for the original provision? The ARSIWA as a whole may well be a mix of codification and progressive development, making it 'difficult to say which article partakes more of one or the other'.[261] It is clear that Article 8 was not codification. Yet automatically saying that it must consequently be progressive development is an all too easy route for those wishing to maintain this mainstream approach to attribution and wanting to escape from acknowledging its full history and incoherent application in practice.

The debates surrounding Article 8 have contributed to ambiguity, inconsistency and uncertainty about its requirements. Yet the circumstances in which it is intended to apply can occur with great frequency, especially because of our globalised world where new and ever-changing types of non-state actors partake in state policy. A significant aspect of the provision is that at present it appears only to cover express factual ties between states and non-state actors, in that a non-state actor can only be regarded as acting for a state if the state was instructing or directing it, which are forms of express authority being exercised. The problem with this approach is that there are numerous other forms of *implied* relationships that do not turn on state instructions, where non-state actors may still be acting in fact on the behalf of states. Article 8 fails to address clear instances of implied state authority, in which there could be evidence establishing that a non-state actor had acted in fact on behalf of a state. An example of an implied nexus between a state and a non-state actor would be one based on dependence, ownership or employment. Yet the former test only triggers attribution if a non-state actor is deemed to be 'completely' dependent on a state – whatever that means. What about non-state actors that are dependent on states, yet not completely, but may still be acting on their behalf without being subject to any precise power and authority? The difficulty in answering this question is why states can, and do, preserve and chase after their own interests via conduct that is sometimes contrary to international rules, through an actor with which there is no official link. Another point to consider is that in dealing with non-state actors only through the medium of them being established as de facto state organs suggests

[260] ibid.

[261] DD Caron, 'The ILC Articles on State Responsibility: The Paradoxical Relationship between Form and Authority' (2002) 96 *American Journal of International Law* 857, 873.

that such non-state actors are part of the state structure. There needs to be a more comprehensive approach to attribution where a non-state actor does not need to be transformed into being viewed as a state organ or be 'effectively controlled' by a state in order to attach its conduct to that state. Exploring rules beyond Article 8 and complete dependence is thus part of providing a more robust attribution framework to help address situations where non-state actors act in fact on behalf of states.[262]

The original test within Draft Article 8 could serve as a part of this purpose, in particular because other attribution tests appear to be little more than indicators of this overarching test that can manifest itself in multiple ways. Ago took the position that 'private natural or legal persons – while definitely remaining such – are entrusted by the public authorities with the provision of a service or the performance of a specific task'.[263] He was correct to view non-state actors as separate from the state, but realised that in such a capacity they could still be in a position to act for the state without having to be incorporated into the wider state machinery as either an organ or an entity exercising governmental authority. This is why Article 8-type attribution is important, as it concerns the means intended to deal with factual relations between states and non-state actors, where the former utilises the latter. The Dutch courts have managed to alter how the effective control test can be read, which could be read into applications of Article 8 in the future. If the international law in this area is to progress in line with contemporary state activity, it is important that attribution is not applied over-precisely so as to discount questions of state responsibility in circumstances where a non-state actor may have in fact acted on behalf of a state.

If this chapter has shown anything, it is that there are different realities with respect to perceptions of what the law in this field is and what it is perceived to be depending on what weight is ascribed to a particular source commenting on matters of state responsibility. There appear to be deeply ingrained perceptions of the international law applicable to determining state responsibility for the conduct of non-state actors, especially with respect to attribution and what has come to be understood as state 'control' in this context. There are camps that can, and do, declare provisions of the ARSIWA to be customary international law despite scant state practice and opinio juris. Alternative camps may centre around the premise that state-empowered entities, such as the ILC and ICJ, are actually responsible for creating the 'international' 'law' in this field, where proponents of these institutions will point to the influence that they bring to bear on questions relating to the existence of international rules. Then there may be camps acknowledging that the law in this field is actually created through a variety of actors that are considered legitimate in the eyes of whoever happens to be making such judgments in a particular instance. Whatever the camp, which may well extend beyond these characterisations, it is important that echo chambers do not develop or continue without challenge.

[262] Some possibilities are proposed in chapter 8.
[263] Third Report, Ago (1971) 263.

4

State Responsibility for Previous Conduct as a Non-state Actor

THE PREVIOUS TWO chapters have shown the extent to which the state responsibility framework through the lens of the ARSIWA can engage with questions concerning state responsibility for the conduct of non-state actors. What they show is that attribution performs a key function, yet is limited at present in three overarching ways. First, although the test of governmental authority is a matter that is regulated by the international law applicable to the field of state responsibility, domestic law is the key factor in determining whether non-state actor conduct can be attributed to a state. Non-state actors that fall into this category therefore differ very little from the perspective of attribution, if at all, from state organs, as both types of actor are provided mandates under domestic law to officially perform roles on the behalf of states. Second, where domestic law does not provide such a mandate to exercise governmental authority, non-state actors may have to act out of necessity in situations where states fail to discharge particular tasks that are considered public in character. This means determining any subsequent international responsibility of states in such settings is limited by circumstance. Third, the mainstream tests for determining whether a non-state actor has acted in fact on behalf of a state rest on whether states issue instructions to non-state actors regarding specific conduct, or whether non-state actors are perceived to be completely dependent on states when carrying out their conduct. Whether other tests can be applied in this regard remains open to question, in particular because the two mainstream tests appear not to be based on positive law, but instead are inventions of judicial discretion, afforded deference for different reasons. So what happens if non-state actors share other connections with states? In particular, what happens if a non-state actor undertakes conduct contrary to an international rule and then becomes part of the official state structure? Retroactivity can be a controversial and tricky concept when applied as part of a legal framework – yet the ILC navigated it in the context of attribution. This chapter examines settings in which non-state actors are successful in forming new governments within states, or when they create new states, and how such outcomes factor into considerations that aim to determine state responsibility for non-state actor conduct.

1. RETROACTIVITY AS A BASIS FOR ATTRIBUTION OF CONDUCT

Article 10 of the ARSIWA states:

> *Conduct of an insurrectional or other movement*
>
> 1. The conduct of an insurrectional movement which becomes the new Government of a State shall be considered an act of that State under international law.
> 2. The conduct of a movement, insurrectional or other, which succeeds in establishing a new State in part of the territory of a pre-existing State or in a territory under its administration shall be considered an act of the new State under international law.
> 3. This article is without prejudice to the attribution to a State of any conduct, however related to that of the movement concerned, which is to be considered an act of that State by virtue of articles 4 to 9.[1]

This provision governs non-state actor conduct that forms part of creating a new government, or a new state. There are thus two separate but related attribution tests under this provision. The first applies to settings where an insurrectional movement establishes a new government. The second applies to settings where insurrectional or other movements establish new states. Article 10 is silent on circumstances affecting international responsibility should a non-state actor fail to create a new government or state.[2] To an extent this makes sense because such matters would concern the international responsibility of non-state actors, save settings in which it were questioned whether a state could have attempted to prevent any wrongdoing that may have occurred at the hands of non-state actors trying to establish a new government or state. Non-state actors that fall within the scope of Article 10 include those that engage in rebellious activity against a state, in an attempt to affect change by replacing state organs with their own. The premise forming the foundations of this provision is that international law should account for public power not being beyond reproach from previous conduct that occurred during efforts towards becoming that public power.

1.1. Creation and Development of the Provision

Article 10 was shaped from a starting premise that states should bear some international responsibility for violent protests, rebellions and similar occurrences. Garcia-Amador identified this issue towards the beginning of his work whilst examining 'exonerating, extenuating or aggravating circumstances' that have bearing on questions of state responsibility.[3] His perspective on such matters centred on the failure of states to prevent or suppress violent movements.[4] He also acknowledged that 'mere occurrence' of an insurgency was not enough to establish state responsibility,

[1] ARSIWA, Art 10.
[2] ibid Commentary, para 16.
[3] Report, Garcia-Amador (1956) 208.
[4] ibid and 228–29; See also Second Report, Garcia-Amador (1957) 121, Draft Article 12; Sixth Report, Garcia-Amador (1961) 48 and 53, Draft Article 16.

but that this could change depending on whether the 'insurgent or revolutionary forces ... succeed in taking over authority and become the Government of the State'.[5] The matter of 'successful' insurgencies thus began to gain a foothold in the work of the ILC.[6] Ago brought this perspective forward, whilst clarifying that groups that could be categorised as insurrectional movements should be viewed as separate from the state for attribution purposes, thereby separating the state from those opposed to its current form and/or way of governance.[7] Although the question of whether insurrectional movements themselves could commit internationally wrongful acts was considered,[8] this line of thinking was deemed to fall outside the scope of the ARSIWA.[9]

The ILC thus focused on how such movements could be linked to states for attribution purposes depending on the outcomes in situations such as internal disturbances and conflicts. These outcomes can be broken down into three main categories:

- A previous government being replaced, in full or in part, by members of an insurgency.
- A change to the pre-existing territorial power and authority of a state over a particular geographical area, in that it would be ceded without necessarily creating a new state.
- The creation of a completely new state.

Ago dealt with these matters by focusing on their common feature as identified by Garcia-Amador: movements taking over the governance of a state.[10] Determining the international responsibility of a state on the basis of attribution in such settings thus hinges on the continuity between the non-state actor movement and the new government or state. The development of this idea was rooted in practice.[11]

The ILC formally adopted this 'retroactive' approach to attribution in 1973.[12] Reference to 'retroactive' is a reminder that the conduct being attributed to the state is that which occurred when members of the changed or new state's organisational structure existed as a separate non-state actor. This provision remained largely unchanged until it was split in two, dealing with attribution and the creation of a

[5] Report, Garcia-Amador (1956) 208.

[6] Second Report, Garcia-Amador (1957) 128.

[7] Third Report, Ago (1971) 205.

[8] Fourth Report, Ago (1972) 129; ILC Report, Twenty-Fifth Session, 7 May–13 July 1973, UNGA, Twenty-Eighth Session, Supp 10 (A/9010/Rev.1), YBILC (1973) vol II, 168. In this context, the predominant consideration was, and still is, whether such a group boasts international legal personality enabling it to be the legal author of a breach.

[9] Fourth Report, Ago (1972) 130.

[10] ibid 131.

[11] ibid 132–51; see also the comments of the Tribunal in *Short v Iran*, Iran–US CTR, Award No 312-11135-3 (14 July 1987) Reports, vol 16 (1987-III) 83, para 28 and 84, para 33; the Tribunal in *Rankin v Iran* also viewed attribution to a state for the conduct of an insurrectional or similar movement becoming a new government as 'an accepted principle of international law' (*Rankin v Iran*, Iran–US CTR, Award No 326-10913-2 (3 November 1987) Reports, vol 17 (1987-IV) 143–44, para 25 and 147, para 30; see also the further practice discussed in G Cahin, 'Attribution of Conduct to the State: Insurrectional Movements' in J Crawford, A Pellet and S Olleson (eds), *The Law of International Responsibility* (Oxford, Oxford University Press, 2010), 247, 248–52.

[12] ILC Report, Twenty-Fifth Session (1973) 171 and 189.

new government, and the creation of a new state, separately.[13] From here Crawford undertook his work.[14] A point that he picked out for scrutiny was the lack of a definition for 'insurrectional movement',[15] to which he made some observations.[16] The first was that international legal personhood should not affect attribution, as 'insurgency movements' may or may not have such a status depending on the circumstances.[17] The second was that from the perspective of attribution, the distinction between 'dissident' groups and 'national liberation movements' was not necessary, even though affirmation of one instead of the other could change applicable primary rules.[18] Attribution considerations were thus considered blind to the type of group that opposes the state and whether it had some measure of international legal personality. Crawford proposed the merging of the two separate draft articles into one, which addressed insurrectional movements that were successful in creating a new government or a new state.[19] This proposal was adopted by the ILC, reflecting the form in which Article 10 stands today.[20]

2. THE SCOPE OF RETROACTIVE ATTRIBUTION

With respect to the applicable scope of the provision, the Netherlands interpreted Article 10 to mean that:

> This article, taken in conjunction with article 7 [now Article 9], leads to the conclusion that every internationally wrongful act of an insurrectional movement which does not succeed in becoming the new government will immediately be directly attributed in full to the State.[21]

This reading is contrary to that developed in the preparatory history, which indicates that in order to attribute to a state the conduct of a non-state actor that aimed to change that state by incorporating its own organs into the state, or attempting to

[13] ILC Report, Twenty-Seventh Session, 5 May–25 July 1975, UNGA, Thirtieth Session, Supp 10 (A/10010/Rev.1), YBILC (1975) vol II, 60.

[14] It should be noted that in 1988 Germany objected to the construction of the draft articles relating to insurrectional movements, making a general criticism in that they raised 'many problems relating to the legality of insurrectional movements. In its present formulation it is not acceptable and is not in line with present international law' (Comments and observations of Governments on part one of the draft articles on State responsibility for internationally wrongful acts, A/CN.4/414, YBILC (1988) vol II(1), 3). A similar point was also made by Austria in 1998 (State Responsibility, 50th Session of the ILC (1998), Agenda Item 2, Comments and observations received by Governments, A/CN.4/488 and Add 1–3, 109).

[15] States continue to have reservations about the term. See, for example, the remarks of Kuwait in Responsibility of States for internationally wrongful acts, Comments and information received from Governments, UN Doc. A/62/63 (9 March 2007) 2.

[16] The former Czechoslovakia raised this point: Comments of Governments on part one of the draft articles on State responsibility for internationally wrongful acts, A/CN.4/342 and Add.1-4, YBILC (1981) vol II(1) 73.

[17] First Report, Crawford (1998) 52.

[18] ibid 53.

[19] ibid 54.

[20] ILC Report, Fifty-Second Session, 1 May–9 June 2000 and 10 July–18 August 2000, UNGA, Fifty-Fifth Session, Supp 10 (A/55/10), YBILC (2000) vol II(2) 66.

[21] State Responsibility, Fifty-Third Session of the ILC (2001), Comments and Observations received from Governments, A/CN.4/515 and Add 1–3, 50.

create a new state, the non-state actor in question must be successful in doing so, implying that should the non-state actor fail in this regard, its conduct cannot be attributed to the state. Is this how the provision applies? As already seen with respect to other provisions, the ILC standpoint on matters of attribution can be different to that of some states. Yet it may well be that the position of the Netherlands is an outlier relative to the views of other states, indicating to an extent why the ILC rested the attribution threshold of Article 10 on the success of a particular non-state actor creating a new government or state. This factor of a new government or state coming into formation certainly appears to be the decisive factor for attribution purposes. For example, the UK reiterated that: 'It is desirable that a new Government should not be able to escape international responsibility for the acts that brought it to power.'[22] However, Sudan has stated the idea behind Article 10 'should be reconsidered', and its views point towards an understanding that a state should not bear 'any responsibility for the conduct of insurrectional movements, whatever they may be, on its territory'.[23]

In theory, attribution under Article 10 should flow relatively naturally, as conduct of persons of an insurrectional or similar movement are attributable to the new government or state by default. As Crawford has pointed out: 'It is as if the state represented by the successful insurgents is precluded from denying attribution to it of their conduct in the course of the insurgency.'[24] And although attribution may not occur should such a movement not create a new government or state, this does not mean that other avenues that can assess state or non-state actor responsibility under international law are prevented from being explored. For example, the responsibility of individual members of an insurrectional movement can be determined through the application of international criminal law, and the responsibility of the state can still be determined through the application of due diligence or complicity assessments.[25] Nevertheless, these are separate matters from those concerning attribution of conduct.

Although Article 10 has been criticised for an apparent lack of pragmatism,[26] and the situations in which it could apply may be seen as exceptional at present, especially in light of the limited practice that has mentioned the provision since its adoption,[27] it could become more relevant in the future should states not address

[22] State Responsibility, Fiftieth Session of the ILC (1998), Agenda Item 2, Comments and observations received by Governments, A/CN.4/488 and Add 1–3, 131.

[23] Responsibility of States for internationally wrongful acts, Comments and information received from Governments, UN Doc. A/74/156 (12 July 2019) 6.

[24] J Crawford, *State Responsibility: The General Part* (Cambridge, Cambridge University Press, 2013) 171.

[25] *Ampal-American Israel Corporation and others v Egypt*, (ICSID Case No ARB/12/11, Decision on Liability and Heads of Loss (21 February 2017); *Asian Agricultural Products Ltd v Sri Lanka*, (ICSID Case No ARB/87/3), Award (27 June 1990); see also K Greenman, 'The Secret History of Successful Rebellions in the Law of State Responsibility' 6(9) *ESIL Reflection* (25 September 2017) www.esil-sedi.eu/sites/default/files/ESIL%20Reflection%20Greenman.pdf.

[26] J D'Aspremont, 'Rebellion and State Responsibility: Wrongdoing by Democratically Elected Insurgents' (2009) 58 *ICLQ* 427.

[27] *Application of the Convention on the Prevention and Punishment of the Crime of Genocide* (*Croatia v Serbia*), Judgment, 3 February 2015, ICJ Rep [2015] 3; *R v TRA* [2018] EWCA Crim 2843, paras 67 and 68; *R v Reeves Taylor* [2019] UKSC 51, paras 54 and 55. For commentary on the latter case, see H Woolaver, 'R v Reeves Taylor (Appellant). [2019] UKSC 51' (2020) 114 *American Journal of International Law* 749.

public dissatisfaction in how they are governed, in particular with respect to who that governance actually benefits.[28] Should there be more of the type of events envisaged by the ILC when creating Article 10, its applicable scope will likely become more practically relevant. Due to the near absence of practice, assessing this scope is currently tricky. Nonetheless, it is still possible to see how attribution factors into the creation of new governments and new states when examining questions of international responsibility.

2.1. The Creation of New Governments

The first test under Article 10 is that if an insurrectional movement successfully creates a new government, then its conduct can be attributed to the state.[29] Attribution here is similar to that under Article 4, because satisfying the attribution threshold of Article 10 depends on the conduct of state organs – albeit conduct from a point in time where the now new government organ held a different status as a type of non-state actor. In other words, the non-state actor in question belonged to the private sphere of a society during a setting such as a rebellion, and a shift occurred placing it in the public sphere afterwards. In so far as this transformation is concerned, attribution assessments under Article 10 consider similar factors to those under Article 9, in that both provisions address conduct of non-state actors that become state officials for a period of time.

In order to attribute conduct of a non-state actor to a state under Article 10(1), the precondition is that the insurrectional movement must replace the government it once opposed. So long as an insurrectional movement that once fought a state creates a new government, its conduct will be attributable to that state. The caveat to consider here is that 'becoming the new government' does not mean that a total change of government needs to occur in order to satisfy the attribution threshold of the provision. What is the key focal point is that although the state remains the same, it is changed in terms of who governs it.[30] The retroactive element in such instances bears importance in being part of efforts aimed at holding to account actors that undertook conduct contrary to international rules during a conflict or period of instability and end up forming part of a new government.[31] Yet the form of accountability that is pursued need not be based on international law through the rubric of international responsibility.

The ILC was aware of reflecting on forms of accountability that extend beyond the application of particular sets of legal rules, and that state responsibility is but one consideration to balance against others in the context of insurrectional or other movements forming new governments.[32] It is emphasised in the commentary

[28] N O'Connor, 'Three Connections between Rising Economic Inequality and the Rise of Populism' (2017) 28 *Irish Studies in International Affairs* 29.

[29] ARSIWA, Art 10, para 1.

[30] ARSIWA, Art 10, Commentary, para 5.

[31] ibid.

[32] ibid para 7.

to Article 10 that the provision 'should not be pressed too far',[33] reflecting what may be construed as good policy and/or best practices when deciding on whether conduct that can be attributed to a state and was contrary to an international rule should always result in establishing international responsibility. The context of this stance refers to the reconciliation processes that can occur upon the conclusion of periods of violence, in particular where agreements between parties to a conflict have been reached. The rationale applied by the ILC in such settings is that states 'should not be made responsible for the conduct of a violent opposition movement merely because, in the interests of an overall peace settlement, elements of the opposition are drawn into a reconstructed government'.[34] This means although sufficient continuity may exist in order to attribute to a state conduct of a non-state actor that was contrary to international rules, meaning international responsibility through the application of Article 10(1) could be established, such an outcome may not be pursued due to being less desirable than matters relating to postconflict resolution.

What the precise normative underpinning of this framing of the ILC towards the apparent trade-off between establishing state responsibility and what can be broadly understood as peacebuilding is unclear. However, it is possible to grasp the logic behind the ILC's thinking. It is important to consider the possible or likely effects of applying a particular rule in a particular context. With respect to the contexts in which Article 10(1) can apply, doing so could affect matters of wider interest to a society, such as political stability. Where persons of a non-state actor movement become incorporated into the same government, meaning a partial change in government occurs – not a complete change of government – attributing the conduct of those persons to the state for the purposes of establishing its international responsibility may make little sense. This is because the state in such situations would be internationally responsible for conduct it only had an attributable connection with because it agreed to the persons who undertook that conduct in the capacity as non-state actors acting against the state, becoming part of the official state structure in order to avoid future conflict. Reconciling differences between governments and those they attempt to govern through such a process is favourable in a setting where at a previous point in time an insurrectional movement was party to violence affecting society within the state, and perhaps further afield. Avoiding the deterioration of friendly relations is a priority for states in such situations. And even if not through the avenue of attribution under Article 10(1), state responsibility is not precluded from being established on other grounds, such as for due diligence failings. Although this consideration is rooted in a fuzzy idea of policy priorities and avoiding conflict, which is not always possible, it is orientated in pragmatism. The ILC was not explicit about this matter, but there is an insinuation that some things are more important than strict adherence to the applicable law in a particular context.

[33] ibid.
[34] ibid.

2.2. The Creation of New States

The second test under Article 10 is that if an insurrectional or other movement successfully creates a new state, then its conduct can be attributed to that state. Governments can, and do, change relatively frequently. In comparison, it is a rarer occurrence that a new state is created.[35] A new state can emerge by a non-state actor defeating the old state it opposed, by creating a new state in a territory formerly held by the state it partially defeated, or by agreement between the predecessor state and the non-state actor. In these instances the insurrectional movement displaces the previous state's structures with its own. The process can be viewed as one of 'secession or decolonization'.[36] The successful insurgents in this instance will therefore no longer be subject to the sovereignty of the predecessor state (if it still exists).[37] Instead, such non-state actors become sovereign by becoming independent and no longer subject to the public power and the administrative authority structures of the previous state.

Croatia v Serbia before the ICJ is one of apparently few cases that have referred to Article 10(2).[38] The claim in this case sought to establish state responsibility for genocide. The relevance of Article 10(2) arose with respect to Croatia's argument that conduct of non-state actors 'controlled by the movement that later proclaimed the FRY [Federal Republic of Yugoslavia] as a State ... must be regarded as acts of the FRY for the purposes of State responsibility'.[39] The ICJ addressed Article 10(2).[40] However, as the application of the provision was in the context of admissibility and jurisdictional questions, the Court did not provide an opinion on its potential scope.[41] The use of Article 10(2) did not result in any analysis because the provision 'is concerned only with the attribution of acts to a new State; it does not create obligations binding upon either the new State or the movement that succeeded in establishing that new State'.[42] Discussion on Article 10(2) thus went no further.

The absence of practice relating to Article 10(2) has led to a proposition by Patrick Dumberry of four theories on how it might apply.[43] The first is continuity of government.[44] This idea contends that the connection between the new state and the insurgents arises because during the hostilities the insurgents were organised and acted like a de facto government. Therefore, when the insurgency is successful, there already exists continuity owing to the formal structures of the movement being in place, thereby satisfying the attribution threshold under Article 10(2).[45] The second

[35] South Sudan and East Timor are two examples. See generally: J Vidmar, 'South Sudan and the International Legal Framework Governing the Emergence and Delimitation of New States' (2012) 47 *Texas International Law Journal* 541.

[36] ARSIWA, Art 10, Commentary, para 8.

[37] ibid.

[38] *Application of the Convention on the Prevention and Punishment of the Crime of Genocide* (*Croatia v Serbia*), Judgment, 3 February 2015, ICJ Rep [2015] 3; see also the practice analysed in P Dumberry, 'New State Responsibility for Internationally Wrongful Acts by an Insurrectional Movement' (2006) 17 *European Journal of International Law* 605, 612–17.

[39] *Croatia v Serbia*, Judgment, 3 February 2015, para 82.

[40] ibid paras 102–05.

[41] ibid para 105.

[42] ibid para 104.

[43] Dumberry (n 38) 609–12.

[44] ibid 609–10.

[45] ibid.

theory is that the rebel group has undertaken a 'legitimate struggle'.[46] Here the efforts of the insurgents against the predecessor state demonstrate the desire to change the authority in power and seek independence, meaning conduct during the struggle is attributable to the new state upon its creation.[47] The third is that of 'state resurrection'.[48] This theory specifies that the creation of a 'new' state was merely the resurrection of an old one, 'which only ceased to exist as an independent entity for a certain period of time'.[49] Under this theory continuity relates to the 'new' state bearing obligations it used to have before it did not exist. The fourth theory is that of 'organic' continuity.[50] The argument behind it is that insurgents can be an embryonic form of a state, which either dissolves or becomes a state proper.[51]

Although these suggestions point to four ways in which Article 10(2) could operate, they also highlight the matter of whether there has been the actual commission of internationally wrongful acts by any new state for its previous conduct when it existed as an insurrectional or similar movement. Attribution may well be relatively straightforward. The four theories certainly suggest so, especially when coupled with the commentary to Article 10.[52] However, whether the new state owes legal obligations and internationally wrongful acts have been committed is another matter.[53] If non-state actors are successful in creating a new state, then attributing their conduct to that state appears straightforward, meaning attempts to determine state responsibility by applying Article 10(2) are unlikely to be hindered by attribution considerations. However, the circumstances in which the provision could become relevant mean that settling questions regarding the international responsibility of any new state rests on statehood and recognition. Although separate from attribution, these considerations concern determining state responsibility for the conduct of non-state actors through the use of Article 10(2). Conduct of a non-state actor can be attributed to a new state for the purposes of determining its international responsibility, but what if that state is not considered as such in the first place? How can conduct be attributed to a state that does not exist?

3. STATEHOOD AND RECOGNITION

What does it take to create a state from the perspective of international law? The significance of this question in the context of international responsibility on the basis of Article 10(2) is that in order to attribute conduct to a state, a state needs to exist.[54]

[46] ibid 610–11.
[47] ibid.
[48] ibid 611.
[49] ibid; see also VD Degan, 'Création et disparition de l'Etat (à la lumière du démembrement de trois fédérations multiethniques en Europe)' (1999) 279 *Recueil des cours* 195, 293.
[50] Dumberry (n 38) 611–12.
[51] ibid.
[52] ARSIWA, Art 10, Commentary, paras 6, 8 and 13.
[53] See C Hillgruber, 'The Admission of New States to the International Community' (1998) 9 *European Journal of International Law* 491, 494–99.
[54] Related questions arise with respect to the recognition of governments. See F Paddeu and N Pavlopoulos, 'Between Legitimacy and Control: The Taliban's Pursuit of Governmental Status' *Just Security* (7 September 2021) www.justsecurity.org/78051/between-legitimacy-and-control-the-talibans-pursuit-of-governmental-status/.

If no state is formed from a setting in which a non-state actor movement attempted to create one, then international responsibility considerations will instead concern the non-state actors themselves and/or the state in which they operated. This section therefore briefly engages with the applicable international law on statehood and recognition to show what it would take for a non-state actor movement to create a new state, where it would then be possible to attribute the conduct of that movement to the new state for the purpose of determining its international responsibility.

3.1. Criteria for Statehood

Should non-state actors attempt to create a new state, the Montevideo Convention sets out what criteria may need to be satisfied so that a new state can be recognised as such.[55] This treaty states:

> The state as a person of international law should possess the following qualifications: (a) a permanent population; (b) a defined territory; (c) government; and (d) capacity to enter into relations with other states.[56]

Although further requirements have been advanced,[57] it has been questioned whether the legal criteria for statehood bear much relevance on whether an entity is recognised as a state.[58] Should a non-state actor movement attempt to create a new state, the international law on statehood offers some guidance on how such an outcome might be lawfully achieved. What the law in this area shows is that there are significant hurdles that must be overcome for a non-state actor movement to be considered as a new state. The international responsibility of such states for their previous conduct as non-state actors rests on such matters, more so than those relating to attribution as envisaged by the ILC under Article 10(2). This is because attribution is an automatic process under this provision, in that so long as a state exists as such, then conduct of the non-state actors that created the state can be attributed to that state. Attribution and international responsibility therefore depend on international recognition in such cases where a determination of the international responsibility of a new state is being sought.

3.2. Recognition of States that Were Once Non-state Actor Movements

Although recognition of competing governments within the same state appears not to alter the international obligations of that state, meaning it is still possible to determine its international responsibility for any potential internationally wrongful acts,[59]

[55] For further commentary, see M Riegl and B Dobos (eds), *Unrecognized States and Secession in the 21st Century* (Cham, Springer, 2017).

[56] Montevideo Convention on the Rights and Duties of States (signed 26 December 1933, entered into force 26 December 1934) 165 LNTS 19, Art 1.

[57] See D Akande, 'The Importance of Legal Criteria for Statehood: A Response to Jure Vidmar' *EJIL: Talk!* (7 August 2013) www.ejiltalk.org/the-importance-of-legal-criteria-for-statehood-a-response-to-jure-vidmar/.

[58] J Vidmar, *Democratic Statehood in International Law: The Emergence of New States in Post-Cold War Practice* (Oxford, Hart, 2013) 241.

[59] *R v Reeves Taylor* [2019] UKSC 51, paras 56–59; *Kadic v Karadic*, US Court of Appeals, Second Circuit [1995] 70 F3d 232, 245.

a state needs to exist in order to assess questions of state responsibility. And whether a state exists rests to a considerable extent on it being recognised as such by other states and intergovernmental organisations. The declaratory and constitutive theories of international recognition show what would likely need to occur in order for a non-state actor movement to attain statehood.[60] It is also worth noting, considering Article 10(2) states the possibility of establishing a new state 'in part of the territory of a pre-existing state',[61] that if secession forms part of a non-state actor movement's attempt to create a new state, unilaterally doing so presents some questions.

There currently appears to be no right to unilateral secession under international law.[62] There is also no general prohibition against it, although secession appears to be prohibited if it is carried out through conduct contrary to other rules of international law that are considered peremptory.[63] This is significant in cases of insurrectional movements attempting to create a new state through secession, because depending on the means they adopt in doing so, they could undertake conduct that is contrary to one of these rules. Should this occur, secession would not be in compliance with international law. However, this does not necessarily mean recognition would not occur, even if international law implies that it should not occur.

If a right to secession does exist under international law, it appears to be coupled with the right to (external) self-determination, in which case what is understood as remedial secession could be enabled by, for example, a state oppressing the non-state actor movement that is attempting to create a new state.[64] Unilaterally seceding from a state is not, however, unlawful under international law, even in the absence of a right to do so.[65] Any future attempts of non-state actor movements attempting to secede from a state would thus likely sit in a middle ground where secession is neither prohibited by international law nor created as a right under this body of law. Secession in any such case would also be political, meaning negotiations between the applicable non-state actor and state may need to occur to hash out differences, in particular with respect to the principle of territorial integrity.[66] This principle stipulates that

[60] J Crawford, *The Creation of States in International Law*, 2nd edn (Oxford, Oxford University Press, 2006) 17–28; see also H Kelsen, 'Recognition in International Law: Theoretical Observations' (1941) 35 *American Journal of International Law* 605.

[61] ARSIWA, Art 10.

[62] M Milanovic, 'Arguing the Kosovo Case' in M Milanovic and M Wood (eds), *The Law and Politics of the Kosovo Advisory Opinion* (Oxford, Oxford University Press, 2015) 21; G Anderson, 'Unilateral Non-colonial Secession in International Law and Declaratory General Assembly Resolutions: Textual Content and Legal Effects' (2020) 41 *Denver Journal of International Law & Policy* 345.

[63] *Accordance with International Law of the Unilateral Declaration of Independence in Respect of Kosovo*, Advisory Opinion, 22 July 2010, ICJ Rep [2010] 403; M Milanovic, 'A Footnote on Secession' *EJIL: Talk!* (26 October 2017) www.ejiltalk.org/a-footnote-on-secession/; M Weller, 'Secession and Self-determination in Western Europe: The Case of Catalonia' *EJIL: Talk!* (18 October 2017) www.ejiltalk.org/secession-and-self-determination-in-western-europe-the-case-of-catalonia/; LS Eastwood, Jr, 'Secession: State Practice and International Law after the Dissolution of the Soviet Union and Yugoslavia' (1993) 3 *Duke Journal of Comparative & International Law* 299, 344.

[64] Milanovic (ibid); See also J Vidmar, 'Remedial Secession in International Law: Theory and (Lack of) Practice' (2010) 6 *St Anthony's International Review* 37.

[65] *Kosovo*, Advisory Opinion [2010] para 81; [1998] 2 SCR 217, para 155; see also J Vidmar, 'Catalonia: The Way Forward Is Comparative Constitutional Rather than International Legal Argument' *EJIL: Talk!* (24 October 2017) www.ejiltalk.org/catalonia-the-way-forward-is-comparative-constitutional-rather-than-international-legal-argument/.

[66] J Vidmar, 'Territorial Integrity and the Law of Statehood' (2012) 44 *George Washington International Law Review* 101, 110–13; C Bell, 'International Law, the Independence Debate, and Political Settlement

states 'shall refrain from any action aimed at the partial or total disruption of the national unity and territorial integrity of any other State or country'.[67] According to the ICJ, the principle is a rule of customary international law.[68] It is unclear whether non-state actors are bound by it due to them not being states. This raises questions as to whether states' right to territorial integrity imposes a legal obligation on non-state actors, and thus whether this right of states exists vis-à-vis non-state actors, as the principle of territorial integrity, according to the ICJ, 'is confined to the sphere of relations between States'.[69] That said, the ICJ has also indicated that this same principle applies between a state and a 'non-self-governing territory'.[70]

In cases of a non-state actor movement attempting unilateral secession and declaring independence from the power and authority of a state, such a state would have a political counterclaim to territorial integrity, the politics of which could influence whether any new state was recognised as such by the international community. In these instances, the burden would be placed on the non-state actor to overcome such a counterclaim, for example, by convincing the international community that it is not an issue, which could be achieved by conducting and maintaining relations with states and intergovernmental organisations without any involvement from organs of the state from which secession occurred.[71] The applicable international law to secession is bound to the politics involved in these processes, which is particularly significant with respect to a challenging aspect of statehood – whether international recognition is granted.

3.2.1. Declaratory Theory

The declaratory theory stipulates that recognition is a political act, in that it is merely a formality that occurs upon the legal requirements of statehood being fulfilled.[72] Hersch Lauterpacht argued that:

> A State exists as a subject of international law – as a subject of international rights and duties – as soon as it 'exists' as a fact, that is, as soon as it fulfills the conditions of statehood as laid down in international law. Recognition merely declares the existence of that fact.[73]

If a non-state actor movement aiming to create a new state were to satisfy the requirements of statehood, then, according to Crawford, it would be 'unacceptable' for other

in the UK' in A McHarg et al (eds), *The Scottish Independence Referendum: Constitutional and Political Implications* (Oxford, Oxford University Press, 2016) 197, 208–10.

[67] Declaration on Principles of International Law Concerning Friendly Relations and Co-operation Among States in Accordance with the Charter of the United Nations, UNGA Res 2625 (XXV), UN Doc. A/RES/2625 (24 October 1970) 1214.

[68] *Kosovo*, Advisory Opinion [2010] para. 80.

[69] ibid.

[70] *Legal Consequences of the Separation of the Chagos Archipelago from Mauritius in 1965*, Advisory Opinion, 25 February 2019, ICJ Rep [2019] 95, para 160.

[71] Vidmar (n 66) 113.

[72] Crawford (n 60) 22–26; H Lauterpacht, 'Recognition of States in International Law' (1944) 53 *Yale Law Journal* 385, 423–33.

[73] Lauterpacht (ibid) 423.

states and the rest of the international community to deny recognition.[74] Yet, unacceptable as such an outcome may be, satisfying all the requirements of statehood does not necessarily mean recognition will occur, even if the crucial 'prerequisite' of independence shows that a new sovereign state in fact exists.[75]

3.2.2. Constitutive Theory

The constitutive theory stipulates that recognition is a legal act, which means a state exists exclusively via recognition by other states.[76] New states do not always emerge automatically upon fulfilling the legal criteria of statehood.[77] They emerge from political processes in which they are accepted by other states.[78] As Jure Vidmar has shown:

> [S]tates grant recognition even when the statehood criteria *are not* met and withhold it where they *are* met [which] indicates that state practice does not accept that statehood would depend on the Montevideo criteria. These criteria do not produce any direct legal effects. To some degree, they can only influence the international practice of acceptance or non-acceptance of claims for independence.[79]

A non-state actor movement aimed at creating a new state could therefore result in such a state being recognised by the international community. The question is *who* needs to recognise such an entity for it to exist as a state. This problem is inherently political. For example, Belize, North Macedonia and Liechtenstein exist as states, but at least for some time were not recognised as states by Guatemala, Greece and the Czech Republic, respectively.[80] The constitutive theory therefore presents statehood as relative. Hans Kelsen argued that a 'state exists legally only in its relations to other states. There is no such thing as absolute existence.'[81] The politics of recognition is thus a key factor, one that can be challenging, with states likely aligning their decision to recognise or not based on their own interests and values.[82]

It cannot be known what states and intergovernmental organisations would do regarding recognition if a non-state actor were to attempt to create a new state. It can be predicted with perhaps some accuracy with reference to the legal requirements of statehood and how a particular entity measures up against them, or whether states indicate in advance that they will grant recognition. However, there is no way to guarantee that states and/or intergovernmental organisations would not change their tune. The constitutive theory allows for the possibility of a non-state actor movement

[74] Crawford (n 60) 27.
[75] ibid 89.
[76] ibid 19-22; Lauterpacht (n 72) 433–42.
[77] Vidmar (n 58) 63, 137, 238–41.
[78] ibid 62 and 237.
[79] ibid 240.
[80] See Crawford (n 60) 20–21.
[81] Kelsen (n 60) 609.
[82] E Tourme-Jouannet, 'The International Law of Recognition' (2013) 24 *European Journal of International Law* 667; M García-Salmones Rovira, 'The Politics of Interest in International Law' (2014) 25 *European Journal of International Law* 765; EA Posner, 'Do States Have a Moral Obligation to Obey International Law?' (2003) 55 *Stanford Law Review* 1901, 1919.

attempting to create a new state being recognised as such even if the legal criteria for statehood are not met. Although it is ultimately up to states what they choose to do with this power, the applicable international law sets what may be seen as acceptable and legitimate parameters for the political aspects of recognition to operate within. The role of international law as part of a non-state actor movement attempting to create a new state that is recognised as such may nevertheless be minimal. Yet the legality of a process aimed at attaining statehood could affect its perceived legitimacy and influence decisions on the granting of recognition. Equally, being recognised as a state could still occur even if achieved through means that are deemed to be illegitimate and/or unlawful,[83] however arguably unlikely.[84] Whether a non-state actor movement attempting to create a new state is actually recognised as a state thus depends on answers to questions that lie beyond the application of legal rules and analysis.

4. CONCLUSION

The irregularity of circumstances in which Article 10 could be applicable may cause its value to be questioned. However, its worth to the law of state responsibility as it applies to non-state actors does not lie in its potential frequency for application. The provision provides a basis for ensuring that an avenue exists in international law that can be used in attempts to establish a form of accountability should non-state actors undertake conduct contrary to international rules in the process of becoming a new government or state. In one way at least, whether a new government or state is formed does not prevent previous non-state actors from answering for past wrongs. That the ILC chose to focus on this matter at all speaks to the importance of having various means to help ensure that state responsibility for non-state actor conduct is not avoided. The theory and practice behind Article 10 show that the ARSIWA attribution framework would be poorer without such a provision. That said, although the theory behind Article 10 is suggestive of attribution being a relatively straightforward process under both tests, other considerations mean determining international responsibility is not so simple, or necessarily desirable depending on the circumstances. Political realities have considerable bearing on both tests under this provision. Should attribution be considered under paragraph 1 in the event of a new government being formed, it may be unhelpful to bother determining and establishing state responsibility because the new government has only partially changed, and did so in order to provide a means of settling a conflict between the non-state actor movement and the state it opposed. Attribution under the second paragraph can also flow smoothly, yet whether attribution should occur in the first place rests on a non-state actor movement successfully creating a new

[83] On the one hand, it has been argued that 'premature' recognition in international law may be unlawful (see Lauterpacht (n 72) 392, n 7). On the other hand, see footnote below.

[84] States do not always meet the legal criteria for statehood under international law and yet this does not prevent them from being internationally recognised as such (see Vidmar (n 58) 98).

state and it being recognised as such. Determining state responsibility for previous conduct of actors when they operated as non-state actors paradoxically depends on factors that are separate from international law and responsibility, in particular those concerning peacebuilding, political stability, statehood, and recognition. These considerations that lie beyond the application of what is perceived to be positive international law is a component that is also held in common with the final attribution provision of the ARSIWA.

5

Conduct of Non-state Actors that is Acknowledged and Adopted by States

ATTRIBUTION CAN BE a relatively straightforward process within international law. The previous chapter has highlighted as much. However, at the same time, it also becomes clear that considerations outwith the law of state responsibility are those that resolve questions regarding whether the international responsibility of a state can be determined, regardless of how simple attribution may appear in theory under a particular test. New governments can be created within states, and the conduct of non-state actors that helped create such governments can be attributed to the applicable states. Yet whether doing so is worthwhile becomes a matter of politics and strategy, in particular when a partial change in government occurs. Entirely new states can also be created. Similarly, the conduct of non-state actors that helped create such states can be attributed to them. Yet a state existing as such from the perspective of international law rests on it fulfilling the legal criteria for statehood and/or being recognised as a state. A state needs to exist in order to attribute conduct to it for the purposes of determining state responsibility. The two attribution tests under Article 10 are thus unlikely to be applied with any great frequency because of the irregularity of circumstances that could warrant their application. It is not every day that non-state actor movements rebel against states in attempts to create new governments or states. While this could change in the future, the trait of rarity in application is held in common with the final attribution provision of the ARSIWA: Article 11. Why is this the case? What is the attribution test under this provision? This chapter explores these questions to show that Article 11 is a particularly unique component of the state responsibility framework, one that instils an important value into the international law applicable to determining state responsibility for the conduct of non-state actors.

1. DEVELOPING ACKNOWLEDGEMENT AND ADOPTION AS AN ATTRIBUTION TEST

Article 11 was designed to apply to situations in which a non-state actor undertakes conduct contrary to an international rule, where such conduct is not necessarily attributable to a state at the time of commission, but can become attributable to a state in retrospect if it is established that the state acknowledged and adopted that conduct of the non-state actor as its own. The provision reads:

> Conduct which is not attributable to a State under the preceding articles shall nevertheless be considered an act of that State under international law if and to the extent that the State acknowledges and adopts the conduct in question as its own.[1]

There can be explicit instances of state acknowledgement and adoption, whereby a state expressly acknowledges and adopts the conduct of a non-state actor as its own. There can also be implicit instances, where attribution is determined by the responses of a state towards a situation involving the conduct of a non-state actor, without the state expressly acknowledging and adopting such conduct as its own. The previous attribution tests that have been addressed so far in the previous chapters can be satisfied regardless of how or whether a state responds to the conduct of a non-state actor after the fact. Conversely, whether the attribution threshold under Article 11 is satisfied rests on the reactions of states towards the conduct of non-state actors.

The idea behind Article 11 came into formation later in the development of the ARSIWA when compared with the other attribution provisions. Garcia-Amador made one reference to states adopting responsibility in his first report.[2] Ago did not examine the possibility of attributing non-state actor conduct to states based on their acknowledgement and adoption. He did consider the issue of state support of non-state actor activities, but as it related to state organs acting outside their competence.[3] There was thus no transcription of the test now covered in Article 11 when the Draft Articles of the ILC were adopted on first reading. A provision addressing state 'ratification' of non-state actor conduct was not proposed until 1998:

> A State might subsequently adopt or ratify conduct not otherwise attributable to it; if so, there is no reason why it should not be treated as responsible for the conduct. Adoption or ratification might be expressed or might be inferred from the conduct of the State in question. This additional possibility needs to be considered.[4]

From this point there was general agreement within the ILC that a provision was needed to address the possibility that a state could adopt the conduct of a non-state actor as its own.[5] The Drafting Committee thereby created Draft Article 15*bis*,[6] which became the provision finally adopted as Article 11. During the period from proposal to final provision, no state raised any objections to its inclusion or content.[7]

There were a number of cases that had concerned the issue of state acknowledgement and adoption of non-state actor conduct. In the *Lighthouses* case, Greece was

[1] ARSIWA, Art 11.

[2] Report, Garcia-Amador (1956) 190.

[3] Fourth Report, Ago (1972) 101.

[4] First Report, Crawford (1998) 54.

[5] ILC Report, Fiftieth Session, 20 April–12 June 1998 and 27 July–14 August 1998, UNGA, Fifty-Third Session, Supp 10 (A/53/10), YBILC (1998) vol II(2), 87.

[6] Draft Articles provisionally adopted by the Drafting Committee: Arts 1, 3, 4 (Part One, ch I), 5, 7, 8, 8 bis, 9, 10, 15, 15 bis and A (chap II), A/CN.4/L.569, YBILC (1998) vol I, 288.

[7] It appears only the Netherlands chose to provide comment on what became Art 11: State Responsibility, Fifty-Third Session of the ILC (2001), Comments and Observations received from Governments, A/CN.4/515 and Add 1–3, 50.

held responsible for endorsing a breach of a concession agreement.[8] In the *Adolf Eichmann* case, Israel was involved in the kidnapping, detention, trial and execution of the former Nazi SS lieutenant colonel.[9] Non-state actors, of whose plan to do so Israel was apparently unaware, allegedly kidnapped Eichmann.[10] Crawford has noted that evidence within a relevant UNSC resolution 'by its terms implies that Israel was at the very least aware of and consented to the abduction'.[11] Israel also accepted custody of Eichmann, and then proceeded to give him a trial that led to his execution by the state, which 'may be taken as adoption of the abduction'.[12] A clearer manifestation of the test now enshrined in Article 11 appeared in the *Tehran Hostages* case.[13] Here the ICJ considered Iran's response to the actors that overran the US embassy in Tehran during the revolution towards the end of the 1970s. A key feature of the case was that in the course of these events, the Court found that for a period of time Iranian authorities were absent and no attempt was made by state organs to rescue the hostages.[14] The US claim, in part, argued that the conduct of the non-state actors involved was attributable to Iran because the 'official attitude' of Iran approved and upheld their conduct.[15] The Court noted that Iran had endorsed and approved of the militant activities and helped perpetuate them by not preventing the hostage situation.[16] However, the Court ruled that Iran's responses to the events did not 'alter the initially independent and unofficial character of the militants' attack on the Embassy'.[17] The ICJ held Iran responsible for its failure to prevent the breaches of its applicable international obligations.[18] That said, the Court's view on Iran's lack of response was 'highly significant in another context' – that being whether Iran was responsible for the militant's conduct on the basis of attribution.[19] Crawford argued that although the attacks were independent from the state as a matter of fact, 'the legal consequences which flowed from that fact were altered by the approval and adoption such that the attacks could now be attributed *a posteriori* to the Iranian state'.[20]

The final commentary to Article 11 reflects the position taken in these cases.[21] This provision was a late addition to the ARSIWA, having been proposed around three years before they were finalised. Despite not having gone through the same process of drafting and scrutiny as other attribution provisions that were introduced at an earlier

[8] *Lighthouses Arbitration between France and Greece* (1956) Claims Nos 11 and 4, 23 ILR 81, 91–93.

[9] *A-G (Israel) v Eichmann* (1961) 36 IRL 18 (District Court) and *A-G (Israel) v Eichmann* (1962) 36 IRL 277 (Supreme Court).

[10] UNSC Res 138 (23 June 1960) UN Doc S/4349.

[11] J Crawford, *State Responsibility: The General Part* (Cambridge, Cambridge University Press, 2013) 183.

[12] ibid.

[13] *United States Diplomatic and Consular Staff in Tehran (United States of America v Iran)*, Judgment, 24 May 1980, ICJ Rep [1980] 3.

[14] ibid paras 62–68.

[15] Crawford (n 11) 184.

[16] *Tehran Hostages*, Judgment, 24 May 1980, para 74.

[17] ibid para 59.

[18] ibid paras 60 and 61.

[19] Crawford (n 11), 185; see also *Tehran Hostages*, Judgment, 24 May 1980, paras 69–75.

[20] Crawford (ibid).

[21] ARSIWA, Art 11, Commentary, paras 3–6.

point in time during the work of the ILC, Article 11 now forms part of the legal framework on attribution. How important a part becomes clearer from examining not so much the application of the provision in legal practice, but from recognising the roots that appear to have underpinned its creation. Nevertheless, there are insights to be gained from observing how Article 11 has applied so far in practice, especially with respect to determining its applicable scope and what is required in order to satisfy its attribution threshold. Before turning to the normative significance of the provision, it is helpful to grasp how it has been interpreted in practice.

2. APPLYING ARTICLE 11 IN PRACTICE

There are a few other cases that occurred before the ARSIWA was finalised that raise questions about attribution based on state acknowledgement and adoption of non-state actor conduct. In the *Priebke* case the Military Tribunal of Rome attributed conduct of partisans to Italy on the basis that the state encouraged their actions and officially recognised them at the end of the Second World War.[22] In the *JT* case The Hague District Court questioned how far a state could be held responsible for conduct of a resistance movement after liberation, which was organised with the consent of the state.[23] Here it was not concluded whether prior state consent implied subsequent acknowledgement and adoption of non-state actor conduct. In the *Tadić* case the ICTY pointed out that states can be considered internationally responsible for conduct of non-state actors if their acts are publicly endorsed or approved retroactively by the state.[24] Since the ARSIWA was finalised, there have been minimal applications of an attribution test based on the contents of Article 11. One case before the Seabed Disputes Chamber of ITLOS cited the provision as an example of an instance where the conduct of a non-state actor can be attributed to a state.[25] Similarly, three ICSID arbitrations refer to Article 11, with the Tribunal in the *Saint-Gobain* case noting:

> In contrast to cases of mere State support, endorsement or general acknowledgment of a factual situation created by private individuals, attribution under this rule requires that the State clearly and unequivocally '*identifies the conduct in question and makes it its own*'.[26]

The Tribunal in the *Mondev International* case also cites the provision without engaging with its content.[27] There were also two cases before the PCA that cite Article 11 without much analysis, save a note in the *Luigiterzo Bosca* case indicating that in

[22] *Priebke* case (1996) Military Tribunal of Rome, Italy, L'Indice penale, 959–1000, para 27.
[23] *JT v The Netherlands*, District Court of The Hague (13 April 1949) para 28.
[24] *Tadić*, paras 118 and 137.
[25] ITLOS, Seabed Disputes Chamber, Advisory Opinion (1 February 2011) para 182.
[26] *Saint-Gobain Performance Plastics Europe v Venezuela*, ICSID Case No ARB/12/13, Decision on Liability and the Principles of Quantum (30 December 2016) para 461 (emphasis original); see also *Unión Fenosa Gas, SA v Egypt*, ICSID Case No ARB/14/4, Award (31 August 2018), paras 9.120–9.121; *Bernhard von Pezold and others v Zimbabwe*, ICSID Case No ARB/10/15 (Award, 28 July 2015) paras 447–49.
[27] *Mondev International Ltd v United States of America*, Case No ARB(AF)/99/2), Award (11 October 2002) para 115, n 47.

situations where a state 'endorses' the conduct of a non-state actor, such conduct may be attributable to that state.[28] Legal practice in which there was more detailed treatment of Article 11 can be found in the case of *Makuchyan and Minasyan* before the ECtHR.[29] Here the Court began its assessment of the provision with a statement that its attribution threshold is 'very high' and 'very stringent'.[30] The reasoning provided for this stance was that the threshold 'is not limited to the mere "approval" and "endorsement" of the act in question, which, in the words of the ILC Commentary, "do not involve any assumption of responsibility"'.[31] The Court observed that the attribution test under Article 11 is cumulative and needs to be 'clear and unequivocal' that the state in question acknowledges *and* adopts the conduct of the non-state actor 'as its own'.[32]

While reiterating that case-law is 'scarce' and that the ARSIWA are 'still subject to debate amongst States', 'do not have the status of treaty law' and are 'not binding on States', the Court infers that it views Article 11 as an existing rule of customary international law, feeling the need to state that 'the Court's assessment in the present case must be limited to the existing rules of international law'.[33] The Court appeared to be unsure as to the status of Article 11 under international law, but in any case chose to apply the provision as though it were a legal rule. In doing so, it considered that the response of Azerbaijan (including the decision to pardon the person whose conduct was at issue, promote them during a public ceremony and award them years of salary in arrears) demonstrated the state's 'approval' and 'endorsement' of the conduct in question – a beheading.[34] The Court then went on to rule that is was 'unable to conclusively find that such "clear and unequivocal" "acknowledgement" and "adoption" indeed took place' for the purposes of satisfying the attribution threshold under Article 11.[35] Although it was considered 'beyond any doubt' that Azerbaijan in some sense approved of the beheading, in 'applying the very high threshold set by Article 11', the Court concluded:

> [I]t has not been convincingly demonstrated that the State of Azerbaijan 'clearly and unequivocally' 'acknowledged' and 'adopted' 'as its own' R.S.'s deplorable acts, thus assuming, as such, responsibility for his actual killing of G.M. and the preparations for the murder of the first applicant. The Court places emphasis on the fact that this assessment is undertaken on the basis of the very stringent standards set out by the existing rules of international law, as they stood at the material time and stand today, from which the Court sees no reason or possibility to depart in the present case.[36]

[28] *Luigiterzo Bosca v Lithuania*, UNCITRAL, PCA Case No 2011-05, Award (17 May 2013) para 128, n 114; *Clayton and Bilcon of Delaware Inc v Canada*, UNCITRAL, PCA Case No 2009-04, Award on Jurisdiction and Liability (17 March 2015) paras 321–24.

[29] *Makuchyan and Minasyan v Azerbaijan and Hungary*, App No 17247/13 (ECtHR, Judgment, 26 May 2020). For further commentary on the case, see M Milanovic and T Papic, 'Makuchyan and Minasyan v Azerbaijan and Hungary' (2021) 115 *American Journal of International Law* 294.

[30] *Makuchyan and Minasyan* (ibid) para 112.

[31] ibid.

[32] ibid.

[33] ibid para 114.

[34] ibid para 117.

[35] ibid para 118.

[36] ibid.

Aside from repeating that the ECtHR views the apparent attribution threshold of Article 11 set by the ILC as being 'very high' and 'very stringent', a view held in common with others,[37] the ruling provides an illustration of the 'line between an expression of state approval for a certain course of conduct and an expression of the state's will to adopt that conduct as its own'.[38] The importance of differentiating between these two stances for attribution purposes lies in the normative difficulty of justifying why expressions of approval and/or endorsement by a state of a particular act or omission of a non-state actor 'should result in the retrospective attribution' of that conduct to the state.[39] An entity, including a state, 'can approve of many things without necessarily assuming responsibility for doing those things'.[40]

In *Makuchyan and Minasyan* the ECtHR also referred to another case that used Article 11.[41] The *Nikolić* case before the ICTY applied the provision by analogy when considering an incident where 'unknown individuals [had] arrested the Accused in the territory of the FRY and brought him across the border with Bosnia and Herzegovina and into the custody of SFOR [a NATO-led stabilisation force]'.[42] Examining attribution was relevant to the proceedings because the conduct of the 'unknown individuals', if deemed attributable to SFOR, affected the Tribunal's jurisdiction.[43] The key issue was that the accused had been detained by unidentified actors whose conduct benefited SFOR and, consequently, the ICTY. The Defence argued:

> [W]hen SFOR personnel took custody of the accused, they had knowledge, actual or constructive, that the accused had been unlawfully apprehended and brought from Serbia against his free will, that his freedom of movement had been unlawfully restricted, that he had been unlawfully deprived of his liberty and that he had been, and remains, detained against his will.[44]

It was argued that SFOR made a choice to 'take advantage' of this setting by arresting and transferring the accused to the ICTY.[45] The Prosecution rebutted, arguing that SFOR was not involved in the unlawful acts of the unknown actors, but instead it was a 'fortuitous recipient' of their conduct: '[T]he mere subsequent *acceptance* by the Prosecution of custody of the Accused cannot in and of itself satisfy the required level of "collusion" or "official involvement" on the part of the Prosecution.'[46]

[37] C Ryngaert and K Istrefi, 'An Azeri Kills an Armenian Soldier at a NATO Training in Budapest: The ECtHR Decides a Rare Case of State Responsibility and Presidential Pardon' *Strasbourg Observers* (29 June 2020) https://strasbourgobservers.com/2020/06/29/an-azeri-kills-an-armenian-soldier-at-a-nato-training-in-budapest-the-ecthr-decides-a-rare-case-of-state-responsibility-and-presidential-pardon/.

[38] M Milanovic, 'Attribution, Jurisdiction, Discrimination, Decapitation: A Comment on Makuchyan and Minasyan v Azerbaijan and Hungary' *EJIL: Talk!* (10 July 2020) www.ejiltalk.org/attribution-jurisdiction-discrimination-decapitation-a-comment-on-makuchyan-and-minasyan-v-azerbaijan-and-hungary/.

[39] ibid.

[40] ibid.

[41] See *Makuchyan and Minasyan* (Judgment, 2020) para 37.

[42] *Prosecutor v Dragan Nikolić ("Sušica Camp")*, Decision on Defence Motion Challenging the Exercise of Jurisdiction by the Tribunal (Trial Chamber II), Case No IT-94-2-PT, 9 October 2002, para 57.

[43] ibid para 56.

[44] ibid para 58.

[45] ibid.

[46] ibid para 59 (emphasis in original).

The Tribunal saw it best to focus on 'the possible attribution of the acts of the unknown individuals to SFOR'.[47] Article 11 was deemed to be applicable:

> As a general matter, conduct will not be attributable to a State under article 11 where a State merely acknowledges the factual existence of conduct or expresses its verbal approval of it. In international controversies States often take positions which amount to 'approval' or 'endorsement' of conduct in some general sense but do not involve any assumption of responsibility. The language of 'adoption', on the other hand, carries with it the idea that the conduct is acknowledged by the State *as, in effect, its own conduct*.[48]

Taking into account this commentary it was held that SFOR and the Prosecution were the 'mere passive beneficiary' of the 'fortuitous (even irregular) rendition', which did not amount to 'adoption' and 'acknowledgement' of the unknown actors' conduct as their own.[49] The ICTY's interpretation of Article 11 highlights that in cases of implicit/inferred forms of state acknowledgement and adoption of non-state actor conduct, a state benefiting from a non-state actor's conduct is not sufficient to attribute that conduct to the state under this provision.

There is an additional layer to this understanding that can be grasped from examining the Commentary to Article 11, where it is pointed out that a state's endorsement of a non-state actor's conduct may be sufficient to satisfy the provision so long as the state in question is simultaneously *facilitating the continuance* of a situation through its own acts or omissions in which conduct contrary to an international rule originating from a non-state actor is ongoing.[50] According to the ILC, in such cases an 'inference may readily be drawn that' the state 'has assumed responsibility for' the conduct of the non-state actor.[51] The ILC also states: 'The phrase "acknowledges and adopts the conduct in question as its own" is intended to distinguish cases of acknowledgement and adoption from cases of mere support or endorsement.'[52] On reading these passages together, it appears conduct of a non-state actor can be attributed to a state so long as that conduct is still ongoing at a time in which the state is endorsing it. In other words, state endorsement and/or approval of non-state actor conduct will not satisfy the attribution threshold of this provision on its own, but can do if (1) the conduct of the non-state actor is still occurring, and (2) the state is conducting itself in such a manner whereby the conduct of the non-state actor is made easier or is not being hindered.

Facilitating the continuance of non-state actor conduct is a determinative factor that can be taken into consideration when interpreting the attribution test under Article 11 in light of applicable facts. A potential method for assessing whether the attribution threshold of this provision is satisfied would be to determine whether the state in question has at the very least not attempted to stop conduct of a non-state actor that it is simultaneously supporting in some form. Attribution would thus occur

[47] ibid para 61.
[48] ibid para 63 (emphasis original).
[49] ibid paras 66–67.
[50] ARSIWA, Art 11, Commentary, para 3. See also the last paragraph in para 4 of the Commentary.
[51] ibid para 3
[52] ibid para 6.

if the conduct of the non-state actor is ongoing and is made easier because of the state's actions or lack of actions, so long as state organs are also issuing communications showing that the state approves of the conduct of the non-state actor. Whether both private (unofficial) and public (official) forms of state communications would be satisfactory in this regard is unclear. The type of state communication at issue could also affect attribution (for example, an internal memorandum of a government department versus a public announcement at a press conference by a state official).

Some useful insights are provided by examining the cases that were used by the ILC as a form of substantiation to support the creation of Article 11 and help formulate its requirements, in addition to those before the ECtHR and ICTY, where the provision has been analysed since the ARSIWA was finalised. Yet, even where considered applicable or noteworthy, as in the cases before the PCA, ITLOS and ICSID panels, there has been minimal engagement from dispute settlement bodies regarding the applicable scope of Article 11. At this time there also appears to be no state practice that could come close to confirming that the provision forms part of customary international law, despite some views to the contrary that are not from states.[53] Again, assuming states actually create what can be known as international law, then mutually reinforcing decisions of courts and tribunals are not evidence of Article 11 existing in the form as a customary rule, despite their rulings adding perceived weight to such claims.

A reason for this absence of practice and engagement with Article 11 may be because 'states are loath to adopt conduct which is not their own'.[54] The lack of state practice in this respect is understandable from the perspective of state policy. In some instances, states explicitly choosing to acknowledge and adopt the conduct of non-state actors as their own could amount to official validation of that conduct. Yet this practice in which states do not explicitly acknowledge and adopt conduct of non-state actors can justify criticism.[55] Both of these positions present a rationale that all conduct has consequences, meaning that when factoring in the dynamics of intra- and inter-state relations in a specific context, states may view the actual and potential costs of acknowledging and adopting non-state actor conduct as their own not being worth the actual and potential benefits coinciding with such a decision (assuming the state in question views such matters in terms of cost–benefit, which it might not).

Although they may be infrequent or non-existent in the future, instances of explicit state acknowledgement and adoption of non-state actor conduct would, if nothing else, offer a chance to send clear messages regarding why particular conduct occurred, whilst providing the opportunity to agree with or challenge the attribution thresholds set by courts, tribunals and the ILC. Such outcomes would provide further clarity as to the applicable scope of Article 11 and when its test is likely to be satisfied.

[53] See, for example, *Saint-Gobain Performance Plastics Europe v Venezuela* (2016) para 456.

[54] Crawford (n11) 182.

[55] Examples may be found in the practice surrounding states' interventions in Syria. See T Ruys, 'Of Arms, Funding and "Non-lethal Assistance" – Issues Surrounding Third-State Intervention in the Syrian Civil War' (2014) 13 *Chinese Journal of International Law* 13; see also M Fisher and K Sukumar, 'Syria's Tangled Proxy Wars: A Simple Visual Guide' *Vox* (3 November 2015) www.vox.com/world/2015/11/3/9664606/syria-war-visual-guide.

States may attribute non-state actor conduct to themselves because they want others to know that they perceive themselves as the true legal author of a particular line of conduct. Why they would want to do so where such conduct was contrary to a rule (or rules) of international law would not necessarily be clear, unless states were transparent in their reasoning. Yet the ILC hints at a potential reason that could be behind such rationalisations.[56] Despite the implicit forms of state acknowledgement and adoption of non-state actor conduct that have been addressed by courts and tribunals, taking the view that states will not explicitly do so of their own volition raises questions concerning why Article 11 came to form part of the ARSIWA attribution framework, and wherein lies the value of this provision.

3. THE VALUE OF ARTICLE 11

There exists some value in the application of Article 11 to settings in which a state may have implicitly acknowledged and adopted non-state actor conduct as its own, for example, if it facilitated the continuance of such conduct whilst simultaneously communicating in some form that the state supports and/or approves of it. In this respect, Article 11 is no different from the other attribution provisions of the ARSIWA, in that it sets out an additional test comprising requirements that vary in substance and clarity, which can be used to determine the international responsibility of a state for the conduct of a non-state actor. The value of these attribution provisions is thus tied to the value of determining the international responsibility of a state for the conduct of a non-state actor in general terms. If assessed in such a way, each attribution test under the ARSIWA has the same value, even if they set out different criteria to be applied. Each attribution threshold of each provision is no more or less demanding/undemanding than the others in the abstract. Context, facts and perspectives applying normative yardsticks determine whether an attribution test is considered to have a 'high', 'low' or 'acceptable' threshold. Any opinion asserting or arguing that an attribution test has whatever level of threshold (eg high/low, stringent/flexible, narrow/broad, restrictive/expansive) will be subject to the questions of 'compared to what?' and 'on what basis?'

What distinguishes Article 11 from the other attribution provisions within the ARSIWA are its normative roots. These roots form part of instances in which a state explicitly acknowledges and adopts the conduct of a non-state actor that was contrary to an international rule. The ILC indicated its hope that states would attribute non-state actor conduct to themselves based on their explicit acknowledgement and adoption.[57] But why would a state do so? The ILC hints at an answer: because such a state would want to accept 'responsibility for conduct of which it did not approve, which it had sought to prevent and which it deeply regretted'.[58] While there may be other reasons behind a state acknowledging and adopting non-state actor

[56] See section 3 (below).
[57] ARSIWA, Art 11, Commentary, paras 6–8.
[58] ibid para 6.

conduct as its own, such as in an attempt to appease the majority of an electorate in order for a current administration to remain in power, the language used by the ILC, in particular that of regret, is telling of an approach towards state responsibility that extends beyond the confines of legalisms.

The extent of the (un)likelihood that a state will explicitly acknowledge and adopt conduct of a non-state actor as its own may lead to questions over the value of Article 11. In doctrinal terms, the value of the provision thus lies in it addressing instances of implicit state acknowledgement and adoption, where attribution is determined by the past opinions of the ILC, as well as those originating from the judgements of courts and tribunals, and perhaps the odd commentator. But what if attribution rested on states doing the right thing?[59] Recall that although states do sometimes attempt to distance themselves from the repercussions of non-state actors' conduct, they also raised concerns over the ARSIWA attribution framework being 'restrictive' and 'narrow',[60] indicating normative judgments that point to respect for the notion that international responsibility should not be avoided. It can thus be reasonable to envisage similar hopes to those of the ILC, in which states acknowledge and adopt non-state actor conduct as their own when they consider it the right thing to do in a particular circumstance. But when would this be the case, where states take responsibility for wrongdoing out of some reverence for morality?

3.1. Answerability for Involvement in the Wrongful Conduct of Non-state Actors

There are underlying assumptions that are worked within when prescribing matters of morality to assess state conduct. A key one is whether such considerations are even appropriate for determining what does and does not justify state conduct in a particular setting.[61] Another is whether states are moral agents.[62] In engaging further with the matter of states explicitly acknowledging and adopting the conduct of non-state actors as their own, the line of reasoning below works off the premise that insights regarding moral responsibility are both suitable and helpful when assessing state conduct, and that states are moral agents that owe moral duties not only to their own residents, but to other states as well, from which they can be held to account for their conduct.[63] What have such considerations got to do with attribution under Article 11? A fair bit, at least from one perspective.

[59] See generally MJ Sandel, *Justice: What's the Right Thing to Do?* (New York, Farrar, Straus & Giroux, 2010).

[60] See, for example, State Responsibility, Fiftieth Session of the ILC (1998), Agenda Item 2, Comments and observations received by Governments, A/CN.4/488 and Add 1–3, 108 (France); State Responsibility, Fifty-Third Session of the ILC (2001), Comments and Observations received from Governments, A/CN.4/515 and Add 1–3, 48–49 (Japan).

[61] R de Sousa, 'Forget Morality: Five Reasons Why Moral Philosophy Is Distracting and Harmful' *Aeon Magazine* (23 July 2021) https://aeon.co/essays/five-reasons-why-moral-philosophy-is-distracting-and-harmful.

[62] GL Scott and CL Carr, 'Are States Moral Agents?' (1986) 12 *Social Theory and Practice* 75.

[63] B Williams, 'State Morality in International Relations' (1923) 17 *American Political Science Review* 17; V Held, 'Morality, Care, and International Law' (2011) 4 *Ethics & Global Politics* 173; L Lee, 'Ethics and Morality in International Relations' in E Kavalski (ed), *Encounters with World Affairs: An Introduction to International Relations* (Abingdon, Routledge, 2015) 63.

The premise behind states acknowledging and adopting non-state actor conduct as their own appears to be grounded in the concept of responsibility as answerability.[64] Answerability stipulates that actors can be called to account for their conduct, in which blameworthiness extends to the extent of their involvement in wrongdoing.[65] Responsibility 'as answerability is at work at the point in the legal process *before* it has been decided one way or another whether a breach of international law has taken place'.[66] This understanding fits well with the test under Article 11 because attribution of conduct considerations are also determined before, or at least separate from, any assessment as to whether an international legal obligation of a state has been breached. Should a state take seriously the notion of responsibility as answerability, then if it were involved in conduct of a non-state actor that was contrary to an international rule it may perceive it has an interest and/or sees value in putting itself in a position to be held to account by attributing to itself that wrongful conduct of the non-state actor.[67] As the ILC notes, such a state may 'acknowledge and adopt conduct only to a certain extent. In other words, a State may elect to acknowledge and adopt only some of the conduct in question.'[68] Whatever the extent to which a state attributes non-state actor conduct to itself, which may depend on the extent to which the state views itself as being the true author of the conduct in question and/or for other reasons, such as those relating to politics, the state would be undertaking a process in which it rationalised its conduct that involved it with the conduct of the non-state actor, came to terms with its contribution to wrongdoing and decided to declare that it was the legal author of some or all of that conduct in light of the extent of its involvement.[69]

Although it may be unsurprising in some respects 'that states behave badly',[70] some justice could be found in settings where states assume responsibility for conduct that was contrary to international law to which they contributed. Courts and tribunals have set their own thresholds for when conduct of a non-state actor can be attributed to a state. Whether labelled 'effective control', 'partial dependency' or 'majority influence', attribution tests are created to set a threshold that if met results in a state becoming the legal author of conduct that was contrary to an international rule. States can internalise their own method for doing the same, which could align with the concept of responsibility as answerability. States can implement criteria that account for this concept when deciding if and when they should acknowledge and adopt conduct of non-state actors as their own. When doing so, a state would be signifying that it perceives itself as responsible for the conduct that was contrary to international law, which 'can be attributed to [it] in a way that makes [it] eligible for

[64] J Lucas, *Responsibility* (Oxford, Oxford University Press, 1993) 5–12.

[65] CV Blatz, 'Accountability and Answerability' (1972) 2 *Journal for the Theory of Social Behaviour* 101.

[66] J Crawford and J Watkins, 'International Responsibility' in S Besson and J Tasioulas (eds), *The Philosophy of International Law* (Oxford, Oxford University Press, 2010) 283, 284 (emphasis original).

[67] J Gardner, 'The Mark of Responsibility' (2003) 23 *OJLS* 157, 169–70.

[68] ARSIWA, Art 11, Commentary, para 8.

[69] Gardner (n 67) 162.

[70] P Allott, 'State Responsibility and the Unmaking of International Law' (1988) 29 *Harvard International Law Journal* 1, 14.

certain distinctively moral responses on its basis'.[71] The responses that might occur as a result may be the same as those that could occur should state responsibility be established by applying a different attribution test, whether through the ruling of a court or tribunal, or by another state invoking responsibility.

In situations where states flout 'relationship-defining demands' by relying on non-state actors as proxies to undertake conduct that is contrary to international rules, they can choose to put themselves in a position 'to be susceptible to being held to account'.[72] In this sense, Article 11 represents possibility. By acknowledging and adopting conduct of non-state actors as their own, states would be showing their willingness to answer for their involvement in past injustices, a path that is currently not well trodden.[73] It may be labelled naïve to approach state responsibility in such a manner, yet so long as it is possible to do so it is possible that changes occur whereby states breathe more life into the notion of responsibility as answerability through their own practices. By envisaging and implementing means to promote state conduct that conforms with this concept, perhaps the international legal order can evolve with a 'broader moral and political climate'[74] that assists in drawing out justifications from states for their contributions to conduct of non-state actors that is contrary to international rules, whilst providing avenues to atone for such conduct.[75]

Over ten years before the ARSIWA was completed, Philip Allott highlighted some of the ways in which the ILC approach towards state responsibility was problematic.[76] It is true that states can, and do, conduct themselves immorally, including acting and reacting out of pre-emptive immorality, such as in cases of anticipatory or pre-emptive self-defence.[77] International law plays a role in these processes and outcomes, as it is used as a medium of communication to attempt justifying, by adding perceived societal legitimacy to, particular acts or omissions, regardless of whether such conduct is actually lawful.[78] One of the functions of international law appears to be legitimising unlawful and sometimes immoral conduct by engaging in discourse and using language that refers to actual and perceived rules of international law.[79] International law also appears to be more adept at ensuring that the international responsibility of states for the conduct of non-state actors is not established than it is at ensuring the inverse. However, states can conduct their affairs out of due

[71] AM Smith, 'Responsibility as Answerability' (2015) 58 *Inquiry* 99, 103.

[72] D Shoemaker, 'Attributability, Answerability, and Accountability: Toward a Wider Theory of Moral Responsibility' (2011) 121 *Ethics* 602, 623.

[73] See, for example, P Oltermann, 'Germany Agrees to Pay Namibia €1.1bn Over Historical Herero-Nama Genocide' *The Guardian* (28 May 2021) www.theguardian.com/world/2021/may/28/germany-agrees-to-pay-namibia-11bn-over-historical-herero-nama-genocide.

[74] Crawford and Watkins (n 66) 298.

[75] See, for example, ARSIWA, Art 31; Z Badawi, 'Reparations from Former Slave-Owning Countries Are Long Overdue' *Financial Times* (28 July 2021) www.ft.com/content/d47cc0e1-4dab-4f35-ada5-a3e653b62131.

[76] Allott (n 70).

[77] J Nabulsi, 'Risky Business: A Model of Sufficient Risk for Anticipatory Self-defence' (2020) 19 *Journal of Military Ethics* 292.

[78] See N Simons, 'The Legality Surrounding the US Strikes in Syria' *Opinio Juris* (25 April 2017) http://opiniojuris.org/2017/04/25/the-legality-surrounding-the-us-strikes-in-syria/.

[79] HH Koh, *The Trump Administration and International Law* (Oxford, Oxford University Press, 2018) 11 and 105.

consideration for what is right. The wrongdoing that international law contributes to and propagates on a daily basis can be ameliorated through components of its corpus applying differently. Article 11 is one such component. Where conduct originating from a non-state actor was contrary to international law and to which a state contributed, that state can acknowledge and adopt some or all of the conduct in question as its own. Occurrences of this sort could arise when a state considers itself, at least in part, morally duty-bound to put itself in a position to be answerable for wrongs to which it views itself as responsible, whether completely or partially. The conduct it attributes to itself would then form the basis for assessing its international responsibility and what outcomes are appropriate in response. Therefore, at least in one way, the ARSIWA attribution framework has the potential to contribute to international law providing an ever so slightly thicker form of justice.[80] By examining the normative groundwork upon which Article 11 appears to be based, the provision can be viewed as less like a rule of international law and more of a moral ideal to be called upon by states that appreciate the significance of answerability.

4. CONCLUSION

Ownership of wrongdoing is a value instilled in the minds of children from a young age. Taking responsibility for involvement in the consequences of conduct has a long history across societies. Although individual human beings are dissimilar from abstract states, the same normative yardsticks can be applied to both entities when assessing their conduct. Just as it is wrong for the professor to arbitrarily kill the student, so it is wrong for the state in which they teach to do the same. To an extent, the ILC appears to follow similar reasoning, providing indications that it was applying a normative yardstick in its work on Article 11, namely, the concept of responsibility as answerability. As an outcome of this process, there exist two forms by which conduct of a non-state actor can be attributed to a state based on its acknowledgement and adoption: implicitly (whereby the state is judged by another actor) and explicitly (whereby the state judges itself). If the ILC did not see the potential in states themselves deciding to acknowledge and adopt conduct of non-state actors as their own, then it could have created an attribution test that only accounts for implicit forms of state acknowledgement and adoption, to be determined by the actor(s) judging the state in question. Whether that actor is a court, a person or another state, could this world use more judgments being rendered against states for their involvement in conduct that was contrary to international law, or, in addition, could it use more states deciding for themselves to acknowledge as much and then put themselves in positions to be answerable for as much by adopting conduct as their own? States can be quick to take credit for when things go right, but they also need to answer for when things go wrong. While the implicit form of the acknowledgement and adoption attribution test is no different from the other attribution tests within the

[80] SR Ratner, *The Thin Justice of International Law: A Moral Reckoning of the Law of Nations* (Oxford, Oxford University Press, 2015) 408–34.

ARSIWA in terms of its value, as all perform the same function of setting a threshold that allows a determination to be made about whether a state should or should not be considered the legal author of conduct originating from its factual author, the explicit form is distinct. Not only does the element of state choice set it apart, but it also promotes an ideal that states step-up and do the right thing. Article 11 signifies potential – the potential to foster state behaviour that in the most basic sense is an appeal to buck up, admit the truth, act accordingly and let the chips fall where they may. And, equally significantly, the potential wielded by those imagining and creating the frameworks that are aimed at regulating state behaviour. Yet it is not enough that actors merely wield this potential; they must also exercise it in order for anything to happen. Non-state actors need not lie beyond the purview of the international law applicable to state responsibility. In fact, the following chapters show the ways in which this legal framework is already developing and can be developed to better accommodate the interactions between states and non-state actors.

6

State Complicity in the Wrongdoing of Non-state Actors

WHAT THE PREVIOUS chapters have shown is that the legal framework regulating state responsibility that revolves around the ARSIWA does engage with non-state actors. It does so through attribution provisions that consist of different tests for determining when states should be considered the legal author of conduct that has originated from the acts or omissions of non-state actors. These creations of the ILC have had a significant influence on legal practice before courts and tribunals, and will likely continue to do so. Further state practice involving the ARSIWA attribution provisions may also develop, whether aligned with the approaches of the ILC and ICJ or otherwise. While any such practice may enrich or replicate understandings relating to state responsibility and the conduct of non-state actors, it is important that attribution considerations alone do not inflate to the point where they crowd out the space for developing additional approaches to determining state responsibility for non-state actor conduct. Preventing such development would be problematic. Building on the work of the ARSIWA in its engagement with non-state actors means that a shortcoming of the current framework can be addressed: attribution only accounts for determining the direct responsibility of a state for the conduct of a non-state actor. There is no avenue under the ARSIWA in which matters of indirect state responsibility for non-state actor conduct are addressed. By the very nature of attribution it cannot address indirect forms of state responsibility in wrongdoing, as the process of applying attribution tests either results in a state being deemed the legal author of conduct or not. There is no in-between in this process. Yet if a state is not considered to be the legal author of conduct that was contrary to an international rule, does this mean its responsibility cannot be determined when it was in fact involved in that conduct? Is state responsibility for the conduct of non-state actors limited to attributability? What about situations where states are not the authors of wrongdoing but contribute towards it? These questions connect with the concept of complicity, which assists in determining responsibility for participation in wrongdoing, and can do so when applied to the interactions between states and non-state actors. State aid or assistance connected to the wrongful conduct of non-state actors raises a number of issues, which this chapter examines. It reflects on the history of the ILC's work regarding state complicity in non-state actor wrongdoing, as well as analysing the requirements of a test that determines state responsibility for complicity in the wrongful conduct of non-state actors. The chapter then proceeds to scrutinising how an international rule on complicity would operate in practice when applying it to the interactions between states and non-state actors, whilst showing the extent to which complicity can, and already does, apply to these interactions.

1. INCORPORATING NON-STATE ACTORS INTO THE LEGAL FRAMEWORK ON COMPLICITY

The ILC was not only mindful of state complicity in wrongdoing but undertook significant work on this matter. These efforts culminated in encapsulating complicity as 'aid or assistance in the commission of an internationally wrongful act'.[1] Article 16, the end product of the ILC's efforts on state complicity, can give the impression that determining state responsibility on such a basis should be a straightforward process:

> *Aid or assistance in the commission of an internationally wrongful act*
>
> A State which aids or assists another State in the commission of an internationally wrongful act by the latter is internationally responsible for doing so if:
>
> (a) that State does so with knowledge of the circumstances of the internationally wrongful act; and
>
> (b) the act would be internationally wrongful if committed by that State.[2]

Yet, as with the tests addressing attribution of conduct, looking past the text of the provision reveals issues that are nuanced. Some of these have attracted attention.[3] In building on the understandings regarding state complicity that have already been developed, this section examines how complicity generally applies to circumstances involving state aid or assistance to non-state actors that undertake conduct contrary to international rules.[4] In benefiting from the blueprint constructed by the ILC that is Article 16, it is possible to offer insights into how state responsibility can be determined for complicity in non-state actor wrongdoing.[5] However, as this creation of the ILC was limited to the interactions between states, the approach below is aimed at forming part of the understandings relating to the application of an analogue test that incorporates non-state actors.

1.1. Reflecting on Work that Remains Unfinished

The evolution of the test for state complicity that ultimately became Article 16 underwent noteworthy changes during drafting. Ago envisaged the creation of such a

[1] ARSIWA, Art 16.

[2] ibid.

[3] M Milanovic, 'Intelligence Sharing in Multinational Military Operations and Complicity under International Law' (2021) 97 *International Law Studies* 1269, 1274–1323; V Lanovoy, *Complicity and its Limits in the Law of International Responsibility* (Oxford, Hart, 2016); M Jackson, *Complicity in International Law* (Oxford, Oxford University Press, 2015); HP Aust, *Complicity and the Law of State Responsibility* (Cambridge, Cambridge University Press, 2011).

[4] R Mackenzie-Gray Scott, 'State Responsibility for Complicity in the Internationally Wrongful Acts of Non-State Armed Groups' (2019) 24 *Journal of Conflict & Security Law* 373.

[5] For further details regarding these conditions see ibid 384–406.

test as a response to the need to address issues where an array of actors were involved in wrongdoing.[6] A key characteristic that contributed to complicity being siphoned off by the ILC for specific treatment was questions regarding whether, and if so how, states could incur international responsibility for conduct contrary to an international rule of which they are not the legal author, but were nonetheless implicated. The work Ago undertook during drafting helps clarify that state responsibility could be established on the basis of complicity, including in conduct originating from actors other than states.[7]

However, the premise that a future complicity rule should address state interactions with non-state actors remained absent in the subsequent drafts of the provision that ultimately became Article 16. In light of the stance taken by the ILC that state responsibility could be determined on the basis of attribution considering whether a non-state actor acted on the behalf of a state, why did this happen? What are the reasons for creating the bases upon which direct state responsibility for non-state actor conduct can be assessed, but failing to do so with respect to the bases upon which indirect state responsibility for such conduct might rest? There is little indication from the preparatory work as to why there was such an omission:

> We shall take into consideration only the case of complicity of a State in an international offence committed by another State, *even though it may well be presumed that the same principles would apply if one of the protagonists were a subject of international law other than a State*.[8]

Although discussed at length within the ILC,[9] the draft provision on complicity remained unchanged for almost twenty years, forming 'part of the Draft Articles adopted on First Reading in 1996'.[10] During this period it appears no efforts were made to address the reality that just as a state can be complicit in state conduct that is contrary to an international rule, so too it can be complicit in non-state actor conduct that does the same. A number of states provided varied feedback on the draft provision, which could have prompted discussion regarding its exclusion of non-state actors.[11] In working through these responses from states, Crawford came to an understanding that the draft provision was not precise enough.[12] It was thus altered, but

[6] Seventh Report, State Responsibility, Roberto Ago, A/CN.4/307 and Add 1 & 2 and Corr 1 & 2, YBILC (1978) vol I(1), 52.

[7] ibid 52–60.

[8] ibid 60 (emphasis added).

[9] ILC Report, Thirtieth Session, 8 May–28 July 1978, UNGA, Thirty-Third Session, Supp No 10 (A/33/10), YBILC (1978) vol II(2), 99, 104 and 105.

[10] Aust (n 3) 102.

[11] See, for example, those of Austria and Mali in Observations and comments of Governments on chapters I, II and III of Part I of the draft articles on State responsibility for internationally wrongful acts, A/CN.4/328 and Add 1–4, YBILC (1980) vol II(1), 91 and 101, respectively; see also Sweden in Comments of Governments on part one of the draft articles on State responsibility for internationally wrongful acts, A/CN.4/342 and Add 1–4, YBILC (1981) vol II(1), 77; The Netherlands and Venezuela in Comments and observations of Governments on part one of the draft articles on State responsibility for internationally wrongful acts, A/CN.4/351, Add 1–2 & Add 2/Corr 1, Add 3 & Corr 1, YBILC (1982) vol II(1), 18 and 19, respectively; Germany in Comments and observations of Governments on part one of the draft articles on State responsibility for internationally wrongful acts, A/CN.4/414, YBILC (1988) vol II(1), 4; Comments and observations received by Governments, A/CN.4/488 and Add 1–3 (1998) 128–29; Comments and observations received from Governments, A/CN.4/492 (1999) 107.

[12] Second Report, State Responsibility, James Crawford, A/CN.4/498 and Add 1–4 (1999) 47–51.

still did not incorporate non-state actors. The two major amendments were elaborating further on the components of the mental requirement and introducing what is now known as the opposability requirement.[13]

After further dialogue in the ILC, what became the final provision only differed slightly from Crawford's proposal.[14] The opportunity to articulate the ways in which indirect state responsibility for non-state actor conduct could be assessed were thus left unrealised by the ILC. This does not mean, however, that insights cannot be gained by reflecting on what the ILC did produce on complicity. Upon doing so it becomes all the more clear that incorporating non-state actors into the legal framework regulating state responsibility would not be that problematic a task. It is even possible to grasp how the requirements of complicity would likely play out if applied to settings in which indirect state responsibility for non-state actor conduct were a consideration.

1.2. Requirements for Determining State Complicity in Non-state Actor Wrongdoing

The requirements that appear to be part of determining state responsibility for complicity are more than meet the eye. There are four key elements that present distinct sets of difficulties:

- The allegedly complicit state must actually provide aid or assistance.
- There must be a nexus between the aid or assistance provided by the state and the conduct in question that is contrary to an international rule.
- The state providing the aid or assistance must fulfil the mental requirement of state complicity, which depends on applying and satisfying one of three thresholds: knowledge, wilful blindness or intent (either direct or indirect).
- The state providing the aid or assistance is bound by the international rule that is applicable to the conduct in question that is contrary to it.

Each requirement is addressed in turn. The analysis below thus offers something of a how-to guide, in that it teases out key factors that likely need to be accounted for in order to determine the international responsibility of a state for complicity in the wrongdoing of a non-state actor.

1.2.1. Rendering Aid or Assistance to Non-state Actors

What constitutes aid or assistance for the purposes of establishing state responsibility for complicity in wrongdoing? The words 'aid' and 'assistance' appear to be indistinguishable and can thus be used interchangeably or collectively.[15] The term

[13] Lanovoy (n 3) 82–83.
[14] Second Report, Crawford (1999) 56.
[15] Aust (n 3) 197; see also UK comment in Comments and observations received from Governments, A/CN.4/515 and Add 1 (2001) 52.

'aid or assistance' encompasses a broad range of acts.[16] The current mainstream understanding is that state conduct constituting aid or assistance for the purposes of determining state complicity comes in the form of acts, not omissions.[17] However, some take the view that this position may be changing.[18]

1.2.1.1. Conduct Constituting Aid or Assistance

Aid or assistance can be a state providing materials, logistical support, technical assistance or financial backing to non-state actors. State practice examples include the provision of weapons,[19] training of personnel,[20] intelligence sharing,[21] export credit guarantees,[22] and financing armed groups or private military companies.[23] This provides a general flavour for the types of state conduct that could qualify as aid or assistance. Compiling lists 'of typical forms of aid or assistance will, however, not lead to satisfactory results' because the scope of 'aid or assistance' was created in the abstract and therefore depends on the circumstances present in each particular case.[24] A helpful insight provided by Harriet Moynihan is that 'it must be actual "aid or assistance"; mere expressions of approval, or refraining from disapproval, in a political forum would not normally qualify', nor does aid or assistance include 'encouragement or moral support'.[25] But the term can be, and is, interpreted to encompass a wide variety of acts. Gauging whether state conduct constitutes 'aid or assistance' thus appears to turn on the genuine provision of something, not necessarily material, by a state to a non-state actor.

1.2.1.2. The Matter of Omissions

Whether an omission could qualify as 'aid or assistance' is a problematic question, one that barely featured in the work of the ILC.[26] The final commentary to the

[16] ARSIWA, Art 16, Commentary, paras 1, 7, 8, 9; Jackson (n 3) 154; J Crawford, *State Responsibility: The General Part* (Cambridge, Cambridge University Press, 2013) 401–02.

[17] Crawford (ibid) 403–05.

[18] Lanovoy (n 3) 96–97 and 184; Jackson (n 3) 156–58; Aust (n 3) 195 and 230; V Lanovoy, 'Complicity in an Internationally Wrongful Act' in A Nollkaemper and I Plakokefalos (eds), *Principles of Shared Responsibility in International Law: An Appraisal of the State of the Art* (Cambridge, Cambridge University Press, 2014) 134, 145–50.

[19] L Green and D Hamer, 'The Legality of the UK/Saudi Arabia Arms Trade: A Case Study' *EJIL: Talk!* (20 July 2017) www.ejiltalk.org/the-legality-of-the-uk-saudi-arabia-arms-trade-a-case-study/; A Asteriti, 'The Use of Cluster Munitions by Saudi Arabia in Yemen and the Responsibility of the United Kingdom' *EJIL: Talk!* (7 March 2017) www.ejiltalk.org/the-use-of-cluster-munitions-by-saudi-arabia-in-yemen-and-the-responsibility-of-the-united-kingdom/.

[20] Amnesty International, *Libya's Dark Web of Collusion: Abuses Against Europe-Bound Refugees and Migrants* (2017) 8, 35, 43–45, 47, 49, 52, 59, www.amnesty.org/en/documents/mde19/7561/2017/en/.

[21] D Akande, 'UK Case on Complicity by UK Intelligence Agencies in Torture Abroad' *EJIL: Talk!* (5 July 2011) www.ejiltalk.org/uk-case-on-complicity-by-uk-intelligence-agencies-in-torture-abroad/.

[22] Lanovoy, 'Complicity in an Internationally Wrongful Act' (n 18) 143.

[23] H Moynihan, 'Aiding and Assisting: Challenges in Armed Conflict and Counterterrorism', Chatham House Research Paper (2016) 23; Aust (n 3) 199.

[24] Aust (ibid).

[25] Moynihan (n 23) 8.

[26] Ago's seventh report to the ILC briefly mentioned omissions in the context of complicity: Seventh Report, Ago (1978) 53.

ARSIWA complicity provision does not make any reference to state responsibility for complicity arising from omission. Helmut Aust ascribes this absence to the matter escaping 'the attention of the ILC or the ILC saw no reason to deviate from its general rule'[27] contained in Article 2.[28] Miles Jackson argues that the idea of omissions being considered as aid or assistance 'has less to do with the ILC and more to do with the ICJ's holding in the *Bosnian Genocide* case'.[29] Here the Court saw it necessary to emphasise the distinction between the positive obligation to prevent genocide and complicity in genocide.[30] The ICJ presents the issue as clear-cut, in that establishing state responsibility for complicity in the form of omissions is not possible.[31]

The critique of this finding consists of two arguments. First, state conduct that could be construed as complicity cannot be limited to actions because state responsibility can be established for state actions or omissions.[32] This argument proceeds along the lines that to discard the possibility of establishing state complicity in cases where the complicit state conduct was an omission would alter the general qualification of an internationally wrongful act.[33] If only actions satisfy a complicity test, then this apparently 'replaces' the elements of a wrongful act, which can consist of either acts or omissions.[34] The accuracy of this rationale is questionable. There is a difference between state responsibility arising from a wrong, whether through act or omission, and complicity in that wrong. The requirements for determining complicity in a principal wrong do not need to be the same as the requirements for determining an internationally wrongful act. They are two distinct matters. A complicity test can operate as an exception to the general elements contained in Article 2 of the ARSIWA. It would only be if omissions were excluded from being considered internationally wrongful acts would the requirement under Article 2 be modified.

Second, Vladyslav Lanovoy argues that the ruling of the ICJ did not apply to complicity under the general international law of state responsibility, but was limited to the context of genocide under the Convention.[35] However, Jackson and Crawford have both suggested that the ICJ's reasoning and understanding of complicity applies beyond the context of genocide to a general international rule.[36] This makes sense considering the point made by the ICJ, seeing 'no reason to make any distinction of substance between "complicity in genocide" ... and the "aid or assistance" of a State in the commission of a wrongful act'.[37] When the ICJ ruled that state complicity considerations should not apply to instances of state omission, it appears the Court was opining broadly on the concept of complicity in international law, and not limiting its scrutiny of state complicity by omission to contexts in which the matter of

[27] Aust (n 3) 226–27.

[28] ARSIWA, Art 2: 'There is an internationally wrongful act of a State when conduct consisting of an action *or omission* ...' (emphasis added).

[29] Jackson (n 3) 156.

[30] *Bosnia Genocide*, Judgment, 26 February 2007, para 432.

[31] Aust (n 3) 230.

[32] ARSIWA, Art 2, Commentary, para 4.

[33] Lanovoy, 'Complicity in an Internationally Wrongful Act' (n 18) 145.

[34] ibid.

[35] ibid 146.

[36] Jackson (n 3) 156; Crawford (n 16) 403–05.

[37] *Bosnia Genocide*, Judgment, 26 February 2007, para 420.

genocide was at issue. While the argument that state aid or assistance can come in the form of omissions can be theoretically coherent, it can pose problems if applied in practice and become conceptually confusing when referring to other concepts, in particular due diligence.[38]

Even though such confusions can be avoided by exercising care when applying the two concepts, including omissions in state complicity assessments is not the most practical of approaches towards the provision of aid or assistance requirement of state complicity.[39] The additional problem is that determining state responsibility for complicity becomes conflated with determining state responsibility for a due diligence failure. The failure of a state to exercise diligence does not mean that it is complicit in conduct that is contrary to an international rule.[40] It means the state is responsible for its own failure to prevent, suppress or address the wrongs of a non-state actor, whereas complicity is based on being actively involved in the wrongdoing of a non-state actor. Should the opposability requirement as formulated by the ILC hold, then establishing state responsibility for complicity rests on the conduct of an assisted non-state actor breaching an international rule, resulting in the commission of an internationally wrongful act.[41] This is not the same for establishing state responsibility for a due diligence failure, in which the conduct of the non-state actor in question need not have amounted to an internationally wrongful act. This distinction becomes particularly important if a general due diligence rule were to develop in international law.[42]

Even if such a general rule does not come to exist in positive law, there remains the matter of conflating complicity by omission under the law of state responsibility with obligations that arise under primary rules. Neither the text nor commentary of Article 16 mentions a general obligation that legally binds states not to aid nor assist actors that undertake conduct contrary to international rules.[43] Although the preparatory work of this provision examined specific primary rules that do impose such prohibitions, this does not automatically suggest that a general rule of such a nature exists. Considering the state practice and jurisprudence referred to in the drafting, it could be argued that Article 16 did not codify international law.[44] Germany and Switzerland also expressed doubts as to whether such a general obligation had 'a solid foundation' in international law.[45] As noted by the ILC, the work undertaken on state complicity

> presupposed the existence of a general rule of international law that prohibited the rendering of aid or assistance in the commission of an internationally wrongful act. It was doubtful that any such rule existed, at least in customary international law.[46]

[38] See R Mackenzie-Gray Scott, 'Due Diligence as a Secondary Rule of General International Law' (2021) 34 *Leiden Journal of International Law* 343, 367–70.

[39] See M Jackson, 'Freeing *Soering*: The ECHR, State Complicity in Torture and Jurisdiction' (2016) 27 *European Journal of International Law* 817, 829.

[40] For more on this point see M Hakimi, 'State Bystander Responsibility' (2010) 21 *European Journal of International Law* 341, 353–54.

[41] ARSIWA, Chapter IV, Commentary, para 4.

[42] See chapter 7.

[43] ARSIWA, Art 16, Commentary, para 7.

[44] See Lanovoy (n 3) 77–80.

[45] Comments and observations received by Governments, A/CN.4/488 and Add 1–3 (1998) 128.

[46] ILC Report, Fifty-First Session, 3 May–23 July 1999, UNGA, Fifty-Fourth Session, Supp 10 (A/54/10), YBILC (1999) vol II(2), 70.

A context where there appears to be a general obligation on states not to aid or assist wrongdoing is when the breach at issue concerns an international rule that is considered peremptory.[47] Yet complicity under the law of state responsibility does not impose an obligation on states not to aid or assist conduct contrary to international law; rather, it determines when the international responsibility of a state for complicity in that conduct can be established.[48] This understanding of complicity under the general international law of state responsibility helps avoid it being confused with primary rules and due diligence. While it is not inconceivable to include omissions as forms of state aid or assistance, this requirement of providing something is the least challenging aspect of the state complicity test. States frequently provide things to non-state actors. This does not mean they are necessarily complicit in wrongdoing when they do so. Regardless of what possible form complicit conduct of a state comes in, the more imperative consideration when determining the international responsibility of a state for complicity is the link between the aid or assistance provided by a state and the conduct of the non-state actor in question.

1.2.2. The Nexus Requirement

The next requirement for determining state responsibility for complicity is that the state aid or assistance provided must link to the conduct in question that is contrary to an international rule. As emphasised by the ILC, an 'assisting State will only be responsible to the extent that its own conduct has caused or contributed to the internationally wrongful act'.[49] A finding of state complicity rests on there being a sufficient nexus between the state aid/assistance and the wrongdoing in question. However, 'it remains unclear what the link (nexus) between the aid or assistance and the principal wrongful act should be in order to trigger responsibility'.[50] The preparatory work of Article 16 provides a hazy account of what link is required, arising from the inability of the ILC to pin down a clear yardstick, hence the two thresholds of 'caused' or 'contributed' referred to in the commentary.[51] This difficulty was encapsulated during a meeting of the ILC:

> [P]articipation must be active and direct. It must not be too direct, however, for the participant then became a co-author of the offence, and that went beyond complicity. If, on the other hand, participation were too indirect, there might be no real complicity. For instance, it would be difficult to speak of complicity in an armed aggression if the aid and assistance given to a State consisted in supplying food to ensure the survival of the population for humanitarian reasons.[52]

The idea of 'direct' participation in a wrong poses a key issue of distinguishing between complicity and co-perpetration. In other words, when would complicity

[47] ARSIWA, Art 41(2), Commentary, paras 11 and 12; see also Chapter IV, Commentary, para 9.
[48] ARSIWA, Art 16, Commentary, para 9.
[49] ARSIWA, Art 16, Commentary, para 1.
[50] Lanovoy (n 3) 165; see also 184.
[51] ARSIWA, Art 16, Commentary, para 1.
[52] 1519th Meeting of the ILC, A/CN.4/307 and Add l and 2 and Add 2/Corr l, YBILC (1978) vol I, 239 (Ushakov).

considerations be engaged instead of, or as well as, those of co-perpetration?[53] And what amounts to 'contribution' for the purposes of establishing state responsibility for complicity, and 'contribution' for the purposes of establishing state responsibility for co-perpetration? The difficulties in answering this question can be credited to indications of either being forms of participation in wrongdoing. A clearer aspect of the nexus requirement is that it has a de minimis component, excluding conduct of an allegedly complicit state that is too remotely related to the wrongdoing.[54] The overarching component of satisfying the nexus requirement appears to be the sufficiency of an assisting state's conduct in its contribution to the wrongdoing at issue, or whether it caused the wrongdoing to occur.[55] Yet two distinct thresholds remain that require closer inspection: causality and contribution.

1.2.2.1. Causality

The nexus requirement of state complicity is not limited to a 'but for' test. There is little indication to support such a threshold applying, including in the work of the ILC.[56] Setting such a threshold would require a causal link between the state aid or assistance and the wrongful conduct in question – the former (cause) being essential for the completion of the latter (effect). If the nexus requirement were only satisfied upon confirming causation, there would be little to distinguish complicity from co-perpetration. The oscillation between state conduct that could trigger international responsibility for complicity and conduct that could trigger international responsibility for co-perpetration would mean assessments attempting to determine either would be problematized by applying a 'but for' threshold. The line between direct and indirect state responsibility could be blurred to the point of non-recognition. One solution to this issue is viewing the nexus requirement through a lens of proximity/remoteness to the wrongful conduct in question, in that the sufficiency of the state contribution to the wrongdoing would be determined by examining how close or far removed the state conduct was from the conduct of the non-state actor. While it is true that 'some causative connection is required' between state aid or assistance and wrongdoing,[57] complicity assessments stand 'apart from the standard cause-and-effect analysis'.[58] A more appropriate approach towards questions regarding the nexus requirement is thus to examine the degree of contribution to wrongdoing by the state in question.

1.2.2.2. Contribution

The contribution of a state to conduct that is contrary to international law is a key reason why the idea of state responsibility for complicity was developed by the ILC.[59]

[53] See ARSIWA, Art 47 and Commentary.

[54] G Nolte and HP Aust, 'Equivocal Helpers – Complicit States, Mixed Messages and International Law' (2009) 58 *ICLQ* 1, 10.

[55] ARSIWA, Art 16, Commentary, paras 5 and 10.

[56] ibid. A similar stance is taken in Moynihan (n 23) 8.

[57] Moynihan (ibid).

[58] Lanovoy, 'Complicity in an Internationally Wrongful Act' (n 18) 161.

[59] Seventh Report, Ago (1978) 52.

Examining the nexus requirement from the perspective of state contributions to wrongdoing also helps address the complicity versus co-perpetration issue. If state aid or assistance is facilitating a wrong, making it easier for the assisted non-state actor to commit it, then state responsibility for complicity would be the more appropriate consideration, whereas co-perpetration does not necessarily imply that the wrongdoing was made easier by the involvement of the state. Complicity in a wrong means that the state provided an ingredient helping it to take place, whereas co-perpetration denotes the state played a larger role in that wrong. However, if the wrongdoing of a non-state actor is being *maintained* by the provision of state aid or assistance, then the line between complicity and co-perpetration becomes less clear.[60] Clarifying how the nexus requirement can be satisfied in the abstract is a fluid process. To really pin down concrete understandings requires its application to established facts in a specific context. Yet even in the abstract, guidance on the nexus requirement can be found in analyses of the mental requirement.

1.2.3. *The Mental Requirement*

The *mens rea* aspect of determining state responsibility for complicity presents challenges and 'is not as straightforward as it seems at face value'.[61] At present, there are three overarching ways to read this requirement, all of which set different thresholds for determining the international responsibility of a state for complicity in wrongdoing. The first rests on establishing that a state knew of the wrongdoing to which it was assisting (knowledge). The second rests on establishing that a state turned a blind eye to the wrongdoing to which it was assisting (wilful blindness). The third rests on establishing that a state intended to facilitate the wrongdoing in question (intent). As related to considerations of the attribution tests explored in the previous chapters, preference towards one threshold will indicate the application of a normative yardstick in which construing a particular reading of the mental requirement as 'narrow', 'broad', etc, will depend on comparisons to other readings undertaken in the same context.

However, this section does not address the question of why one particular threshold should be applied instead of another. Answering this question is particularly difficult because the three current thresholds are interconnected. There is little agreement as to the 'correct' threshold to apply or the 'right' way to interpret each threshold.[62] Further clarity on these matters will become clearer the more state complicity is assessed in practice. At this time, however, because there is little practice relating to the mental requirement, the aim here is to show some of the simplicities and difficulties of applying each threshold, which can be used to help decide what one of the three, if any, would make the most sense to apply in practice. That said, it

[60] See ARSIWA, Art 41, Commentary, para 11.

[61] R Mackenzie-Gray Scott, 'Torture in Libya and Questions of EU Member State Complicity' *EJIL: Talk!* (11 January 2018) www.ejiltalk.org/torture-in-libya-and-questions-of-eu-member-state-complicity/.

[62] See the disagreement between, for example, Aust (n 3) 230–49 and Lanovoy (n 3) 218–40; or Crawford (n 16) 407–08 and Jackson (n 3) 159–62; see also Nolte and Aust (n 54) 13–15 and Moynihan (n 23) 21–22.

might be that all three will be utilised in the future when state complicity in non-state actor wrongdoing becomes a consideration. This would not necessarily be a problem, save perhaps for playing a part in creating more ambiguity within a legal framework where legal certainty is already scarce.

1.2.3.1. Knowledge

Knowledge is an essential component of the mental requirement, and determinations of whether a state is responsible for complicity in the wrongdoing of a non-state actor can rest on state knowledge. But knowledge of what? Under the state-to-state conceptualisation of complicity as enshrined in Article 16, it appears that the knowledge required by a state is that of illegality.[63] A state that is to be held responsible for complicity 'must indeed have knowledge not merely of the circumstances of the act but also of its wrongfulness'.[64] Under this reading of the mental requirement, so long as a state providing assistance to a non-state actor has knowledge of an internationally wrongful act committed by that non-state actor, then the requirement would be satisfied.[65] Yet this understanding presents problems. First, determining whether a state has knowledge of wrongdoing undertaken by a non-state actor that it assists can be hard to assess before or after the fact.[66] Second, although an analogue to Article 16 that encompasses non-state actors need not adhere to the opposability requirement, assessing whether conduct of a non-state actor amounts to an internationally wrongful act will not be possible in cases where non-state actors do not have international legal personality, meaning they cannot breach international rules because they are not bound by them in the first place. Although this second problem can be addressed by advancing an alternative understanding to the opposability requirement, the first issue remains.[67]

Applying a knowledge threshold alone could also risk ascribing international responsibility for complicity to states where states are aware of wrongdoing undertaken by non-state actors, but not necessarily contributing to it.[68] A key consequence here is that if the international responsibility of states for complicity is established in such settings, doing so could compromise cooperation.[69] If it becomes more likely that states will be considered internationally responsible for complicity in non-state actor wrongdoing when they have knowledge of that wrongdoing, then states may be deterred from providing aid or assistance that in some cases might be beneficial for the societies in which the non-state actors operate, because although states may not intend to contribute to wrongdoing through such aid or assistance, providing it may inadvertently do so. The requisite level of knowledge needed to be held by a state in

[63] ARSIWA, Art 16, Commentary, para 4.

[64] Statement of John Dugard, 2577th Meeting of the ILC, YBILC (1999) vol I, 69.

[65] Jackson (n 3) 159–62; Crawford (n 16) 406.

[66] For details on this point, see Mackenzie-Gray Scott (n 4) 391–92.

[67] See section 1.2.4 (below).

[68] Aust (n 3) 230–49.

[69] For examples, see Mackenzie-Gray Scott (n 4) 392.

order to satisfy the knowledge threshold is not clear.[70] Whether actual, near certain or constructive knowledge is sufficient, or that knowledge needs to encompass a degree of intent, are matters yet to be resolved in practice.

An argument favouring a knowledge threshold applying as part of the mental requirement of state complicity is that this was the threshold used for the final text of Article 16, which was adopted by the ILC. Giorgio Gaja points out that:

> As a general rule, giving greater weight to the text of the articles where there are discrepancies with the commentaries reflects the much more detailed attention that the ILC devotes to the adoption of the articles.[71]

This is a conclusion taking into consideration the procedure of adopting provisions in the ARSIWA. The draft commentaries to the articles of the ARSIWA are debated less rigorously, sometimes if at all, than the draft texts themselves. Voting in the ILC also pertains to the texts of the provisions, not their commentaries. Yet, as has been shown with respect to those concerning attribution, it is helpful to read provisions of the ARSIWA in conjunction with their commentaries in order to better grasp how particular tests are considered to apply. Further, although a knowledge threshold may be favoured for a state-to-state complicity test, an analogue addressing state-to-non-state actor interactions need not follow the reasoning that because the ILC decided to adopt this threshold for the former test enshrined in Article 16, a separate test should do the same.

1.2.3.2. Wilful Blindness

The next threshold that can be applied to the mental requirement is that of wilful blindness, which can be defined as a state consciously turning a blind eye to credible information that points to wrongful conduct of a non-state actor to which it is aiding or assisting.[72] Should this threshold be applied in practice, it is worth giving due regard to information that is in the public domain, as 'evidence may be clear to some parts of the international community but not to others'.[73] Just because something is clear to state officials in one state does not mean the same holds true for state officials in another state. The relevance of this caution is that the wilful blindness threshold overlaps with the knowledge threshold. A state may claim it did not have knowledge of non-state actor wrongdoing, but this may because it chose to avoid such knowledge. Reading a wilful blindness threshold into assessments on the mental requirement addresses this type of situation where relevant information is ignored by states that proceed with their provisions of aid or assistance to non-state actors undertaking conduct contrary to international rules. Yet a state may be genuinely

[70] D Bethlehem, 'The Secret Life of International Law' (2012) 1 *Cambridge Journal of International & Comparative Law* 23, 34; H Moynihan, 'Aiding and Assisting: The Mental Element Under Article 16 of the International Law Commission's Articles on State Responsibility' (2018) 67 *ICLQ* 455, 467.

[71] G Gaja, 'Interpreting Articles Adopted by the International Law Commission' (2015) 85 *British Yearbook of International Law* 10, 20.

[72] Mackenzie-Gray Scott (n 61).

[73] Moynihan (n 23) 14.

unaware of certain circumstances of which another state is fully aware. In such cases the wilful blindness threshold would not be met.

The concept of wilful blindness is closely connected with those of reckless participation, negligence and due diligence.[74] This could cause conceptual difficulties in the application of this threshold, such as blurring the line between primary and secondary rules.[75] Complicity assessments adopting a wilful blindness threshold can also become mixed with due diligence assessments.[76] An example is the ruling of the ECtHR in the *El-Masri* case:

> The Macedonian authorities *not only* failed to comply with their positive obligation to protect the applicant from being detained in contravention of Article 5 of the Convention, *but they actively facilitated* his subsequent detention in Afghanistan by handing him over to the CIA, despite the fact that they *were aware or ought to have been aware of the risk of that transfer*.[77]

A further point is whether there is a conflict with applying a wilful blindness threshold and a position advanced by the ILC when commenting on the mental requirement of Article 16: 'If the assisting or aiding State is unaware of the circumstances in which its aid or assistance is intended to be used … it bears no international responsibility.'[78] This insight indicates the application of a knowledge threshold, in which a state that is considered to be wilfully blind to non-state actor wrongdoing would not satisfy the mental requirement of state complicity. That said, although much can be learned from the ILC's engagement with the nuances of the mental requirement, the same approach to assessing whether the mental requirement has been satisfied need not be adopted for an analogue complicity test incorporating non-state actors, especially in light of the fact that states have argued for different thresholds of the mental requirement to apply.[79]

The value of reading wilful blindness into complicity considerations means that there is a potential safeguard to satisfying the knowledge threshold should an allegedly complicit state claim that it did not know of the non-state actor wrongdoing in question. If states are accused of aiding or assisting conduct of non-state actors that is contrary to international rules, it will be harder to argue against allegations of wilful blindness the more reliable information becomes available pointing towards such conduct, especially if the information is widely known and other states have responded to it. This information could come from reports of states, intergovernmental organisations, NGOs, court judgments or investigative journalism. Whether states are genuinely aware or unaware of particular conduct undertaken by non-state actors to which they provide aid or assistance cannot be determined in the abstract. Yet in deciding on claims of wilful blindness, a determinative factor would be to consider whether the state providing assistance was likely aware that the assisted non-state

[74] Jackson (n 3) 162.

[75] For details on this point, see Mackenzie-Gray Scott (n 4) 394.

[76] See Nolte and Aust (n 54) 15.

[77] *El-Masri v The Former Yugoslav Republic of Macedonia*, App No 39630/09 (ECtHR, 13 December 2012) para 239 (emphasis added).

[78] ARSIWA, Art 16, Commentary, para 4.

[79] See Comments and observations received from Governments, A/CN.4/515 and Add 1 (2001) 52.

actor would undertake conduct contrary to the international rule at issue in the ordinary course of events. For example, if a state provides weapons to a non-state actor that has an established history of undertaking conduct that makes a mockery of the right not to be arbitrarily deprived of life, then the wilful blindness threshold would likely be met. Yet in the same scenario, if the non-state actor had no such history, and out of the blue arbitrarily took life with those weapons, then the wilful blindness threshold would likely not be met. In the most general sense, the more information that is available to a state indicating that conduct contrary to international rules originates from a particular non-state actor, the less likely an argument of that state being unaware of such conduct is going to be rational and reasonable should its responsibility for complicity be called into question for providing aid or assistance to that actor. The Netherlands took this understanding a step further when advocating for applying the threshold that a state 'should have known' of wrongdoing when assessing whether the mental requirement has been satisfied.[80]

1.2.3.3. Intent

According to the ILC, the mental requirement sets a threshold in which the provision of state aid or assistance must be done 'with a view to facilitating' the commission of the conduct contrary to the international rule at issue.[81] This phrase reflects the opinions of some states that appear to show preference towards a threshold including an assessment of intent, rather than knowledge alone.[82] A comment made by Germany reflects this stance: 'The requirement of intent in aiding and assisting the commission of an unlawful act also needs to be incorporated more clearly and unequivocally.'[83] Although applying an intent threshold to the mental requirement has attracted criticism, such an approach need not be problematic.[84] Although it is worth exercising caution when approaching the ruling on this matter,[85] the ICJ has held that intent forms part of the mental requirement in state complicity assessments.[86] The intent of a state can be determined by reference to its explicit rationale for providing aid

[80] Comments and observations received from Governments, A/CN.4/515 and Add 1 (2001) 52.

[81] ARSIWA, Art 16, Commentary, paras 1, 3 and 5.

[82] Comments and observations received from Governments, A/CN.4/515 and Add 1–3 (2001) 52 (UK and US); Comments and observations of Governments on part one of the draft articles on State responsibility for internationally wrongful acts, A/CN.4/351, Add 1–2 & Add 2/Corr 1, Add 3 & Corr 1, YBILC (1982) vol II(1), 19 (former USSR); Comments and observations of Governments on part one of the draft articles on State responsibility for internationally wrongful acts, A/CN.4/414, YBILC (1988) vol II(1), 4 (Germany); Comments and observations received by Governments, A/CN.4/488 and Add 1–3 (1998) 128 (Germany and UK), 129 (US); Comments and observations received from Governments, A/CN.4/492 (1999) 107 (Japan); Comments and observations received from Governments, A/CN.4/515 and Add 1–3 (2001) 51 and 52 (Denmark, Finland, Norway, Sweden, Iceland, UK and US).

[83] Comments and observations received by Governments, A/CN.4/488 and Add 1–3 (1998) 128.

[84] A Boivin, 'Complicity and Beyond: International Law and the Transfer of Small Arms and Light Weapons' (2005) 87 *International Review of the Red Cross* 467, 471–72; B Graefrath, 'Complicity in the Law of International Responsibility' (1996) 2 *Revue Belge de Droit International* 371, 375.

[85] See the reasons for this in Mackenzie-Gray Scott (n 4) 395–96.

[86] *Bosnia Genocide*, Judgment, 26 February 2007, para 421.

or assistance to a non-state actor.[87] This means that should an intent threshold be read into it, determinations on the mental requirement are less likely to encounter difficulties relating to the knowledge of a state in correlation with the timing of the aid or assistance rendered.[88] While it may be difficult to demonstrate that a state had knowledge of non-state actor wrongdoing in a particular case before or after any aid or assistance was provided to that non-state actor, demonstrating intent during such periods would be more straightforward where the state has expressed its intentions to facilitate the wrongdoing of the non-state actor in question, regardless of what point in time the wrongdoing took place in correlation to the provision of aid or assistance. Critics of utilising an intent threshold have so far not taken into consideration this factor.[89] However, intent can be hard to establish, even if it comes in a direct form. There is also the question that if the direct intent of a state were established, whether such a finding would be more akin to establishing state responsibility for co-perpetration rather than for complicity.[90] While it may be that establishing the direct intent of a state could lead to the state being considered the legal author of the non-state actor conduct in question, this does not preclude intent from also forming part of the mental requirement when assessing state complicity.[91]

Intent can manifest itself in indirect forms. Oblique intent can thus play a role when interpreting the mental requirement.[92] Oblique intent can be when 'a particular consequence is to be regarded as intended if the relevant state organ is aware that it will occur in the ordinary course of events'.[93] Insights from international criminal law provide guidance on adopting an intent threshold in mental requirement assessments, which can be analogised for the purposes of applying to situations where determining the international responsibility of a state is at issue.[94] As there currently exists minimal guidance on the different degrees of intent with respect to the mental requirement of complicity under the law of state responsibility, reference to international criminal law can assist in outlining how this aspect of the mental requirement could apply in practice.

Article 30(2) of the Rome Statute of the ICC states:

> For the purposes of this article, a person has intent where:
>
> (a) In relation to conduct, that person means to engage in the conduct;
>
> (b) In relation to a consequence, that person means to cause that consequence or is aware that it will occur in the ordinary course of events.[95]

[87] In practice there will not always be such explicit statements, which is why indirect intent serves an important purpose (see below).

[88] For further details, see Mackenzie-Gray Scott (n 4) 396.

[89] Lanovoy (n 3) 227–34; J Quigley, 'Complicity in International Law: A New Direction in the Law of State Responsibility' (1987) 57 *British Yearbook of International Law* 77, 111.

[90] See Mackenzie-Gray Scott (n 4) 396–98.

[91] See section on instigation in chapter 8.

[92] Quigley (n 89) 111.

[93] Mackenzie-Gray Scott (n 61).

[94] According to Moynihan, such a technique should 'be employed with care' in light of state responsibility and international criminal law being 'different areas of international law with different histories and characteristics' (Moynihan (n 23) 19).

[95] Rome Statute of the International Criminal Court (adopted 17 July 1998, entered into force 1 July 2002) 2187 UNTS 3, Art 30, para 2.

The first part of subparagraph (b) is a form of direct intent. However, the second part is a form of indirect intent. In applying this provision, the ICC has held:

> [Direct intent] requires that the suspect knows that his or her acts or omissions will bring about the material elements of the crime and carries out these acts or omissions with the purposeful will (intent) or desire to bring about those material elements of the crime. According to the *dolus directus in the first degree*, the volitional element is prevalent as the suspect purposefully wills or desires to attain the prohibited result.[96]

In addition to this direct intent, the Court ruled:

> *Dolus directus in the second degree* does not require that the suspect has the actual intent or will to bring about the material elements of the crime, but that he or she is aware that those elements will be the almost inevitable outcome of his acts or omissions, *i.e.*, the suspect 'is aware that ... [the consequence] will occur in the ordinary course of events' (article 30(2)(b) of the Statute). In this context, the volitional element decreases substantially and is overridden by the cognitive element, *i.e.* the awareness that his or her acts or omissions 'will' cause the *undesired* proscribed consequence.[97]

These passages show that intent can arise in a number of forms, and that establishing oblique forms of intent are sufficient for satisfying a mental requirement that adopts an intent threshold. This understanding is underlined in other cases,[98] and, as pointed out by the ICC, is also 'relied on by the jurisprudence of the ad hoc tribunals and commonly accepted in the legal literature'.[99] Transposing these insights into the law of state responsibility means an intent threshold could be satisfied even if a state does not desire to bring about the consequence of conduct undertaken by a non-state actor that is contrary to an international rule. In other words, such a result was not the purpose behind the aid or assistance provided by the state, but, because of the overall context of the situation, the state is considered to be aware that the conduct of the non-state actor is likely to be the almost inevitable outcome of its aid or assistance. When determining state intent, it therefore does not need to be established why a state provided aid or assistance, but that it did so whilst being aware that conduct contrary to an international rule (or rules) would likely occur upon doing so, which is a threshold that fits with practice.[100]

The interpretative guidance provided by the Rome Statute and jurisprudence of the ICC help highlight how oblique intent can be applied to mental requirement assessments. Utilising these insights when determining state complicity can help build on those gained from the work undertaken by the ILC on this matter. What the above analysis also demonstrates is that applying an intent threshold can incorporate a knowledge threshold, and vice versa, meaning the two thresholds can be

[96] *Prosecutor v Jean-Pierre Bemba Gombo*, Pre-Trial Chamber (II), ICC-01/05-01/08, Decision Pursuant to Article 61(7)(a) and (b) of the Rome Statute on the Charges of the Prosecutor Against Jean-Pierre Bemba Gombo (15 June 2009) para 358 (emphasis in original).

[97] ibid para 359 (emphasis and format original).

[98] *Prosecutor v Thomas Lubanga Dyilo*, Pre-Trial Chamber (I), ICC-01/04-01/06, Decision on the confirmation of charges (29 January 2007) paras 350–55.

[99] *Prosecutor v Germain Katanga and Mathieu Ngudjolo Chui*, Pre-Trial Chamber (I), ICC-01/04-01/07, Decision on the confirmation of charges (30 September 2008) para 530.

[100] See Fourth Report, Ago (1972) 128; see also Crawford (n 16) 408.

intertwined. For instance, in cases where a state has actual knowledge of conduct that is contrary to an international rule, 'intent may be imputed' to that state as part of a complicity assessment.[101] There is also a significant interaction between the nexus requirement and the mental requirement, in particular with respect to what threshold is applied and satisfied for each in the course of a particular complicity assessment. A key factor in deciding on whether the nexus requirement has been met in a particular case is the sufficiency of the state aid or assistance rendered in contributing to the conduct at issue. But is this threshold the same should the direct intent of the state be established? Does the degree of contribution required under the nexus requirement change depending on the threshold applied to the mental requirement? If it were established that a state possessed direct intent when aiding or assisting a non-state actor that undertook conduct contrary to an international rule, then, conceivably, the sufficiency of its contribution to the conduct of that non-state actor may not need to be established because it would be clear that the purpose of the state aid or assistance was to facilitate the occurrence of that conduct. Applying this rationale to another example, if it were established that the aid or assistance provided by a state caused the conduct of the non-state actor to occur, then the intentions of the state may be considered irrelevant. The general point here is that if a relatively more demanding threshold is applied and satisfied on the nexus requirement, then that would mean having to apply and satisfy a relatively less demanding threshold on the mental requirement, and vice versa.

1.2.4. The Opposability Requirement (and the Potential in Tweaking It)

The final requirement for determining state responsibility for complicity is that of opposability, which stipulates that the state providing aid or assistance to the recipient that undertakes the conduct that is contrary to an international rule is bound by the obligation applicable to that rule. In both the state-to-state and state-to-non-state actor conceptualisations of complicity, adhering to the opposability requirement as constructed by the ILC means that the aided/assisted state or non-state actor must breach an international obligation, and the aiding/assisting state must be bound by the same obligation that was breached. This requirement of state complicity was not created until the second reading of the ARSIWA.[102] Before this time, it was considered that the international responsibility of a state for complicity could still be established without the state that provides the aid or assistance being bound by the legal obligation corresponding to the right that was breached by the conduct of the assisted actor.[103] The rationale behind the creation of the opposability requirement is that 'a State cannot do by another what it cannot do by itself'.[104] If an analogue to the complicity test created by the ILC were to incorporate this construction of the

[101] Crawford (ibid) 408; see also Jackson (n 3) 160; S Talmon, 'A Plurality of Responsible Actors: International Responsibility for Acts of the Coalition Provisional Authority in Iraq' in P Shiner and A Williams (eds), *The Iraq War and International Law* (Oxford, Hart, 2008) 185, 218–19.
[102] Second Report, Crawford (1999) 51.
[103] Crawford (n 16) 409.
[104] ARSIWA, Art 16, Commentary, para 6.

requirement, then satisfying it would depend on the respective international obligations held by any state providing aid or assistance and any non-state actor receiving aid or assistance.[105]

This construction of the opposability requirement has been criticised for being restrictive and unpractical,[106] including to the extent that its application could reduce compliance with international rules.[107] A counterargument in favour of the opposability requirement is that in its absence there would be a risk of states incurring international responsibility in the absence of being bound by an international obligation. Although the requirements for determining complicity in an internationally wrongful act do not have to be the same as the requirements for determining an internationally wrongful act, there remains a question whether removing the opposability requirement would alter the requirements of an internationally wrongful act, as in doing so the international responsibility of a state could be established without the state in question being bound by the obligation at issue. While the way in which the ILC constructed the opposability requirement was not supported by some states,[108] it need not be constructed in the same manner for an analogue complicity test that incorporates non-state actors, especially to an extent in which doing so 'shuts the door' to the possibility of establishing state responsibility for complicity when states aid or assist non-state actors that undertake conduct contrary to international rules.[109]

Other issues that the opposability requirement raises have been examined by Jackson, who shifted the debate on its existence/inexistence to matters of 'whether there are principled and policy reasons for extending responsibility for complicity to situations where the assisting state is not so bound' by the applicable rule or rules at issue.[110] Yet the approach of the ILC towards the opposability requirement need not be departed from entirely when determining state complicity in non-state actor wrongdoing, only tweaked. It is worth noting at this point that the existence of the opposability requirement in terms of positive law is far from established, and there remains an 'absence of concrete international practice on this precise matter'.[111] Although state practice could well change these in the future, there are two reasons why opposability need not amount to an impediment on state complicity assessments involving non-state actors. First, generally speaking, it is more likely that a state will be bound by an international legal obligation than a non-state actor.[112] On this balance of probability, if a non-state actor satisfies the requirements of an internationally wrongful act, because it has breached an international legal obligation to which it is bound, then, in general terms, it will be likely that any state aiding or assisting the commission of this wrongdoing is also bound by that same rule.[113]

[105] ibid paras 7–10.
[106] Lanovoy, 'Complicity in an Internationally Wrongful Act' (n 18) 160.
[107] Lanovoy (n 3) 240–58.
[108] See ibid 248–49.
[109] Lanovoy, 'Complicity in an Internationally Wrongful Act' (n 18) 159.
[110] Jackson (n 3) 164.
[111] Aust (n 3) 266.
[112] An exception to this generalisation finds itself within the confines of international humanitarian law, whereby this body of law can bind states and non-state armed groups equally.
[113] For further explanation, see Mackenzie-Gray Scott (n 4) 402–06.

So long as a non-state actor has breached an international obligation, then so long as a state is bound by that same obligation, its international responsibility can be established for complicity if the other requirements are also met. The opposability requirement to an analogue complicity test incorporating non-state actors would thus apply in the same manner as it applies under Article 16.

Second, this construction analogised from that of the ILC can be tweaked. While a state that provides aid or assistance to a non-state actor would need to be bound by the international obligation in question, so that, in the words of Article 16(b), 'the act would be internationally wrongful if committed by that State', the non-state actor need not be bound by, and thus be in a position to breach, the applicable legal obligation. What would instead suffice is that the conduct of the non-state actor was contrary to the applicable international rule, meaning if the assisting state were to take the place of the non-state actor and undertake the same conduct, the state would be committing an internationally wrongful act. The opposability requirement under an analogous complicity rule that incorporates non-state actors would thus be satisfied or not by determining the following:

> Whether the state providing the aid or assistance would be bound by an international legal obligation relating to the conduct that was contrary to an international rule if it were to take the place of the actor receiving the aid or assistance that undertook that conduct.

This construction better accommodates the current reality that non-state actors in general do not have international legal personality, and therefore cannot be bound by and subsequently breach international rules. The key issue here is how the international responsibility of a state can be determined for complicity in conduct that does not technically breach the rule at issue, even though if the state were to perpetrate that conduct it would breach that rule. If such a construction were to apply in practice it is unclear whether doing so would change the requirements of an internationally wrongful act, or whether a finding of state complicity that satisfies the other requirements would amount to a separate internationally wrongful act in and of itself. Further, while there is currently not a legal obligation under the law of state responsibility that binds states to refrain from aiding or assisting non-state actors that undertake conduct contrary to international rules, one could develop that incorporates this construction of the opposability requirement. However any of these ideas pan out, the opposability requirement would remain the same on the end of the assisting state, in that it would need to be bound by an international legal obligation that it would breach if it were to take the place of the assisted non-state actor and undertake that same conduct. While this proposal may be deemed something along the lines of too radical a departure from the mainstream ILC construction of the opposability requirement, the only real difference between the two is pieces of paper (eg legislation and a contract) under the domestic laws of a particular state stipulating that an actor is a state organ. Why should it matter to state complicity assessments under international law if an actor is categorised as a state organ or not under domestic law, if the conduct of that actor is contrary to an international rule and has been aided or assisted by a state?[114]

[114] This question is engaged with further in section 3.1 below.

2. THE OPERATION OF STATE COMPLICITY IN NON-STATE ACTOR WRONGDOING

Having set out the requirements for a state complicity test that incorporates non-state actors, it is worthwhile confirming how this test would operate in practice, thereby engaging in the discourse regarding how the concept of complicity applies to state interactions with non-state actors. The debate here consists of two predominant positions. The first is that complicity should operate as a basis for attribution, functioning like Articles 4–11 of the ARSIWA, which determine the direct responsibility of a state for a non-state actor's conduct. This understanding runs contrary to that which underpins the analysis of the requirements in the previous section, yet provides a number of helpful insights, including with respect to the matter of special attribution tests that can develop independently of those under the general state responsibility framework.[115] The second is that complicity operates as a basis separate from attribution, one that determines the indirect responsibility of a state for involvement in a non-state actor's conduct, which is the understanding upon which the requirements set out above are based. This section presents and addresses these positions in turn, before concluding on the more appropriate operation to adopt at this time.

2.1. The Attribution Approach to Complicity

Complicity applying as a basis for attribution of conduct has been expressed by a number of people.[116] The idea here is that a complicity test could be applied to relationships between non-state actors and states in a way similar to other attribution tests, such as those under Articles 4–11 of the ARSIWA. Applied in this manner, complicity would operate as a test for determining direct state responsibility for non-state actor conduct, thereby making states the legal author of conduct originating from non-state actors when the applicable test is satisfied. Lanovoy appears to centre this argument on accepting that complicity is a hybrid of 'direct and derivative responsibility'.[117] Daniele Amoroso considers complicity applying as an attribution test to be suitable compared to the alternatives regarding how complicity could apply to engage with matters of determining state responsibility for non-state actor conduct, namely: the failure of a state to exercise due diligence; a breach of a primary rule; and complicity as a distinct basis of responsibility.[118] Christian Tams advances

[115] For further insights, see M Milanovic, 'Special Rules of Attribution of Conduct in International Law' (2020) 96 *International Law Studies* 295.

[116] CJ Tams, 'The Use of Force against Terrorists' (2009) 20 *European Journal of International Law* 359; D Amoroso, 'Moving towards Complicity as a Criterion of Attribution of Private Conducts: Imputation to States of Corporate Abuses in the US Case Law' (2011) 24 *Leiden Journal of International Law* 989; Lanovoy (n 3) 306–29; A Nollkaemper, 'Attribution of Forcible Acts to States: Connections Between the Law on the Use of Force and the Law of State Responsibility' in NM Blokker and NJ Schrijver (eds), *The Security Council and the Use of Force: Theory and Reality – A Need for Change?* (Brill, Nijhoff, 2005) 160.

[117] Lanovoy (ibid) 309.

[118] Amoroso (n 116) 991–94.

an argument that is based on state practice in the context of use of force against non-state actors considered to be terrorists:

> [A] territorial state has to accept anti-terrorist measures of self-defence directed against its territory where it is responsible for complicity in the activities of terrorists based on its territory – either because of its support below the level of direction and control or because it has provided a safe haven for terrorists. In short, pursuant to this more moderate re-reading, modern practice points towards a special standard of imputability in relations between terrorist groups and host states.[119]

In order to comply with the inter-state reading of circumstances in which the use of force is permissible in self-defence, states have creatively interpreted the law in this area so as to lawfully permit force in response to the activities of non-state actors.[120] As Nancy Simons argues, 'states have increasingly construed the exceptions to the prohibition on the use of force in innovative ways'.[121] The idea that self-defence can be taken up by a state against a non-state actor is contentious with respect to the international law governing the use of force.[122] In using force against non-state actors, states attempt to keep within the state-to-state UN Charter-based framework by arguing that they are acting in self-defence because the 'host' state has failed to prevent or suppress the non-state actor carrying out attacks. Attribution presumably factors into such considerations because the non-state actor's conduct needs to be linked under international law to the state in order to permit lawful force, meaning the complicity of the host state lies in its failure to prevent or suppress such conduct, which, according to arguments favouring complicity operating as an attribution test, ties the conduct of the non-state actor to the state, thereby making the state directly responsible for its wrongdoing. Proponents of this position also consider state aid or assistance to encompass omissions, hence the references to states failing to do something, as opposed to doing something. Taking this premise onto the plane of the general international law on state responsibility presents difficulties. Recall the unlikelihood of state aid or assistance by omission being part of a complicity test, which means a state's failure to act would more likely be caught under an applicable primary rule, or, if one exists, a general due diligence rule.[123]

Arguments favouring complicity operating through the attribution of conduct route have predominantly arisen in the use of force context.[124] Complicity can be

[119] Tams (n 116) 385.

[120] FI Paddeu, 'Use of Force against Non-state Actors and the Circumstance Precluding Wrongfulness of Self-defence' (2017) 30 *Leiden Journal of International Law* 93; A Banerjee, 'Indian Surgical Strikes: Accelerating the Emergence of Nascent Norms of Use of Force Against Non-state Actors' *Cambridge International Law Journal* (6 September 2017) http://cilj.co.uk/2017/09/06/indian-surgical-strikes-accelerating-the-emergence-of-nascent-norms-of-use-of-force-against-non-state-actors/.

[121] N Simons, 'The Legality Surrounding the US Strikes in Syria' *Opinio Juris* (25 April 2017) http://opiniojuris.org/2017/04/25/the-legality-surrounding-the-us-strikes-in-syria/.

[122] T Ruys, *'Armed Attack' and Article 51 of the UN Charter: Evolutions in Customary Law and Practice* (Cambridge, Cambridge University Press, 2010).

[123] See chapter 7.

[124] V Lanovoy, 'The Use of Force by Non-state Actors and the Limits of Attribution of Conduct' (2017) 28 *European Journal of International Law* 563 and V Lanovoy, 'The Use of Force by Non-state Actors and the Limits of Attribution of Conduct: A Rejoinder to Ilias Plakokefalos' (2017) 28 *European Journal of International Law* 595.

understood as a transformative test here, in that it generates an appearance that a state is directly responsible for the conduct of a non-state actor to which it has ties, either by mere association, for example, because the non-state actor operates out of the state's territory, or because the state facilitates the non-state actor, whether actively, for example, by providing it with weapons, or passively, by having the means available to prevent its conduct but not doing so. In such settings the state can be considered to be the legal author of the conduct undertaken by the non-state actor, which then provides apparent justification by reference to international law for another state to act in self-defence. Tams argues that the application of a complicity test offers a 'lower' attribution threshold compared to the 'effective control' test, whilst emphasising that a 'lower' threshold is not necessarily beneficial or desirable, especially considering the context that is essentially about what is legally permissible armed violence that results in death and destruction.[125] Lanovoy builds on this line of reasoning, arguing that the adoption of a complicity test with a supposedly lower attribution threshold is beneficial and desirable.[126] The supporting rationale is that because a complicity test apparently has a lower threshold than a control test, it allows attribution to apply more expansively. In the view of Lanovoy, this means responsibility gaps are more likely to be reduced because non-state actor conduct can now be attributed to states, making it less likely that responsibility cannot be established.[127] However, within such arguments there are conflations between the general international law governing state responsibility and the international law governing the use of force.

2.2. Complicity as a Distinct Basis for Determining Indirect State Responsibility

Complicity operating as a distinct basis for determining indirect state responsibility finds itself in the preparatory work of the ARSIWA, practice and literature.[128] Although this process can be termed attribution, it is not that of attribution *of conduct*, but that of attribution *of responsibility*. These are two separate processes for determining state responsibility, which can be conflated. Attribution of responsibility can be understood in either one of two ways within the international law applicable to determining state responsibility for non-state actors. The first is that the conduct of a non-state actor is attributed to the state through the application of an attribution of conduct test (eg one of those under Articles 4–11 of the ARSIWA), *and* that conduct has breached a primary rule obligation of the state in question,

[125] Tams (n 116) 385 and 381–87.
[126] Lanovoy (n 3) 307-329; Lanovoy (n 124).
[127] ibid.
[128] Fourth Report, Ago (1972) 128; Seventh Report, Ago (1978) 52–60; ILC Report, thirtieth session, 8 May–28 July 1978, UNGA, Thirty-Third Session, Supp No 10 (A/33/10), YBILC (1978) vol II(2), 99–105; Second Report, Crawford (1999) 47–51; KN Trapp, 'The Use of Force against Terrorists: A Reply to Christian J Tams' (2010) 20 *European Journal of International Law* 1049; KN Trapp, *State Responsibility for International Terrorism* (Oxford, Oxford University Press, 2011) 34–62; Crawford (n 16), 395–401; Jackson (n 3) 176–200; I Plakokefalos, 'The Use of Force by Non-state Actors and the Limits of Attribution of Conduct: A Reply to Vladyslav Lanovoy' (2017) 28 *European Journal of International Law* 587.

the combination of both leading to the attribution of responsibility to that state.[129] The second is that the state itself has breached a primary rule obligation, by, for example, failing to suppress or address conduct of a non-state actor that *is not* attributable to the state, meaning the international responsibility of the state is established through the content of the primary obligation in question. Both of these operations distinguish between *direct* state responsibility *for* wrongdoing and *indirect* state responsibility for *involvement in* wrongdoing.

Kimberley Trapp has emphasised that in drawing a distinction between direct and indirect state responsibility, complicity as basis for determining international responsibility belongs to the latter.[130] It is also worth restating that to do the opposite would be to blur, if not disregard, the distinction between primary and secondary rules. In this respect Ago's contribution to the law of state responsibility has been acknowledged as a 'stroke of genius'.[131] The conceptual clarity that comes with this distinction permits assessments regarding state responsibility for the conduct of non-state actors from becoming tangled in the primary rules that change depending on the issue at hand, whilst providing the opportunity for secondary rules to be applied consistently.[132] The distinction between primary and secondary rules thus appears to exist as an analytical tool to help 'navigate through the maze of conceptual confusion' that can arise when distinct bodies of law become applicable to a particular situation.[133] Conceptual clarity is at the heart of arguments favouring complicity operating as a distinct basis for determining indirect state responsibility, separate from that of attribution of conduct.

Monica Hakimi has also addressed the problems that come with conflating primary and secondary rules, particularly when applying complicity.[134] This work helps grasp the significance behind the point made by Jackson that complicity operates independently of agency relationships, to which the tests concerning attribution of conduct are related.[135] Attribution tests, including those under the ARSIWA, are 'conceptually distinct' from 'state complicity in the wrongdoing of another', as they 'do not seek to tie the accomplice to a separate wrong committed by a principal actor. Instead, they attribute the conduct of the principal actor to the state and, in doing so, give rise to state responsibility for that conduct in terms of the state's own primary obligations.'[136] Complicity allows for a determination to be made regarding the international responsibility of states for *their own* conduct that aided or assisted a principal wrong originating from a separate actor. To argue or assert that such involvement means that the applicable conduct of a non-state actor becomes the

[129] ARSIWA, Art 2, Commentary, paras 3–6.

[130] Trapp, *State Responsibility for International Terrorism* (n 128) 45 and 61.

[131] Trapp, 'The Use of Force against Terrorists: A Reply to Christian J. Tams' (n 128) 1055.

[132] CJ Tams, 'The Use of Force against Terrorists: A Rejoinder to Federico Sperotto and Kimberley N Trapp' (2010) 20 *European Journal of International Law* 1057, 1061; See also KN Trapp, 'Back to Basics: Necessity, Proportionality, and the Right of Self-defence against Non-state Terrorist Actors' (2007) 56 *ICLQ* 141.

[133] Plakokefalos (n 128) 589.

[134] Hakimi (n 40) 353–76.

[135] Jackson (n 3) 176–200.

[136] ibid 200.

conduct of the state providing aid or assistance to it would render states directly responsible for conduct that they did not perpetrate through one of their agents.[137]

2.3. Moving the Debate Along

State responsibility is a body of law in which rules 'are general and residual in their application'.[138] Complicity under the general international law of state responsibility operates independently of primary rules. Yet the creation of Article 16 drew on primary rules for inspiration.[139] The debate regarding how complicity should operate is understandable in light of such findings. In the hope of moving the debate along regarding complicity applying as an attribution test or as a distinct basis for determining indirect state responsibility for involvement in the wrongdoing of another actor, this section attempts to clarify how complicity should operate under the law of state responsibility as it applies to non-state actors, taking into account the arguments provided above.

State responsibility for complicity becomes a consideration when a state has provided aid or assistance to another actor that undertakes conduct contrary to an international rule or rules. The responsibility being assessed in any such case is that of the state rendering something that might have been a component of wrongdoing. The responsibility of the actor that was provided aid or assistance is relevant only with respect to the occurrence of a wrongful act for the assisting state to be complicit in. The relevant conduct of an allegedly complicit state is that of its own agent (providing the aid or assistance), which is attributable to it via one of the provisions within the ARSIWA or another attribution test.[140] The next component is the breach of a primary rule, which has occurred through the conduct of the assisted actor, resulting in the commission of an internationally wrongful act. Through its aid or assistance, the state has helped breach this primary rule, thus contributing to the principal wrong. It is this combination of conduct originating from one actor that was contrary to an international rule and the provision of aid or assistance by a state to that actor, which raises questions of state responsibility for complicity. Ago considered it 'impossible to conclude that the treatment by international law of complicity of any kind in a given act is necessarily the same as its treatment of the act itself'.[141] Complicity was treated by the ILC 'as an autonomous wrongful act' and continues to be considered as such at this time,[142] meaning the conduct of the actor that undertakes the principal wrong is not attributed to the state on the basis of a complicity test.[143] This is why

[137] ibid.

[138] Plakokefalos (n 128) 588.

[139] ARSIWA, Art 16, Commentary, para 2.

[140] This would function differently for omissions, where such questions would turn on whether a primary rule positive obligation had been breached, whether the omission itself could qualify as aid or assistance, or whether a state failed to exercise due diligence.

[141] Seventh Report, Ago (1978) 60.

[142] Graefrath (n 84) 380.

[143] V Lowe, 'Responsibility for the Conduct of Other States' (2002) 101 *Journal of International Law & Diplomacy* 1, 4.

complicity cases concern the indirect responsibility of assisting states, as they are not the principal wrongdoers.[144]

Alternatively, to have complicity apply as an attribution test would shift indirect responsibility to direct. Arguments favouring this approach can become strained if applied to the general international law governing state responsibility. This is particularly so when attempting to discern the difference between complicity and co-perpetration. It would be conceptually and practically difficult to differentiate between state responsibility for complicity and state responsibility for co-perpetration, if a complicity test were to operate under the law of state responsibility as one of attribution of conduct, as assessments for either complicity or co-perpetration would concern direct responsibility for wrongdoing. Should the attribution approach to complicity be adopted, there would exist no ground in which state responsibility could be determined for *involvement in* wrongdoing, whereas there are already a number of ways to determine state responsibility *for* wrongdoing through the application of one of the attribution tests under the ARSIWA or otherwise. Complicity may be viewed as conceptually 'analogous to' attribution in some respects, but this does not make them the same.[145] Nor does it mean they operate similarly.

A road towards the acceptance of complicity operating as an attribution test, one that would also prevent the conflation of primary and secondary rules,[146] is if such a test were *lex specialis* in nature, meaning it would not form part of the general international law on state responsibility, but would become part of whatever sub-field of international law was deemed appropriate.[147] This is where a complicity test in use of force in self-defence contexts becomes more plausible.[148] There exists evidence in state practice to show that 'non-state entities engaged in armed activities depend upon the active support, connivance, acquiescence, or collusion of a state to be able to subsist, flourish, and launch attacks against their targets'.[149] It may be considered 'undesirable' to have attribution of conduct tests that are primary rule-dependent, yet this does not mean it cannot happen.[150] Article 55 of the ARSIWA is a testament to the premise that primary rule-specific attribution tests can develop. While such tests appear to be developing,[151] attribution is a core component of the international law governing state responsibility, 'where *lex specialis* should not be accepted lightly'.[152]

144 ARSIWA, Art 16, Commentary, para 11.

145 Second Report, Crawford (1999) 47.

146 E de Wet, 'The Invocation of the Right to Self-defence in Response to Armed Attacks Conducted by Armed Groups: Implications for Attribution' (2019) 32 *Leiden Journal of International Law* 91.

147 N Tsagourias, 'Self-defence against Non-state Actors: The Interaction between Self-defence as a Primary Rule and Self-defence as a Secondary Rule' (2016) 29 *Leiden Journal of International Law* 801, 806–07.

148 M Hmoud, 'Are New Principles Really Needed? The Potential of the Established Distinction Between Responsibility for Attacks by Nonstate Actors and the Law of Self-defense' (2013) 107 *American Journal of International Law* 576.

149 IM Lobo De Souza, 'Revisiting the Right of Self-defence against Non-state Armed Entities' (2015) 53 *Canadian Yearbook of International Law* 202, 203.

150 M Milanovic, 'Self-defense and Non-state Actors: Indeterminacy and the Jus ad Bellum' *EJIL: Talk!* (21 February 2010) www.ejiltalk.org/self-defense-and-non-state-actors-indeterminacy-and-the-jus-ad-bellum/.

151 Milanovic (n 115).

152 Milanovic (n 150).

One reason for this is that if more special attribution tests develop in other fields of international law, then the law governing state responsibility will become more fragmented. Instead of having a set of attribution tests that are generally applicable to an array of different instances concerning the international responsibility of states, which apply independently of what primary rules are at issue, there could exist different tests across each sub-field of international law. The law of state responsibility in such a reality would begin to become an indistinct field of international law, one that would be dependent upon what other international rules were applicable in a particular case. Although the current general framework of state responsibility is not always applied consistently, it is a constant. One that helps maintain a measure of cohesion in a legal order that aspires to be universal in some sense.

Another issue with special attribution tests, including one based on a complicity test under the international law governing use of force in self-defence, is the foggy normative foundations that justify their existence and application.[153] Why should a specific attribution test, whether based on a complicity assessment or otherwise, exist in the international law governing the use of force, but not exist in the international law governing, say, human rights? And if such tests existed, why should they differ in the threshold that determines when a state should be considered the legal author of conduct? While arguments favouring the application of special attribution tests may be focused on reducing or eradicating responsibility gaps, it is hard to grasp why such gaps should only be addressed if particular primary rules are applicable. Perhaps if there are sector-specific rules considered by some to be hierarchically more important than others they could have corresponding attribution tests that were tailored to reflect their comparatively higher level of importance?[154] Yet a risk with such an approach to attribution is responsibility gaps not being appropriately addressed, if at all, depending on the sub-field at issue, with a different treatment occurring each time there was a change in the applicable sector-specific rule. In addition, although prevalent, attribution is not the be all and end all of the applicable law that can be brought to bear on questions of state responsibility for the conduct of non-state actors and the occurrence of responsibility gaps. Even if conduct of a non-state actor is not attributable to a state, this does not automatically mean a responsibility gap will exist. Primary rules themselves can address such gaps through applicable positive obligations.[155]

There are further issues with applying complicity as an attribution of conduct test. One assumption that supposedly supports this operation is knowledge being 'all' that would be required to attribute the conduct of a non-state actor to a state, which, apparently, sets a 'lower' attribution threshold than 'effective control'.[156] However, if the above analysis has shown anything, it is that establishing the requisite degree of knowledge held by a state can be difficult. Relating to the discussion in chapter 5, when considered in the abstract, a complicity test adopting a threshold of

[153] For further engagement with this matter, see Milanovic (n 115) 385–88.

[154] See P Weil, 'Towards Relative Normativity in International Law?' (1983) 77 *American Journal of International Law* 413.

[155] See also Mackenzie-Gray Scott (n 38).

[156] Lanovoy (n 3) 328–29.

knowledge alone under the mental requirement is also no more or less likely to result in attribution taking place than if Article 8 of the ARSIWA were applied to assess the same relationship between a state and a non-state actor, or if any of the other attribution tests under the ARSIWA or elsewhere were applied, which is a consideration that such arguments can overlook.[157] Likelihood of attributability is determined by the specific sets of facts upon which attribution tests can be applied.[158] Even if a complicity-based attribution test did have a 'less demanding' threshold than other tests when comparing them, why would such an attribution threshold be desirable in the abstract, and, more importantly, in specific contexts, for example, those determining whether the use of force is considered to be legally permissible?

Attribution determines on what basis a state can be considered the legal author of conduct, the tests for which decide when a particular actor is or is not acting on behalf of a state.[159] This legal authorship approach to determining state responsibility is not the same as complicity. Complicity addresses state responsibility for involvement in wrongdoing, in particular when a state has provided something to another actor that can be construed as aid or assistance.[160] Those favouring an attribution of conduct operation of complicity appear to oppose the idea of a test analogous to Article 16 that incorporates non-state actors because of the general inability of non-state actors to bear international legal obligations.[161] However, such an approach is not 'largely unworkable' in settings where non-state actors do bear international legal obligations.[162] It is also worth considering the potential that comes with tweaking the opposability requirement. Instead of requiring that the non-state actor in question be bound by and breach an international rule, it would instead be required that if the assisting state were to take the place of the assisted non-state actor, the same conduct would breach the applicable international rule at issue because that state has a legal obligation under it. Considering that the ILC and others understand state responsibility for complicity as a distinct internationally wrongful act, it seems to be superfluous to require that in order for such an internationally wrongful act to occur, another, separate internationally wrongful act needs to occur.

On the whole, when considering the operation of a complicity test under the law of state responsibility as it applies to non-state actors, it suffices to say that this consideration comes down to the distinction between direct and indirect international responsibility and that between primary and secondary rules. While there are reasons to be hesitant towards the outright rejection of the idea that complicity can operate as an attribution test,[163] in light of the analysis above it is now hopefully

[157] R Mackenzie-Gray Scott, 'Complicity and its Limits in the Law of International Responsibility' (2017) 66 *ICLQ* 1009, 1010.

[158] See chapter 8, section 1.

[159] R Lawson, 'Out of Control. State Responsibility and Human Rights: Will the ILC's Definition of the "Act of State" Meet the Challenges of the 21st Century?' in M Castermans-Holleman, F Van Hoof and J Smith (eds), *The Role of the Nation-State in the 21st Century: Human Rights, International Organisations and Foreign Policy – Essays in Honour of Peter Baehr* (The Hague, Kluwer, 1998) 91, 93–98.

[160] Crawford (n 16) 395-401.

[161] Lanovoy (n 3) 309; Lanovoy, 'Complicity in an Internationally Wrongful Act' (n 18) 159; Amoroso (n 116) 994.

[162] This point is explored further below.

[163] See Jackson (n 3) 200.

clearer that under the international law applicable to determining state responsibility for the conduct of non-state actors, it is more appropriate for complicity to operate as a secondary rule used to determine the indirect responsibility of a state for ancillary involvement in conduct that is contrary to an international rule.

3. THE FOUNDATIONS OF A GENERAL COMPLICITY RULE THAT INCORPORATES NON-STATE ACTORS

Having now shown what the requirements would likely be for determining state responsibility for complicity in conduct undertaken by a non-state actor that is contrary to an international rule, and offering some insights that hopefully clarify how complicity operates under the general international law applicable to determining state responsibility for the conduct of non-state actors, the contours of a complicity test that incorporates non-state actors can be examined. This section first canvasses a premise underpinning the creation of such a test, before assessing how far it would likely extend in the international law of today. The extent to which non-state actors were included in the preparatory work of Article 16 is then considered further, providing an appreciation for the antecedents of a complicity test that addresses the relationships between states and non-state actors. Finally, in order to get a better handle on whether this proposed test is an actual rule of international law, an examination of state practice is conducted with respect to state aid or assistance rendered to non-state actors that undertake conduct contrary to international rules

3.1. Premise behind an Analogue to Article 16

The idea behind an analogue test to Article 16 that incorporates non-state actors, and such a test being workable, stems from several factors. The ARSIWA was not intended to be, and is not, an all-embracing reflection of all the possible rules governing state responsibility. The law in this area need not be sclerotic, and would do well not to fall victim to the consequences of inertia. When reflecting on the material analysed by the ILC, it is evident that the ARSIWA provisions are wide-ranging, but not exhaustive. There exists the possibility for new rules to develop within the general framework governing state responsibility. New rules are developing in other areas addressing international responsibility, as evidenced by the creation of the ARIO. Article 14 of the ARIO in particular addresses complicity with respect to an intergovernmental organisation that provides aid or assistance to a state or another intergovernmental organisation that undertakes conduct contrary to an international rule.[164]

[164] ARIO, Art 14, which reads: 'An international organization which aids or assists a State or another international organization in the commission of an internationally wrongful act by the State or the latter organization is internationally responsible for doing so if: (a) the former organization does so with knowledge of the circumstances of the internationally wrongful act; and (b) the act would be internationally wrongful if committed by that organization.'

To theoretically exclude the inverse defies logic: if the international responsibility of an intergovernmental organisation can be established for the commission of an internationally wrongful act, there is no reason why the international responsibility of a state cannot be established for complicity if it aided or assisted its commission, which is why Article 58 of the ARIO addresses this matter.[165] Going a step further, why should this logic end at intergovernmental organisations, and not extend to relationships between states and non-state actors?

States are no longer the only entities that bear international legal obligations. During the drafting of the ARSIWA, the question of whether, and the extent to which, non-state actors have international legal obligations was more contentious than it is today.[166] Although at this time non-state actors are not generally bound by international law, there are specific settings whereby they do bear international legal obligations.[167] Even the ICJ, the choirmaster of the mainstream voices of international law, appears to provide further space for the international law governing state responsibility for complicity to develop in order to better address state complicity in non-state actor wrongdoing. The Court in its engagement with the obligation of the prohibition on genocide shows that the Genocide Convention prohibits complicity in genocide, regardless of what status the actor that commits genocide is considered to be from the perspective of international law, whether a state, non-state actor or otherwise.[168] The ICJ also directed Serbia to

> ensure that any military, paramilitary or irregular armed units which may be directed *or supported* by it, as well as any organizations and persons which may be subject to its control, direction *or influence*, do not commit any acts of genocide.[169]

It is important to note that this position of the ICJ was based on the text of the Genocide Convention and not on a secondary complicity rule. Although there is minimal indication from this ruling that non-state actors can bear international obligations generally, even if they do so regarding the prohibition on genocide, as far as state responsibility for complicity is concerned, this consideration of whether the actor perpetrating conduct has breached an international legal obligation appears not to matter. What matters for the purposes of determining state responsibility for complicity in genocide is that acts of genocide occur, and the state in question has somehow aided or assisted those acts.[170] This understanding fits with the tweaking

[165] ARIO, Art 58, which reads: '1. A State which aids or assists an international organization in the commission of an internationally wrongful act by the latter is internationally responsible for doing so if: (a) the State does so with knowledge of the circumstances of the internationally wrongful act; and (b) the act would be internationally wrongful if committed by that State. 2. An act by a State member of an international organization done in accordance with the rules of the organization does not as such engage the international responsibility of that State under the terms of this article.'

[166] R Goodman and V Lanovoy, 'State Responsibility for Assisting Armed Groups: A Legal Risk Analysis' *Just Security* (22 December 2016) www.justsecurity.org/35790/state-responsibility-aiding-assisting-armed-groups-legal-risk-analysis/.

[167] See chapter 1, section 2.1.

[168] *Bosnia Genocide*, Judgment, 26 February 2007, paras 419–21.

[169] *Bosnia Genocide*, Order for Provisional Measures, 8 April 1993, ICJ Rep [1993] 3, para 52 (emphasis added).

[170] For further analysis on state complicity in genocide, see Jackson (n 3) 202–14.

of the opposability requirement outlined above, again highlighting that the international responsibility of a state for complicity in conduct contrary to an international rule undertaken by a non-state actor may be established even if the non-state actor in question cannot technically breach the applicable rule at issue.

Even if this proposal on the tweaking of the opposability requirement is considered to be unworkable and/or too radical by those that decide what creations become part of international law or not, non-state actors can still be bound by international obligations, meaning international responsibility can be established for complicity if states aid or assist these actors in such breaches. The mainstream approach to the opposability requirement under an analogue test to Article 16 that incorporates non-state actors therefore remains feasible considering the international obligations borne by non-state actors today.[171] Yet it has been noted that states and non-state actors are 'rarely if ever bound by the same obligations'.[172] While there are examples that can prove and disprove this point, perhaps a middle ground between those that believe the international law on state responsibility for complicity should extend no further than governing the interactions between states, and those that believe the international law on state responsibility for complicity should also govern the interactions between states and non-state actors, can be that wherever 'international law imposes obligations on non-state actors, so state complicity in violations thereof would give rise to international responsibility'.[173]

What a state can do through the conduct of an actor considered to be acting on its behalf, whether this actor is labelled a state organ, official or agent, a non-state actor can do. States and non-state actors can, and do, commit materially similar acts.[174] The state-centric version of the international law story is a fairly popular one, so much so that when considering the notion that states can be involved in wrongdoing without undertaking the wrongdoing themselves, the ILC decided to limit the complicity test it created to the interactions between states. Yet the abstract state has not existed for as long as actors that can be considered to be non-state actors, such as human beings. The key difference between an actor that is considered to officially represent a state and one that is considered not to is another intersubjective construct: a law. Whether this law is domestic, stipulating that a particular actor should be considered to be a state organ, or international, stipulating that the actor is deemed to be acting on behalf of the state because the threshold of a particular attribution test has been satisfied, states and non-state actors need not be different – they are just classified differently by those that wield the power (but not necessarily the authority) to do so by implementing ideas such as arbitrary line-drawing on maps and calling them borders on the assumption they should be treated as such.[175] So long as domestic law stipulates that a particular actor

[171] See, for example, those under international humanitarian law and (arguably) human rights law respectively in S Sivakumaran, *The Law of Non-International Armed Conflict* (Oxford, Oxford University Press, 2012) and A Clapham (ed), *Human Rights and Non-State Actors* (Cheltenham, Edward Elgar, 2013).

[172] Lanovoy, 'Complicity in an Internationally Wrongful Act' (n 18) 159.

[173] Jackson (n 3) 202. This logic is also supported in Art 16, Commentary, para 11.

[174] E de Wet, 'Complicity in Violations of Human Rights and Humanitarian Law by Incumbent Governments Through Direct Military Assistance on Request' (2018) 67 *ICLQ* 287.

[175] See J McLean, 'Problems of Translation – The State in Domestic and International Public Law and Beyond' in H Charlesworth, M Chiam, D Hovell and G Williams (eds), *The Fluid State: International*

officially acts on behalf of the state, then the actor in question can be anything, whether a robot community support officer, a military service dog or a piece of malware – not that this last one is likely to be encoded in domestic law in a way that signifies the software officially represents the state (but you never know). If there is no domestic law stipulating that a particular actor acts on behalf of a state, then international law might be able to show the same if the threshold of a particular attribution test is satisfied.

The point being made is that even if applicable domestic and international laws are stripped away, actors can be exactly the same, and undertake exactly the same conduct. It is questionable why it should matter so much to the international law applicable to determining state responsibility for complicity what status an actor holds in the eyes of the creations under a particular domestic legal system, if that actor is undertaking conduct that is contrary to an international rule and the state in question appears to be aiding or assisting it. Examined in such a light, the version of the complicity test created by the ILC and enshrined in Article 16 could understandably be conceived as limited. By the time the ILC finalised the ARSIWA, the state-centric story of international law was already beginning to crumble. States continue to be 'joined by powerful non-state actors as potential violators of fundamental international norms'.[176] Upon reflecting on the history of the development of complicity under the law of state responsibility it remains difficult to this day to disagree with the point made by Vaughan Lowe in 2002 regarding the efforts of the ILC, namely that the Commission

> laboured throughout half a century in which the archetypal nation State, the building-block of classical international law, was at its zenith, only to produce its Draft Articles on State Responsibility at a time when it had become painfully clear that the nation State was already in terminal decline.[177]

States do not retain a monopoly on conduct that legal rules attempt to regulate. A general complicity test that incorporates non-state actors reflects this reality. Yet whether such a test becomes an actual rule of international law is for others to decide. In so doing, the analysis below may be worth a swatch.

3.2. Further Considerations in Light of the Preparatory Work on Article 16

The idea of a complicity test under the law of state responsibility applying to non-state actors was instilled in the work of the ILC. Ago highlighted instances of practice showing states that assisted non-state actors that undertook wrongful conduct.[178]

Law and National Legal Systems (Sydney, Federation Press, 2005) 210, 226; TJ Bassett, 'Cartography and Empire Building in Nineteenth-Century West Africa' (1994) 84 *Geographical Review* 316.

[176] Jackson (n 3) 215.

[177] Lowe (n 143) 2.

[178] Fourth Report, Ago (1972) vol II, 102, 103, 120; Fifth Report, State Responsibility, Roberto Ago, A/CN.4/291 and Add 1 & 2 and Corr 1, YBILC (1976) vol II(1), 36, 37, 50; Eighth Report, State Responsibility, Roberto Ago, A/CN.4/318 and Add 1–4, YBILC (1979) vol II(1), 32.

However, at that time these wrongs did not constitute internationally wrongful acts, prompting recognition that:

> Cases in which a State incurs international responsibility for the act of a subject of international law other than a State (eg an international organization or an insurrectional movement), although intellectually conceivable, are not covered, because there are no known cases in which this has actually happened.[179]

The notion of non-state actors bearing international legal obligations during the time in which Article 16 was being drafted was not settled, which appears to be a key reason why they remained excluded from drafts of the provision, even though actors other than states were recognised as subjects of international law bearing some measure of legal personality. It was also noted:

> The study of international practice could, however, show that the acts of private individuals are never taken into account in determining the international responsibility of the State unless they are accompanied by certain actions or omissions of organs of the State. This should not automatically lead us to exclude the possibility of attributing the action of an individual to the State. Inded [sic], it could be so attributed, but only in cases where it it [sic] specifically characterized by a measure of participation or complicity on the part of State organs. There is no need, at this juncture, to establish the forms that such 'participation' or 'complicity' should take, but only to emphazise [sic] that the acts in question should, of course, really conform to such definitions. Nor should time be spent discussing the objection, already referred to above, that, since a private individual cannot violate an international obligation, complicity between the individual and the State for the purpose of such a violation would be inconceivable. As has already been shown, when the State endorses the act of an individual it is the State itself which acts, both through the individual and through the organs which are 'accomplices'; the idea of such complicity would thus be quite conceivable. What should really be pointed out however, is that the conclusion envisaged should always include the idea that the State endorses the act of the individual as such, where certain State organs have in some way connived at that act. The action of an individual would be the basis of the internationally wrongful conduct of the State, and the State would violate an international obligation through the action of an individual in which certain organs were merely accomplices.[180]

Although complicity and attribution were mixed together here, the general premise of the provided reasoning was open to the idea that a complicity assessment could apply to the interactions between states and non-state actors when determining state responsibility.[181] Riphagen also acknowledged the possibility of a complicity test that incorporated non-state actors when he questioned whether aid or assistance provided by a state to peoples that had survived colonial oppression could, in the course of emancipating themselves from the coloniser state in a way that threatened

[179] Eighth Report (ibid) 5.

[180] Fourth Report, Ago (1972) 96.

[181] This approach was similar to that of arbitral tribunals in the nineteenth and twentieth century: *Cotesworth and Powell* (*Britain v Colombia*, 1875) 2 *International Arbitrations* 2050, 2082; *The Montijo* (*United States v Colombia*, 1875) 2 *International Arbitrations* 1421, 1438; *Poglioli* (*Italy v Venezuela*, 1903) 10 *Reports of International Arbitral Awards* 669, 689; *Narcisa de Hammer* (*United States v Venezuela*, 1885) 3 *International Arbitrations* 2969; *Janes and others* (*United States v Mexico*, 1925) 4 *Reports of International Arbitral Awards* 82, 89–90.

its territorial integrity and political independence, incur issues regarding state responsibility for such aid or assistance.[182] Arangio-Ruiz also pointed to an example of possible state complicity in non-state actor wrongdoing that concerned the former Yugoslavia's 'assistance to irregular Serbian units' participating in acts of aggression.[183]

Crawford took a different view. His reports make no indication towards a complicity test applying outside state-to-state parameters. He was against incorporating non-state actors, primarily because of their general inability to function as subjects of the international legal system that are capable of bearing and breaching direct legal obligations.[184] Although there are exceptions and things could change further into the future, resting an argument against the incorporation of non-state actors on them not having the same measure of legal personality as states misses a point. The discussion focused on tweaking the opposability requirement highlights that so long as there has been conduct contrary to an international rule and a state has aided or assisted its commission, a general complicity test can apply to determine the international responsibility of that state regardless of the status of the actor that undertook the conduct, which as noted previously depends on necessary, but sometimes nonetheless arbitrary, distinctions being made through domestic or international law. Whether the debates surrounding the idea of non-state actors bearing international legal obligations put a leash on the discourse within the ILC when creating its complicity provision, its final text and commentary do not reflect the extent to which non-state actors were considered in the preparatory stages. Although critiques regarding 'the limited ambition of Article 16' are understandable,[185] should a complicity rule that incorporates non-state actors come into existence within the law of state responsibility, the efforts of the ILC will form part of its antecedents. The question remaining is if such a test exists as part of positive law today.

3.3. Evidence of a Developing Complicity Rule that Incorporates Non-state Actors

States render aid or assistance to a variety of non-state actors. It can come in the form of providing military equipment to groups opposing a government, offering diplomatic protection to private investors, or humanitarian assistance to workers of non-governmental organisations. When outcomes occur in which assisted non-state actors have undertaken conduct that is not contrary to international rules, states in turn do not risk their international responsibility being established for complicity. But when non-state actors do undertake conduct that is contrary to international rules that has been facilitated by states providing aid or assistance to them, state responsibility for complicity becomes a concern. Situations of this type are not

[182] Fourth Report on the content, forms and degrees of international responsibility by Willem Riphagen, A/CN.4/366 and Add 1 & Add 1/Corr 1, YBILC (1983) vol II(1), 13.

[183] Seventh Report, State Responsibility, Gaetano Arangio-Ruiz, A/CN.4/469 and Add 1–2, YBILC (1995) vol II(1), 19.

[184] Goodman and Lanovoy (n 166).

[185] ibid.

uncommon. For example, it has been reported that Russia has provided weapons, logistical support and training to non-state actors operating in Eastern Ukraine that have killed thousands and displaced millions.[186] Another example is the United States training and arming non-state actors fighting in Syria that have been involved in possible breaches of rules under international humanitarian law.[187] China provides fishing vessels that are non-state actors with intelligence information, which are part of the state's so-called 'maritime militia' that reportedly harasses vessels from other states.[188] Colombia appeared to support Chiquita Brands, which was accused of being involved in killing hundreds of its workers.[189]

The method of examining state practice has a number of potential benefits in light of these situations and many others. It can help discern the extent to which there is a need for a general complicity rule that incorporates non-state actors, whilst uncovering whether an analogue to Article 16 would apply in a similar manner as the ILC intended this provision to apply. This is particularly important with respect to clarifying whether a new rule would impose an international obligation on states not to aid or assist non-state actors that undertake conduct contrary to international rules, or would instead be used to determine state responsibility for complicity based on the application of the requirements examined above and/or others. If the former, difficulties could arise in assessing whether any state claim (along the lines of 'states should not aid or assist non-state actors undertaking conduct contrary to international rules') arose because of their belief in an existing general rule and thereby indicating opinio juris, or because it is considered to be a good policy choice. If the latter however, in that such a rule would not impose any legal obligations not to aid or assist wrongdoing but instead be used to determine international responsibility for doing so, then it would be simpler to distinguish such a rule from policy. For instance, if a state or a group of states were to claim that another state should be held internationally responsible for its assistance to a non-state actor that undertook wrongdoing, that would be more indicative of a possible rule than claims along the lines that states should not provide aid or assistance to non-state actors undertaking wrongdoing, which is ambiguous, and could mean the existence of an obligation (and not necessarily one that is secondary in nature), or a principled policy choice, in that states should not aid or assist non-state actors committing wrongs, or that are likely to commit wrongs, because it is bad policy, including in terms of the potential political or other repercussions that could ensue from doing so. The other related difficulty in examining state practice is differentiating between whether states consider aid or

[186] Council on Foreign Relations, Global Conflict Tracker, 'Conflict in Ukraine' (2 March 2018) www.cfr.org/interactives/global-conflict-tracker?marker=7#!/conflict/conflict-in-ukraine.

[187] Council on Foreign Relations, Global Conflict Tracker, 'Civil War in Syria' (2 March 2018) www.cfr.org/interactives/global-conflict-tracker?marker=7#!/conflict/civil-war-in-syria.

[188] AS Erickson, 'Understanding China's Third Sea Force: The Maritime Militia' (8 September 2017), Fairbank Center for Chinese Studies, Harvard University, https://medium.com/fairbank-center/understanding-chinas-third-sea-force-the-maritime-militia-228a2bfbbedd; see also AS Erickson and CM Kennedy, 'China's Maritime Militia: What It Is and How to Deal With It *Foreign Affairs* (23 June 2016) www.foreignaffairs.com/articles/china/2016-06-23/chinas-maritime-militia.

[189] Associated Press, 'Victims of Colombian Conflict Sue Chiquita Brands' *New York Times* (15 November 2007) www.nytimes.com/2007/11/15/business/worldbusiness/15chiquita.html.

assistance to conduct that is claimed to be internationally wrongful because of a new secondary complicity rule developing, or because of a breach of an applicable primary rule.

Nonetheless, the method of scrutinising state practice has the potential to offer authoritative evidence on two matters that are presently obscure. The first is whether the opposability requirement would form part of a general complicity rule at all, or whether it would apply akin to the ILC approach, the tweaking approach set out above or something else. If states consider one another to have been involved in what they term violations/breaches/infringements of international law for aid or assistance rendered to non-state actors that are not bound by the same (or any) rules as the assisting state in question, then this would indicate that states do not view the opposability requirement as necessary under a general complicity rule. Although this may be unlikely considering the perceived need for there to be an occurrence of an internationally wrongful act on the part of the assisted actor in order for state responsibility for complicity to ensue as a matter of general international law, should some understanding develop among states that aligns with the tweaking approach to the opposability requirement, then the occurrence of an internationally wrongful act would still exist on the part of states that render aid or assistance to non-state actors that undertake conduct contrary to international rules, even if such non-state actors do not bear international legal obligations with respect to those rules.

3.3.1. A New and Emerging Complicity Rule?

There is some state practice evidencing the possible formation of new complicity rule as part of customary international law that engages with the issue of state complicity in non-state actor wrongdoing. This practice is separate from that referred to in the preparatory work of Article 16. A widespread piece of such practice is the adoption of UNGA Resolution 2625, which states:

> Every State has the duty to refrain from organizing, instigating, assisting or participating in acts of civil strife or terrorist acts in another State or acquiescing in organized activities within its territory directed towards the commission of such acts.[190]

Such resolutions are helpful in establishing the existence of an international customary rule and opinio juris.[191] A key factor with this resolution is that the conduct of non-state actors within this resolution is qualified, to the extent that such conduct relates to the use of force. Its language also points to the possibility that an international legal obligation is imposed on states not to aid or assist non-state actors that

[190] UNGA Res 2625 (XXV), UN Doc A/RES/25/2625 (24 October 1970).

[191] *Legality of the Threat or Use of Nuclear Weapons*, Advisory Opinion, 8 July 1996, ICJ Rep [1996] 226, paras 70–71; see also LR Helfer and IB Wuerth, 'Customary International Law: An Instrument Choice Perspective' (2016) 37 *Michigan Journal of International Law* 563, 576–603; SM Schwebel, 'The Effect of Resolutions of the UN General Assembly on Customary International Law' (1979) *Proceedings of the ASIL Annual Meeting*, vol 73, 301; J Higashi, 'The Role of Resolutions of the United Nations General Assembly in the Formative Process of International Customary Law' (1982) 25 *Japanese Annual of International Law* 11.

are engaged in violent conduct. This potential obligation is also referred to later in the resolution: '[N]o State shall organize, assist, foment, finance, incite or tolerate subversive, terrorist or armed activities directed towards the violent overthrow of the regime of another State, or interfere in civil strife in another State.'[192] An issue with this example is the difficulty of not being able to clarify that the rule is primary or secondary, although this resolution could well be evidence suggestive of both. Resolution 2625 was adopted without a vote, pointing towards at least some measure of its content being accepted by states. Yet it cannot be established from this UNGA resolution alone whether the complicity rule it appears to suggest existed at that time, which maybe still exists today, addresses the use of force exclusively or is more general in nature, extending to the law governing state responsibility for the conduct of non-state actors, or both.

A clearer example is General Comment 36,[193] which states: 'States also have obligations under international law not to aid or assist activities undertaken by other States and non-State actors that violate the right to life.'[194] Those involved in formulating General Comment 36 provide further insight on this statement in an interview.[195] In this interview it was asked:

> The Comment [shown above] does not cite prior Concluding Observations or Views of the Committee in the note accompanying this proposition, but instead refers to the International Law Commission's Articles on State Responsibility and the International Court of Justice's Bosnia Genocide Case. Is it fair to read General Comment 36 as recognition that as a matter of customary international law the rule in Article 16 of the Articles of State Responsibility may also apply to State aid and assistance to non-State actors?[196]

The answer:

> To the extent that international law imposes on non-state actors' obligations to respect and ensure the right [to] life, the Committee was of the view that there is no reason to limit the duty on state parties not to aid or assist to violations of relevant obligations by other states only. In adopting this approach, the Committee has followed the decision of the ICJ in Genocide (Bosnian & Herzegovina v Serbia), which similarly drew inspiration from article 16 to analyze the notion of complicity in genocide. Although it did not purport to offer a new interpretation of article 16, its position can be regarded as supportive of the need for such a new interpretation.[197]

These insights on General Comment 36 show that as a matter of international custom, a general complicity rule that incorporates non-state actors appears to be developing and is perceived as necessary. It also suggests that such a rule could end up mirroring

[192] UNGA Res 2625 (1970).
[193] General Comment No 36 on Article 6 of the International Covenant on Civil and Political Rights, on the right to life, CCPR/C/GC/36 (30 October 2018).
[194] ibid para 63.
[195] R Goodman, 'Human Rights, Deprivation of Life and National Security: Q&A with Christof Heyns and Yuval Shany on General Comment 36' *Just Security* (4 February 2019) www.justsecurity.org/62467/human-life-national-security-qa-christof-heyns-yuval-shany-general-comment-36/.
[196] ibid.
[197] ibid.

the opposability requirement under Article 16, in that the international responsibility of states for complicity in non-state actor wrongdoing would be limited to instances in which non-state actors bear and breach an international legal obligation. This example from practice is also limited to state responsibility for complicity in non-state actor conduct that concerns the legal obligations pertaining to the human right not to be arbitrarily deprived of life, even though the Committee used Article 16 for inspiration. This means the apparent complicity rule expounded here does not in and of itself equal the existence of a general rule on complicity under the law of state responsibility, especially considering the former sets out a primary legal obligation not to aid or assist wrongdoing and the latter would be a secondary rule for determining international responsibility should states end up doing so.

However, there are further examples from practice that support the possibility that a general complicity rule that incorporates non-state actors is developing. Within the context of the Syrian conflict, Austria issued a position paper concerning a proposal to lift a EU arms embargo.[198] Austria considered it to be the case that if the embargo was lifted, EU 'Member States supplying arms to the Syrian opposition would incur State responsibility for aiding and assisting in the commission of internationally wrongful acts'.[199] Austria envisages this complicity rule being similar in form to Article 16, as it refers to the provision's requirements ('principles'), but applies them by analogy to determining state complicity in the wrongful conduct of non-state actors:

> When applying these principles to the envisaged supply of arms to the Syrian opposition, it is to be considered that war crimes, including murder, extrajudicial killings and torture, are perpetrated by anti-Government armed groups in Syria, as reported by the UN Commission of Inquiry, as well as suicide bombings and attacks against and hostage-taking of UNDOF peacekeeper, as is known from the daily news. Should supplied arms be used by armed opposition groups in Syria in the commission of internationally wrongful acts, the States who had supplied these arms and had knowledge of these acts would incur State responsibility for their aid and assistance in the commission of such acts.[200]

The position of Austria could not be clearer. As with General Comment 36, it is based on the premise that so long as an internationally wrongful act occurs, the international responsibility of a state can be established for complicity in that act, regardless of the legal status of the actor committing the wrongdoing. This example of state practice and opinio juris shows that should non-state actors breach an international rule, any state that has knowledge of such conduct and supplies aid or assistance to those actors can have its international responsibility established for complicity.

It appears that no other EU Member State publicly denounced or challenged the Austrian statement,[201] which could indicate their tacit consent and acceptance by

[198] J Borger, 'The Austrian Position on Arms Embargo in Syria – Official Document' *The Guardian* (15 May 2013) www.theguardian.com/world/julian-borger-global-security-blog/interactive/2013/may/15/austria-eu-syria-arms-embargo-pdf.

[199] ibid 3.

[200] ibid.

[201] EU Council Decision 2013/109/CFSP amending Decision 2012/739/CFSP concerning restrictive measures against Syria (28 February 2013).

acquiescence of the rule set out by Austria.[202] The acquiescence of states towards the position of another state can be evidence of a developing customary rule.[203] In discerning whether such a rule in fact exists, according to Anthea Roberts and Sandesh Sivakumaran, the approach that 'makes most sense' is when states 'initially acting assert that this is the law (whether they believe it to be or not) and, if others accept that assertion as law, it becomes so'.[204] Austria clearly articulated what it considers the law to be with respect to state responsibility for complicity in the wrongdoing of non-state actors, setting out a threshold of what is and is not lawfully permissible in terms of state aid or assistance to non-state actors, and appears to have conducted itself in this context under the pretext of, and in line with, an existing international rule, instead of its conduct 'being undertaken merely out of courtesy or comity'.[205] While there are issues with a handful of states creating customary rules that other states 'tacitly accept' or 'acquiesce' to through their own lack of response, this process is currently part of lawmaking at the international level.[206] Although the apparent tradition of customary law being 'made by a few interested states for all' should change so that states can have a fuller say in shaping international rules that affect the lives of those they govern, a developing rule can come to become considered customary by way of state silence.[207] Reflected on in this light, the Austrian position on the arms embargo could be pointing to nascent custom of a complicity rule that incorporates non-state actors.

More ambiguous state practice can be found in the accusations of Guinea against Liberia and Burkina Faso for their alleged complicity in attacks on border villages resulting in hundreds of deaths.[208] These killings occurred at the hands of non-state 'armed insurgents', which Guinea claimed were supported by the two states.[209] Guinea used the precise language of 'complicity' when alluding to the international responsibility of Liberia and Burkina Faso for their apparent involvement in the wrongdoing of the non-state actors.[210] Although the precise accusation of complicity is telling, there is not much more in this case that is suggestive of a general rule governing state aid or assistance to non-state actors existing in positive international law.

Another less clear example comes from the High Court of Ireland in the *Horgan* case, which concerned the use of force by the United States and the United Kingdom in the context of the Iraq war.[211] A claim was brought against Ireland for its alleged

[202] Establishing customary international law in this way is significant and has the potential to affect the legality of a broad spectrum of state conduct. See, for example, E Schweiger, 'The Risks of Remaining Silent: International Law Formation and the EU Silence on Drone Killings' (2015) 1 *Global Affairs* 269.

[203] J Kammerhofer, 'Uncertainty in the Formal Sources of International Law: Customary International Law and Some of its Problems' (2004) 15 *European Journal of International Law* 523, 533; DJ Bederman, 'Acquiescence, Objection and the Death of Customary International Law' (2010) 21 *Duke Journal of Comparative & International Law* 31, 34–45.

[204] A Roberts and S Sivakumaran, 'The Theory and Reality of the Sources of International Law' in MD Evans (ed), *International Law*, 5th edn (Oxford, Oxford University Press, 2018) 89, 96.

[205] ibid.

[206] Helfer and Wuerth (n 191) 570.

[207] JI Charney, 'Universal International Law' (1993) 87 *American Journal of International Law* 529, 538.

[208] UN Yearbook (2000) vol 54, 182.

[209] ibid.

[210] ibid.

[211] *Horgan v Ireland* [2003] IEHC 64.

complicity in conduct that was contrary to international rules. During proceedings it was pointed out that a state 'cannot provide aid or assistance to a belligerent engaged in armed conflict unless it has concluded that the involvement of that belligerent in the armed conflict is lawful'.[212] As the Court did not elaborate on this point, whether the 'belligerents' referred to can include non-state actors is unclear. In addition, the term 'cannot provide' appears to show that the references to state complicity arose from applicable primary rules and not a general complicity rule. A separate case involving the question of whether states not party to an armed conflict can have their international responsibility established for aid or assistance rendered to parties of the conflict raised similar points before the German courts.[213]

A clearer example provided by examining domestic law is the *McDonald* case.[214] This case concerned the alleged complicity of Libya in the internationally wrongful acts of the Provisional Irish Republican Army:

> PIRA bombing utilized Semtex as the primary explosive ingredient against the Alien Plaintiffs and the unarmed British population constitute crimes against humanity in violation of the law of nations. ... Throughout the 1980s and 1990s, this campaign by the PIRA was widespread and systematic against the civilian population. Libya, through its officials, employees, and agents including but not limited to Qadhafi, Senoussi, Kusa, Ashour, and Bazelya, knowingly, intentionally and directly aided and abetted, intentionally facilitated, and/or recklessly disregarded crimes against humanity in violation of the law of nations.[215]

Other factors in this case exhibiting potential state complicity in the wrongdoing of non-state actors were the provision of weapons, ammunition, training and training facilities, which Libya allegedly knew would be used to commit conduct contrary to international rules.[216] Two facets relating to the international responsibility of Libya for complicity were thus the commission of conduct contrary to international law by PIRA and the state '[k]nowingly assisting such a group'.[217]

3.3.2. How Far Does this Developing Rule Currently Extend?

At this time, it cannot be said with confidence that a general complicity rule that incorporates non-state actors exists as part of positive international law. The limited state practice and opinio juris suggest that such a rule is currently developing. Yet the need for such a rule is much clearer in light of two key factors. First and foremost, there is abundant practice of states providing aid or assistance to non-state actors, including to those that undertake conduct contrary to international rules. Second, because they have a measure of international legal personality, some of these non-state actors are bound by and therefore can (and do) breach international rules, meaning they commit internationally wrongful acts. The analysis of practice,

[212] ibid para 62.

[213] *Attorney of the Federal Armed Forces v Anonymous (a Major of the Armed Forces)*, Final appeal, BVerwG 2 WD 12.04 (2005).

[214] *McDonald et al v Libya*, US District Court for the District of Columbia, 06-0729 JR (21 April 2006).

[215] ibid paras 313–20.

[216] ibid para 322.

[217] A Clapham, 'Focusing on Armed Non-state Actors' in A Clapham and P Gaeta (eds), *The Oxford Handbook of International Law in Armed Conflict* (Oxford, Oxford University Press, 2014) 766, 808.

including that referred to in the preparatory work undertaken on Article 16, suggests that if a complicity rule under the law of state responsibility exists today, if it were to extend to non-state actors, it would likely only go so far as to include non-state actors that actually bear international obligations, such as non-state armed groups.

Over time it is possible that a general complicity rule could extend to all non-state actors, with the tweaking of the opposability requirement meaning that state responsibility for complicity could still be established for aid or assistance to non-state actors that undertake conduct contrary to international rules, even if those actors are not legally bound by those rules. Whatever happens, the people working for states will continue to intuit complicity as a test for determining the indirect international responsibility of states for the conduct of non-state actors. Whether states view aid or assistance rendered to non-state actors that undertake conduct contrary to international rules being a matter for international law to resolve rests on state choice. Should they claim or invoke state responsibility in cases where a state has aided or assisted a non-state actor that has either breached an international rule, or undertaken conduct that is contrary to an international rule, then it would be much clearer that they consider the complicity test addressed in this chapter to be a rule of customary international law.

Bearing in mind the ongoing practice of states rendering aid or assistance to non-state actors, there exists a vacuum for a general complicity rule to fill. This will remain the case unless (1) some type of treaty is created, which is not necessarily desirable; (2) such a rule crystallises as custom, which may never happen; or (3) courts and tribunals do what they have been doing with the attribution tests under the ARSIWA for decades – applying them, even though their customary status is far from evident. Why should a complicity test be any different? Domestic courts in particular are in a unique position to actually develop the international law regarding state complicity in the wrongdoing of non-state actors. The current nuances and ambiguities surrounding complicity under state responsibility allow for courts and tribunals to offer their own two pennies' worth on this subject, and it is important that they be left sufficient room to do so.[218] Domestic courts and tribunals are not bound to applying creations of international institutions. These participants in international lawmaking need not strictly follow the blueprints of the ILC, but can forge their own path, formulating new and useful insights in the process. While such conduct could result in various understandings emerging on state complicity, such practice would instead give a more accurate and possibly messy picture of what a general international complicity rule looks like. With the development of such a tapestry, perhaps the international law applicable to determining indirect state responsibility for non-state actor conduct would be in a better position to help address more of the realities that ruin this world. In so doing, perhaps the law in this area could also become a wee bit more international, shaped by diversity of opinion from across states, and a wee bit less … exclusive.[219]

[218] For some reasons why this is important, see chapter 8, section 1.3.2.

[219] See chapter 8, section 1.3.2.

When considering the uncertainty surrounding whether Article 16 itself is reflective of customary international law, there exists time to build on this provision. In light of the historical and contemporary practice of states rendering aid or assistance to other states and non-state actors, it is arguably more appropriate that if any general test on complicity were to apply under the law of state responsibility, then it should incorporate state–non-state actor interactions as well as those between states. Alternatively, a separate, general complicity test that incorporates non-state actors could apply alongside Article 16. The restraints on such a rule depend on approaches towards international legal personality, in particular its (ir)relevance with respect to actors that are aided or assisted by states, the opposability requirement, and the connections between the two. Although at this time it appears to be a safer estimate to say that a complicity test addressing state aid or assistance to non-state actors will likely only extend to situations where the non-state actor in question actually bears and has breached an international legal obligation, such a test need not be so bound, either now or in the future.

4. CONCLUSION

Complicity serves as an additional basis for determining state responsibility for involvement in the wrongs undertaken by non-state actors. Understood as such, a complicity test is no more or less than an alternative option that can be used instead of applying an attribution test, thereby laying out a possible route for the determination and establishment of indirect state responsibility, including if the routes towards direct responsibility are not possible. There thus could exist a further avenue to pursue in attempting to prevent the occurrence of responsibility gaps under international law. Complicity under the law of state responsibility as it applies to the conduct of non-state actors therefore serves the function of being part of a fuller framework of tests that are not all-embracing, but can be called upon to assess whether a state can be considered to be internationally responsible for the conduct of a non-state actor that was contrary to an international rule.

Learning from and building on the work of the ILC shows that the legal framework for determining indirect state responsibility is largely unrealised. Yet bases for assessing indirect international responsibility when a state has been involved in conduct that is contrary to an international rule have an important part to play in the international legal order, especially when considering the current challenges posed by non-state actors across the globe. Complicity is one base, but one that has been held back in its application to governing the relationships between states and non-state actors. Hopefully it is clearer that such a situation need not continue, nor should it. If a state can help another state undertake conduct that is contrary to an international rule, then it can help a non-state actor do the exact same thing. This understanding formed part of the work undertaken on Article 16, yet was dissolved the further the provision developed.

Today, however, looking to practice provides evidence of a general complicity rule that appears to be developing to incorporate non-state actors within it. Yet regardless of whether such a test ever forms part of positive international law, courts and tribunals can apply it. Such an outcome would be far from abnormal. Look no further than the prominence afforded to the attribution tests under the ARSIWA, all of which were created by the ILC and continue to find themselves lacking in state practice and opinio juris. Yet that is the kicker: the brand stamp of the ILC, or any other institution that people agree to be the declaratory authority on a subject. While the efforts of the ILC remain considerable, it is not unfair to say that the resulting outputs it produces can result in more deference than is always justifiable. Although two heads can be better than one, there exist tipping points in which too many cooks spoil the broth. While the research behind this chapter did not set out to provide an opinion on whether the approach taken towards state responsibility for complicity within the ILC reached such a tipping point, it appears that the final complicity broth that became part of the ARSIWA was not so much spoiled as it lacked depth of flavour. It is a bit like Scottish porridge made by traditionalists, with oats, salt and water. Fine, sure. But bland, beige, and probably made better by a smidgen of something else. While there is nothing necessarily wrong with things bland or beige, recipes can be developed. So too can they be complemented. Complicity is but one test for determining the indirect responsibility of a state for its involvement in wrongful conduct carried out by a non-state actor. Are there others? And, if so, what do they offer the law of state responsibility in terms of engaging with non-state actors?

7

Due Diligence Failings of States that Contribute to the Wrongdoing of Non-state Actors

WHILE IT IS clear that complicity is currently a distinct basis for determining the indirect international responsibility of a state for its contribution to the conduct of a non-state actor that is contrary to an international rule, the test for state complicity need not stand alone in this regard. There exist further opportunities to develop the state responsibility framework so that it can more meaningfully engage with the problems posed by non-state actors. As with attribution and complicity, the efforts of the ILC help shed light on paths that have remained largely untrodden since the ARSIWA was completed. The process that shaped the ARSIWA is at least equally important, if not more so, than the final product that was produced. The rich substance that was grappled with during this process reveals a further matter that has been touched upon in previous chapters, but calls for more attention: the extent to which the ILC drew inspiration from primary rules when constructing the provisions of the ARSIWA. A key consideration here is the methodology that was adopted in doing so, in particular the potential to be found in its further use. This chapter shows that the use of this same method uncovers how another distinct basis for determining indirect state responsibility for the conduct of non-state actors can be theoretically formulated and practically applied. This alternative basis is rooted in a concept that is as prominent across a number of fields as it is ambiguous: due diligence. Yet this concept does not currently form part of the general legal framework governing state responsibility. Why? What even is due diligence? And how does it apply to the interactions between states and non-state actors? In engaging with these questions, a further part of the picture begins to emerge of the ways in which the law of state responsibility can evolve to better address the difficulties posed by non-state actors.

1. DUE DILIGENCE IN THE PREPARATORY WORK OF THE ARSIWA

Although due diligence formed a significant part of the preparatory work undertaken on the ARSIWA, the concept ultimately did not form part of the ILC's final product.[1] Why this happened is due to a combination of factors, perhaps the most predominant

[1] The concept is referred to once, in the commentary. See ARSIWA, Art 2, Commentary, para 3.

one being that the ILC when drafting the ARSIWA was making an attempt to ensure its provisions embodied secondary rules. This section begins to unpack an argument that the concept of due diligence has much to offer the general international law applicable to determining state responsibility for non-state actors.[2] But before delving into how due diligence could be formulated and potentially applied as a secondary rule, it is helpful to reflect on the history surrounding the considerable efforts of the ILC that focused on due diligence. As with the complicity test set out in the previous chapter, by looking back at how due diligence formed part of the work undertaken on the ARSIWA, it becomes easier to appreciate how past efforts can help shape future initiatives within the law of state responsibility.

1.1. The Potential of Garcia-Amador's Initial Work

The ILC began addressing due diligence through the work of Garcia-Amador.[3] He contributed to shedding light on how due diligence could be used to determine the international responsibility of states for the conduct of non-state actors.[4] His position was that should a state through its own conduct fail to exercise due diligence with respect to ties that state had with a non-state actor, 'imputability' became a consideration, in that state responsibility would become a consideration for the conduct of that non-state actor.[5] Garcia-Amador envisaged this process to play out in the following way: '[W]hat is in essence imputed to the State is not really the act or deed which causes the injury, but rather the non-performance of a duty.'[6] He was of the view that international responsibility on the basis of a due diligence assessment should take into consideration any fault or culpability on the part of states when examining their relationships with non-state actors.[7]

From these understandings began the development of a 'rule of "due diligence"'.[8] The rule that Garcia-Amador worked towards creating appeared to be aimed at imposing an obligation on states to 'guarantee the safety of persons and property', which he argued was 'recognised as an integral part of the international law relating to responsibility'.[9] It was made clear at this stage that establishing the international responsibility of states for due diligence failings rested on the legal obligations held by them, as going beyond this basis was considered an issue that could 'open the door to wholly unjustified claims'.[10] Garcia-Amador considered due diligence to be a key element of the international law applicable to state responsibility, one that could be called upon to help ensure that international responsibility is not avoided

[2] See also R Mackenzie-Gray Scott, 'Due Diligence as a Secondary Rule of General International Law' (2021) 34 *Leiden Journal of International Law* 343.
[3] First Report, International Responsibility, FV Garcia-Amador, A/CN.4/96, YBILC (1956) vol II.
[4] ibid 187.
[5] ibid.
[6] ibid; see also 208.
[7] ibid 209.
[8] Second Report, International Responsibility, FV Garcia Amador, A/CN.4/106, YBILC (1957) vol II, 104.
[9] ibid 106.
[10] ibid.

'whenever the circumstances genuinely justify a claim against the State for negligence in the discharge of its essential functions'.[11] This perspective to an extent portrays due diligence as the inverse of negligence.

Although it will be shown that due diligence not only entails the absence of negligence, the two concepts share a connection. In chapter 1 it was shown that much, if not most, of Garcia-Amador's work was shelved by the ILC. Yet it is debatable whether this extended to his insights on due diligence. Even if these insights were officially not taken forward, they appeared to instil a mindset that kept due diligence considerations in mind during the drafting process of the ARSIWA, not so much in the forefront of these efforts, but lingering in the background. Before completing his tenure as special rapporteur, Garcia-Amador sought to clarify in general terms how due diligence should apply in international law, which consists of acting as basis for determining the international responsibility of a state where it either fails to prevent, suppress or address conduct of a non-state actor that was contrary to an international rule to which the state is bound.[12]

1.2. Taking Forward the Enduring Efforts of Garcia-Amador

When taking over from Garcia-Amador, Ago built on the insights surrounding due diligence. By examining practice involving due diligence components, his work added further details to an emerging blueprint that articulates how due diligence could be applied as part of the general international law applicable to determining state responsibility. There were a number of cases that shed more light on how to determine state responsibility for a failure to exercise due diligence.[13] One was the *Bernadotte* case, where Israel was considered to be responsible for 'failure to exercise due diligence and to take all reasonable measures for the prevention of' an assassination.[14] Another was the *Romanian Legation* case, which involved a claim for reparation regarding an attack on diplomats in Switzerland, on the grounds that the authorities had not anticipated the attack, did not arrest those who perpetrated the attack without delay, and did not help the injured driver of the delegation quickly enough.[15] This argument was rejected because it was deemed 'impossible either to anticipate or prevent the aggression … the police had taken all steps which the circumstances required', the driver was taken to hospital upon being found by the authorities, and Switzerland stated it 'would prosecute the perpetrators of the attack, who were in fact sentenced to rigorous imprisonment, deprivation of civic rights and expulsion from Swiss territory'.[16]

[11] ibid; see also Third Report, International Responsibility, FV Garcia-Amador, A/CN.4/111, YBILC (1958) vol II, 54.

[12] Fifth Report, International Responsibility, FV Garcia-Amador, A/CN.4/125 and Corr 1, YBILC (1960) vol II, 63.

[13] See Fourth Report, State Responsibility, Roberto Ago, A/CN.4/264 and Add.1, YBILC (1972) vol II, 131–38.

[14] ibid 118.

[15] ibid.

[16] ibid.

The analysis of practice undertaken by Ago highlighted that states were essentially being assessed on their vigilance when their international responsibility was called into question for not preventing, suppressing or addressing conduct of non-state actors that was contrary to international rules. Two key findings were made during this time. First, exercising due diligence does not equate to preventing every incident without exception.[17] Second, if proven that the exercise of due diligence by a state might have prevented the wrongful conduct in question from occurring, then the international responsibility of that state can be established for not having done so.[18] In taking these insights forward, Ago proposed Draft Article 23, which read:

> There is no breach by a State of an international obligation requiring it to prevent a given event unless, following a lack of prevention on the part of the State, the event in question occurs.[19]

This draft provision was based on practice.[20] The commentary clarifies its scope:

> Clearly, a State cannot be alleged to have breached its obligation to prevent a given event so long as the event has not actually occurred, and the same is true where the feared event has occurred but cannot be ascribed to a lack of foresight on the part of certain State organs. In other words, neither the occurrence of the event without there having been any negligence on the part of State organs nor such negligence without the occurrence of any event in itself constitutes a breach of the international obligation. Only the combination of these two elements permits the conclusion that there has been such a breach.[21]

Had it been retained, this provision would have applied as a secondary rule that included a due diligence assessment. Although it would have interfaced with whatever primary rule was at issue in a particular case, Ago emphasised the intention to apply Draft Article 23 'without seeking to determine the conditions for the occurrence of such a breach in the various hypothetical cases'.[22] This work was well-received during this stage of drafting the ARSIWA, with the Drafting Committee and the ILC adopting the draft provision the same year it was proposed.[23] After its adoption, Ago continued to make the effort of showing that the draft provision was based on legal practice, examining more cases involving due diligence in his final report.[24]

[17] ibid 133 and 137.

[18] ibid 135–36. For example: 'The British Foreign Office also sent to its consular officers abroad the following instruction, which was transmitted to the United States Ambassador in Mexico City by the British Minister in 1913: "Where claims are made for compensation for damages done by insurgents in armed insurrections against a government which was unable to control them, claimants should be reminded that His Majesty's Government do not regard a government as liable in such cases *unless* that government were negligent and *might have* prevented the damage arising"' (emphasis added).

[19] Seventh Report, State Responsibility, Roberto Ago, A/CN.4/307 and Add 1 & 2 and Corr 1 & 2, YBILC (1978) vol I(1), 37.

[20] ibid 32–37.

[21] ibid 32.

[22] ibid 36.

[23] ILC Report, Thirtieth Session, 8 May–28 July 1978, UNGA, Thirty-Third Session, Supp No 10, A/33/10, YBILC (1978) vol II(2), 81; Draft Articles on State responsibility: Text adopted by the Drafting Committee: Articles 23–27 and title of Chapter IV of the draft – reproduced in A/CN.4/SR.1513 and SR.1524, A/CN.4/L.271 and Add 1, YBILC (1978) vol I, 206.

[24] Eighth Report, State Responsibility, Roberto Ago, A/CN.4/318 and Add 1–4, YBILC (1979) vol II(1), 63–64.

After this time, the work undertaken on Draft Article 23 appeared to be dormant for a period. Following from Ago as the next special rapporteur, Riphagen did refer to due diligence in his work, but it seems only once.[25] When Arangio-Ruiz began, due diligence was addressed in more detail, but insofar as it related to making reparations assessments.[26] The draft provision therefore remained unaltered and was adopted by the ILC on first reading.[27] Of the comments received, it appears states favoured the draft provision forming part of the ARSIWA.[28] That said, some states made it clear that the provision in their view required further refinement.[29] Germany, for example, stated that Draft Article 23 in its then current form was 'too abstract'.[30] The United Kingdom also thought it required further work, but expressed that the draft provision was 'uncontroversial'.[31] France held a different position, which was that Draft Article 23 concerned 'rules of substantive law, which classify primary obligations', and thus, according to France, had 'no place in a draft of this kind and should be deleted'.[32] Despite this explicit call for deletion, the general position of states at the time appeared to favour retaining the draft provision.[33]

1.3. The Beginning of the End for Due Diligence Forming Part of the ARSIWA

Crawford was faced with the task of bringing together all the work undertaken up to his appointment as the last special rapporteur and examining it in light of the comments received by states. In doing so, considerations regarding due diligence went no further in the final stages of the ARSIWA's drafting process. A key reason for this outcome becomes clearer in light of the perspective put forward by Crawford with respect to Draft Article 23: that there was 'clearly a strong case for simply deleting' the draft provision.[34] His reasons for this recommendation were threefold. First, Draft Article 23 had apparently 'been criticized by a number of Governments as over-refined'.[35] Second: 'They [draft Articles 20, 21, paragraph 1, and 23] have been widely criticized in the literature'.[36] Third: 'Their [draft Articles 20, 21, paragraph 1, and 23] relationship to similar concepts under national law is

[25] Seventh Report, State Responsibility, Willem Riphagen, A/CN.4/397 and Corr 1 & 2 and Add 1 & Corr 1, YBILC (1986) vol II(1), 8.

[26] Second Report, State Responsibility, Gaetano Arangio-Ruiz, A/CN.4/425 & Corr 1 and Add 1 & Corr 1, YBILC (1989) vol II(1), 6, 15, 16, 26, 27.

[27] ILC Report, Forty-Eighth Session, 6 May–26 July 1996, UNGA, Fifty-First Session, Supp No 10, A/51/10, YBILC (1996) vol II(2), 60.

[28] Observations and comments of Governments on Chapters I, II and III of Part I of the Draft Articles on State responsibility for internationally wrongful acts, A/CN.4/328 and Add 1–4, YBILC (1980) vol II(1), 92, 93, 100, 101, 103; Comments of Governments on part one of the Draft Articles on State responsibility for internationally wrongful acts, A/CN.4/342 and Add 1–4, YBILC (1981) vol II(1), 75.

[29] Comments and observations received from Governments, A/CN.4/488 and Add 1–3 (1998) 123.

[30] ibid.

[31] ibid 126.

[32] ibid.

[33] Second Report, State Responsibility, James Crawford, A/CN.4/498 and Add 1–4 (1999) 27.

[34] ibid 28.

[35] ibid.

[36] Second Report, Crawford (1999) 28.

obscure and even contradictory'.[37] However, there existed a tension between these three points and two others. The first is that the criticisms of states centred on the under-refinement of the draft provision, hence the claims that it was 'too abstract' and required further work.[38]

The second is that the references used to support the final two points did not appear to reflect any wide criticism of Draft Article 23 specifically.

It is clear that Crawford saw some value in Draft Article 23: 'the commentaries to articles 20, 21 and, *especially*, 23 are useful, although they are in need of modification'.[39] His reluctance towards his own proposal of deleting the draft provision was also apparent:

> The case for deletion is a formidable one, but still there must be a hesitation, given the currency of the terms used, their value in some cases, e.g. in determining when a breach has occurred, and the relative poverty of the conceptual framework of international law in matters relating to breach of obligation.[40]

Although the considerable efforts of Crawford and those of the other special rapporteurs, as well as the ILC more broadly, could have further teased out the due diligence components of Draft Article 23, it is understandable that this did not occur. Pragmatism could be said to be a reason behind this outcome. The ILC may not have retained a draft provision that included a due diligence assessment,[41] and little remains of this work in the final version of the ARSIWA,[42] but due diligence formed part of their preparatory work. This concept can therefore be taken forward from its historical context within the area of state responsibility, meaning that even though the ARSIWA contains no due diligence provision, the final product of the ILC does not prevent the creation of a new international rule that is also based on the premise of it being generally applicable across sub-fields of international law. Furthermore, it becomes clear that the very methodology preferred by the ILC provides an avenue towards formulating and potentially applying due diligence as a secondary rule.

2. FORMULATING DUE DILIGENCE AS A SECONDARY RULE

Considering what secondary rules are said to be in the area of state responsibility, in that they set out general conditions for determining international responsibility for wrongful conduct, it is somewhat surprising that the ILC did not ultimately create a due diligence provision for inclusion in the ARSIWA. This is because the ILC relied on primary rules as inspiration in its attempts to create secondary rules.[43]

[37] ibid 28–29.

[38] See Comments and observations received from Governments, A/CN.4/488 and Add 1–3 (1998), at 123–26.

[39] Second Report, Crawford (1999) 29 (emphasis added).

[40] ibid.

[41] ILC Report, Fifty-First Session, 3 May–23 July 1999, UNGA, Fifty-Fourth Session, Supp No 10, A/54/10, YBILC (1999) vol II(2), 50; State responsibility: Titles and texts of draft articles adopted by the Drafting Committee: Articles 16 to 26 bis (chapter III), 27 to 28 bis (chapter IV) and 29 to 35 (chapter V) – reproduced in document A/CN.4/SR.2605, para 4, A/CN.4/L.574 [and Corr 1 and 3], YBILC (1999) vol I, 275.

[42] See ARSIWA, Art 14 and Commentary, in particular para 14.

[43] See analysis in section 2.1 (below) and also J Vidmar, 'Some Observations on Wrongfulness, Responsibility and Defences in International Law' (2016) 63 *Netherlands International Law Review* 335, 349.

As a consequence, numerous ARSIWA provisions also reflect the content of primary rules.[44] Considering this point, there exists an opportunity to show how a new due diligence rule can be created to form part of the secondary rules governing state responsibility for non-state actor conduct.

2.1. The Extrapolation Method as a Part of International Lawmaking

Extrapolation is a method of international lawmaking that consists of examining the content of one concept in one or multiple forms, and reproducing it in a different form. Utilising it allows international rules that are sector-specific to be mashed together, from which a general international rule can be created.[45] Extrapolating from specific international rules was the methodology adopted by the ILC when creating the ARSIWA. Yet this method of lawmaking 'is by no means particular' to state responsibility,[46] nor is the thinking relating to it restricted to international law.[47] Sivakumaran has shown that the ILC used extrapolation to craft Article 16 of the ARSIWA:

> The ILC provides for a general rule on complicity – a state aiding or assisting another state in the commission of an internationally wrongful act by the latter – on the basis of international law rules on complicity in the specific areas of aggression, circumvention of sanctions imposed by the UN Security Council and human rights violations. From these three very particular subject areas, a generalized rule on complicity was formulated.[48]

It is not only Article 16 that was created using extrapolation. Article 6 was based on human rights and international trade law.[49] Human rights law and international humanitarian law was used to create Article 7, where rules of the latter body are acknowledged in the commentary as 'corresponding' to the provision's attribution test.[50] Although it was the ICJ that created the effective control test under Article 8, the ILC made an attempt to show its existence in other areas by referring to case-law from human rights law and investment law.[51] The commentary to Article 9 shows that the 'principle underlying' the provision is based on rules of international

[44] Vidmar (ibid) 350.

[45] S. Sivakumaran, 'Techniques in International Law-Making: Extrapolation, Analogy, Form and the Emergence of an International Law of Disaster Relief' (2017) 28 *European Journal of International Law* 1097, 1108–16.

[46] ibid 1112. For example, in creating the Draft Articles on the Expulsion of Aliens, the ILC combined 'aspects of traditional customary international law, human rights lat [sic], refugee law' and extrapolated 'current trends' to 'restate' the law in this area (*Harvard Human Rights Journal*, Forum on the International Law Commission's 'Draft Articles on the Expulsion of Aliens', Introduction, http://harvardhrj.com/forum-essays/).

[47] JD Dana, Jr, 'General and Specific Rules: A Mechanism Design Approach' (2005) 161 *Journal of Institutional and Theoretical Economics* 347; C Engel, 'General and Specific Rules' (2005) 161 *Journal of Institutional and Theoretical Economics* 350.

[48] Sivakumaran (n 45) 1112.

[49] ARSIWA, Art 6, Commentary, paras 2–7.

[50] ARSIWA, Art 7, Commentary, paras 4–6.

[51] ARSIWA, Art 8, Commentary.

humanitarian law.[52] Article 21 replicates the law on the use of force regarding self-defence under the UN Charter.[53]

There exists a sliding scale of reliance on primary rules to form the basis of attempts to create secondary rules by the ILC. At one end of this scale there are provisions of the ARSIWA that have no or little connection with primary rules. At the other end are provisions that in theory are meant to embody secondary rules but remain primary rules. The in-between on this scale are provisions that contain components of related primary rules and provisions that are based on similar normative foundations as primary rules. Although utilising extrapolation does not come without its share of problems,[54] secondary international rules can be created by reference to primary international rules. The ILC used this method to construct the ARSIWA. By grouping together characteristics that were held in common across different primary rules, it became possible to distil these into a provision that encapsulated them in a generalised form. The same can be done with respect to due diligence. Examining the application of this concept across primary rules and domestic law allows a template to be crafted that helps show how it could apply as a secondary rule part of the general international legal framework applicable to determining state responsibility.

2.2. Combining the Content of Primary Rules and Domestic Law

The preparatory work on what could have developed into a due diligence provision within the ARSIWA shows that a general understanding of the concept existed before it began to develop across primary rules; as did it exist before the distinction between primary and secondary rules was made.[55] Since this distinction was adopted by the ILC, the idea that due diligence could be formulated and applied as a secondary rule within the law of state responsibility has heretofore rested on the fringes of international law. Transporting this idea into the mainstream rests, in part, on showing that there are rules that can be brought together in a generalised form. The prevalence of due diligence in both international and domestic law suggests that there are such rules to work with, whilst at least initially indicating the potential for the extrapolation method to work in this particular instance.

[52] ARSIWA, Art 9, Commentary, para 2.

[53] ARSIWA, Art 21 and Commentary.

[54] See Mackenzie-Gray Scott (n 2) 349–50.

[55] It is unclear from where the ILC got the distinction. The terminology might have been adopted from Hart, who made this distinction in the context of domestic law: HLA Hart, *The Concept of Law* (Oxford, Clarendon Press, 1961). However, it should be noted that 'the ILC's distinction between primary and secondary norms may *prima facie* appear, to a large extent, to be influenced by HLA Hart's Concept of Law; nevertheless, Hartian thought should not be considered as the origin of the distinction' (A Gourgourinis, 'General/Particular International Law and Primary/Secondary Rules: Unitary Terminology of a Fragmented System' (2011) 22 *European Journal of International Law* 993, 1016).

2.2.1. *Due Diligence in Primary Rules*

Numerous sub-fields of international law contain due diligence as part of their frameworks. The concept is well-used in environmental,[56] humanitarian,[57] human rights[58] and investment law.[59] It is also part of efforts aimed at addressing issues in newly developing areas, such as cyberspace,[60] forms part of the governance of outer space,[61] as well as being utilised to bolster protections with respect to suppressing terrorism[62] and domestic abuse.[63] The short story of due diligence in international law is that it spans a diverse array of fields and has an extensive history dating back to at least the nineteenth century.[64] Daria Davitti argues that the 'specific content of the due diligence principle can be traced back to the 1920s'.[65] This period saw the emergence of practice where states were assessed on their own conduct with respect to protecting against wrongful conduct of non-state actors.[66]

This practice clarified that state responsibility for non-state actor conduct could be established for a failure to ensure protection,[67] or for not 'diligently prosecuting and properly punishing'.[68] The ICJ also contributed to the development of due diligence with its insights in the *Tehran Hostages* case, where the Court considered Iran to be responsible for its failure to take action against rebels that attacked the US embassy.[69] It held that Iran had failed to take 'appropriate steps' to protect the premises, staff and archives of the US embassy from attack, in addition to failing to put an end to the wrongdoing at issue.[70] In determining whether a state has

[56] R. Yotova, 'The Principles of Due Diligence and Prevention in International Environmental Law' (2016) 75 *Cambridge Law Journal* 445.

[57] A Boivin, 'Complicity and Beyond: International Law and the Transfer of Small Arms and Light Weapons' (2005) 87 *International Review of the Red Cross* 467, 479 and 489–90; RP Barnidge, Jr, 'The Due Diligence Principle Under International Law' (2006) 8 *International Community Law Review* 81, 92 and 120.

[58] See case-law of the Inter-American Court of Human Rights (IACtHR) and European Court of Human Rights (ECtHR) (below).

[59] Y Levashova, 'Fair and Equitable Treatment and Investor's Due Diligence Under International Investment Law' (2020) 67 *Netherlands International Law Review* 233; E De Brabandere, 'Host States' Due Diligence Obligations in International Investment Law' (2015) 42 *Syracuse Journal of International Law and Commerce* 319.

[60] MN Schmitt and S Watts, 'Beyond State-Centrism: International Law and Non-state Actors in Cyberspace' (2016) 21 *Journal of Conflict & Security Law* 595, 602–07.

[61] UNGA Res A/RES/21/2222, Treaty on Principles Governing the Activities of States in the Exploration and Use of Outer Space, including the Moon and Other Celestial Bodies, Art 6.

[62] T Becker, *Terrorism and the State: Rethinking the Rules on State Responsibility* (Oxford, Hart, 2006) 119–30 (reviewing practice on this issue); RB Lillich and JM Paxman, 'State Responsibility for Injuries to Aliens Occasioned by Terrorist Activities' (1977) 26 *American University Law Review* 217, 251–76.

[63] *Goekce v Austria*, UN Doc CEDAW/C/39/D/5/2005 (2007) paras 12.1.2–12.1.4; *Opuz v Turkey*, App No 33401/02 (ECtHR, 9 June 2009) paras 165 and 200; L Hasselbacher, 'State Obligations Regarding Domestic Violence: The European Court of Human Rights, Due Diligence, And International Legal Minimums of Protection' (2010) 8 *Northwestern Journal of Human Rights* 190.

[64] *Alabama claims of the United States of America against Great Britain*, Award (14 September 1872) RIAA, vol XXIX, 125–34.

[65] D Davitti, 'On the Meanings of International Investment Law and International Human Rights Law: The Alternative Narrative of Due Diligence' (2012) 12 *Human Rights Law Review* 421, 445.

[66] Barnidge (n 57) 98–99.

[67] *Thomas H Youmans (USA) v United Mexican States*, UNRIAA (1926) vol IV, 110, para 11.

[68] *Massey v United Mexican States*, UNRIAA (1927) vol IV, 155, para 159.

[69] *United States Diplomatic and Consular Staff in Tehran (United States of America v Iran)*, Judgment, 24 May 1980, ICJ Rep [1980] 3.

[70] ibid para 63.

exercised due diligence, the ICJ has also ruled that the available resources of a state are an imperative factor to consider when assessing international responsibility.[71] In the *Nicaragua* case, although Nicaragua had not prevented weapons crossing its territory from being trafficked into El Salvador, the ICJ assessed the extent of due diligence required from the state in the broader context of the ongoing activities in the region.[72] Due diligence was thus assessed through a lens of reasonableness. There were non-state actors in Nicaraguan territory undertaking conduct contrary to international law, yet because other states that had more resources at their disposal had not prevented the non-state actors from undertaking this conduct, it was ruled unreasonable to expect Nicaragua, a state with comparatively fewer resources at its disposal, to do more in attempting to prevent the weapons trafficking.[73] The *Pulp Mills* case also forms a part of the practice relating to due diligence.[74] Here the ICJ ruled that a state should 'use all the means at its disposal in order to avoid activities which take place in its territory, or in any area under its jurisdiction, causing significant damage'.[75] From this reading it can be taken that states must do everything they can to prevent non-state actor conduct from doing harm.[76] The ICJ saw a crucial part of this process to entail states undertaking assessments as to how they should conduct themselves in order to ensure that non-state actors do not cause harmful outcomes through their conduct.[77]

In addition to international tribunals and the ICJ, regional human rights courts have furthered understandings of due diligence. The IACtHR has held that states are obligated to exercise due diligence in preventing non-state actors from undertaking conduct that is contrary to an individual's rights.[78] In the *Velasquez Rodriguez* case the IACtHR made a number of pronouncements on this matter,[79] including that Honduras failed to exercise due diligence because it 'did not take effective action' to ensure that the rights it owed could be 'freely and fully' exercised.[80] Other judgments of the IACtHR have followed this precedent.[81] The ECtHR has also

[71] *Military and Paramilitary Activities in and against Nicaragua (Nicaragua v United States of America)*, Judgment, 27 June 1986, ICJ Rep [1986] 14, paras 157–60.

[72] ibid para 157.

[73] ibid.

[74] *Case Concerning Pulp Mills on the River Uruguay (Argentina v Uruguay)*, Judgment, 20 April 2010, ICJ Rep [2010] 14.

[75] ibid para 101.

[76] This stance takes insights from the work of the ILC in its Draft Articles on Prevention of Transboundary Harm from Hazardous Activities (2001), UN Doc A/RES/56/82 (2001), 56 UN GAOR Supp (No 49) 498, Supp (No 10) A/56/10 (V.E.1). It should be noted that these provisions apply 'to activities not prohibited by international law' (see Art 1, Commentary, paras 1–17) and thus concern international liability, which is a separate issue from international responsibility for conduct that *is* prohibited by international law. See NLJT Horbach, 'The Confusion About State Responsibility and International Liability (1991) 4 *Leiden Journal of International Law* 47.

[77] *Pulp Mills*, Judgment (20 April 2010) para 205.

[78] *Velasquez Rodriguez v Honduras* (Ser C) No 4 (IACtHR, 29 July 1988) para 166.

[79] ibid paras 79, 172–82.

[80] ibid paras 180 and 167, respectively.

[81] See, for example, *Caso 19 Comerciantes* (Ser C) No 109 (IACtHR, 5 July 2004) paras 29, 30, 112, 140, 203; *'Mapiripán Massacre'* (Ser C) No 122 (IACtHR, 15 September 2005) paras 226, 246, 304; *Pueblo Bello Massacre* (Ser C) No 140 (IACtHR, 31 January 2006) paras 126, 139, 140, 151, 170, 201; *Masacres de Ituango* (Ser C) No 148 (IACtHR, 1 July 2006) paras 134, 291, 310, 315, 316, 317, 328, 330, 399, 402, 417; *Masacre de La Rochela* (Ser C) No 163 (IACtHR, 11 May 2007) paras 2, 111, 149, 150, 155–164, 165, 172, 194, 199, 202, 203, 209, 288, 293, 297.

made similar pronouncements.[82] This collection of precedents taps into one of the overarching aims of applying due diligence, which is that states are expected to put in place measures that set out to achieve, or at the least attempt to realise, a common goal that is set by legal obligations part of a particular framework. These obligations predominantly concern preventing, suppressing or addressing conduct that is contrary to the corollary rights at issue. In the human rights field, as stressed by the ECtHR, the obligations regarding the exercise of due diligence by states are ones 'of conduct' not 'of result'.[83] This is true of due diligence under international law more generally,[84] where states tend to 'have obligations of conduct, rather than result'.[85]

Examining due diligence through primary rules helps formulate a general precedent that states should implement measures that at a minimum endeavour to protect the legal obligations they owe to others, whether individuals, businesses or other states. This does not mean an international legal obligation exists that binds states to prevent all conduct of non-state actors that is contrary to international rules. Instead, this formulation begins setting the parameters of an international due diligence rule that is general in nature. These parameters, when coupled with insights from domestic law, help show how due diligence could function as a distinct basis for determining the international responsibility of states for the conduct of non-state actors.

2.2.2. *Due Diligence in Domestic Law*

It is beyond doubt that the concept of due diligence forms part of primary rules. And the same is true for domestic law. Within legal systems across states, due diligence is linked to the duty of care principle, foreseeability and negligence, which form part of tort, delict and contract law.[86] Cases in these areas turn on the scope and exercise of an actor's duty of care, which is assessed through a lens of reasonableness.[87] The extent of required due diligence conferred on an actor and

[82] See, for example, *Lopes De Sousa Fernandes v Portugal*, App No 56080/13 (ECtHR, 19 December 2017) paras 31, 47, 49, 64; *Ilaşcu and Others v Moldova and Russia*, App No 48787/99 (ECtHR, 8 July 2004) paras 322–52; *Tahsin Acar v Turkey*, App No 26307/95 (ECtHR, 8 April 2004); *Slivenko v Latvia*, App No 48321/99 (ECtHR, 9 October 2003); *Kudła v Poland*, App No 30210/96 (ECtHR, 26 October 2000) paras 109 and 129; *Osman v United Kingdom*, App No 87/1997/871/1083 (ECtHR, 28 October 1998) para 116.

[83] *Lopes De Sousa Fernandes* (ibid) para 31.

[84] N White, 'Due Diligence Obligations of Conduct: Developing a Responsibility Regime for PMSCs' (2012) 31 *Criminal Justice Ethics* 233.

[85] T Christakis, 'Challenging the "Unwilling or Unable" Test' in A Peters and C Marxsen (eds), *Self-defence Against Non-state Actors: Impulses from the Max Planck Trialogues on the Law of Peace and War* (MPIL Research Paper Series No 2017-07) 18; See also P-M Dupuy, 'Reviewing the Difficulties of Codification: On Ago's Classification of Obligations of Means and Obligations of Result in Relation to State Responsibility' (1999) 10 *European Journal of International Law* 371, 376–78; J Crawford, 'Revising the Draft Articles on State Responsibility' (1999) 10 *European Journal of International Law* 435, 440–42.

[86] R Versteeg, 'Perspectives on Foreseeability in the Law of Contracts and Torts: The Relationship Between "Intervening Causes" and "Impossibility"' (2011) 5 *Michigan State Law Review* 1497; J Bonnitcha and R McCorquodale, 'The Concept of "Due Diligence" in the UN Guiding Principles on Business and Human Rights' (2017) 28 *European Journal of International Law* 899, 902–03.

[87] *Hadley v Baxendale* [1854] EWHC J70; *Blyth v Birmingham Waterworks Co* [1856] 11 Ex Ch 781; *Palsgraf v Long Island Railroad* (NY, 1928) 162 NE 99; *Smith v Littlewoods* [1987] UKHL 18; *Fairchild v Glenhaven Funeral Services Ltd* [2002] UKHL 22; *D v East Berkshire Community Health NHS Trust* [2005] 2 WLR 993.

its execution of conduct meeting that threshold determines liability. An example is the relationship between a doctor and their patient, whereby the former 'must do everything that a reasonable person and competent physician can do in order to look after a patient. But a doctor has no obligation, in the strict meaning of the term, to heal or cure the patient'.[88]

As clarified above, the concept of due diligence can be associated with obligations of conduct, which under domestic law require the actor owing the obligation in question to ensure actions are taken that endeavour to achieve a certain outcome. Even if the desired outcome is not achieved, the obligation will not be breached so long as the actor did everything it reasonably could to protect the corollary rights arising from the corresponding obligation at issue. Domestic law across legal systems portrays due diligence in this way.[89] Domestic laws alone could also form the basis to transpose the concept of due diligence into general international law.[90] However, bringing together the domestic and international law relating to due diligence not only assists in formulating the concept in general terms, but also shows that doing so fits with previous practice.

2.2.3. Generalising Insights from Domestic and International Law

The ICJ in the *Corfu Channel* case formulated due diligence in general terms,[91] which developed from an understanding that states should not knowingly permit their territory to be used in a way that results in other states being injured.[92] This precedent built on that from the *Trail Smelter* case, where it was ruled that a state 'owes at all times a duty to protect other States against injurious acts by individuals from within its jurisdiction'.[93] Further practice pointing to a generalised conception of due diligence can be found in a district court case in the United States, where it was held that the 'law of nations requires every national government to use "due diligence" to prevent a wrong being done within its own dominion to another nation'.[94]

[88] Dupuy (n 85) 375.

[89] For some examples, see C Bright, D Lica, A Marx and G Van Calster, 'Options for Mandatory Human Rights Due Diligence in Belgium', Leuven Centre for Global Governance Studies (2020); R McCorquodale, L Smit, S Neely and R Brooks, 'Human Rights Due Diligence in Law and Practice: Good Practices and Challenges for Business Enterprises' (2017) 2 *Business and Human Rights Journal* 195; T Baudesson, R Lindsay, C-H Boeringer and A Constans, 'New French Law Imposing Due Diligence Requirements in Relation to Human Rights, Health and Safety, and the Environment', Briefing Note (Clifford Chance, 3 March 2017); N Ahiauzu and T Inko-Tariah, 'Applicability of Anti-Money Laundering Laws to Legal Practitioners in Nigeria: NBA v FGN & CBN' (2016) 19 *Journal of Money Laundering Control* 329; M Conway, 'A New Duty of Care? Tort Liability from Voluntary Human Rights Due Diligence in Global Supply Chains' (2015) 40 *Queen's Law Journal* 741; Decree n 8.420 (2015), Art 42, XIII (Brazil).

[90] C Eggett, 'The Role of Principles and General Principles in the "Constitutional Processes" of International Law' (2019) 66 *Netherlands International Law Review* 197.

[91] *Corfu Channel Case (United Kingdom v Albania)*, Judgement, 9 April 1949, ICJ Rep [1949] 4, para 22.

[92] JA Hessbruegge, 'The Historical Development of the Doctrines of Attribution and Due Diligence in International Law' (2004) 36 *Journal of International Law & Politics* 265, 275.

[93] *Trail Smelter Case (United States, Canada)*, UNRIAA (1941) vol III, 1905, 1963; see also C Eagleton, *The Responsibility of States in International Law* (New York, New York University Press, 1928) 80.

[94] *United States v Hasan and ors*, Decision on motion to dismiss (29 October 2010) No 2:10 cr56 [ED VA] para 72.

A similar ruling was made in *R (on the application of Gentle and another)*.[95] In this case the House of Lords held:

> In reality, all that the nation state can do is to use its best endeavours to conform its actions to international law, just as all that anyone else can do is to use their best endeavours to conform their actions to the law. … [T]he Government should have taken reasonable care ('used due diligence') to ascertain whether the war was lawful before ordering its troops into battle. Of course we all hope that Governments will take reasonable care, especially before making such momentous decisions as this. But the point of taking reasonable care is to discover what you can and cannot do.[96]

This ruling can be linked to the pronouncements made by the ICJ in the *Corfu Channel* case and those of domestic courts regarding the duty of care principle. It is clear that the House of Lords assessed due diligence through a lens of reasonableness, which appears to be a common approach when applying the concept.[97]

What the combined insights of domestic and international law also show is that due diligence can exist as a distinct basis for determining legal responsibility. For the purposes of determining the international responsibility of states for the conduct of non-state actors, there thus exists potential to apply due diligence as a secondary rule that would sit alongside others within this general framework that currently revolves around the ARSIWA. Although the ILC sheds light on the generalisable nature of due diligence,[98] these efforts did not culminate in the creation of any new rule. Yet this outcome need not prevent such a rule from coming into existence by other means. What becomes crucial at this stage is addressing whether the formulation of a new secondary due diligence rule by way of extrapolation is legitimate, regardless of the fact that this method was utilised by the ILC to create provisions of the ARSIWA.

2.2.4. *The Legitimacy of a Secondary Due Diligence Rule Created via Extrapolation*

It is clear that due diligence exists across many primary rules of international law and in a number of areas of domestic law across states. For the purposes of creating a new international rule on due diligence this factor of prevalence is significant. Sivakumaran has shown that it is more straightforward to extrapolate from a series of rules where there exists considerable practice,[99] as is it possible 'to generalize from a series of consistent domestic laws … where they are sufficiently numerous and similar in content'.[100] Due diligence thus ticks both boxes in this respect. Within international law there is considerable practice on due diligence across a variety of sub-fields. Similarly, within domestic laws, due diligence is prevalent. Considering

[95] *R (on the application of Gentle and another)* [2008] UKHL 20.
[96] ibid para 59.
[97] See also US Federal Securities Act (1933); Bonnitcha and McCorquodale (n 86) 906.
[98] Report, Garcia-Amador (1956) 190.
[99] Sivakumaran (n 45) 1116.
[100] ibid.

this practice showing the application of due diligence across numerous areas of international, regional and domestic law, a suggestion presents itself that due diligence can be generalised into a secondary international rule.

Upon amalgamating the dominant trends of due diligence that become apparent from its use, it is possible to extrapolate from this template. Whether this is a legitimate approach to creating a new rule rests, in part, on 'an assessment as to whether generalization and extrapolation is appropriate in a particular circumstance'.[101] Although due diligence exists as a matter of positive law in a number of fields, it does not currently exist within the general legal framework applicable to the international responsibility of states. This space combined with the adoption of extrapolation highlights that the notion of applying due diligence as a secondary rule rests on reasonable foundations. Legal rules can 'without a proper explanation' be adopted and used 'out of habit or convenience'.[102] And it has been argued that in 'many respects, this is a normal part of law-making'.[103] However, it is 'more legitimate to refer to a standard that already exists than to "invent" one'.[104] The due diligence rule that is being proposed here is 'not going beyond what can be based on existing law'.[105] It is instead based on what law already exists, but presented in an alternative form, for the purposes of being applied as part of an existing legal framework in which it does not currently form part, and thus would apply differently to current applications of due diligence across primary rules of international law and domestic law.

Due diligence applying in the form of a new secondary rule under the law of state responsibility has the potential to contribute to the same cohesion sought by the application of a general rule on complicity and those concerning attribution, as opposed to relying on divergent special rules across sub-fields of international law to address questions of state responsibility for the conduct of non-state actors through the lens of due diligence. The process of generalising due diligence in international law could converge the fragmented practice applying this concept, with its key elements being condensed. The international law applicable to determining the international responsibility of states for the conduct of non-state actors could benefit from more consistency. But is consistency the only reason behind why a new secondary rule of due diligence should be created? What, if any, are other potential benefits?

2.3. Further Factors Favouring a Secondary Due Diligence Rule

Perhaps the most significant factor that arguably points towards the creation of a new secondary due diligence rule is that the current international responsibility framework applicable to addressing questions of indirect state responsibility for the conduct of non-state actors is close to non-existent. A complicity test that

[101] ibid.
[102] ibid 1115.
[103] ibid.
[104] ibid.
[105] ibid 1126; see also W Kälin, 'The Guiding Principles on Internal Displacement – Introduction' (1998) 10 *International Journal of Refugee Law* 557, 561–62.

incorporates non-state actors goes some way towards addressing this matter. However, as of yet, there remains no general test for assessing international responsibility in cases where states contribute to wrongful conduct of non-state actors because of their failures to act. The omissions of states are a significant feature of international responsibility considerations – one that can be better addressed.[106]

A further factor that favours a new international rule on due diligence is that considerable uncertainty surrounds the concept, with it being labelled 'one of the most ambiguous terms in the contemporary discourse on international liability and state responsibility'.[107] Is this owed to the splintered and widespread application of due diligence across many different areas of domestic, regional and international law? Possibly, if not probably. It is not easy to assess what something is when there are multiple opinions on that something. Yet this does not necessarily mean the concept at issue is meaningless purely because its parameters are unclear.[108] Instead, what can happen is uniformity being overshadowed by indeterminacy. This is where the issues with applying due diligence through primary rules becomes apparent. Across primary rules it can be hard to clarify what conduct is required from a state in order for due diligence to have been considered exercised.[109] Even in specific cases there can be multiple ways to interpret what constitutes a state exercising due diligence.[110] This indeterminacy presents a challenge to states in their attempts to navigate what they should do in terms of protecting against non-state actors undertaking conduct that is contrary to international law.[111] The amount and diversity of primary rules that bind states alter the requirements for meeting the threshold of exercising due diligence.[112] This in turn can contribute to perpetuating and aggravating fragmented practice.[113] Rosana Garciandia has argued that the ICJ can assist in addressing this

[106] See GA Christenson, 'Attributing Acts of Omission to the State' (1991) 12 *Michigan Journal of International Law* 312.

[107] J Kulesza, *Due Diligence in International Law* (Leiden, Brill, 2016) 1; see also R Pisillo-Mazzeschi, 'The Due Diligence Rule and the Nature of the International Responsibility of States' (1992) 35 *German Yearbook of International Law* 9.

[108] See D Hyde and D Raffman, 'Sorites Paradox' in EN Zalta (ed), *The Stanford Encyclopedia of Philosophy* (2018) https://plato.stanford.edu/archives/sum2018/entries/sorites-paradox/.

[109] E Askin, 'Due Diligence Obligation in Times of Crisis: A Reflection by the Example of International Arms Transfers' *EJIL: Talk!* (1 March 2017) www.ejiltalk.org/due-diligence-obligation-in-times-of-crisis-a-reflection-by-the-example-of-international-arms-transfers/.

[110] This point is also emphasised in N McDonald, 'The Role of Due Diligence in International Law' (2019) 68 *ICLQ* 1041, 1054.

[111] RP Barnidge, Jr, 'States' Due Diligence Obligations with Regard to International Non-State Terrorist Organisations Post-11 September 2001: The Heavy Burden that States Must Bear' (2005) 16 *Irish Studies in International Affairs* 103.

[112] To the extent that human rights treaty bodies have considered claims for such differentiation, they appear unwilling to accept it: see, for example, Human Rights Committee, Concluding Observations: Algeria, UN Doc CCPR/C/79/Add.95 (1998) para 3 ('a general climate of violence heighten the responsibilities of the State party to re-establish and maintain the conditions necessary for the enjoyment and protection of fundamental rights'); Human Rights Committee, Concluding Observations: Tanzania (1992) para 5; See also L Rajamani, *Differential Treatment in International Environmental Law* (Oxford, Oxford University Press, 2006) 20.

[113] A Peters, 'The Refinement of International Law: From Fragmentation to Regime Interaction and Politicization' (2017) 15 *International Journal of Constitutional Law* 671; G Hafner, 'Pros and Cons Ensuing from Fragmentation of International Law' (2004) 25 *Michigan Journal of International Law* 849.

fragmentation by advancing judicial integration regarding the state responsibility framework and how it is applied.[114] Another way to contribute to integration leading to uniformity in the application of a particular concept is to have rules that can be applied across primary rules without them changing. Just as the attribution tests part of the ARSIWA are a good example of what can be achieved in this respect, so too could a secondary due diligence rule serve the same function. Seen from this perspective, due diligence appears to have more to offer the international law applicable to determining state responsibility if it were to apply as a secondary rule.

Such a rule would not place any international legal obligation on states. What it would do is act as an alternative basis for determining the international responsibility of states in settings where conduct of a non-state actor was contrary to international law. It would do this by prescribing the requirements for assessing whether a state can be considered internationally responsible for a particular omission of its own. The failure of states to act in attempting to regulate the conduct of non-state actors would finally be addressed by the legal framework governing international responsibility. Due diligence would thus sit alongside the secondary rules on attribution and complicity, whilst ensuring conceptual and practical viability by maintaining the distinction between these three bases for determining state responsibility, despite their links and the potential for them to overlap.[115] The significance of this ties back into the law of state responsibility being in a position to properly address issues of both direct and indirect responsibility with respect to the wrongdoing of non-state actors. There are a host of possible scenarios where a nexus between a state and a non-state actor has contributed to conduct contrary to an international rule, but where establishing state responsibility for, or involvement in, that conduct may not be possible through the application of attribution or complicity tests. The research of Hakimi still rings true today in that the 'attribution approach targets a narrower range' of wrongdoers, meaning non-state actors may not be 'sufficiently connected to any state for their conduct to be attributable to a state'.[116] Recall also from chapter 6 the difficulties that come with attempting to satisfy the requirements for establishing state responsibility for complicity in non-state actor wrongdoing. A due diligence secondary rule would thus help address state conduct that contributes to non-state actor conduct that is contrary to international law where the two entities share a connection, but 'short of the [state] participation necessary for attribution' or complicity to establish international responsibility.[117] A due diligence test might thus catch what complicity and attribution tests fail to catch.

[114] R Garciandia, 'State Responsibility and Positive Obligations in the European Court of Human Rights: The Contribution of the ICJ in Advancing Towards more Judicial Integration' (2020) 33 *Leiden Journal of International Law* 177.

[115] See Mackenzie-Gray Scott (n 2) 367–71.

[116] M Hakimi, 'State Bystander Responsibility' (2010) 21 *European Journal of International Law* 341, 349; See also Communication No 17/2008 (29 July 2011), UN Doc CEDAW/C/49/D/17/2008; Communication No. 1020/2001 (19 September 2003), UN Doc CCPR/79/D/1020/2001.

[117] Hakimi (ibid) 354.

Unshackling from the state-centric approach of the ILC towards international responsibility is also a significant factor that favours the development of new rules that can complement the ARSIWA. Considering the frequency with which states act in consort with, use, enable or allow non-state actors to undertake wrongful conduct, and the impact this has on individuals, communities, businesses and societies more generally, why settle for the mainstream position regarding the determination of state responsibility? It is not easy to envisage how non-state actors can be further incorporated within the scope of this legal framework unless it is allowed to develop in line with contemporary practice. The ARSIWA was never intended to be an exhaustive reflection of the international law applicable to state responsibility. Nor need it take up so much space in this area despite its many merits. But this cannot change unless new suggestions are put forward. The due diligence rule proposed here is nothing more than one such suggestion – one that is aimed at having a new tool in part of the toolbox that is opened up when addressing questions of state responsibility for the conduct of non-state actors. The next question is how would this new tool apply in practice, and what are the requirements that would need to be satisfied to establish state responsibility for a failure to exercise due diligence?

3. APPLYING A SECONDARY DUE DILIGENCE RULE

As due diligence has yet to apply as a secondary rule of international law, the content here draws on the constituent elements of the concept when it has been applied in domestic, regional and international legal practice. These elements are drawn out from examining their prevalence across primary rules and domestic laws, the identification of which is possible by recognising their consistent treatment in due diligence assessments. This is not to say that the elements identified here are exhaustive, there could well be others. But what is clear is that four are predominant in determining the exercise of due diligence, which are interlinked and couple up quite neatly. The first of these pairs of elements are power and authority. The second are foreseeability and precaution. What ties them together is that they all appear to be assessed through a lens of reasonableness. This helps set out the requirements and their respective thresholds for determining whether a state has exercised due diligence. In turn, by offering analysis that assesses whether a state exercised due diligence in a particular case involving conduct of a non-state actor that was contrary to an international rule, it becomes easier to see what due diligence is in the context of international responsibility.

3.1. Reasonableness as a Lens that Helps Assess the Requirements of Due Diligence

States' capabilities are a prominent factor when assessing what is required from them in due diligence terms regarding the relationships they share with non-state actors.[118]

[118] See *Prosecutor v Stanislav Galic* (Judgement and Opinion), Case No IT-98-29-T (5 December 2003) para 58.

These capabilities are relative between states and are taken into consideration with respect to due diligence assessments.[119] They also share a connection with reasonableness in setting expectations of what states should do in particular circumstances. In *R (Smith)*, the UK Supreme Court held:

> Troops on active service are at risk of being killed despite the exercise of due diligence by those responsible for doing their best to protect them. Death of a serviceman from illness no more raises an inference of breach of duty on the part of the State than the death of a civilian in hospital.[120]

States need to do enough in their efforts to address, suppress or prevent a particular outcome in order to be considered to have exercised due diligence. But that threshold of 'enough' is contextual and dependent on what state is being scrutinised for what outcome. The application of reasonableness to due diligence assessments also means that state responsibility would not necessarily turn on the state actually preventing conduct of a non-state actor that was contrary to an international rule. The idea underpinning the concept of reasonableness when applied to considerations of state responsibility is that states are assessed on whether it was feasible for them to address, suppress or prevent the conduct of non-state actors.

States 'have myriad measures' for regulating non-state actors.[121] However, these measures, and the feasibility of implementing them, vary from state to state. This is because states do not have the same capabilities and capacities for regulating non-state actors with the aim of addressing, suppressing or preventing conduct that is contrary to international rules. Non-state actors themselves also play a significant role in what states are able to accomplish in this respect, particularly if they wield and exercise more power and influence than many, most or maybe all states.[122] It is a quaint idea that states are the epicentre of global power structures. Nevertheless, the law of international responsibility will likely continue to hobble along with its prevalent focus on states until the international law project as a whole comes to terms with, and starts adequately addressing, other actors. That said, although states vary in terms of their economic, legislative, military, moral and technological robustness, they currently remain able to shape the conduct of non-state actors. This relative competency must be accounted for should a secondary due diligence rule end up applying in practice. Relative competency comprises two inseparable elements, which are also the first pair of requirements for determining whether a state has exercised due diligence: power and authority.

3.1.1. Power and Authority

If due diligence were to apply as a secondary rule, a state would be assessed on whether they did everything that was reasonably within their power and authority

[119] See Fourth Report, Ago (1972) 134 and 138.

[120] *R (on the application of Smith) and Equality and Human Rights Commission (intervening) v Secretary of State for Defence* [2010] UKSC 29, para 84.

[121] Hakimi (n 116) 371.

[122] M Babic, E Heemskerk and J Fichtner, 'Who Is More Powerful – States or Corporations?' *The Conversation* (10 July 2018) https://theconversation.com/who-is-more-powerful-states-or-corporations-99616.

to address conduct of a non-state actor that was contrary to an international rule.[123] This would mean that to avoid falling foul of this rule, states would need to conduct themselves diligently towards non-state actors with which they share a connection.[124] However, this expectation is limited to the state in question having the authority to exercise its power, which depends on the circumstances of each case, including the 'means reasonably available' to the state and 'the degree of influence' it wields over the non-state actor in question.[125] The type of nexus shared between a state and a non-state actor thus factors into determining whether there has been a failure to exercise due diligence.

For those who may consider this to seem a bit fuzzy, it can be helpful to consider an example. If the non-state actor is a company that has been employed by a state to carry out a particular function, say, conduct military operations abroad, the expectation of exercising due diligence would be relatively higher for the employer state compared to the state that the company is physically operating within, which would be relatively lower because, say, that state does not have the economic and military power to influence the company that is operating within its borders, even though it has the authority to do so owing to the very fact that the company is operating on its territory.[126] The due diligence required by a state with respect to the conduct of a non-state actor thereby decreases the further the capabilities and capacity of the state to act are impaired by circumstance, which is influenced by a state's power over, authority to regulate, and nexus to, a non-state actor.

Due diligence consists of the 'efficiency and care used by governmental instrumentalities'.[127] This is particularly important when states delegate public functions to autonomous non-state actors. In terms of preventing responsibility gaps, the difficulties in pinpointing the domestic law that empowers non-state actors to exercise governmental authority means that determining state responsibility by way of attribution may not be possible, but doing so via a due diligence assessment might be. Such delegation is a helpful example of how the power and authority dynamic plays out as a requirement for establishing a due diligence failure. Should a state delegate to a non-state actor in order to carry out a particular task or fulfil a particular function, this brings with it a higher expectation of exercising due diligence compared to that which is expected with respect to other non-state actors to which the state did not delegate. This is because of the pre-existing arrangement between the state and the non-state actor in question. Such arrangements demonstrate the state has power over the non-state actor, as delegation presupposes the ability to exert influence, and has the authority to exercise that power, as provided by the very domestic law that creates the official relationship with the non-state actor to which tasks and functions are delegated.

[123] Convention (I) for the Amelioration of the Condition of the Wounded and Sick in Armed Forces in the Field. Geneva, 12 August 1949, Commentary (2016) paras 118 and 153.

[124] ibid para 135.

[125] ibid paras 150 and 165.

[126] M Turcan and N Ozpinar, '"Who Let the Dogs Out?": A Critique of the Security for Hire Option in Weak States' (2009) 2 *Dynamics of Asymmetric Conflict* 143; G Cronogue, 'Rebels, Negligent Support, and State Accountability: Holding States Accountable for the Human Rights Violations of Non-State Actors' (2013) 23 *Duke Journal of Comparative & International Law* 365.

[127] Second Report, Garcia-Amador (1957) 122.

It is important when states are assessed on whether they have exercised due diligence that their duties in other settings are taken into consideration because a balance needs to be struck that ensures states can act 'without abandoning other responsibilities that ought not to be abandoned'.[128] This balancing act is the lens of reasonableness in operation when examining the power and authority a state had to act in a particular situation where the conduct of a non-state actor was contrary to an international rule, which is a process that is apparent in international practice.[129] In the *Bosnia Genocide* case the ICJ clarified that a state 'does not incur responsibility simply because the desired result is not achieved'.[130] The Court then held that 'responsibility is however incurred if the State manifestly failed to take all measures to prevent genocide which were within its power'.[131] Relative competency pops up again, which to restate is the varying power and authority that states have to adopt measures that can at least attempt to prevent, or actually suppress or address, conduct originating from non-state actors that is contrary to international rules. The ICJ provides further clarification, emphasising that 'the capacity [of the state] to influence effectively the action of persons likely to commit, or already committing' the wrong in question, 'which varies greatly from one State to another', should be taken into consideration when determining state responsibility for a failure to do something.[132] A further insight provided by the Court is that:

> This capacity itself depends, among other things, on the geographical distance of the State concerned from the scene of the events, and on the strength of the political links, as well as links of all other kinds, between the authorities of that State and the main actors in the events.[133]

The proximity or remoteness between a state and a non-state actor is thus also determinative in due diligence assessments, yet perhaps not only in the sense of time and space, but in other respects as well, such as legislatively. For example, there will exist more legislative proximity between a company domiciled in a state compared to one that is not. Similarly, there will exist more remoteness between an extremist group and a state that they do not operate within compared to the state in which they do. The facts of each individual case will set the expectations as to whether due diligence should have been exercised. In general, if a state has knowledge, or should have knowledge, that a space subject to its power and authority is being, or will be, used to carry out conduct contrary to international law, it should deploy its best

[128] JW Nickel, 'How Human Rights Generate Duties to Protect and Provide' (1993) 15 *Human Rights Quarterly* 77, 81.

[129] *Nicaragua*, Judgment, 27 June 1986, para 220; *Armed Activities on the Territory of the Congo (Democratic Republic of the Congo v Uganda)*, Judgment, 19 December 2005, ICJ Rep [2005] 168, paras 211 and 345; *Legal Consequences of the Construction of a Wall in the Occupied Palestinian Territory*, Advisory Opinion, 9 July 2004, ICJ Rep [2004] 136, paras 158–59; UNSC Res. 681 (20 December 1990) UN Doc S/RES/681, para 5.

[130] *Application of the Convention on the Prevention and Punishment of the Crime of Genocide (Bosnia and Herzegovina v Serbia and Montenegro)*, Judgment, 26 February 2007, ICJ Rep [2007] 43, para 430.

[131] ibid.

[132] ibid.

[133] ibid.

efforts 'to put an end to [the] threat, even if the outcome cannot be ensured'.[134] If a state conducts itself along these lines, then its international responsibility for failing to exercise due diligence will likely not be established, even if the conduct of the non-state actor that was contrary to an international rule ultimately took place.

3.1.2. Foreseeability and Precaution

The second pairing of elements that form part of the due diligence concept are foreseeability and precaution. When examined through the lens of reasonableness, it becomes clearer how they would apply alongside power and authority as requirements of a secondary due diligence rule. Similar to power and authority, foreseeability and precaution share a connection in the context of determining international responsibility for due diligence failings. Foreseeability is in a basic sense about making a prediction about the likely result of conduct, thus concerning the knowledge and perception of the present in order to anticipate the future. The concept is used to judge the consequences of conduct as to whether they were predictable, examined through the lens of reasonableness. Reasonable foreseeability is used as a test in order to determine liability for negligence.[135] The concept of foreseeability has formed part of due diligence assessments for centuries, which has been part of carving out a distinct basis for establishing responsibility that accounts for 'what should have been foreseen by a diligent' person but 'was not foreseen', or perhaps foreseen but not acted upon.[136]

The ILA has contributed to how foreseeability fits into due diligence considerations, showing that establishing a state's failure to exercise due diligence depends on being able to demonstrate that the state did not 'prevent foreseeable significant damage, or at least minimize the risk of such harm'.[137] This premise builds on the work that the ILC has undertaken on the prevention of transboundary harm, which highlights that:

> [D]ue diligence is manifested in reasonable efforts by a State to inform itself of factual and legal components that relate foreseeably to a contemplated procedure and to take appropriate measures, in [a] timely fashion, to address them.[138]

Appropriate measures are where the concept of precaution comes in. Implementing measures that at least have the potential to prevent reasonably foreseeable outcomes entails a degree of precaution involved in the preparation of planned conduct. An example is hard hats being mandatory for workers operating on construction sites. While the likelihood of being hit on the head with a brick or whatnot while doing manual labour will vary depending on where someone is working, a hard hat is a precaution to help protect people from outcomes that may not even reach the

[134] Christakis (n 85) 18.

[135] D Keeley. 'The Test of Reasonable Foreseeability: As Applied to Intervening Negligence Rather Than the Particular Act Constituting the Negligence' (1961) 13 *Hastings Law Journal* 160.

[136] Justinian, *The Digest of Roman Law: Theft, Rapine, Damage and Insult* (London, Penguin, 1979) 91.

[137] ILA Study Group on Due Diligence in International Law, First Report (7 March 2014) 26.

[138] Draft Articles on Prevention of Transboundary Harm from Hazardous Activities (2001) Art 3, Commentary, para 10; see also paras 5 and 18.

threshold of being reasonably foreseeable.[139] Another example is if a person is going to give a kid a gun to play around with they remove all the bullets from the weapon beforehand, or risk the reasonably foreseeable outcome (ie shooting and killing someone by accident).[140] While on the topic of killing people, foreseeability is also ingrained in a sub-field of international law that concerns how to deliberately and lawfully kill people: international humanitarian law.

The foreseeability of a breach of a rule from international humanitarian law and the knowledge thereof determines whether a state is responsible for failing to ensure respect for that particular rule.[141] The prohibition on disproportionate attacks stipulates that 'launching an attack which may be expected to cause incidental loss of civilian life … which would be excessive in relation to the concrete and direct military advantage anticipated, is prohibited'.[142] The use of 'expected' and 'anticipated' put forward the rationale that this principle is embedded with characteristics of the foreseeability concept. There is also the principle of precautions in attack, which sets a requirement of taking all feasible precautions, where 'feasible' means 'practicable' or 'practically possible' in the circumstances.[143] This requires belligerents to take preliminary measures before conducting military operations, which includes assessing the apparent nature of the situation and conducting the operation in a manner that is expected to have the least amount of damage.[144] Breaches can occur when the conduct of belligerents was not carried out with precaution in the planning and decisions regarding the methods of warfare used throughout the course of the particular operation. In correlation with the concept of foreseeability, the importance of the precautionary principle is that it intends to minimise damage, which can be catalysed and amplified if foreseeable consequences of conduct are not considered in the preparatory stages of planned conduct.

In another sub-field of international law, the principle of non-refoulement concerns the likelihood of people being persecuted should they be forced to return to a state.[145] Foreseeability and precaution are intertwined when making assessments in these cases, as it is taken into account what could happen to the person in question if they are forced to return to a particular state and weighing that up alongside the precautionary measure of allowing them to remain in a different state. In domestic

[139] W Ibbs and P Razavi, 'Foreseeability in Construction' (2016) 6 *Journal of Legal Affairs and Dispute Resolution in Engineering and Construction* 1.

[140] J Diaz, 'High Gun Sales and More Time at Home Have Led to More Accidental Shootings by Kids' *NPR* (31 August 2021) www.npr.org/2021/08/31/1032725392/guns-death-children.

[141] Convention (I) for the Amelioration of the Condition of the Wounded and Sick in Armed Forces in the Field, Geneva, 12 August 1949, Commentary (2016), para 150.

[142] ICRC, Customary IHL Database, Rule 14 https://ihl-databases.icrc.org/customary-ihl/eng/docs/v1_cha_chapter4_rule14.

[143] ICRC, Customary IHL Database, Rule 15 https://ihl-databases.icrc.org/customary-ihl/eng/docs/v1_rul_rule15.

[144] I Robinson and E Nohle, 'Proportionality and Precautions in Attack: The Reverberating Effects of Using Explosive Weapons in Populated Areas' (2016) 98 *International Review of the Red Cross* 107.

[145] J. Pirjola, 'Shadows in Paradise – Exploring *Non-Refoulement* as an Open Concept' (2008) 19 *International Journal of Refugee Law* 639.

law, the precedent set in the *Donoghue v Stevenson* case also highlights the interwoven nature of foreseeability and precaution, where it was held that: 'You must take reasonable care to avoid acts or omissions which you can reasonably foresee would be likely to injure your neighbour.'[146] Similarly, ITLOS has ruled that:

> [T]he precautionary approach is also an integral part of the general obligation of due diligence of sponsoring States. ... The due diligence obligation of the sponsoring States requires them to take all appropriate measures to prevent damage that might result from the activities of contractors that they sponsor, [including in] situations where scientific evidence concerning the scope and potential negative impact of the activity in question is insufficient but where there are plausible indications of potential risks.[147]

Determining state responsibility for a due diligence failure involves an assessment regarding whether there was a 'failure of agents of the State to foresee the consequences' of their inaction.[148] The approach of the ICC towards determining recklessness also takes into account whether a party 'foreseeing the occurrence of the undesired consequences as a mere likelihood or possibility' of its conduct proceeds regardless (ie without taking any precautions).[149]

Should a secondary due diligence rule one day apply to determine the international responsibility of states for the conduct of non-state actors, foreseeability and precaution would likely be part of its requirements. The two concepts form an important component of state decision-making, one that, if realised, aligns with the exercise of due diligence. If states take into account the reasonably foreseeable outcomes of their inaction and implement precautionary measures in order to attempt preventing those outcomes from occurring, then they do not risk their international responsibility being established on the basis of a due diligence failing. Although it will not always be a simple process for states to draw a 'line between the foreseeable and the unforeseeable in the world of everyday affairs' before they carry out their choices,[150] the benefit of hindsight after these choices have been put into practice will allow courts, states and other actors to assess whether states accounted for reasonably foreseeable outcomes in the planning of those choices. This approach to determining the exercise of due diligence could further compel states to carefully consider the potential future consequences of their decisions, and take precautions in contexts where there exists the likelihood of non-state actors undertaking conduct that is contrary to international rules, lest they risk the possibility of their international responsibility being established.

[146] *Donoghue v Stevenson* [1932] UKHL 100.

[147] *Responsibilities and obligations of States sponsoring persons and entities with respect to activities in the Area*, Advisory Opinion, No 17, 1 February 2011, ITLOS Rep [2011] 10, para 131.

[148] Sixth Report, International Responsibility, FV Garcia Amador, A/CN.4/134 and Add 1, YBILC (1961) vol II, 41; see also H Moynihan, 'Aiding and Assisting: The Mental Element Under Article 16 of the International Law Commission's Articles on State Responsibility' (2018) 67 *ICLQ* 455, at 464.

[149] *Prosecutor v Bemba*, Pre-Trial Chamber, ICC-01/05-01/08, Judgment (15 June 2009) para 363.

[150] L Green, 'Foreseeability in Negligence Law' (1961) 61 *Columbia Law Review* 1401, 1413; see also I Plakokefalos, 'Causation in the Law of State Responsibility and the Problem of Overdetermination: In Search of Clarity' (2015) 26 *European Journal of International Law* 471.

3.2. So What Is Due Diligence?

Due diligence will mean different things to different individuals and collectives depending on their perspectives in a particular context. Therefore, the suggestion put forward below as to what due diligence is in the context of determining the international responsibility of states for the conduct of non-state actors is in no way intended to be prescriptive to other contexts, even if it might serve as a guiding reference. Furthermore, although it ultimately falls to states and other actors that influence states to decide whether to create criteria for defining when state conduct does and does not meet the threshold of exercising due diligence when determining international responsibility, it is important to offer a counterbalance against leaving states complete discretion in defining for themselves what constitutes due diligence in this context. A crucial factor to bear in mind here is the nexus between a state and a non-state actor, which can also take into account the severity and scale of the wrongdoing undertaken by the non-state actor.[151] However, the elements that are arguably not optional when determining state responsibility for non-state actor conduct on the basis of a due diligence failing are power, authority, foreseeability and precaution. Due diligence can thus be considered to be a state exercising its power to implement precautionary measures for the purpose of attempting to prevent or suppress reasonably foreseeable conduct of a non-state actor that would be contrary to an international rule in situations where the state has the authority to conduct itself in such a manner. In short, due diligence is the exercise of power within the bounds of authority that takes precautions with the aim of preventing foreseeable outcomes from transpiring.

Generally speaking, states have power and authority over many non-state actors, meaning they can exert influence to prevent, or attempt to prevent, these non-state actors from undertaking conduct that is contrary to international rules.[152] Yet a state must have both the power and the authority to act in such a way. Not conflating these two elements is crucial. A state may have the power to do something, but that does not mean it has the authority to do it, and vice versa. For example, one state may have the power to enter another state for the purpose of putting an end to conduct of a non-state actor that is contrary to an international rule, but this does not automatically signify the presence of the authoritative basis for doing so, such as the provision of domestic legislation and the consent of the state it entered into. On the flip side, a state may have the authority to put an end to wrongful conduct of a non-state actor that operates out of its territory, but may lack the power to do so. With respect to the elements of foreseeability and precaution, their presence as requirements of a secondary due diligence rule would mean states being assessed on whether they considered the potential future consequences of their inaction, and

[151] See, for example, *Da Penha v Brazil*, Case 12.051, IACHR, Report No 54/01 (2000) para 56; *Opuz v Turkey*, App No 33401/02 (ECtHR, 9 June 2009) paras 91–106 and 132; *Saadi v Italy*, App No 37201/06 (ECtHR, 28 February 2008); *Ilaşcu and Others v Moldova and Russia*, App No 48787/99 (ECtHR, 8 July 2004) paras 28–185, 380–82, 393–94. However, see also Committee on the Elimination of Discrimination Against Women, Communication No 6/2005: *Yildirim v Austria*, UN Doc CEDAW/C/39/D/6/2005 (2007) para 12.1.2.

[152] ILA Study Group on Due Diligence in International Law, First Report (7 March 2014) 26.

what they did to attempt averting those consequences. The combination of these two requirements accounts for what states knew or ought to have known in terms of realising that non-state actor conduct contrary to an international rule would likely occur in the ordinary course of events if due diligence were not exercised.[153]

These four requirements of a secondary due diligence rule are considered through the lens of reasonableness, whether taken individually or collectively. This should not be mistaken to mean that due diligence is reasonableness, but instead that determinations of state responsibility for non-state actor conduct on the basis of a secondary due diligence rule should be considered within a margin of reasonableness. Such assessments will be relevant to cases where states are passively implicated in the wrongdoing of non-state actors, but not necessarily actively contributing to that wrongdoing. A secondary due diligence rule would therefore determine the international responsibility of a state for a distinct wrongful act that is owed to its own failure to at least attempt preventing, suppressing or addressing conduct of a non-state actor that is contrary to an international rule. Having this rule would mean a new basis for determining indirect state responsibility for non-state actor conduct would exist under general international law, of which the test could read:

> A state shall be considered internationally responsible for failing to exercise due diligence in connection with the conduct of a person or entity if:
>
> (a) The state did not exercise the power it had in an attempt to prevent, suppress or address the conduct of that person or entity;
> (b) The state had the authority to exercise the power in question;
> (c) The conduct of the person or entity was foreseeable in the ordinary course of events;
> (d) The state did not implement precautionary measures relative to its nexus with that person or entity;
> (e) The conduct of the person or entity was contrary to an international rule, meaning the state had an international obligation corresponding to the rule of international law that the conduct of the person or entity would have breached if that person or entity bore the same international obligation as the state with respect to the applicable rule.

4. CONCLUSION

There is a conceptual density that comes with determining the international responsibility of states for the conduct of non-state actors on the basis of a due diligence test – one to which centuries of practice and insights across domestic, regional and international law have contributed. These historic efforts make it easier to envisage how due diligence can be formulated as a secondary rule of international law. Putting

[153] Restatement (Third), *Foreign Relations Law of the United States* (1987) s 711 n 2B; FV García-Amador, LB Sohn, and RR Baxter, *Recent Codification of the Law of State Responsibility for Injuries to Aliens* (Leiden, Nijhoff, 1974) 27; Committee on the Elimination of Discrimination against Women, Communication No 5/2005: *Goekce v Austria*, UN Doc CEDAW/C/39/D/5/2005 (2007) para 12.1.4; *Osman v United Kingdom*, para 116; *Soering v United Kingdom*, App No 14038/88 (ECtHR, 7 July 1989) paras 88, 91, 92, 98, 111.

this idea into practice also rests on the adoption of a methodology that the ILC utilised to help build its influential ARSIWA. Yet this component of the state responsibility framework need not be considered to represent its whole. Sector-specific rules have already shown that the ARSIWA is not exhaustive and does not prevent new rules from developing and applying in the future. The same can be said for general rules. This is apposite when considering due diligence, as there is no basis at present under the current law of state responsibility that considers the general conditions for determining the international responsibility of states for their failures to act in circumstances where non-state actors have undertaken conduct contrary to international rules. There is thus an existing opportunity to forge such a basis with the hope of equipping this area of international law with a new tool to confront the problems put before it.

Applying due diligence as a secondary rule also offers the promise of injecting a wee bit more unity into a legal order that is fragmented, in some respects to the point of incoherence. There is a key reason why some consider the due diligence concept to be one of the most ambiguous in contemporary discussions about international law: it means different things across different sub-fields. However, when these differences taken together with those from domestic law are sifted through, commonalities begin to appear that can coalesce to form a coherent account of due diligence. Whether a secondary due diligence rule encapsulates this concept in its best possible form is for others to judge. Through such judgment it will also become clearer whether and how this rule should apply in practice, as well as whether it will come to form part of the positive law in this area. Yet on this latter point it is worth recalling the influence that provisions of the ARSIWA have had through their digestion by courts, tribunals and other actors that are not states. Not forming part of positive international law is not necessarily equal to not forming part of international practice. In terms of the bases that are currently utilised in legal practice to engage with questions of state responsibility for the conduct of non-state actors, it appears not to matter all that much whether a so-called rule of international law rests on the foundations of state practice and opinio juris. Sometimes regardless of what states say or do, what appears to be of greater influence is *who* advances an assertion or argument based on their own perceptions and agendas. As with many things in this weird world, branding and status hold (too) much sway. Truth can be communicated by any source, but whether it is received as such partly depends on the platform provided to that source. An assertion from an ICJ judge will likely trump an argument from an 'ordinary' member of the public in terms of its perceived accuracy. Stamping the brand of the ILC on an output would likely result in its contents being considered more robust than if it were portrayed to be the research of a solitary professor.

The overarching point here is that a secondary due diligence 'rule' need not be any different from other 'rules' under the ARSIWA (or elsewhere), in that they need not actually exist as international rules in order to be used in practice. A different way to think about the bases for determining state responsibility for the conduct of non-state actors is that they are tests that set out different avenues for approaching this undertaking. They form part of a blueprint. And blueprints can always be changed. Facilitating the development of legal practice focused on questions of state responsibility for non-state actor conduct depends on the construction of visions setting out where the law should venture, and why. It is perhaps past time that the law of state responsibility included a basis for determining indirect international responsibility when states fail to act. In so doing, the other bases for determining direct and indirect state responsibility for non-state actor conduct would be supplemented. There are limits as to what can be expected from attribution and complicity in working towards outcomes in which states can be held to account under international law for their involvement in the wrongdoing of non-state actors. Up to this point in time, attribution has been relied on to do most of the heavy lifting here. Whether this continues depends on recognising and addressing the dearth of secondary rules applicable to determining indirect international responsibility. Should due diligence fill up further space alongside complicity in this regard, this is far from the end of the story. There are other aspects of the fringes of the international law applicable to state responsibility for non-state actors that can still be cast into the foreground.

8

New Tests for New Futures

THERE EXISTS A tapestry of content from international law that can be used to engage with matters concerning state responsibility for non-state actors. In terms of the current framework of secondary rules, these predominantly consist of the ARSIWA provisions on attribution, for the time being at least. There is also the possibility of building on these tests, which form the basis for determining direct international responsibility. By referring to the concepts of complicity and due diligence, further bases for determining international responsibility can be developed, which, crucially, provide avenues towards addressing indirect state responsibility for non-state actor conduct. In addition to applicable general rules, sector-specific rules can apply within sub-fields of international law, as was discussed with respect to the use of force by states in self-defence against non-state actors. Although there is no defined framework governing state responsibility for non-state actor conduct, the aforementioned content can be combined to form the beginnings of one. The cumulative examination of the tests concerning attribution, complicity and due diligence may therefore convey the impression that there is little left to say on questions of state responsibility for non-state actors, at least from the perspective of general international law. However, an uncertainty remains as to whether this content is exhaustive. Pursuing this question reveals other features of the international law on responsibility, which can be brought to bear on issues in which states act in consort with, use, enable or allow non-state actors to undertake conduct that is contrary to international rules. These insights assist in envisaging how the law of state responsibility for non-state actors could function in the future, whilst unearthing some considerations about the processes part of international lawmaking.

1. A DEFAULT APPROACH TO NON-STATE ACTORS IN MATTERS OF STATE RESPONSIBILITY

As was shown in previous chapters, the attribution provisions under the ARSIWA can sometimes be described as restrictive, stringent or narrow. Perhaps such descriptions arise because of the likelihood that a particular attribution test will not capture conduct of states in which they participate in conduct of non-state actors that is contrary to international law. However, much depends on the establishment of facts in a given case and the normative underpinnings of views scrutinising the extent of the capture of an attribution test in that instance. The questions of 'compared to what?' and 'on what basis?' arise when a particular test is considered to be broad or narrow, flexible or stringent, expansive or restrictive. For example, Article 5 could be considered narrow/restrictive/stringent when compared to Article 8 because the latter test does not require the existence of domestic law in order for its attribution threshold to be satisfied. Yet if the domestic law existed in a particular case the same might not be said, or the opposite could be considered true, in that Article 8 is considered more narrow/restrictive/stringent than Article 5, for example, because there was no evidence of instructions being provided by the state to the non-state actor. The point being made is that in the abstract, the threshold for each attribution test under the ARSIWA is no more or less demanding/undemanding than another, as what shapes considerations on the extent of capture of an attribution test is the context it is applied in, including facts and normative judgments relating to those facts.

This is different to the refinement of a particular attribution test during its drafting, in which certain terms are used in order to qualify the test being created. There are a number of such terms within the attribution provisions of the ARSIWA, such as 'empowered by the law' under Article 5 or 'instructions' under Article 8. The ICJ also created its own term of 'complete dependence' in order to qualify what it considers to be de facto state organs.[1] These terms create the criteria that need to be met in order to satisfy the attribution threshold of each test. As there are multiple terms creating different criteria, so there exist multiple attribution tests, which the ARSIWA portrays in Articles 4–11. With respect to state organs, the attribution test under Article 4 is comparatively less precise than the attribution tests under Articles 6 and 7, which also address state organs. Article 4 stipulates that whenever a state organ acts in its official capacity, any of its conduct is always attributable to the state.[2] Article 4 is thus the starting point for determining direct state responsibility for the conduct of state organs, of which there exist more precise denominations under Articles 6 and 7. But what is the starting point for determining direct state responsibility for the conduct of non-state actors? Or to put it another way, is there an Article 4 equivalent for non-state actors? Not under the final version of the ARSIWA at least.[3] Yet the ILC came close to adopting such a provision, one that has remained largely unnoticed to this day.

1.1. Displacing the Starting Point for Attribution Considerations

Whether conduct of an actor that is deemed to be part of the official state structure can be attributed to the state for the purposes of determining international responsibility depends on two factors: first, whether domestic law shows that the actor carrying out the conduct is part of that official structure; and second, whether that actor was acting in an official capacity or 'in an apparently official capacity, or under

[1] *Bosnia Genocide*, Judgment, 26 February 2007, paras 392, 393, 395, 397, 400, 406; see also *Nicaragua*, Judgment, 27 June 1986, paras 109–10.

[2] ARSIWA, Art 4 and Commentary, paras 6, 7 and 13.

[3] Instead, six precise tests are presented to choose from (Arts 5 and 7–11).

[the] colour of [state] authority'.[4] Article 4 covers actors acting on behalf of the state in an official capacity, in that domestic law stipulates this is their professional role, meaning they are attached to the official state structure through domestic law. These actors are labelled 'state organs'. But what about a similar test for actors that are not state organs but still act on behalf of the state, even if there is no domestic law to indicate as much? As the final version of the ARSIWA does not provide an answer, only denominations of a possible answer in Articles 5 and 7–11, further denominations can arise without their origins being clear. This is exemplified in the practice of the ICJ with its creation of the 'complete dependence' test, considered to be an additional means for attributing conduct of a non-state actor to a state, which if satisfied can result in the non-state actor being labelled a '*de facto* state organ'.[5] Non-state actors operating as part of the wider and unofficial state machinery can thus fall within its scope. But the creation of this test does not answer the question of its origins. Of what is the test of complete dependence a more precise denomination? The answer is also the same for the attribution tests under the ARSIWA.

The ILC conceived an attribution test that was a less precise version of all those that ultimately formed part of the final version of the ARSIWA.[6] Its inclusion in the final draft did not come to fruition for reasons that are cumulative and obscure.[7] The attribution test in question is that from 1974, which read:

> *Attribution to the State of the conduct of persons acting in fact on behalf of the State*
>
> The conduct of a person or group of persons shall also be considered as an act of the State under international law if
>
> (a) it is established that such person or group of persons was in fact acting on behalf of that State.[8]

This draft provision was provisionally adopted that same year and remained unchanged for over twenty years. From the text it is arguable that this provision is not a refined rule. It does not stipulate specific terms qualifying when conduct can be attributed to a state, other than a non-state actor must have been acting in fact on behalf of a state. The extent of this precision/imprecision may explain why the draft provision was changed, despite the apparent lack of positive law warranting this change.[9] The ILC saw no reasons to make alterations until after Crawford reworded the draft provision during his work as Special Rapporteur, which culminated in a different version coming into existence that was more precise than the original formulation, a change now enshrined in Article 8.

[4] ARSIWA, Art 4, Commentary, para 13; see also *Francisco Mallén (United Mexican States) v USA* (27 April 1927) UNRIAA, vol IV, 175–77.

[5] See, for example, S Talmon, 'The Responsibility of Outside Powers for Acts of Secessionist Entities' (2009) 58 *ICLQ* 493, 498; A Cassese, 'The Nicaragua and Tadić Tests Revisited in Light of the ICJ Judgment on Genocide in Bosnia' (2007) 18 *European Journal of International Law* 649, 650; A Abass, 'Proving State Responsibility for Genocide: The ICJ in Bosnia v Serbia and the International Commission of Inquiry for Darfur' (2007) 31 *Fordham International Law Journal* 871, 891.

[6] See chapter 3, section 1.

[7] ibid.

[8] ILC Report, Twenty-Sixth Session, 6 May–26 July 1974, UNGA, Twenty-Ninth Session, Supp 10 (A/9610/Rev.1), YBILC (1974) vol II(1), 283.

[9] See chapter 3, section 1 and conclusion.

These findings are notable for an additional reason to those already explored in chapter 3: the shift appears to have overlooked Article 8 being a denomination of the original provision, replacing it with what may be an indicator of a rule that is the starting point for determining direct state responsibility for the conduct of non-state actors. It is unclear whether the ILC viewed the 'acting in fact on behalf of the state' (AFBS) test from this perspective. What is clear is that Crawford changed this original formulation, making it more precise. Alain Pellet summarised the influence Crawford had in shaping the ARSIWA as 'Anglo Saxon pragmatism'.[10] It is a fair and logical presumption that states might not accept a proposed attribution test that opens an unknown number of doors that could lead to their direct international responsibility being established for the conduct of non-state actors. By making a proposed attribution test more precise than its predecessor in terms that further qualify what conduct it could capture, the likelihood of determining state responsibility for non-state actor conduct on that basis of attribution is reduced. If Crawford in his pragmatic approach towards the drafting of the ARSIWA was aiming to avoid ascriptions of state responsibility that states might not accept, then making provisions that address such matters more precise is a reasonable way of helping address such a concern. Whether states would have ultimately settled on the original drafting of the provision that became Article 8 is hard to say. There is evidence suggesting that some states might have accepted the original formulation and that some might not have accepted it without the terminology being made more precise.[11]

The AFBS attribution test from 1974 to 1998 maintained a presence within the ILC. At present this test appears to be the comparatively least precise test for, and thus rational starting point for, determining direct state responsibility for the conduct of non-state actors. It is worth recalling that it is likely the law did not change in 1998, only the provision that became Article 8.[12] These findings prompt several questions. Does the AFBS test proposed by Ago exist within the state responsibility framework today? Since 1998, when the draft provision changed to the depicted tests of state 'control', 'direction' or 'instructions', has the actual rule remained that of AFBS, which has lain dormant in international law, overshadowed by the work of the ILC in putting forward the final version of Article 8 as it is known today? Has this rule been underlying in the positive law this entire time? If not, does it still apply in practice?

1.2. In Search of Practice

From 1998 onwards there appear to have been no clear instances of state practice relating to the AFBS attribution test under the law of state responsibility.[13] This makes

[10] A Pellet, 'The ILC's Articles on State Responsibility for Internationally Wrongful Acts and Related Texts' in J Crawford, A Pellet and S Olleson (eds), *The Law of International Responsibility* (Oxford, Oxford University Press, 2010) 75, 76 and 83.

[11] See, for example, the comments of Canada in Seventh Report, Riphagen (1986) 10; see also chapter 3, section 1.3,.

[12] See chapter 3, section 1.

[13] But see the test using the language of 'acting on behalf of' under international humanitarian law: Convention (I) for the Amelioration of the Condition of the Wounded and Sick in Armed Forces in the

some sense considering the ARSIWA holds the spotlight in the area of state responsibility; why would states, courts and other bodies apply an attribution test that did not make the ILC's final cut? There is one example that can be found in a judgment from the United Kingdom.[14] In this case it was noted:

> States are artificial legal persons: they can only act through the institutions and agencies of the state, which means, ultimately through its officials *and other individuals acting on behalf of the state*. For international conduct which is so serious as to be tainted with criminality to be regarded as attributable only to the impersonal state and not to the individuals who ordered or perpetrated it is both unrealistic and offensive to common notions of justice.[15]

This passage shows that conduct can be attributable to states where those that undertake the conduct are considered to have done so on the behalf of states, even if the persons involved are not state officials, as determined by domestic law. However, this one example is not sufficient for the purposes of showing that the AFBS test forms part of positive law today. Even in wider commentary there appears to have been similarly scarce reference to this attribution test, including in other contexts concerning international responsibility.[16] Although Ago in his role as a special rapporteur identified this test, and it was accepted by the ILC for at least two decades thereafter, the ILC ultimately supplanted it. An effect of this outcome appears to have been the test being perceived as not forming part of the international law applicable to determining state responsibility for the conduct of non-state actors. What else could account for there being so little practice and commentary since 1998? Grappling with this question puts forward another consideration that could also explain the minimal presence of the AFBS test, in addition to that of perceptions regarding its contemporary (ir)relevance.

A key hurdle in assessing whether rules are developing or exist in positive international law is language, particularly levels of proficiency in different languages. This is one reason why treaties are such an important source of international law, as their content can be easier to identify than customary rules when it is expressed in a language or languages that the reader comprehends. Yet identifying customary rules without relying on the claims of commentators depends on being able to comprehend a multitude of languages that are likely beyond the grasp of any one reader, even those who are polyglots or well-versed in the use of translators or translation software. For those who barely have a grasp of one language, it is difficult to envisage how such readers would be in a position to accurately identify the existence of customary rules, aside from that reflected in multilateral treaties or across a

Field, Geneva, 12 August 1949, Commentary (2016) paras 150, 229, 250, 263, 267, 270; see also *Lubanga*, ICC Trial Judgment (2012) para 541; *Bemba*, ICC Trial Judgment (2016) para 130; *Tadić*, paras 81, 84, 90, 91, 99, 117, 120, 122, 124, 129, 133, 152, 162.

[14] *R, ex parte Pinochet v Bartle and ors* [1999] UKHL 17.

[15] ibid para 51 (emphasis added).

[16] RA Wessel, 'The EU as a Party to International Agreements: Shared Competences, Mixed Responsibilities' in M Maresceau and A Dashwood (eds), *Law and Practice of EU External Relations: Salient Features of a Changing Landscape* (Cambridge, Cambridge University Press, 2008) 152, 181.

sample of bilateral treaties.[17] Sivakumaran makes a point worth remembering, which is particularly pertinent to the state responsibility framework applicable to non-state actors:

> The existence of a customary rule is too often asserted without any proof. At the same time, when proof is provided and the methodology behind the determination set out explicitly, it is open to challenge. The existence of customary international law is thus both easy to assert and easy to deny. With relatively few exceptions, the practice and *opinio juris* of particular states tends to be privileged, not necessarily for ideological reasons but, rather, due to the availability of materials, familiarity with practice and linguistic capability on the part of the identifier.[18]

It could be that the AFBS attribution test has been referred to and applied by states that do not use English as their main working language. But equally, this might not be the case. Although it may be that there is further practice from English-language sources, it cannot be said from those that have been uncovered that the AFBS attribution test currently forms part of customary international law. Nor can it be argued that the AFBS test is a developing rule and could become custom in the future, as may be the case with the complicity test examined in chapter 6. In addition, although rules may become part of positive international law through state silence,[19] there is little practice since 1998 to evidence that a clear legal position has been asserted by a state or states regarding the AFBS approach to attribution, which has then been acquiesced to by other states.[20] Although the customary status of the AFBS test is far from certain, it need not remain unused in practice. The significance of applying this test more frequently is worth setting out in light of it being the starting point for determining direct state responsibility for the conduct of non-state actors.

1.3. Significance of a Default Attribution Test Applicable to Non-state Actors

There are many advantages to giving the law precision. Doing so allows rules to be predictable in their implementation, which assists in satisfying one of the core elements of the rule of law: legal certainty.[21] Clear and precise rules avoid vagueness and creating ambiguity regarding what conduct will result in what legal exposure, which entails assessing the risk of a particular line of conduct contravening a rule and the ensuing establishment of responsibility that might follow. Helen Xanthaki points

[17] RR Baxter, 'Multilateral Treaties as Evidence of Customary International Law' (1965) 41 *British Yearbook of International Law* 275; SM Schwebel, 'The Influence of Bilateral Investment Treaties on Customary International Law' (2004) 98 *Proceedings of the Annual Meeting of the American Society of International Law* 27; BD Lepard, *Customary International Law: A New Theory with Practical Applications* (Cambridge, Cambridge University Press, 2012) 191–207.

[18] S Sivakumaran, 'Techniques in International Law-Making: Extrapolation, Analogy, Form and the Emergence of an International Law of Disaster Relief' (2017) 28 *European Journal of International Law* 1097, 1110.

[19] RB Baker, 'Customary International Law in the 21st Century: Old Challenges and New Debates' (2010) 21 *European Journal of International Law* 173, 176.

[20] A Roberts and S Sivakumaran, 'The Theory and Reality of the Sources of International Law' in MD Evans (ed), *International Law*, 5th edn (Oxford, Oxford University Press, 2018) 89, 96.

[21] Venice Commission, *The Rule of Law Checklist* (Council of Europe, 2016) 25–28.

out that ensuring predictability via precision means those that are 'inclined to comply with the law are offered the tools to understand what is required of them'.[22] Domestic courts can even strike down rules for not being precise enough.[23] However, while desirable from a number of perspectives, attempts to achieve precision in lawmaking can result in overprecision. This can be a problem for a number of reasons, some of which are relevant to the international law applicable to determining state responsibility for non-state actors. With respect to the matter of attribution as it applies to non-state actors, the significance of having a test that strikes the right balance in terms of the extent of its precision should not be understated.

1.3.1. Against Overprecision in International Lawmaking

There are a number of reasons why precision in lawmaking can sometimes be problematic.[24] The focus here is on rules being made precise to the point where they unintentionally create regulatory gaps. In other words, when rules are too precise that they fail to capture eventualities common to a particular practice that the law is aimed at governing. To take a hypothetical example, a treaty provision on environmental protection could read:

> *High Contracting Parties agree not to damage the Fancy Forest located at the border between the Independent State of Foogle and the Technocratic Republic of Gacebook.*

An alternative version of this provision could read something like:

> *High Contracting Parties agree not to burn, bomb, or flood the flora and fauna located within the area known as Fancy Forest approximate to the common border between the Independent State of Foogle and the Technocratic Republic of Gacebook.*

The attempt at precision in the second formulation has excluded other forms of conduct that could damage the forest, such as deforestation. By referring to flora and fauna, this formulation also qualifies the content of the forest that should not be burned, bombed or flooded, leaving out any indigenous peoples that live there and their property and cultural heritage. By attempting to ensure that the provision addresses all eventualities, the second formulation does the opposite. While this hypothetical may be a bit crude for some, it highlights the 'trap of over-exhaustiveness'.[25] Daniel Kahneman, Olivier Sibony and Cass Sunstein point out a pitfall of overprecision:

> [I]f there is a specific list of what counts as wrongdoing, then terrible behaviour that is not explicitly covered by the list will end up being tolerated. Because [some] rules have clear edges, people [and/or other actors] can evade them by engaging in conduct that is technically exempted but that creates the same or analogous harms.[26]

[22] H Xanthaki, *Drafting Legislation: Art and Technology of Rules for Regulation* (Oxford, Hart, 2014), 85.
[23] C Lockwood, 'Defining Indefiniteness: Suggested Revisions to the Void for Vagueness Doctrine' (2009) 8 *Cardozo Public Law, Policy, and Ethics Journal* 255.
[24] See R VanSickle-Ward, *The Devil Is in the Details: Understanding the Causes of Policy Specificity and Ambiguity* (New York, SUNY Press, 2014).
[25] Xanthaki (n 22) 91.
[26] D Kahneman, O Sibony and CR Sunstein, *Noise: A Flaw in Human Judgment* (New York, Little, Brown Spark, 2021) 345.

Seeking to craft an exhaustive list of rules can thus inadvertently exclude content applicable to conduct that the proposed law behind the list is endeavouring to cover.

When reflecting on the issue of overprecision and the ARSIWA provisions on attribution, a different picture emerges on the change that took place within the ILC regarding the AFBS test and the final version of Article 8. In supplanting the original provision with another, more precise version that includes three exhaustive terms (control, direction, instructions), which, recalling from chapter 3, all mean the same thing in practice, the final attribution test adopted by the ILC excludes other types of state conduct that could signify a non-state actor had in fact undertaken conduct on its behalf. The AFBS test appears to be the least precise version of all the attribution tests applicable to non-state actors under the ARSIWA. From this perspective these provisions of the ILC are nothing more than a list of proposed rules, which may be indicators of an overarching rule. The manner in which these provisions were presented can give the impression that they are exhaustive, even if they are not. In this respect one important word is missing in the drafting efforts of the ILC regarding attribution: *including*. The way in which the text of the ARSIWA attribution tests was structured could have thus reflected their non-exhaustive content with the use of this word:

> The conduct of a person or group of persons shall be considered an act of a State under international law if the person or group of persons is acting in fact on behalf of that state, including by acting on the instructions of that state or by exercising elements of the governmental authority of that state.

Taking inspiration from the non-exhaustive method adopted when drafting legislation, which is considered to be good practice,[27] the formulation above clarifies that attribution is not limited to a state issuing instructions or a non-state actor exercising governmental authority, meaning the provision does not exclude other means of attribution where a non-state actor has acted in fact on behalf of a state, such as a state acknowledging and adopting non-state actor conduct as its own, or a state employing a non-state actor to carry out a specific task, or a state owning, or sponsoring the conduct of, a non-state actor that functions for the benefit of that state,[28] or a non-state actor undertaking conduct in complete dependence on a state of which they are 'ultimately merely the instrument'.[29] Should the ILC have structured an attribution provision in this or a similar way, it would have shown that attribution is not limited to the examples provided by the ILC. This is important for other reasons.

First, structuring provisions in a non-exhaustive approach may calibrate the perceptions of readers and appliers of the law in a way that is arguably less likely to lead to conscious and unconscious thinking centred on the provisions being exhaustive of the potentially applicable law.[30] The availability bias means information that

[27] Xanthaki (n 22) 91–92; see also F Schulz, *Principles of Roman Law* (Oxford, Clarendon Press, 1936) 79–80.

[28] UN Convention on the Law of the Sea (adopted 10 December 1982; entered into force 16 November 1994) 1833 UNTS 3, Art 139.

[29] *Bosnia Genocide*, Judgment, 26 February 2007, para 392.

[30] D Kahneman, *Thinking, Fast and Slow* (New York, Farrar, Straus & Giroux, 2011) 79–105, in particular see 85–88.

comes to mind with ease can be misrepresented as that which is representative, such as a group of provisions.[31] The relative ease with which the ARSIWA can be accessed and navigated (whether on a device or in print), its authority and prominence derived from the ILC, and the frequency of its use in practice, all contribute to making its content readily available in the minds of those presented with problems concerning state responsibility and attribution. Second, concentrating on the minutiae of a rule can lead to its purpose being neglected and by extension the law not addressing what it arguably should,[32] which in this context is relationships between states and non-state actors and conduct that is contrary to international rules. Third, it has been argued that overprecision can decrease deterrence, as specificity in the law can result in actors simply avoiding undertaking conduct that would be captured by the rule(s) in question, whereas non-exhaustive rules, despite their potential to diminish legal certainty, tap into the risk aversion of actors because of the uncertainties surrounding what conduct will result in legal exposure and likely sanction.[33] However, the extent to which this reason holds any weight in contexts where the actors are states and the rules are international is unclear, opening up a line of inquiry concerning whether the anticipation of international responsibility being potentially established is a deterrent to states undertaking conduct that will result in the commission of an internationally wrongful act, but may also benefit them in some way.[34] Crawford and Watkins take the view that 'state responsibility seems to be a very poor instrument for discouraging behaviour that is deemed undesirable by the international community',[35] which resonates with other arguments that question the deterrence value of the law of state responsibility.[36] Further research has the potential to confirm or refute assumptions that states refrain from undertaking particular courses of conduct because of the likelihood that their international responsibility will be established, including any correlated consequences arising therefrom.[37]

Aside from the possibility that the use of open-ended rules may increase deterrence of wrongful conduct, there is a further reason why the international law applicable to determining state responsibility for non-state actor conduct could do with applying such a rule. The use of open-ended rules helps steer clear of mutually inconsistent meanings arising in practice,[38] an example from the ARSIWA being the text of Article 5

[31] A Tversky and D Kahneman, 'Availability: A Heuristic for Judging Frequency and Probability' (1973) 5 *Cognitive Psychology* 207.

[32] *R (Quintavalle) v Secretary of State for Health* [2003] UKHL 13, para 8.

[33] Kahneman, Sibony and Sunstein (n 26) 346-349.

[34] B Simone, 'Strong States' Noncompliance, Absence, and Self-interest: How Effective are Treaties Really? *Michigan Journal of International Law Blog* (July 2020) www.mjilonline.org/strong-states-noncompliance-absence-and-self-interest-how-effective-are-treaties-really/.

[35] J Crawford and J Watkins, 'International Responsibility' in S Besson and J Tasioulas (eds), *The Philosophy of International Law* (Oxford, Oxford University Press, 2010) 283, 290.

[36] P Allott, 'State Responsibility and the Unmaking of International Law' (1988) 29 *Harvard International Law Journal* 1, 14.

[37] See F Schauer, 'The Political Risks (if any) of Breaking the Law' (2012) 4 *Journal of Legal Analysis* 83; see also PH Robinson and AA Haque, 'Advantaging Aggressors: Justice & Deterrence in International Law' (2011) 3 *Harvard National Security Journal* 143.

[38] P Gottlieb, 'Aristotle on Non-contradiction' in EN Zalta (ed), *The Stanford Encyclopedia of Philosophy* (2019) https://plato.stanford.edu/entries/aristotle-noncontradiction/.

stipulating that domestic law is needed in order to empower a non-state actor to exercise governmental authority, versus the text of Article 7 implying domestic law is not necessarily needed, in addition to the text of Article 9 signifying that a non-state actor exercising elements of governmental authority is not based on a state empowering it to do so, whether through domestic law or otherwise. While an attribution test that is less precise than those under the ARSIWA and applicable to non-state actors is not a magic wand to wave whenever questions of state responsibility for non-state actor conduct arise, there are a few other factors that favour the use of the AFBS test, which simultaneously speak to broader issues beyond the law of international responsibility.

1.3.2. Making the Law of State Responsibility for Non-state Actors More International

Substantial work has been undertaken showing that what is considered to be international law is not all that international.[39] Rule-makers construct much of international law in order to protect their own interests, with the 'rule takers or passive recipients of international law' having little or no influence in the lawmaking process.[40] The development of international law could be shaped by more states, instead of a handful dictating terms.[41] With respect to the international law governing state responsibility for the conduct of non-state actors, domestic courts could become a more active participant in the development of this area. These judicial bodies hold much promise in being agents of change.[42] As Filiz Kahraman, Nikhil Kalyanpur and Abraham Newman argue, domestic 'courts are not simply passive recipients of international law. They redefine what constitutes global law and are essential to how it unfolds in practice.'[43] Yet in order to shape international law, and not only be 'a channel through which to implement or transpose' it,[44] domestic courts need to be provided the space to be creative.

While there are examples of 'creative judicial approaches to attribution'[45] in domestic[46] and regional[47] courts, fostering such practice requires thinking beyond

[39] J Linarelli, ME Salomon, and M Sornarajah, *The Misery of International Law: Confrontations with Injustice in the Global Economy* (Oxford, Oxford University Press, 2018); A Roberts, *Is International Law International?* (Oxford, Oxford University Press, 2017); KT Gaubatz and M MacArthur, 'How International Is "International" Law?' (2001) 22 *Michigan Journal of International Law* 239.

[40] Linarelli, Salomon, and Sornarajah (ibid) 57.

[41] ibid 34, 76, 93, 181, 267, 273.

[42] S Fatima, *Using International Law in Domestic Courts* (Oxford, Hart, 2005); A Roberts, 'Comparative International Law? The Role of National Courts in Creating and Enforcing International Law' (2011) 60 *ICLQ* 57; A Tzanakopoulos and CJ Tams, 'Introduction: Domestic Courts as Agents of Development of International Law' (2013) 26 *Leiden Journal of International Law* 531.

[43] F Kahraman, N Kalyanpur and AL Newman, 'Domestic Courts, Transnational Law, and International Order' (2020) 26 *European Journal of International Relations* 184, 199.

[44] ibid.

[45] P Webb, 'The Weakest Link of the Troika? The Immunity of Heads of Government in Customary International Law' *EJIL: Talk!* (27 October 2021) www.ejiltalk.org/the-weakest-link-of-the-troika-the-immunity-of-heads-of-government-in-customary-international-law/.

[46] *Re Al M (Fact-finding)* [2021] EWHC 1162 (Fam) paras 152–71.

[47] *Carter v Russia*, App No 20914/07 (ECtHR, 21 September 2021) paras 152 and 162–69.

the confines of the attribution provisions under the ARSIWA. This is not the same as disregarding this output, as courts can resort to practices such as adverse inferences and shifting burdens of proof,[48] as well as creatively interpreting the content of provisions,[49] whilst working within the confines set by the ILC. These practices go some way in counteracting the overprecision within the ARSIWA attribution framework. However, if domestic courts are going to depart from the mainstream approaches to attribution, then they need a starting point, a default rule, from which they can build. This is where the AFBS test comes in. It serves as a starting point for determining whether conduct of a non-state actor can be attributed to a state. It would be up to domestic courts to determine – and thus refine – what amounts to a non-state actor acting in fact on behalf of a state for attribution purposes. In having a default reference point to begin analyses on questions of state responsibility for non-state actor conduct that is less precise and general compared to various optional starting points that are all more precise and specific, domestic courts would have the space to decide what elements should be present in order for attribution to occur in a particular case.

Providing domestic courts more space to develop attribution from the starting point of the AFBS test is also a bottom-up approach of developing the international law on determining state responsibility for non-state actors (ie national practice shaping international practice), with the top-down approach being international institutions such as the ILC and ICJ deciding what rules should be created and applied, sometimes regardless of the positions of states. The reasons behind why more bottom-up approaches to developing the international law in this area through domestic courts are desirable in addition to those top-down approaches are twofold and interconnected. First, there is the issue of international institutions lacking diversity. With respect to the ILC and ICJ, two entities that have shaped much if not most of the international law on state responsibility, the lack of diversity is stark. Three per cent of ILC members from 1947 to 2022 have been women.[50] What about the ICJ? Josephine Jarpa Dawuni provides the answer: '[I]t is noteworthy that historically, out of the 108 judges since the court was established, only four have been women, representing 3.7%.'[51] These statistics make the apparent steppingstone/'staging post'[52] culture of ILC members becoming ICJ judges all the more questionable – notable

[48] See M Milanovic, 'European Court Finds Russia Assassinated Alexander Litvinenko' *EJIL: Talk!* (23 September 2021) www.ejiltalk.org/european-court-finds-russia-assassinated-alexander-litvinenko/.

[49] See, for example, the 'implicit instructions' test proposed in N Tsagourias and M Farrell, 'Cyber Attribution: Technical and Legal Approaches and Challenges' (2020) 31 *European Journal of International Law* 941.

[50] P Pillai, 'Representation of Women at the International Law Commission' *Opinio Juris* (7 October 2021) http://opiniojuris.org/2021/10/07/symposium-on-gender-representation-representation-of-women-at-the-international-law-commission/; see also P. Pillai, 'Women in International Law: A Vanishing Act?' *Opinio Juris* (3 December 2018) http://opiniojuris.org/2018/12/03/women-in-international-law-a-vanishing-act/.

[51] JJ Dawuni, 'Disrupting Global Patriarchy: Why Gender Diversity at the International Court of Justice Matters for Africa and the World' *Opinio Juris* (17 November 2020) http://opiniojuris.org/2020/11/17/disrupting-global-patriarchy-why-gender-diversity-at-the-international-court-of-justice-matters-for-africa-and-the-world/.

[52] D Akande, 'Outcome of 2016 Elections to the International Law Commission + Trivia Questions' *EJIL: Talk!* (5 November 2016) www.ejiltalk.org/outcome-of-2016-elections-to-the-international-law-commission/.

examples relevant to the development of the law of state responsibility being Ago and Crawford.[53] Perhaps a more accurate title for this book would be *The Men's Law of State Responsibility for Non-State Actors: Stuck in the Past*. Although the composition of domestic courts in all states may not necessarily be more diverse in terms of gender than the ILC and ICJ,[54] by the very fact that domestic courts are located in different states, there will be more diversity in terms of culture, ethnicity, race and religious (and other) beliefs, although not necessarily in terms of age, class, disability and sexual orientation.[55] This diversity contributes to differences in viewpoints, meaning there exist opportunities to develop the international law on attribution in potentially dissimilar ways, which could then be balanced out against one another when taken collectively.

This diversity under the broad brush of nationality is also distinct to the national diversity presented in international institutions in at least one respect: operationally. By originating from separate entities across different states, judgments from domestic courts when taken in the aggregate are not going to be the product of any groupthink, which has been shown to occur in settings where an assembly of people work together under the mandate of a singular entity.[56] This problem does not necessarily implicate the practice of the ILC, especially considering its review procedure of work product in which states provide comments that are taken into account in discussions and can be worked into changes of draft provisions, but raises questions about what content that contributes to the development of international law gets traction and why.[57] The interpretation of state responsibility by the ILC and ICJ influencing how this area is approached can be supplemented by more insights from domestic courts. Although prominent, the reasoning and/or judgments of international institutions such as the ILC and ICJ need not always be followed by domestic courts.[58] Varied comparative case-law could emerge as a result of such practices. Identifying the commonalities in such case-law would mean that if there was consensus across domestic courts in different states on a particular approach to attribution, then it might indicate developing international custom. The international law on determining state responsibility for the conduct of non-state actors could consequently become more international, united in its diversity.

The second related reason favouring a bottom-up approach to crafting the international law in this area through domestic courts relates to the separation of powers

[53] ICJ, Members of the Court past and present (2021) www.icj-cij.org/en/all-members.

[54] JJ Dawuni, 'To "Mother" or Not to "Mother": The Representative Roles of Women Judges in Ghana' (2016) 60 *Journal of African Law* 419, 423; see also, for example, the UK, where '32% of court judges and 47% of tribunal judges were women as at 1 April 2020' (Ministry of Justice, Diversity of the judiciary: Legal professions, new appointments and current post-holders, 2020 statistics) 16.

[55] AJ Kang, MC Kittilson, V Hoekstra and MC Escobar-Lemmon, 'Diverse and Inclusive High Courts: A Global and Intersectional Perspective' (2020) 8 *Politics, Groups, and Identities* 812.

[56] CR Sunstein and R Hastie, *Wiser: Getting Beyond Groupthink to Make Groups Smarter* (Boston, MA, Harvard Business School Press, 2014); see also Kahneman, Sibony and Sunstein (n 26) 94–106.

[57] D Azaria, 'The Working Methods of the International Law Commission: Adherence to Methodology, Commentaries and Decision-Making' in UN (ed), *Seventy Years of the International Law Commission: Drawing a Balance for the Future* (Leiden, Brill/Nijhoff, 2020) 172, in particular at 181–83.

[58] D Azaria, '"Codification by Interpretation": The International Law Commission as an Interpreter of International Law' (2020) 31 *European Journal of International Law* 171; R Rosenstock, 'The ILC and State Responsibility' (2002) 96 *American Journal of International Law* 792.

within domestic legal systems.[59] Constitutional law protects against domestic courts bending to the will of governments.[60] The government of a state should not be able to influence the decision-making and rulings of judicial bodies within that state, beyond arguing their side of cases before such bodies. However, in international forums, such as the ILC, states can exert comparatively more influence over decisions and outcomes that shape international law.[61] As exerting influence is a normal part of diplomacy, the ILC can be limited by this power in expanding international law beyond the constraints of the politics at play regarding state preferences. It may also be that the ILC depends on such practice to maintain its institutional legitimacy from the perspective of states, as it gives them a voice (referring to 'representation and influence of a state in the decision-making of an international institution').[62] A problematic factor in this regard is if a state exerts influence over a particular ILC member that happens to be particularly influential within the group of members because, for example, of 'their ability to make and explain their judgments with confidence',[63] as cascade effects can occur in which the position of the influential member on a particular point can result in other members following that position, even if they disagree with it.[64] The contextual significance here is if members of the ILC in pragmatic attempts to appease states and foster consensus water down or alter proposed rules for the benefit of certain states.[65] Laurence Boisson de Chazournes notes that the 'political sensitivity' associated with a certain topic can also contribute to final outputs not being produced.[66] But aside from leaving more space to potentially foster bottom-up approaches to developing the international law on state responsibility for non-state actors through domestic courts, at least in addition to those top-down approaches that already occur, which in turn could help this area become more international, why else could the law in this area do with a less refined attribution rule?

1.3.3. Non-state Actors as an Elementary Consideration

Keeping pace with contemporary realities and being prepared to effectively engage with possible futures are matters with which the law can struggle.[67] These matters

[59] See B Ackerman, 'The New Separation of Powers' (2000) 113 *Harvard Law Review* 633.

[60] Venice Commission, *The Rule of Law Checklist* (2016) 33–38.

[61] Z Trávníčková, 'The International Law Commission and the International Law Codification Market' in UN (n 57) 351, 360–64.

[62] J Tallberg and S Verhaegen, 'The Legitimacy of International Institutions among Rising and Established Powers' (2020) 11 *Global Policy* 115, 116.

[63] Kahneman, Sibony and Sunstein (n 26) 228.

[64] Sunstein and Hastie (n 56) 109–44; Kahneman, Sibony and Sunstein (n 26) 94–106.

[65] WA Schabas, *The International Criminal Court: A Commentary on the Rome Statute*, 2nd edn (Oxford, Oxford University Press, 2016) 19.

[66] LB de Chazournes, 'The International Law Commission in a Mirror – Forms, Impact and Authority' in UN (n 57) 133, 148.

[67] GE Marchant, BR Allenby and JR Herkert (eds), *The Growing Gap Between Emerging Technologies and Legal-Ethical Oversight* (Cham, Springer, 2011); L Finlay and C Payne, 'Why International Law Is Failing to Keep Pace with Technology in Preventing Cyber Attacks' *The Conversation* (19 February 2019) https://theconversation.com/why-international-law-is-failing-to-keep-pace-with-technology-in-preventing-cyber-attacks-111998.

are particularly acute with respect to the law of state responsibility in its approach towards non-state actors. From a historical perspective non-state actors existed before the abstract state came into being. These actors are not a recent phenomenon across societies. Yet non-state actors to the law of state responsibility can, by way of definition, be perceived as exceptional to this framework. Challenging the apparent exceptional nature of non-state actors within this area of international law is significant for many reasons, some of which were explored in chapter 1. The ARSIWA attribution framework treats non-state actors as exceptional because it sets out specific exceptions to the general premise that state responsibility is limited to conduct of actors that domestic law stipulates are undertaking their roles officially on the behalf of states.[68] This creates a perception that conduct of actors not linked to the state structure though domestic law should only be attributed to states in 'exceptional circumstances'.[69] Yet such actors could still be undertaking conduct on the behalf of states, even if not officially, as determined by the existence/inexistence of applicable domestic law.

Reviving the AFBS test to apply in practice factors in this reality whilst pushing back against the perception that non-state actors should somehow be considered as exceptions when addressing matters of state responsibility, even though states are intersubjective constructs and artificial legal persons that require physical entities to interact on their behalf with the world. The alternative is maintaining the status quo, in which the levels of specificity provided by the ILC/ICJ position in setting out some attribution tests do not capture the realities of the current world and likely future in which non-state actors undertake myriad functions on the behalf of states, even to extents where states are sometimes dependent on non-state actors in order to be in a position to properly respond to issues in the public interest.[70]

Keeping pace with technology developed and maintained by non-state actors but used by states is one component of multiple possible futures in which non-state actors will be undertaking conduct on the behalf of states. The overprecision of the mainstream attribution tests provides less space for the law to change when compared to a less precise test. Meeting the challenges presented by novelty requires adaptability. Being too precise in attempting to regulate a practice today in light of practices from yesterday limits the possibilities of effectively regulating similar practices tomorrow should unforeseen (or foreseen but unheeded) events transpire. Whether a state-owned

[68] See chapter 1, section 1.2.

[69] J Crawford, *State Responsibility: The General Part* (Cambridge, Cambridge University Press, 2013) 125.

[70] JK Wither, 'Outsourcing Warfare: Proxy Forces in Contemporary Armed Conflicts' (2020) 31 *Security & Defence Quarterly* 17; H Warrell and N Fildes, 'Amazon Strikes Deal with UK Spy Agencies to Host Top-Secret Material' *Financial Times* (25 October 2021) www.ft.com/content/74782def-1046-4ea5-b796-0802cfb90260; F Foer, 'What Big Tech Wants Out of the Pandemic' *The Atlantic* (July 2020) www.theatlantic.com/magazine/archive/2020/07/big-tech-pandemic-power-grab/612238/; D Sabbagh and A Hern, 'UK Abandons Contact-Tracing App for Apple and Google Model' *The Guardian* (18 June 2020) www.theguardian.com/world/2020/jun/18/uk-poised-to-abandon-coronavirus-app-in-favour-of-apple-and-google-models.

enterprise reduces the bottom line of a private investor, or a private military company employed by a state uses an autonomous robot that ends up killing a civilian, or a hacker paid by one state shuts off the utilities in another state, or a consulting detective for a police force goes rogue from using too much Ritalin and tortures a suspect, or a company deploys tracking software on mobile devices the data from which it then sells to the highest-bidding state in order for it to keep tabs on perceived undesirables, non-state actors will likely continue to play far from exceptional roles across societies, raising the question why the law of state responsibility should treat them as exceptions if this body of international law hopes to keep pace with developments in other sectors of societies.

The default rule of attribution for non-state actors that is the AFBS test accounts for the non-exceptional nature of non-state actors' involvement in everyday intra- and inter-state affairs. Ago put a reality squarely before the ILC in his work, which is 'private natural or legal persons – while definitely remaining such' – being 'entrusted by' states 'with the provision of' services.[71] Adopting the AFBS test would complement those listed under the ARSIWA, providing a more comprehensive approach towards attribution, thus contributing to the creation of a robust toolkit for tackling the multifaceted interactions that occur between states and non-state actors. Striking the right balance in the refinement of proposed rules can help cultivate regulatory effectivity in practice. The AFBS test could help in this respect considering the above analysis. In a world in which states do not do many things for themselves, but delegate and outsource to get things done, the implementation of state policy by proxy demands that non-state actors are envisaged as an elementary part of the law of state responsibility.

1.4. Going Forward: New Tests for New Futures

Despite the aforementioned promise of the AFBS test, there may not be much of an appetite to rekindle its application in practice, including in domestic courts. Even if this is not the case, questions remain regarding whether complicity and due diligence are the only bases for determining indirect state responsibility for non-state actor conduct. There is also the matter of whether other attribution tests can supplement those under the ARSIWA, which may also be more precise versions of the AFBS test and thus further indicators of this default rule. Any such tests would be significant if the AFBS were not to apply because their application could capture conduct arising in state–non-state actor interactions that the provisions under the ARSIWA might not capture. Potential responsibility gaps resulting from the non-application of the AFBS test could thus be reduced in some instances where questions beyond those envisaged by the ILC are raised. This current and potentially future framework governing

[71] Third Report, Ago (1971) 263.

state responsibility for the conduct of non-state actors is represented in the following diagram:

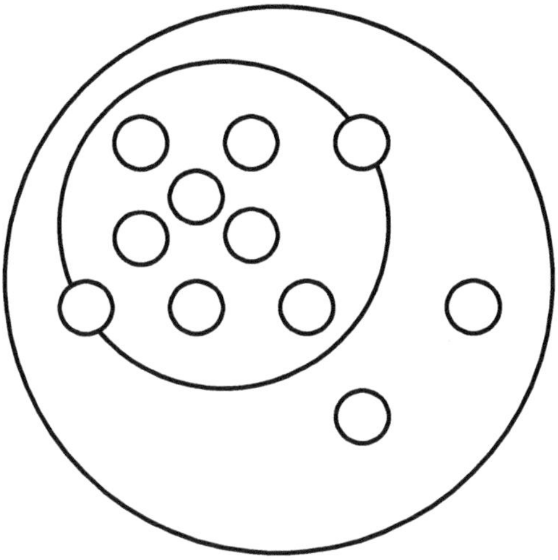

- **Largest circle** = all relationships between states and non-state actors.
- **Second largest circle** = potential capture offered by AFBS test.
- **Circles within second largest circle** = potential capture offered by ARSIWA and other attribution tests such as the ICJ test of complete dependence that are applicable to non-state actors and more refined versions of the AFBS test.
- **Circles outside second largest circle** = bases for determining indirect state responsibility such as the complicity and due diligence tests and their potential capture, which are not attribution tests and thus do not depend on satisfying elements of indicators that a non-state actor was acting on behalf of a state.
- **Circles straddling the divide of second largest circle** = Bases for determining state responsibility that may determine direct or indirect state responsibility and their potential capture, where it is unclear whether they would apply as an attribution test and thus depend on satisfying elements of an indicator that a non-state actor was acting in fact on behalf of a state.

The size of the circles representing more refined versions of the AFBS test within the second largest circle are all equal, indicating that their capture is potentially the same in the abstract, meaning they all share the same potential to address relationships between states and non-state actors when conduct occurs that is contrary to international law. Changes in sizes of the circles within the largest circle would reflect the extent of a particular test's capture in practice, which would depend on how they are interpreted in light of established facts, reflecting the likely change in capture on a case-by-case basis. The above diagram thus represents abstract capture of the tests for determining state responsibility for non-state actor conduct. It is worth recalling that the term capture in this context refers to the state conduct that would fall within the scope of, by satisfying the elements of, a particular test for determining its international responsibility for the conduct of a non-state actor that is contrary to an international rule.

The size of the circle representing the AFBS test is to emphasise that not every relationship between a state and a non-state actor will signify that the non-state actor is acting in fact on behalf of the state with which it shares a connection. The complicity and due diligence tests examined in chapters 6 and 7, respectively, fall outside of the circle representing the AFBS test because they do not concern determining whether a non-state actor has acted on behalf of a state, but rather whether a state contributed through its own actions or omissions to conduct of a non-state actor that was contrary to international law, without the state being considered the legal author of that conduct. Circles that sit within and outwith the parameters of the AFBS test circle indicate an uncertainty as to whether their use would determine indirect state responsibility, applying as tests sitting alongside those on complicity and due diligence, or direct state responsibility, applying as alternative attribution tests to those created by the ILC and ICJ. In the search for whether there are alternative bases for determining state responsibility for non-state actor conduct, there are at least two that appear, both of which could be brought to bear on such questions: state instigation of non-state actor conduct, and state coercion of non-state actors. However, if these bases were adopted as part of the secondary rule framework in this area, it is unclear whether they would apply as new attribution tests, or as separate bases for determining indirect state responsibility.

2. STATE INSTIGATION OF NON-STATE ACTOR CONDUCT

As fleshed out in chapters 6 and 7, a state implicated in conduct of a non-state actor that was contrary to an international rule can be considered to have either (1) contributed to that conduct through its own actions or omissions, establishing its indirect international responsibility for complicity or a due diligence failing, or (2) be considered the author of that conduct, as determined by satisfying the elements of a particular attribution test, establishing its direct international responsibility. In sum, there is a difference between being responsible for something and being responsible for contributing to that thing. As the indirect intent of a state appears to be necessary for the purposes of establishing its international responsibility for complicity in the wrongful conduct of a non-state actor, there remain questions regarding what happens if the direct intent of a state is established. These questions arise in particular if a state desires conduct to come about that is contrary to an international rule as a result of its involvement with a non-state actor. Furthermore, if tweaking the opposability requirement is not considered a viable approach when addressing complicity assessments, then should the conduct of a non-state actor not constitute an internationally wrongful act, state responsibility for complicity cannot be established.[72] A key question is: would such a scenario prevent the establishment of state responsibility even if the state intended the non-state actor to commit the specific wrong that occurred? If establishing a due diligence failure is not possible,

[72] See analysis on the opposability requirement in chapter 6.

nor is attributing the wrongful conduct to the state, then the answer is yes. Given that the state desires the occurrence of the precise conduct that is contrary to an international rule, and has contributed to ensuring it occurs through its own participation, this outcome is perplexing and unsatisfactory. It therefore becomes relevant to consider whether direct intent could be an element of another basis for determining state responsibility, including one of attribution.

A state expressly intending for a non-state actor to undertake a particular course of conduct signifies that the wishes of the two entities are aligned for a moment in time. However, the intentions of a state and its mutual interests shared with a non-state actor need to be manifested in some form in order for international responsibility to become a consideration. Responsibility cannot be established if intentions remain unmanifested (aside from if a future involves versions of being considered responsible for conduct that has not yet occurred but might, as determined by predictions based on thoughts and previous conduct, for example). The Independent State of Foogle cannot be internationally responsible for having the intention of paying a company to carry out microchip injection on its residents for surveillance purposes unless it actually carries out this practice, even if its state officials were thinking about it. Intent thus needs to attach to some other state conduct in order to raise questions of international responsibility. It is here that the concept of instigation brings a considerable amount to unpack, in particular with respect to attribution considerations.[73]

2.1. The ILC Perspective on State Instigation

During the ARSIWA's drafting, Ago revealed that acts of instigation might be sufficient to attribute conduct of a non-state actor to a state:

> Where it can be seen that that Government encourages and even promotes the organization of such groups, that it provides them with financial assistance, training and weapons, and co-ordinates their activities with those of its own forces for the purpose of conducting operations, and so on, the groups in question cease to be individuals from the standpoint of international law. They become entities which act in concert with, and at the instigation of, the State, and perform missions authorized by or even entrusted to them by that State. Such groups then fall into the category of those organs which are linked, in fact if not formally, with the State machinery, and frequently called 'de facto organs'.[74]

The link between attribution and instigation is apparent:

> The possible 'participation' or 'complicity' of organs of the State in the action of an individual do not have the effect of making that individual a member – even an incidental or *de facto* member – of the machinery of the State. *This is therefore a totally different field from that of action committed by certain individuals at the instigation and on behalf of the State*: i.e. the cases, referred to previously, of persons who, without really being organs of the State, act on behalf of the State in certain circumstances, so that their actions would

[73] *Nahminana et al v Prosecutor*, Appeal Judgment, ICTR-99-52-A (28 November 2007) para 480.

[74] Fourth Report, Ago (1972) 120.

> then be attributed to the State in the same way as those of organs in the strict sense of the term.[75]

This passage shows that acts of instigation can be construed to be a separate ground of attribution. The final commentary to the ARSIWA alludes to this understanding.[76] It notes that attribution must 'recognize the autonomy of persons acting on their own account and not at the instigation of a public authority'.[77] Conduct not attributable to a state is thus contrary to conduct instigated by a state. The ILC makes it clear that:

> [T]he general rule is that the only conduct attributed to the State at the international level is that of its organs of government, or of others who have acted under the direction, instigation or control of those organs, i.e. as agents of the State.[78]

According to the ILC, cases where non-state actor conduct could be attributed to a state under this ground will arise 'most commonly' 'where State organs supplement their own action by recruiting or instigating private persons or groups who act as "auxiliaries" while remaining outside the official structure of the State'.[79] Instigation subtly shines through in the ILC's work as a distinct attribution test, even though it is not presented as such within the listed provisions of the ARSIWA.

2.2. International Practice Addressing State Instigation

In commenting on prosecuting those accused of instigating genocide, the former USSR stated:

> It was impossible that hundreds of thousands of people should commit so many crimes unless they had been incited to do so … how, in those circumstances, the inciters and organizers of the crime should be allowed to escape punishment, when they were the ones really responsible for the atrocities committed. The peoples of the world would indeed be puzzled if the Committee, basing its decision on purely political arguments of doubtful validity, were to state that the instigators of genocide, those who incited others to commit the concrete acts of genocide, were to remain unpunished.[80]

Practice from international criminal law provides insights regarding instigation, in particular its potential to apply as a basis for attribution,[81] especially when considering the comparable commander/commanded relationships that exist in the course of state–non-state actor interactions with which the law of state responsibility and international criminal law interact. Practice centring on this matter illustrates that 'instigation', 'incitement' and 'inducement' hold similar meanings, in that they convey an action that contributed to a planned outcome occurring in the ordinary

[75] ibid 96 (emphasis added).

[76] Ch II, Commentary, para 2; Art 8, Commentary, para 2; Art 55, Commentary, para 3 (n 820).

[77] ibid Ch II, Commentary, para 2.

[78] ibid.

[79] ARSIWA, Art 8, Commentary, para 2.

[80] Sixth Committee, UNGA, Eighty-Fourth Meeting, UN Doc A/C.6/SR.84 (26 October 1948) 219 (Morozov).

[81] The appropriateness of analogising/drawing from international criminal law to help develop state responsibility is discussed in chapter 6.

course of events. These terms can thus be applied and analysed interchangeably for attribution considerations.

In the *Nahimana* case the ICTR pointed out that the '*actus reus* of "instigating" implies prompting another person to commit an offence'.[82] Showing that instigation took place for the purposes of attribution means that the act itself substantially contributed to the conduct of the entity in question.[83] Coupling direct intent to acts of instigation has also been considered necessary for the purposes of establishing responsibility:

> [T]he *mens rea* for instigating is established where the perpetrator acts with either direct intent to prompt another to commit a crime, or with awareness of the substantial likelihood that a crime will be committed in execution of that instigation.[84]

Transposing this into terms of state responsibility means that if a non-state actor's conduct were to be attributed to a state, then the state must have directly intended the outcome that took place through the conduct of the non-state actor to which the state instigated. Domestic case-law adds further insights.[85] One holding involving an alleged patent infringement was:

> [N]ot only the persons who actually took part in the commission of a delict were held liable for the damage caused, but also those who assisted them in any way, as well as those by whose command or instigation or advice the delict was committed. To a similar effect is the passage which was quoted from *Grotius* … that everyone is liable for a delict 'even though he has not done the deed himself, who has by act or omission in some way or other caused the deed or its consequence: by act, that is by command, consent, harbouring, abetting, advising or instigating'.[86]

The ILC has considered state instigation of wrongdoing to be equally as serious as the wrongdoing itself:

> A government official who plans, instigates, authorizes or orders such crimes not only provides the means and the personnel required to commit the crime, but also abuses the authority and power entrusted to [them]. [They] may, therefore, be considered to be even more culpable than the subordinate who actually commits the criminal act.[87]

The understanding portrayed here is that the occurrence of the primary wrong would have been unlikely but for the act of instigation, coming about as a result of the conscious policy choices of the state, which can also be viewed as manifestations of their intent.[88]

[82] *Nahminana et al v Prosecutor*, Appeal Judgment, ICTR-99-52-A (28 November 2007) paras 480 and 660.

[83] ibid; see also E Lauterpacht, CJ Greenwood and AJ Oppenheimer (eds), *International Law Reports*, vol 122 (Cambridge, Cambridge University Press, 2002) 96.

[84] *Nchamihigo v Prosecutor*, Appeal Judgment, ICTR-01-63-A (18 March 2010) para 61.

[85] *McKenzie v Van der Merwe* [1917] AD 41.

[86] *Cipla Medpro (Pty) Ltd v Aventis Pharma SA, Aventis Pharma SA and Others v Cipla Life Sciences (Pty) Ltd and Others* (139/2012, 138/2012) [2012] ZASCA 108, para 34 citing *McKenzie v Van der Merwe*.

[87] Draft Code of Crimes against the Peace and Security of Mankind, adopted by the International Law Commission at its Forty-Eighth Session (1996) A/51/10, YBILC, vol II(2), Art 7, Commentary, para 1.

[88] See WA Schabas, 'State Policy as an Element of International Crimes' (2008) 98 *Journal of Criminal Law and Criminology* 953, 970.

Deciding on the scope of what prompting acts of a state constitute instigation cannot be done in the abstract and depend on the facts in a given case,[89] as it 'can take many different forms'.[90] An example is encouragement.[91] It is also reasonably clear that a state organ instigating the conduct of a non-state actor would not have to be present in the same place in order for that conduct to be attributable to the state.[92] In the *Naulilaa* case Portugal claimed reparations for damage caused by German forces.[93] Here the Tribunal implied that Germany's responsibility could have been established for instigating indigenous locals to revolt, despite it being unclear from the Tribunal's analysis alone about whether this outcome would be based on attribution.[94] A clearer example is the ILC Draft Code of Offences against the Peace and Security of Mankind, which appears to present instigation as a basis for attributing non-state actor conduct to states.[95] Article 2(11) states:

> The following acts are offences against the peace and security of mankind: …
>
> Inhuman acts such as murder, extermination, enslavement, deportation or persecutions, committed against any civilian population on social, political, racial, religious or cultural grounds by the authorities of a State *or by private individuals acting at the instigation* or with the toleration of such authorities.[96]

The commentary to this provision also aligns with the reasoning that instigation could apply as an attribution test:

> The instigation or direction of a Government or any organization or group, which may or may not be affiliated with a Government, gives the act its great dimension and makes it a crime against humanity imputable to private persons or agents of a State.[97]

Although it is ambiguous from this source whether state responsibility would be determined on the basis of attribution, instigation is considered alongside direction, which serves as a current attribution test under Article 8, indicating the comparability and potential for overlap between the two tests.

There are a number of treaties that further signify the presence of instigation in international law. The Treaty on the Non-Proliferation of Nuclear Weapons compels states parties 'not in any way to assist, encourage, or induce any non-nuclear-weapon State to manufacture or otherwise acquire nuclear weapons'.[98] The Ottawa Treaty

[89] *Uwinkindi v Prosecutor*, Decision on Indictment, ICTR-01-75-AR72(C) (16 November 2011) paras 36–38.

[90] Lauterpacht, Greenwood and Oppenheimer (n 83) 96.

[91] Second Report, Crawford (1999) 48.

[92] *Prosecutor v Boskoski and Tarculovski*, Appeal Judgment, ICTY-04-82-A (19 May 2010) paras 125–32.

[93] *Responsabilité de l'Allemagne en raison des actes commis postérieurement au 31 juillet 1914 et avant que le Portugal ne participât à la guerre* (*Portugal v Germany*), Decision of 30 June 1930, reprinted in UNRIAA, vol 2, 1035.

[94] ibid 1071–73; see also I Plakokefalos, 'Causation in the Law of State Responsibility and the Problem of Overdetermination: In Search of Clarity' (2015) 26 *European Journal of International Law* 471, 486–87.

[95] Draft Code of Offences Against the Peace and Security of Mankind (1954) UN Doc. A/2693.

[96] ibid Art 2, para 11 (emphasis added).

[97] Report of the ILC to the UNGA on the Work of its Forty-Eighth Session (1996) Art 18, 5, UN Doc A/51/10.

[98] Treaty on the Non-Proliferation of Nuclear Weapons (adopted 1 July 1968, entered into force 5 March 1970) 729 UNTS 161, Art I.

states that each party 'undertakes never under any circumstances ... To assist, encourage or induce, in any way, anyone to engage in any activity prohibited to a State Party under this Convention'.[99] Similarly, the Chemical Weapons Convention states: 'Each State Party to this Convention undertakes never under any circumstances ... To assist, encourage or induce, in any way, anyone to engage in any activity prohibited to a State Party under this Convention'.[100] The Convention against Torture obligates states to

> prevent in any territory under its jurisdiction other acts of cruel, inhuman or degrading treatment or punishment which do not amount to torture as defined in article I, when such acts are committed by *or at the instigation of* or with the consent or acquiescence of a public official or other person acting in an official capacity.[101]

This final rule is also viewed to be reflective of customary international law.[102] Although these treaties concern primary rules, and there does not appear to be a sufficient presence of instigation in specific sub-fields of international law to justify extrapolation,[103] they show how international responsibility can be based on state instigation of wrongdoing undertaken by a non-state actor. Due to these rules being enshrined in treaties, there exists a demonstrable acceptance across states that their international responsibility can be determined on the basis of instigation, including with respect to contexts involving non-state actors.

2.3. Proposed Application of a State Instigation Test

Satisfying an attribution test aimed at addressing state instigation of non-state actor conduct appears to rest on two elements. First, the state explicitly wants the non-state actor to undertake conduct contrary to an international rule, perhaps through a specific course of action (direct intent element).[104] Second, in attempting to ensure that this consequence actually takes place, the state conducts itself in a way so as to bring about that wrongdoing of the non-state actor (instigation element).[105] These elements, when taken collectively, point to a state being the legal author of conduct

[99] Convention on the Prohibition of the Use, Stockpiling, Production and Transfer or Anti-Personnel Mines and on their Destruction (adopted 18 September 1997, entered into force 1 March 1999) 2056 UNTS 211, Art 1(c).

[100] Convention on the Prohibition of the Development, Production, Stockpiling and Use of Chemical Weapons and on Their Destruction (adopted 13 January 1993, entered into force 29 April 1997) 1974 UNTS 45, Art 1(d).

[101] Convention against Torture and Other Cruel, Inhuman or Degrading Treatment or Punishment (adopted 10 December 1984, entered into force 26 June 1987) 1465 UNTS 85, Art 16(1); see also Art 1.

[102] E de Wet, 'The Prohibition of Torture as an International Norm of *Jus Cogens* and its Implications for National and Customary Law' (2004) 15 *European Journal of International Law* 97; see also more specifically the acknowledgement of this rule's customary status by the US in CAT/C/28/Add.5 (9 February 2000) paras 62–63.

[103] See chapter 7, section 2.

[104] WK Timmermann, 'Incitement in International Criminal Law' (2006) 88 *International Review of the Red Cross* 823, 829.

[105] *Prosecutor v Seselj*, Appeal Judgment, MICT-16-99-A (11 April 2018) para 124; SH Kadish, 'Complicity, Cause and Blame: A Study in the Interpretation of Doctrine' (1985) 73 *California Law Review* 323, 342.

that is contrary to an international rule. If taken separately, each element is more akin to a charge of complicity in conduct contrary to an international rule.[106] Instigation absent direct intent way well be an additional basis for establishing the indirect responsibility of a state for the conduct of a non-state actor, which may or may not depend on the application of an opposability requirement like that of complicity, which, even if it were to apply, could also be tweaked to accommodate non-state actors as in the case of the complicity test examined in chapter 6. As noted in the ARSIWA's commentary, 'incitement of wrongful conduct is generally not regarded as sufficient to give rise to responsibility on the part of the inciting State, if it is not accompanied by concrete support'.[107] Nina Jorgensen argues that 'in order for a crime to be attributable to the state, it must be instigated' by that state.[108] While Aust argues '[i]nternational law knows no responsibility for incitement',[109] this is a separate consideration as to whether instigation combined with the direct intent of a state can serve as a basis for attribution.

A starting point for this test applying in practice would be to examine if there was an indication of the state's direct intent for the conduct of the non-state actor to have taken place. The question then becomes whether the state instigated this conduct through its own conduct, which affects the decision-making of the non-state actor, thereby making a particular course of conduct likely in the ordinary course of events. The state essentially sets 'things in motion' by 'planting the idea' of the particular conduct 'in the principal perpetrator's mind'.[110] And because a 'state's actions are to a certain extent signposts which point in the direction of a particular intention',[111] the direct intent of the state shows that the will of the non-state actor was influenced into carrying out the will of the state. If satisfied, these two elements would arguably indicate that the non-state actor's conduct was undertaken on behalf of the state and would therefore be attributable to that state. There would be a shift from the state being considered an accomplice to the actual author of the wrongful conduct.

State instigation absent direct intent would render instigation operating in a manner similar to complicity, which means applying such a test would establish the indirect responsibility of a state for the conduct of a non-state actor without that conduct being attributed to the state.[112] The crucial caveat here is that if instigation were applied in such a way, the non-state actor in question may need to have committed an internationally wrongful act if the state were to be held responsible for instigating it without being considered the legal author of that conduct.[113]

[106] See chapter 6.

[107] ARSIWA, Ch IV, Commentary, para 9.

[108] NHB Jorgensen, *The Responsibility of States for International Crimes* (Oxford, Oxford University Press, 2000) 112.

[109] HP Aust, *Complicity and the Law of State Responsibility* (Cambridge, Cambridge University Press, 2011) 221; see a similar point in C Dominice, 'Attribution of Conduct to Multiple States' in Crawford et al (n 10) 281, 285.

[110] Timmermann (n 104) 846.

[111] Jorgensen (n 108) 111.

[112] M Jackson, 'State Instigation in International Law: A General Principle Transposed' (2019) 30 *European Journal of International Law* 391.

[113] ibid.

The further instigation is applied in practice concerning state responsibility, the further it will become clear as to the appropriateness of applying it as an attribution test or as a basis for determining indirect responsibility. As things stand it can be applied as either, thereby retaining its potential to supplement the secondary rule framework applicable to non-state actors. In this respect, state instigation as a basis for determining state responsibility need not stand alone as a new addition.

3. STATE COERCION OF NON-STATE ACTORS

The idea of state responsibility for coercion arose in Garcia-Amador's first report.[114] His last report also acknowledged that non-state actors could be subject to state coercion.[115] Coercion also linked to Ago's work on complicity and attribution.[116] Ago argued that international responsibility should be established when a state 'in some way connived at that act'.[117] Non-state actors were considered in this setting, but in a manner blurring the distinction regarding whether coercion might apply as either a basis for attribution or for establishing the indirect responsibility of a state:

> The action of an individual would be the basis of the internationally wrongful conduct of the State, and the State would violate an international obligation through the action of an individual in which certain organs were merely accomplices.[118]

The ILC questioned whether 'certain means of coercion' by a state could attribute the conduct of the coerced non-state actor to that state.[119] Coercion did not begin to form as a concept for determining state responsibility for involvement in a principal wrong until 1978.[120] It was during this time that Ago began to separate the concept from state instigation of a wrongful act.[121] At this point it remained unclear whether state responsibility for coercion would be determined on the basis of an attribution test or as a distinct basis for determining indirect responsibility. It was argued that it 'would be wrong' to suggest state coercion over an entity constitutes participation in the primary wrong, as the coercer remains 'entirely foreign' to the primary wrong.[122] However, at the same time, it was pointed out that a state being implicated in the primary wrong for its own conduct 'goes well beyond' participation.[123] Romania, the United States and the United Kingdom agreed that state coercion over another state would mean that the coercing state 'would have

[114] Report, Garcia-Amador (1956) 216–19.
[115] Sixth Report, Garcia-Amador (1961) 3 and 49; this point was later seconded by Ago: Second Report, Ago (1970) 181.
[116] Fourth Report, Ago (1972) 96.
[117] ibid.
[118] ibid.
[119] ILC Report, Twenty-Seventh Session, 5 May–25 July 1975, UNGA, Thirtieth Session, Supp 10, A/10010/Rev.1, YBILC (1975) vol II, 69.
[120] Seventh Report, Ago (1978) 56.
[121] ibid 57.
[122] ibid.
[123] ibid.

had to answer for the act committed by the Government which had been forced to act against its will'.[124] From these insights, Ago proposed Draft Article 28:

> *Indirect responsibility of a State for an internationally wrongful act of another State*
>
> 1. An internationally wrongful act committed by a State in a field of activity in which that State is not in possession of complete freedom of decision, being subject, in law or in fact, to the directions or the control of another State, does not entail the international responsibility of the State committing the wrongful act, but entails the indirect international responsibility of the State which is in a position to give directions or exercise control.
> 2. An internationally wrongful act committed by a State under coercion exerted to that end by another State does not entail the international responsibility of the State which acted under coercion, but entails the indirect international responsibility of the State which exerted it.[125]

This provision was provisionally adopted in 1979.[126] Yet whether direct or indirect responsibility should ensue for state coercion remained debatable. Ago argued that responsibility for coercion was indirect, but the ILC position appeared to differ.[127] The ILC took the view that: '[A] State which commits an internationally wrongful act under coercion by another State is in fact in a situation similar to that of a State which in one area of its activity is subject to the direction or control of another State.'[128] Although it is unclear from the ILC perspective where it considers the tipping point to be for indirect responsibility becoming direct, Crawford later provided a helpful insight that a coercing state is the '*fons et origo* [source and origin] of the conduct' in question, indicating that coercion might be closer to a basis for determining direct state responsibility.[129]

Crawford's analysis also highlighted the connection between state coercion and state instruction as a basis for attribution.[130] The difference between state instructions implying effective control and state coercion is tricky to identify as both concepts signify that the entity undertaking the conduct contrary to international law is the instrument of the state in question. Similar to the instructions issued by a state, the conduct of a coercing state can confine the coerced entity, in a sense obliging it to carry out conduct in a prescribed manner. From the perspective of the coercing state, the conduct of the coerced entity can be predetermined to an extent, which is similar when issuing instructions, assuming they will be followed. Another common denominator is a dynamic based on a form of state dominance over a subordinate. Yet perhaps a key difference is that coercion involves the autonomy of an entity to make its own decisions being removed in part by way of persuasive manipulation, whereas the issuance of instructions does not necessarily mean there is any manipulation involved.

[124] Eighth Report, Ago (1979) 24.
[125] ibid 26–27.
[126] ILC Report, Thirty-First Session, 14 May–3 August 1979, UNGA, Thirty-Fourth Session, Supp 10, A/34/10, YBILC (1979) vol II(2), 93.
[127] ibid.
[128] ibid.
[129] Second Report, Crawford (1999) 45.
[130] ibid 45–48.

What is clear is that Crawford successfully separated the concepts and proposed an amended coercion provision in 1999.[131] The ILC commended the singling out of coercion as a distinct approach to determining state responsibility, but stressed that it 'was entering difficult terrain of defining coercion'.[132] The preparatory work indicates that coercion is not limited to threats, for example that of armed force, but 'should cover any action seriously limiting the freedom of decision of the State which suffers it – any measures making it extremely difficult for that State to act differently from what is required by the coercing State'.[133] These were the foundational understandings of the provision that became Article 18 of the ARSIWA.

3.1. Elements of Coercion According to the ILC

Article 18 states:

> A State which coerces another State to commit an act is internationally responsible for that act if:
>
> (a) The act would, but for the coercion, be an internationally wrongful act of the coerced State; and
> (b) The coercing State does so with knowledge of the circumstances of the act.[134]

Before examining how state coercion could apply as a basis for determining state responsibility for the conduct of non-state actors, it is worth briefly setting out how the ILC intended this concept to apply between states. The requirement under paragraph (a) appears to be that if a state were to undertake the same conduct without being coerced by another state, that conduct would need to satisfy the requirements of an internationally wrongful act. But what happens if a state coerces another and wrongdoing occurs even though the coercion was not necessarily aimed at producing that unlawful outcome? Can the international responsibility of the coercing state still be established in such situations? The ILC commentary suggests not: '[T]he coercing State must coerce the very act which is internationally wrongful. It is not enough that the consequences of the coerced act merely make it more difficult for the coerced State to comply with the obligation.'[135] State coercion in and of itself is not internationally wrongful unless the form of coercion adopted by a state happens to be contrary to a primary rule.[136] This makes sense considering states subject others to various forms of what may amount to coercion in order to fulfil policy objectives without those forms necessarily being unlawful.[137]

[131] ibid 56–57.
[132] ILC Report, Fifty-First Session, 3 May–23 July 1999, UNGA, Fifty-Fourth Session, Supp 10, A/54/10, YBILC (1999) vol II(2), 69.
[133] ibid 72.
[134] ARSIWA, Art 18.
[135] ibid Commentary, para 2.
[136] A Tzanakopoulos, 'The Right to be Free from Economic Coercion' (2015) 4 *Cambridge International Law Journal* 616, 618–23.
[137] ibid; see also VCLT, Arts 51 and 52.

The requirement under paragraph (b) can be read as the coercing state having knowledge that its coercion would likely mean conduct occurring that is contrary to an international rule. What knowledge is required would depend on the situation, but in assessing this requirement the approach used to address the mental requirement of state complicity could be adopted.[138] As with other provisions under the ARSIWA, the text of Article 18 appears straightforward at face value, but issues become apparent when examining its content in greater detail.[139] In general, questions of state responsibility for coercion will arise if the will of an actor has been influenced by pressure exerted over it in a manner implying blameworthiness.[140] A key consideration to look out for is a state compelling another actor to undertake conduct that can be considered wrongful, in which the actor undertaking that conduct is presented the illusion of having no choice but to comply with the demands of the coercing state without being subject to the manifestation of an undesirable threat that is perceived as likely or certain to occur, the anticipation of which lingers over the coerced actor. The ILC characterises state coercion along similar lines: 'Nothing less than conduct which forces the will of the coerced …, giving it no effective choice but to comply with the wishes of the coercing State.'[141] Another way of viewing state coercion is that it involves a state procuring conduct of another actor.[142] As is perhaps already evident, actors that can be subjected to state coercion are not limited to other states, so why limit state responsibility for coercion to situations involving only states?

3.2. Difficulties with Determining State Responsibility for Coercion of Non-state Actors

The formulation of the coercion test under Article 18 indicates that a test analogous to this provision incorporating non-state actors could be workable. This does not necessarily imply that such a test needs to follow the elements of coercion as stipulated by the ILC, but, as with the complicity test analogous to Article 16 that incorporates non-state actors, the work undertaken in creating Article 18 serves as a helpful reference point to guide developments relating to state responsibility for coercion of non-state actors. But perhaps not to the same extent. There was little mention of non-state actors in the preparatory work of Article 18, save to the extent that considerations regarding state coercion were mixed with those concerning attribution.[143]

[138] See chapter 6, section 1.2.3.

[139] See JD Fry, 'Coercion, Causation, and the Fictional Elements of Indirect State Responsibility' (2007) 40 *Vanderbilt Journal of Transnational Law* 611.

[140] J Howard, 'Invoking State Responsibility for Aiding the Commission of International Crimes – Australia, the United States and the Question of East Timor' (2001) 2 *Melbourne Journal of International Law* 1; DG Arnold, 'Coercion and Moral Responsibility' (2001) 38 *American Philosophical Quarterly* 53.

[141] ARSIWA, Art 18, Commentary, para 2.

[142] J Crawford, 'Revising the Draft Articles on State Responsibility' (1999) 10 *European Journal of International Law* 435, 454.

[143] Seventh Report, Ago (1978) 57; Eighth Report, Ago (1979) 25; ILC Report, Thirty-First Session, 14 May–3 August 1979, UNGA, Thirty-Fourth Session, Supp 10, A/34/10, YBILC (1979) vol II(2), 94, 104, 106.

It appears that at only one juncture was the possibility hinted at that a coercion test might apply to interactions between states and non-state actors in a similar manner as it applies between states.[144] However, despite this lack of treatment by the ILC, the rationale behind formulating and applying a coercion test that incorporates non-state actors is comparable to that behind the complicity test that incorporates non-state actors.[145] Conduct of a state that can be construed as coercive is not limited to that which could be exerted over other states. What a state can do to coerce another state, it can do to coerce another type of actor. The ILC recognises this reality in another of its outputs, the ARIO, in which Article 60 addresses international responsibility for state coercion of an intergovernmental organisation.[146] The inverse is also addressed in the ARIO under Article 16.[147] This logic need not end at the relationships between states and intergovernmental organisations, but instead can extend to relationships between states and non-state actors.

The dynamics of coercion are based on power imbalances, with its occurrence implying a power asymmetry, in which dominance of one actor over another is manifested. States have many means to implement their will through non-state actors. By utilising methods such as blackmail, physical violence or psychological abuse, state coercion involves persuading non-state actors to do, or refrain from doing, something that if fulfilled would be contrary to an international rule.[148] It is worth noting that this is an overarching difference between state coercion and state regulation of non-state actors through domestic law, as the latter is undertaken with the aim of ensuring that the conduct of such actors complies with the law, not undertake conduct contrary to it. A more difficult question is whether in compelling a non-state actor to comply with a domestic law, the non-state actor is effectively being coerced by the state because in order to comply with that law it has to carry out conduct that is contrary to an international rule. While this matter will not be addressed in further detail here, such problems boil down to the law actually prescribing behaviour that is right, as conduct being lawful does not equate to that conduct being justifiable on other grounds. Normative assessments are required to consider the differences between state coercion and state regulation, considering laws exist and can be introduced that allow, or even prescribe, wrongdoing.[149] These matters aside, a new coercion test that incorporates non-state actors would thus be grounded in the

[144] Fourth Report, Ago (1972) 96.

[145] See chapter 6, section 3.

[146] ARIO, Art 60, which reads: 'A State which coerces an international organization to commit an act is internationally responsible for that act if: (a) the act would, but for the coercion, be an internationally wrongful act of the coerced international organization; and (b) the coercing State does so with knowledge of the circumstances of the act.'

[147] ARIO, Art 16, which reads: 'An international organization which coerces a State or another international organization to commit an act is internationally responsible for that act if: (a) the act would, but for the coercion, be an internationally wrongful act of the coerced State or international organization; and (b) the coercing international organization does so with knowledge of the circumstances of the act.'

[148] See generally DA Lake, 'Authority, Coercion, and Power in International Relations' in M Finnemore and J Goldstein (eds), *Back to Basics: State Power in a Contemporary World* (Oxford, Oxford University Press, 2013) 55.

[149] See K Pistor, *The Code of Capital: How the Law Creates Wealth and Inequality* (Princeton, NJ, Princeton University Press, 2019) 71–76.

premise that states have the power, and sometimes the authority, to coerce non-state actors that are relatively less powerful.

The need for such a basis to determine state responsibility can be appreciated when reflecting on instances of state coercion of non-state actors. One example is the use of child soldiers.[150] State recruitment of children to participate in violence involves compelling them

> [to follow] orders under threat of severe punishment or death. To coerce children to participate in combat and commit atrocities against civilians, commanders not only use threats of violence against child recruits but also against their families as well as the possibility of torture and death at the hands of the enemy.[151]

State coercion can take many forms, including subjecting children to witness and/or participate in the punishment or killing of other children (such as those accused by a state of desertion), beating people or threatening them with execution for non-compliance with state orders, or instilling fear and guilt in people to the extent that they carry out state requests without question – indoctrinated to the point of mechanization.[152] In situations where states implement incentive-based approaches to prompting conduct that is contrary to international rules, coercion becomes a consideration. Identification of such incentivisation is also what differentiates cases of state coercion from cases of state instigation – although the line between the two is not always clear.[153] Furthermore, should coercion apply as a distinct attribution test, the direct intent of a state would not factor into determinations of state responsibility on this basis, unlike the proposed instigation attribution test, which includes an intent element. However, despite the rationale behind this proposal for a new coercion test to determine state responsibility for non-state actor conduct, in addition to the apparent need for the state responsibility framework to be in a position to address instances of state coercion of non-state actors, there is a question that raises doubts regarding both of these points. What is the difference between state coercion and state control and where does one end and the other begin?

As highlighted in the preparatory work of Article 18, the challenge of differentiating between state coercion and state control remains regardless of whether a distinct basis for determining state responsibility based on the former would be formulated as an attribution test or as a test for assessing indirect international responsibility.[154] State influence over non-state actors varies on a sliding scale from non-existent to total. Depending on the specific relationship between a state and a non-state actor, the state may conduct itself in a manner that is more akin to control rather than coercion being exerted over a non-state actor, and vice versa. This variability poses several questions. What is the impact of fluctuation between state control and state coercion on determining state responsibility for the conduct of a non-state actor? What are

[150] B Beber and C Blattman, 'The Logic of Child Soldiering and Coercion' (2013) 67 *International Organization* 65.

[151] Human Rights Watch, 'Coercion and Intimidation of Child Soldiers to Participate in Violence' (16 April 2008) www.hrw.org/news/2008/04/16/coercion-and-intimidation-child-soldiers-participate-violence.

[152] ibid.

[153] Timmermann (n 104) 839.

[154] See discussion in section 3 (above).

the implications of the effective control/Article 8 attribution test being interpreted flexibly? Engaging with these questions is not helped by the fact that during the drafting of Article 18 the ILC and states used the terms controlled, directed, instructed and coerced interchangeably.[155] Coercion and control could thus be interchangeable in terms of determining state responsibility for non-state actor conduct. And some might assert that the distinction between these terms is one without a difference in this respect.

Coercion could perhaps fall within the scope of the other three terms under Article 8 (control, direction, instructions). Sivakumaran argues:

> There may very well be different degrees of control; however there may also be different levels of control within the effective control standard. The concept need not be a fixed, stagnant one but may be fluid so as to adapt to the different situations to which it is applied. The effective control test is, essentially, context specific.[156]

Dutch domestic courts have provided flexible readings of what 'effective control' can encompass.[157] What comes hand-in-hand with more deviation with respect to what constitutes state control for attribution purposes is more uncertainty on what is distinct about state coercion. The mainstream position of the ILC and ICJ of reading state control as being limited to providing instructions to a non-state actor may therefore provide conceptual clarity. In cases where a state has issued instructions to a non-state actor without the additional element of past conduct lingering over that non-state actor creating a perceived threat, this would likely be more akin to state control, whereas the inverse, where past conduct of the state signifies the existence of a threat of something that is perceived as certain or expected to happen, would likely be more akin to state coercion. The further any such threats fade to the point of non-existence, the more strained state responsibility can be based on a test of state coercion. The perception of an impending threat coming to fruition if state instructions are not carried out is the additional element of a coercion test that does not form part of the attribution test enshrined in Article 8. The actual degree of autonomy held by a non-state actor when it undertakes conduct contrary to an international rule is thus one approach to help distinguish between state control and state coercion.[158] The freedom to exercise choice without fear of reprisal is a crucial factor. State coercion thus makes it more difficult for a non-state actor to resist any instructions that might also be construed as demonstrating control, when compared to state instructions that if not carried out would likely not result in any evident punishment.

[155] See, for example, the comment of Venezuela: Comments and observations of Governments on part one of the draft articles on State responsibility for internationally wrongful acts, A/CN.4/351, Add 1–2 & Add 2/Corr 1, Add 3 & Corr 1, YBILC (1982) vol II(1), 20; Or Mexico and Poland: Comments and observations received from Governments, A/CN.4/515 and Add 1–3 (2001) 53.

[156] S Sivakumaran, 'Application of the Convention on the Prevention and Punishment of the Crime of Genocide' (2007) 56 *ICLQ* 695, 703.

[157] See analysis on the *Nuhanović and Mustafić*, and *Mothers of Srebrenica* cases in chapter 3, section 2.2.

[158] This also raises the issue of ultra vires conduct of a non-state actor being attributed to a state. See chapter 3, section 2.2.2.

3.3. Proposed Application of a State Coercion Test

The interplay between coercion and control can be subtle. The concepts share common traits. The question remaining is whether a coercion test would form a basis for attribution and thus be applied to determine direct state responsibility for the conduct of non-state actors, or as a basis for determining indirect state responsibility. The ILC alludes to both being possible,[159] as do observations provided by states during the ARSIWA's drafting.[160] The way coercion appears to be conceived under the law of state responsibility is that a coercing state is considered responsible for the primary wrong in question. A State that coerces another actor to commit a wrongful act 'is internationally responsible *for that act*'.[161] The ILC made an effort to draw attention to the point that state responsibility for coercion was 'principal and inescapable'.[162] Crawford also pointed out that state coercion over another actor can be considered the source and origin of the wrongful conduct that occurs as a consequence of that actor being coerced.[163] In light of these considerations, state coercion could be formulated as an attribution test. However, whether it would be superfluous to do so is worth further reflection.

State coercion of a non-state actor would likely involve some form of instructions being issued to that actor, which would engage attribution under Article 8. The added element of a lingering threat for non-compliance with those instructions would indicate coercion, and could result in attribution, but this added element would not be needed if the threshold under Article 8 were already satisfied. Coercion applying as an attribution test within the international framework governing state responsibility for the conduct of non-state actors could thus be considered more of a symbolic notion than a practical one, as the issuance of state instructions needed for coercion would be captured by the attribution test under Article 8. The added threat element of situations involving coercion is in addition to the elements under this provision. That is what separates instances of state control over non-state actors from instances of state coercion: a perceived state threat towards a non-state actor. But this element is not needed to attribute the conduct of the latter to the former should state instructions be present, and if the threat element were established attribution would occur all the same. Even if there were no evidence of state instructions being issued and an adverse inference was used because a state appeared to be in a position that is threatening a non-state actor, which would apply a coercion attribution test in a different way, this again would be captured by the attribution test under Article 8, in that state instructions in some form must have been issued because there was state coercion present. In other words, how can state coercion occur without some form of state instructions being issued?

[159] ARSIWA, Ch IV, Commentary, para 6.

[160] Comments and observations of Governments on part one of the draft articles on State responsibility for internationally wrongful acts, A/CN.4/351, Add 1–2 & Add 2/Corr 1, Add 3 & Corr 1, YBILC (1982) vol II(1), 17, 19, 20; Comments and observations received from Governments, A/CN.4/515 and Add 1–3 (2001) 53.

[161] ARSIWA, Art 18 (emphasis added).

[162] ILC Report, Thirty-First Session, 14 May–3 August 1979, UNGA, Thirty-Fourth Session, Supp 10, A/34/10, YBILC (1979) vol II(2), 106.

[163] Second Report, Crawford (1999) 45.

State coercion involves more than the issuance of instructions to a non-state actor, and that element of a perceived threat signifies such an occurrence to be worse in a normative sense than a state issuing instructions that if followed would result in conduct contrary to an international rule. But why should state coercion be considered worse than state control? One answer relates to the existence of a continuous relationship between a state and a non-state actor where the latter is in effect a puppet. A definition of a puppet is an actor whose conduct is determined by an external power.[164] During the drafting of the ARSIWA, Ago undertook some work on the matter of state coercion and puppets.[165] This helps show that relationships where a state exercises dominance over another actor can facilitate coercion.[166] Ago clarifies the link between state dominance and the potential for state coercion:

> [*D*]*e facto* situations include both some relatively stable situations, such as that which comes into existence between a 'dominant' State and a 'puppet' State created on its initiative, and other purely occasional ones, such as that created through coercive action taken by one State against another with the aim of compelling it to adopt a certain line of conduct.[167]

Although Ago focused on states, it can be envisaged how this type of scenario could play out with the involvement of non-state actors. If and when a state is in a dominant position to determine the conduct of a non-state actor, and it actually does so by way of coercion, then the conduct that the non-state actor undertook as a result of the coercion would be attributable to that state, in which it may be 'possible that in certain circumstances the "dominant" state will be called upon to answer for an internationally wrongful act committed by the "puppet"'.[168]

It is the removal of almost any sense of agency and personal autonomy from a non-state actor that makes state coercion worse than state control.[169] A state can provide instructions to a non-state actor to carry out certain conduct, but in doing so it does not necessarily imply that the state has control over the non-state actor in general, but only in the specific setting relating to the conduct that was carried out on the instructions of that state. State coercion on the other hand, implies that the state exercises a general degree of control over the non-state actor that is inherent in that relationship, similar to that which forms part of relationships based on dependency. In this sense the ICJ's attribution test of complete dependence is similar to the proposed state coercion test, meaning if a state and a non-state actor share a relationship based on state coercion, the non-state actor may be considered a de facto state organ. Coercion can occur when states pursue their own policy preferences by restricting the freedom of decision of the actor carrying out the related decision-making so as to best ensure that the state's objectives are fulfilled.[170] What occurs, whether through ultimatums or otherwise, may not always be a direct order, such as

[164] See generally B Ivanel, 'Puppet States: A Growing Trend of Covert Occupation' in TD Gill (ed), *Yearbook of International Humanitarian Law*, vol 18 (Cham, Springer, 2015) 43.
[165] Eighth Report, Ago (1979) 6–36.
[166] ibid 6.
[167] ibid 15.
[168] ibid 22.
[169] JW Moore, 'What Is the Sense of Agency and Why Does it Matter?' (2016) 7 *Frontiers in Psychology* 1272.
[170] Eighth Report, Ago (1979) 22.

an instruction, but an assurance that consequence X will follow if Y is not fulfilled. Coercion can thus present itself in subtle forms involving strategic manipulation by a state. States may present 'choices' to non-state actors, when in fact they are aiming to push them towards a particular line of conduct that is contrary to international law. Where there exist relationships based on state coercion over non-state actors, there will exist the potential to exercise control through the issuance of instructions, including where the will of a state is followed to the letter for fear of reprisals should there be non-compliance.

4. CONCLUSION

To an extent it is rational that non-state actors are considered to be exceptional to the law of state responsibility. States and non-state actors are, after all, distinct legal persons with different obligations and rights. Yet what makes them different are the very laws created by human beings that help make sense of this world, but which have also made life on planet Earth more complicated. International law holds little weight in this regard compared to domestic in differentiating between a state and a non-state actor, making it questionable why rules of international law should treat non-state actors as exceptional in a period of time in which states rely on these actors to carry out a variety of tasks. From contact tracing to imperial conquests, state proxies abound in the course of everyday life. If a state chooses to do so, anything can act on its behalf. It is beyond time that international law factored in this reality. Considering the ARSIWA attribution provisions are a list of possible ways to determine when an actor is acting on behalf of a state, there is no reason to treat this list as exhaustive, no matter the prestige attached to the institution that created it. In this respect the AFBS test could again be utilised in practice, with domestic courts along with other actors determining what state conduct is captured by it and whether, and if so how, to refine it further. The ILC already did this in its own way and other actors can do the same. Although the AFBS test appears not to form part of positive international law, this does not mean it cannot be applied in practice. And for examples of that happening already, the provisions of the ARSIWA provide plenty. In a similar vein, practice shows that the tests of state instigation and state coercion could supplement the ILC framework and apply alongside other tests for determining state responsibility for non-state actors that have been created by international courts and tribunals. Where these tests are those of attribution, they are likely to be more precise versions of the AFBS test and thus further indicators of this general rule. The combination of the two further tests of state instigation and state coercion explored here should in no way be considered exhaustive; as there may be other bases for determining both direct and indirect state responsibility for the conduct of non-state actors. Although adding new tools to a dated toolbox contributes to an enhanced ability to address a wider array of problems, the potential implications resulting from this expansion are also important. Situations may present themselves where it is non-state actors that become the primary issue of concern regarding responsibility assessments, in which questions of state responsibility could simply be a distraction. While issues of non-state actor responsibility do not remove the need to determine state responsibility where a link between the two actors contributed to conduct contrary to international law, the caveat is that any developments in the law governing state responsibility for non-state actors should not negate potential developments in other areas of international law and responsibility. The future, perhaps as much if not more so than the present, will be reliant on such complementarity. In the spirit of coalescing the beginnings of a comprehensive framework applicable to questions of state responsibility for the conduct of non-state actors, thereby building on what the ILC has provided through the ARSIWA, fostering the development of new tests for new futures can provide additional help in tackling some of the problems that this legal framework is likely to encounter and would do well to effectively address.

Conclusion

Exploring the law applicable to determining the international responsibility of states for the conduct of non-state actors reveals a fair amount about a number of things. This process makes it easier to observe and appreciate the current limits and value of the law in this area. It also illustrates why these limitations exist and in what ways they can be addressed. But perhaps above all, studying this subject uncovers the care, effort and efficacy of individuals and collectives in bringing about developments that have the potential to shape a world that is filled with more fairness, justice and respect. The ILC and its members deserve credit in this regard. Without the ARSIWA, the state responsibility framework would be poorer off, if not non-existent. The law in this area has helped maintain some cohesion and stability in a legal order that appears to fluctuate in its fragmentation and convergence, whilst serving as a common denominator that provides objectivity when dealing with different rights and obligations across sub-fields of international law. Yet the objectivity provided need not only be that set by the people selected to sit as part of bodies that have reputable international brands.

New ways of confronting the challenges posed to those that consider the use of international law worthwhile when addressing wrongdoing can be opened up beyond current parameters of thinking. It is important that laws change to reflect the times they apply in; as it is a significant part of lawmaking to make efforts to account for what may lie ahead when reflecting on what has already happened, and that past practice need not be indicative of what the future holds. The continuous endeavour of developing the international law applicable to state responsibility in its engagement with non-state actors relies on recognising that what is and is considered to be positive law at this time does not have all the answers to the questions that arise now and may arise in the future. Taking into account this mix of past, present and possible futures may help overcome the hurdles that present themselves when tackling matters concerning wrongful conduct of non-state actors with which states are involved. While the degree and kind of impact in such cases will continue to vary, the questions regarding how the international responsibility of states can be determined will continue to be a constant. The answers to these questions provide the knowledge needed to operate within the confines of international law, dictate the ability of actors to lawfully respond to being wronged, ascertain the occurrence or not of responsibility gaps, and decide the success or failure of claims before judicial and quasi-judicial bodies. And with the continuation and emergence of numerous trends, questions of state responsibility for non-state actors are probably not going anywhere anytime soon.

Globalisation and the prominence of neoliberal ideals throughout this world have changed the dynamics between the public and private spheres of life, including the line between the two and its evaporation. Economic models, social practices and cultural norms that are embedded with these ideals are also likely to continue changing these dynamics. Whether because of outsourcing, privatisation or lack of state regulation, non-state actors carry out numerous functions that form part of the administration of public life. States are sometimes beholden to these actors, as do they play second fiddle to them in certain scenarios. Issues of transparency, oversight and accountability can present themselves when states and non-state actors collaborate in the pursuit of their respective goals. Yet in the course of these relationships it is often hard to say if the non-state actors form any official part of states' governance structures. The relevance of international law to these occurrences is dependent on domestic law. The municipal laws that change from state to state are a crucial focal point for determining whether an actor is conducting its activities officially on the behalf of a state. When states take steps to vest their powers in actors through the use of domestic law, they are prescribing the authority to officially conduct state business. This means if an actor is empowered by domestic law to act for a state, then so long as it is undertaking its conduct in that capacity or giving the appearance of doing so, including where it may be exceeding the authority it was prescribed by the state, the international responsibility of that state can be established if that conduct was contrary to an international rule. Considering the prominence of domestic law here for the purposes of attribution, the distinction that the ILC and its following attempt to make between actors labelled state organs and other types of actors that also officially act on the behalf of states may be one without a difference in a number of settings. In addition, if it is not obvious whether an actor is officially part of the state machinery, then domestic laws can make it tricky to work this out.

It may not always be possible to access materials containing the law governing ties between states and the actors included within their official structures, due to factors such as confidentiality and national security. The contract in particular is a tool that states can utilise both to empower non-state actors to act for them, and to help avoid international responsibility by relying on domestic law to shield them from legal claims centred on attribution should conduct occur that is contrary to an international rule. Determining whether a non-state actor is exercising governmental authority is largely curbed right now by the likelihood of being able to obtain and examine the required domestic law, highlighting some tension between the municipal laws across states and the associated attribution tests created as part of the international law on state responsibility, namely Articles 5 and 7 of the ARSIWA. Yet a number of states were not in favour of this requirement when it was being created, raising questions regarding why it exists and whether it should continue to exist.

It is noteworthy, then, that the ILC developed further insights that ensure determining the international responsibility of states for the conduct of non-state actors does not end at examining the ties these entities share through domestic law, which is but one element of assessing whether an actor is acting on behalf of a state, and by extension whether its conduct is attributable to the state. The second is where no domestic law appears to exist linking a state to another actor, but that actor may nevertheless be undertaking conduct in fact on behalf of the state. Where non-state actors assume a role that, for the time being at least, can be reasonably perceived as being public in character, state responsibility can be determined on the basis that even if a state did not vouchsafe the authority to act for it, a non-state actor may still be considered to be acting on behalf of that state out of necessity. By serving a public purpose, conduct of non-state actors can be attributed to states in situations where states fail to fulfil that purpose. With state neglect comes the chance for governmental authority to exist by default in actors that govern a particular part of a society. However, the utility of an attribution test accounting for such circumstances is limited by those very circumstances. The ungoverned aspects of societies within states varies across and beyond them, meaning the rarity or not of situations in which non-state actors have to exercise state-like roles because of states' failures to do so differs. Where it is common for police officers to provide safety and security to some members of society in one state, it is less common in another, where actors ranging from drug cartels to militias carry out this role. With migration to realities provided by the Internet, the movement of forums and assemblies from physical locations to those online raises issues regarding the governance of these spaces, which are neither purely private nor public. Should conduct occur from non-state actors that attempts to regulate the digital realm in ways that are considered necessary but may be simultaneously contrary to international rules, it is unclear whether that conduct would be attributable to particular states because of their failures to enact their own regulations. It is settings where non-state actors exercise more power and authority over certain areas than states which call into question the point of attributing their conduct to states for the purpose of determining international responsibility, as such states may no longer have legal obligations that are enforceable against them owing to the questionable nature of how far, if at all, their power and authority to govern extends into a realm governed by non-state actors. With respect to geographic locations, just because a map implies that a particular territory should be presided over by a state does not mean that state actually has any say in how that territory is ruled. It can therefore be somewhat of a misnomer to say Article 9 of the ARSIWA will function as an attribution test in each and every situation to which it might apply, considering attribution is the mechanism used to determine whether an actor is undertaking conduct on behalf of a state, and thus if the state should be considered the legal author of that conduct. Much depends on the context and the extent to which public authority is fragmented or if it is lost entirely. Should a non-state actor find itself in a position where out of necessity it empowers itself to exercise a form of authority that the state it sits within is failing to exercise, it is debatable whether its conduct is being undertaken for the state or in spite of it.

Beyond official state structures lie many non-state actors that carry out the work of states, and not only those that do so out of necessity. Should these actors act on the instructions of states, be completely dependent on them, their conduct be instigated by them, or should they be coerced by them, their conduct can be attributed to states. These tests for determining whether a non-state actor is acting in fact on behalf of a state provide further assistance in addressing cases where states utilise the services of non-state actors with which there is no apparent nexus in domestic law. While others might develop, and only one of these tests so far has been granted the veneer of a treaty provision, that under Article 8 of the ARSIWA, they can all apply as part of legal practice. This may help dampen compulsions towards applying only one test in cases where other possible tests are applicable, all of which are more precise versions of one common denominator that would do well to be taken as the default starting point for attribution assessments. Whether the attribution test referred to is the more precise version of that created by the ILC, the ICJ or another actor, they all appear to be indicators of the same overarching rule, which is that conduct is attributable to a state if it is established that the non-state actor carrying it out was acting in fact on behalf of that state.

In addition to situations where non-state actors act on the behalf of states, whether officially or not, there is the possibility that the international responsibility of a state can be determined for the conduct of a non-state actor where that actor was not necessarily acting on the behalf of the state, but may be considered to have done so in retrospect. Should a non-state actor movement create a new government within a state or a new state, international law provides some answers as to the apportionment of international responsibility should conduct occur that is contrary to international rules during the efforts made towards creating a new polity. It could thus be argued that Article 10 of the ARSIWA extends to governing non-state actor responsibility as well as that of states, albeit retroactively and indirectly. This provision is an indication that even if something changes, whether in name, construction or function, this does not prevent it from being answerable for past wrongs. Yet attribution is only one part of the picture in such settings, and a small one in comparison to others. Determining state responsibility for previous conduct as a non-state actor may not be possible or desirable depending on the circumstances. Recourse to the law is not the solution to every problem. The success or failure of a new government or state in the making rests on factors that may need to put the applicable rules under the law of state responsibility to one side. In resolving conflicts, such rules may sometimes be more of a hindrance than help, getting in the way of what is important. Those that use the law can also make things out to be more complicated than they need to be in order to serve a particular agenda. Should a new government be formed as a result of conduct from non-state actors, if it is a partial change that occurred to settle a conflict it may be unhelpful to bother determining or establishing *state* responsibility, especially when taking into account the interests relating to peacebuilding and political stability. The dynamic may change, however, if an entirely new government is formed as a result of conduct that is contrary to international rules. Should non-state actors embark on the heftier endeavour of attempting to create a new state, its international responsibility as a state ultimately depends on it being considered to exist as a state, meaning matters of statehood, recognition and the associated politics become relevant.

Considerations that lie beyond what international law can offer in terms of addressing situations where the responsibility of a state is at issue are also a key feature of a frequently unaccounted for effort of the ILC, one that incorporates non-state actors into the state responsibility framework. Article 11 of the ARSIWA was a bit of a late bloomer in coming to form part of this framework. And its use today remains uncommon. But its potential to be utilised more in the future should not be understated. One of the two separate strands of this attribution test is what sets it apart from others. As part of the first, attributability may turn on a state facilitating the continuance of conduct from a non-state actor that it is concurrently communicating its approval towards. However, the second strand concerns states taking it upon themselves to acknowledge and adopt conduct of non-state actors as their own. Attribution being based on this choice is rooted in the hope that states will begin a process to do right by those that have been wronged. Why they would do so can be better grasped when reflecting on the philosophy conceptualising responsibility as answerability. By owning up to their involvement in wrongdoing, states can spearhead their own absolution. It is also worth considering that while the law can influence behaviour, including that of states, the behaviour of peers is at least equally influential, if not more so. The way one state behaves can influence the way another behaves, and so on and so forth. International law and those that engage with it can fall into the habit of treating states as though they conduct themselves without the participation of people. And these people are not immune to the practice of monkey see, monkey do. In taking a step of putting itself in a position where it becomes legitimately answerable for wrongful conduct, a state is offering the promise that ownership of wrongdoing can become a principle more readily realised in everyday affairs, with truth and transparency laying the foundations of paths towards trust. Truth is also a constituent element of justice. A measure of justice will thus be found in states being honest about their involvement in wrongdoing and willing to receive the outcomes arising therefrom.

The law will always have its limits. Yet this does not mean those limits cannot change. With respect to that applicable to determining the international responsibility of states for the conduct of non-state actors, although the ARSIWA is a sensible first port of call, despite appearances, this product of the ILC by no means marks the limits of this topic. How state responsibility is determined for involvement in wrongful conduct of non-state actors short of states being considered the legal authors of such conduct is of considerable consequence. Indirect state responsibility is therefore an issue that is ripe for investigating, which is not so much focused on the wrongdoings of non-state actors per se, but on states' contributions and nexus to those acts. Although wrongful non-state actor conduct can occur because of its linkage to some manifestation of state action or omission, that conduct is not, and does not become, that of the state for the purposes of determining indirect international responsibility. The concept of complicity holds much promise to develop international law in this regard. Unbinding complicity to account for interactions beyond those that take place between states aligns with the practice of states providing assistance to non-state actors that carry out conduct contrary to international rules. What at this time appears to be a developing general rule on complicity can be applied more in practice, which would build on ideas that were not fully contemplated at the time they were conceived. The requirements of this complicity test that have been moulded by many over the years supply guidance that can be used to inform decisions regarding if a state should be considered legally complicit in the wrongdoing of a non-state actor. Even though the antecedents of a complicity rule that incorporates non-states actors went adrift in the past, they now fit into a construction composed of theory and practice specifying that if conduct occurs that is contrary to an international rule, the international responsibility of a state can be established for complicity regardless of what status the actor that undertook the conduct is assigned in accordance with domestic law.

Alongside complicity, formulating and applying the concept of due diligence differently can supplement the international law applicable to determining state responsibility for the conduct of non-state actors. What is particularly distinct when considering this proposal is the current dearth of international law addressing the general conditions for determining state responsibility for failing to act in circumstances where non-state actors undertake conduct that is contrary to international rules. In forging a new basis that takes into consideration the link between the omissions of states and the wrongdoing of non-state actors, a further avenue becomes available to analyse whether a state can be considered internationally responsible for the wrongful conduct of a non-state actor. In scrutinising states in light of their relative competency to attempt preventing, suppressing or addressing such conduct, it becomes clearer how the due diligence failings of states can result in their international responsibility being reviewed. In assessing the requirements of this due diligence test through a lens of reasonableness, key features to bear in mind are the power a state has relative to the non-state actor at issue, the authority the state has to exercise that power, the foreseeability of that non-state actor's conduct in the ordinary course of events, any precautionary measures the state took considering its nexus to that non-state actor, and the conduct in question being contrary to an international rule that is binding on the state.

With an increase in the number of bases for determining state responsibility for the conduct of non-state actors, the links between them start to become perceptible. In accounting for how each attribution, complicity and due diligence test relate to each other, commonalities show potential for overlap. As there are a number of ways to attribute conduct of a non-state actor to a state, some of these tests may intersect depending on their interpretation against the facts in a given case. These intersections can also extend to the complicity and due diligence tests that have been analysed. The provision of aid or assistance by a state to a non-state actor might be construed to mean attributable links exist between the two. Information sharing could include the issuance of instructions from a state, constantly supplying arms could be part of an argument that a non-state actor is acting in fact on behalf of the supplier state, providing financial assistance could amount to a finding of complete dependence. The mental requirement of complicity can also link to attribution if a threshold of intent is applied, as such intent forms part of attribution considerations based on state instigation of non-state actor conduct. Drop this requirement from the instigation attribution test and it instead operates as a basis for determining indirect state responsibility for non-state actor conduct, much like complicity. Another threshold of the mental requirement under the complicity test, that of wilful blindness, relates to due diligence. Wilful blindness occurs when a state ignores evidence that suggests wrongful conduct of a non-state actor is occurring, or could transpire, which the state is, or would be, aiding. In such instances the state would be acting negligently, meaning a due diligence evaluation could become bundled up in a complicity evaluation. Whether the necessary wilful blindness of a state is possessed for the purpose of determining its international responsibility for complicity could well turn on findings, or lack thereof, that the state should have known that its aid would be used for wrongful ends, which may indicate that due diligence was or was not exercised. Due diligence is also linked to complicity if state omissions are considered to be forms of aid or assistance, and links to attribution in at least three ways. First, should the effective control attribution test be read to include an assessment on whether a state had the power and authority to prevent the conduct of a non-state actor, which is an element of the due diligence test. Second, should a state be neglectful to an extent creating a situation necessitating that a non-state actor undertake conduct in which it exercises elements of governmental authority by default, as the failure or inadequacy of a state to fulfil its role raises questions of attribution as well as those concerning due diligence and the ability of that state to exercise it in a particular setting. Third, should a state communicate its support for a non-state actor carrying out conduct that the state did not at least attempt to prevent, as if the state facilitated the continuance of that conduct by not doing anything, the attribution test based on implicit state acknowledgement and adoption of non-state actor conduct would share similarities with the due diligence test.

The three overarching bases for determining the international responsibility of states for the conduct of non-state actors (attribution, complicity and due diligence) contain clusters of requirements that can change and present similarly across these bases, which may mean they overlap depending on the facts in a particular case. They can thus be depicted in different ways, for example:

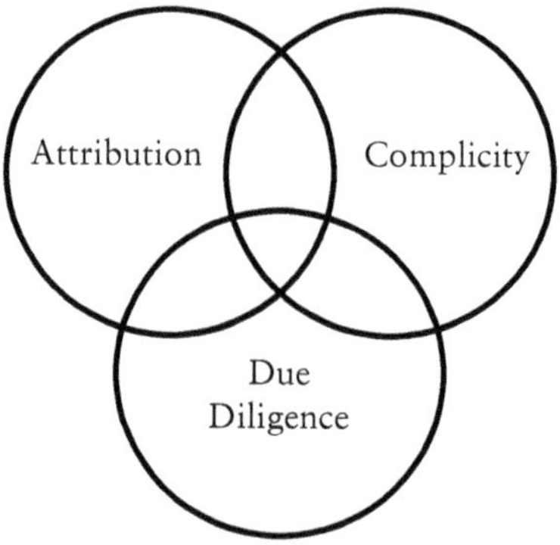

If international responsibility is established on the basis of attribution, this signifies that a state is the legal author of wrongful conduct. If established on the basis of complicity, this signifies that a state participated in wrongful conduct without being considered to have undertaken it. And if established on the basis of a due diligence failure, this signifies that a state made an allowance for wrongful conduct without being considered to have undertaken it or necessarily participated in it. These bases account for the degree and kind of a state's involvement in wrongdoing of a non-state actor, whether it was active or passive, in which this involvement may correlate to the degree and kind of a response upon a finding of international responsibility on a particular basis.

There remain questions about whether and why the difference between direct and indirect responsibility matters. Although there are differences between the kid who threw eggs at the police car, the kid who bought the eggs knowing full well they would not be used for baking, and the kid who did nothing to prevent this from occurring because they fancied an extra bit of running for the week, whether and why such differences matter when assessing how responsibility is determined are not immediately clear. Although distinctions exist between being responsible for something and being responsible for contributing to something, further inquiry presents opportunities to clarify why these matter when assessing how to determine international responsibility, whilst accounting for factors that come into play after state responsibility for non-state actor conduct has been established. This would include what the wronged party is entitled to and its consequent response, raising questions ranging from the type of countermeasures that could be adopted to the reparations requested, all whilst giving appropriate weight to the gravity, nature and scale of wrongdoing and on what basis the responsible state was implicated.

Another question that requires examination concerns what the point is behind determining, establishing or invoking state responsibility in light of the associated processes and outcomes. Assumptions exist signifying that the use of international law is somehow worthwhile in attempting to hold states to account for their involvement in wrongdoing. Yet whether this is an effective use of resources, who it actually benefits and at what costs in what arenas merits further study. The law of state responsibility's deterrent effect on states in particular has been questioned by a number of people. While the anticipation of international responsibility being potentially established may not amount to much in states' decision-making processes, should wrongful conduct transpire, this body of law can provide some measure of accountability. Whether that measure is satisfactory, especially in comparison to others that might be achieved, is a separate matter. But by building on the international law that exists already, a comprehensive legal framework governing state responsibility for the conduct of non-state actors can come into existence. In order for this to happen, space for exploration, discussion and acceptance of alternatives to the ARSIWA is needed. Accommodating the realities posed by non-state actors is a challenge facing those making and shaping the law of state responsibility. Meeting this challenge hinges on the realisation of prospects for the future that this area of international law can provide, which in turn relies on the sources used in this evolution and if they are obdurate or receptive.

There can be no room for growth if debates are overwatered with the type of repetition that results in redundancy. Hoping to keep pace with change requires adaptability. The sources making and shaping the law need not remain the same. Nor should they. Practices such as placing selected sources on pedestals contribute to related laws becoming less responsive and more stagnant than they could be, thus impacting the effectivity of the law. The role and influence of certain sources can become inflated. Yet if they become so, it is because of the status afforded to such inventions through their brand and the consequent responses of people. The shaping of perceptions regarding value currently places too much emphasis on such connections. This is partly the reason behind why the ILC and the ICJ have managed to shape narratives and perceptions concerning the law applicable to determining the international responsibility of states for the conduct of non-state actors to an extent where they become mainstream without the participation of other actors, including states. The relationship between these two institutions in particular is also somewhat akin to a revolving door, one that creates feedback loops starting and ending with one declaring something on the grounds that the other did so. However, more viewpoints can be reflected in the law constructed around the topic of international responsibility.

Diversity of sources is part of ensuring that laws are not merely moulded by the influential and pushed on the masses. The choices taken in responding to the challenges brought about by change require different perspectives being granted platforms that allow them to be recognised. There is no need to agree on everything in order to streamline progress. Reasoned discourse uncovering common ground is not the same as that compelling conformity, which discourages creativity, fosters exclusion and upsets the unity to be found in mutual respect. If such discourse can be achieved, perhaps the interactions between states and non-state actors will pose fewer problems for international law and its students in the future. For now, it is human beings who create the law, which is a reflection of those that hold the power to change it. The law applicable to determining the international responsibility of states for the conduct of non-state actors is no different. If change is what is required in the law, then change is required in the groups of people that make and shape it. And within this area, the experiences of individuals and the statistics that sometimes take them into account speak volumes for what remains to be done in providing opportunities to participate in these practices. The law attempting to address matters of state responsibility for the wrongful conduct of non-state actors lies between futility and functionality. Wherever this precise point currently resides, it will likely shift. In what direction rests with those willing to continue in the good fight.

Bibliography

BOOKS

Ackerly, BA, *Universal Human Rights in a World of Difference* (Cambridge, Cambridge University Press, 2008).

Adler, MD and Fleurbaey, M (eds), *The Oxford Handbook of Wellbeing and Public Policy* (Oxford, Oxford University Press, 2016).

Allott, P, *Eutopia: New Philosophy and New Law for a Troubled World* (Cheltenham, Edward Elgar, 2017).

Alston, P (ed), *Non-state Actors and Human Rights* (Oxford, Oxford University Press, 2005).

Anzilotti, D, *Cours de droit international* (Paris, Librairie de Recueil Sirey, 1929).

Arts, B, Noortmann, M and Reinalda, B (eds), *Non-state Actors in International Relations* (Farnham, Ashgate, 2001).

Aust, HP, *Complicity and the Law of State Responsibility* (Cambridge, Cambridge University Press, 2011).

Becker, T, *Terrorism and the State: Rethinking the Rules on State Responsibility* (Oxford, Hart, 2006).

Bernhardt, R (ed), *Max Planck Encyclopedia of Public International Law*, vol 10 (Amsterdam, Elsevier, 1987).

Besson, S and Tasioulas, J (eds), *The Philosophy of International Law* (Oxford, Oxford University Press, 2010).

Blokker, NM and Schrijver, NJ (eds), *The Security Council and the Use of Force: Theory and Reality – A Need for Change?* (Leiden, Nijhoff, 2005).

Brownlie, I, *International Law and the Use of Force by States* (Oxford, Clarendon Press, 1963).

Brownlie, I, *Principles of Public International Law* (Oxford, Clarendon Press, 1966).

Byres, M (ed), *The Role of Law in International Politics: Essays in International Relations and International Law* (Oxford, Oxford University Press, 2000).

Carlston, KS, *The Process of International Arbitration* (Cambridge, Cambridge University Press, 1946).

Castermans Holleman, M, Van Hoof, F, and Smith, J (eds), *The Role of the Nation State in the 21st Century: Human Rights, International Organisations and Foreign Policy – Essays in Honour of Peter Baehr* (Dordrecht, Kluwer, 1998).

Charlesworth, H, Chiam, M, Hovell, D and Williams, G (eds), *The Fluid State: International Law and National Legal Systems* (Sydney, Federation Press, 2005).

Clapham, A (ed), *Human Rights and Non state Actors* (Cheltenham, Edward Elgar, 2013).

Clapham, A and Gaeta, P (eds), *The Oxford Handbook of International Law in Armed Conflict* (Oxford, Oxford University Press, 2014).

Clapham, A, *Human Rights Obligations of Non state Actors* (Oxford, Oxford University Press, 2006).

Crawford, J, *The Creation of States in International Law*, 2nd edn (Oxford, Oxford University Press, 2006).

Crawford, J, *State Responsibility: The General Part* (Cambridge, Cambridge University Press, 2013).

Crawford, J, Pellet, A and Olleson, S (eds), *The Law of International Responsibility* (Oxford, Oxford University Press, 2010).

Criddle, E (ed), *Human Rights in Emergencies* (Cambridge, Cambridge University Press, 2016).

Donnelly, J, *Universal Human Rights in Theory and Practice*, 3rd edn (Cambridge, Cambridge University Press, 2013).

Douglass, F, *Narrative of the Life of Frederick Douglass, an American Slave* (London, Penguin, 2014).

Dworkin, R, *Law's Empire* (Cambridge, MA, Harvard University Press, 1986).

Eagleton, C, *The Responsibility of States in International Law* (New York, New York University Press, 1928).

Eddo-Lodge, R, *Why I'm No Longer Talking to White People About Race* (London, Bloomsbury, 2018).
Ellis, MS, *Sovereignty and Justice: Balancing the Principle of Complementarity between International and Domestic War Crimes Tribunals* (Newcastle upon Tyne, Cambridge Scholars, 2014).
Evans, MD (ed), *International Law*, 5th edn (Oxford, Oxford University Press, 2018).
Fabri, HR, Wolfrum, R and Gogolin, J, *Select Proceedings of the European Society of International Law*, vol II (Oxford, Hart, 2008).
Fatima, S, *Using International Law in Domestic Courts* (Oxford, Hart, 2005).
Finnemore, M and Goldstein, J (eds), *Back to Basics: State Power in a Contemporary World* (Oxford, Oxford University Press, 2013).
Frankfurt, HG, *On Bullshit* (Princeton, NJ, Princeton University Press, 2005).
Frankopan, P. *The Silk Roads: A New History of the World* (Bloomsbury, 2015).
Freeman, AV *Responsibility of States for Unlawful Acts of their Armed Forces* (Leiden, Nijhoff, 1955).
Gal Or, N, Ryngaert, C and Noortmann, M (eds), *Responsibilities of the Non state Actor in Armed Conflict and the Market Place* (Leiden, Brill, 2015).
Garcia Amador, FV, *The Changing Law of International Claims* (New York, Oceana, 1984).
García Amador, FV, Sohn, LB and Baxter, RR, *Recent Codification of the Law of State Responsibility for Injuries to Aliens* (Leiden, Nijhoff, 1974).
Gill, TD (ed), *Yearbook of International Humanitarian Law*, vol 18 (Cham, Springer, 2015).
Harari, YN, *Sapiens: A Brief History of Humankind* (New York, Vintage, 2015).
Harari, YN, *Homo Deus: A Brief History of Tomorrow* (New York, Vintage, 2017).
Harari, YN, *21 Lessons for the 21st Century* (New York, Vintage, 2019).
Hart, HLA, *The Concept of Law* (Oxford, Clarendon Press, 1961).
Higgins, R, *Problems and Process: International Law and How We Use It* (Oxford, Oxford University Press, 1994).
Hofmann, R (ed), *Non state Actos as New Subjects of International Law: International Law – From the Traditional State Order Towards the Law of the Global Community* (Berlin, Duncker & Humblot, 1999).
Jackson, M, *Complicity in International Law* (Oxford, Oxford University Press, 2015).
Jorgensen, NHB, *The Responsibility of States for International Crimes* (Oxford, Oxford University Press, 2000).
Justinian, *The Digest of Roman Law: Theft, Rapine, Damage and Insult* (London, Penguin, 1979).
Kahneman, D, *Thinking, Fast and Slow* (New York, Farrar, Straus & Giroux, 2011).
Kahneman, D, Sibony, O and Sunstein, CR, *Noise: A Flaw in Human Judgment* (New York, Little, Brown Spark, 2021).
Kavalski, E. (ed), *Encounters with World Affairs: An Introduction to International Relations* (Abingdon, Routledge, 2015).
Keshavjee, MM, *Islam, Sharia & Alternative Dispute Resolution* (Basingstoke, Palgrave, 2013).
Koh, HH, *The Trump Administration and International Law* (Oxford, Oxford University Press, 2018).
Krieger, H (ed), *Inducing Compliance with International Humanitarian Law: Lessons from the African Great Lakes Region* (Cambridge, Cambridge University Press, 2015).
Kulesza, J, *Due Diligence in International Law* (Leiden, Brill, 2016).
Lanovoy, V, *Complicity and its Limits in the Law of International Responsibility* (Oxford, Hart, 2016).
Lauterpacht, H, *The Function of Law in the International Community* (Oxford, Oxford University Press, 2011).
Lauterpacht, E, Greenwood, CJ and Oppenheimer, AJ (eds), *International Law Reports*, vol 122 (Cambridge, Cambridge University Press, 2002).
Letho, M, *Indirect Responsibility for Terrorist Attacks: Redefinition of the Concept of Terrorism Beyond Violent Acts* (Leiden, Nijhoff, 2009).
Lepard, BD, *Customary International Law: A New Theory with Practical Applications* (Cambridge, Cambridge University Press, 2012).
Lewis, R, *Legal Fictions in International Law* (Cheltenham, Edward Elgar, 2021).
Lillich, RB and Magraw, DB (eds), *The Iran–United States Claims Tribunal: Its Contributions to the Law of State Responsibility* (Irvington on Hudson, NY, Transnational, 1998).
Linarelli, J, Salomon, ME and Sornarajah, M, *The Misery of International Law: Confrontations with Injustice in the Global Economy* (Oxford, Oxford University Press, 2018).

Liu, HY, *Law's Impunity: Responsibility and the Modern Private Military Company* (Oxford, Hart, 2015).
Lucas, J. *Responsibility* (Oxford, Oxford University Press, 1993).
Macak, K. *Internationalized Armed Conflicts in International Law* (Oxford, Oxford University Press, 2018).
Machiavelli, N, *The Prince* (London, Penguin, 2004).
Marchant, GE, Allenby, BR and Herkert, JR (eds), *The Growing Gap Between Emerging Technologies and Legal Ethical Oversight* (Cham, Springer, 2011).
Maresceau, M. and Dashwood, A (eds), *Law and Practice of EU External Relations: Salient Features of a Changing Landscape* (Cambridge, Cambridge University Press, 2008).
Marx, K and Engels, F, *The Communist Manifesto* (London, Penguin, 2002).
McConville, M and Chui, WH (eds), *Research Methods for Law*, 2nd edn (Edinburgh, Edinburgh University Press, 2017).
McHarg, A, Mullen, T, Page, A and Walker, N, *The Scottish Independence Referendum: Constitutional and Political Implications* (Oxford, Oxford University Press, 2016).
McNair, AD, *The Law of Treaties* (Oxford, Clarendon Press, 1961).
Milanovic, B, *The Haves and the Have Nots: A Brief and Idiosyncratic History of Global Inequality* (New York, Basic Books, 2011).
Milanovic, M, *Extraterritorial Application of Human Rights Treaties: Law, Principles, and Policy* (Oxford, Oxford University Press, 2011).
Nollkaemper, A and Plakokefalos, I (eds), *Principles of Shared Responsibility in International Law: An Appraisal of the State of the Art* (Cambridge, Cambridge University Press, 2014).
Noortmann, M, Reinisch, A and Ryngaert, C (eds), *Non state Actors in International Law* (Oxford, Hart, 2015).
O'Neil, C, *Weapons of Math Destruction: How Big Data Increases Inequality and Threatens Democracy* (New York, Basic Books, 2016).
Paine, T, *Rights of Man, Common Sense and Other Political Writings* (Oxford, Oxford University Press, 1998).
Paparinskis, M. *The International Minimum Standard and Fair and Equitable Treatment* (Oxford, Oxford University Press, 2013).
Pattaro, E. *A Treatise of Legal Philosophy and General Jurisprudence*, vol 4 (Cham, Springer, 2005).
Pazartzis, P and Merkouris, P (eds), *Permutations of Responsibility in International Law* (Leiden, Brill, 2019).
Perez, CC, *Invisible Women: Exposing Data Bias in a World Designed for Men* (London, Chatto & Windus, 2019).
Pistor, K, *The Code of Capital: How the Law Creates Wealth and Inequality* (Princeton, NJ, Princeton University Press, 2019).
Ragazzi, M (ed), *International Responsibility Today: Essays in Memory of Oscar Schachter* (Leiden, Nijhoff, 2005).
Rajamani, L, *Differential Treatment in International Environmental Law* (Oxford, Oxford University Press, 2006).
Ratner, SR, *The Thin Justice of International Law: A Moral Reckoning of the Law of Nations* (Oxford, Oxford University Press, 2015).
Roberts, A, *Is International Law International?* (Oxford, Oxford University Press, 2017).
Rousseau, J J, *The Social Contract* (Oxford, Oxford University Press, 2008).
Ruys, T. *'Armed Attack' and Article 51 of the UN Charter: Evolutions in Customary Law and Practice* (Cambridge, Cambridge University Press, 2010).
Sandel, MJ, *Justice: What's the Right Thing to Do?* (New York, Farrar, Straus & Giroux, 2010).
Sandel, MJ, *What Money Can't Buy: The Moral Limits of Markets* (New York, Farrar, Straus & Giroux, 2013).
Sandel, MJ, *The Tyranny of Merit: What's Become of the Common Good?* (New York, Farrar, Straus & Giroux, 2020).
Seneca, *On the Shortness of Life* (London, Penguin, 2004).
Schabas, WA, *The International Criminal Court: A Commentary on the Rome Statute*, 2nd edn (Oxford, Oxford University Press, 2016).
Schachter, O, *International Law in Theory and Practice* (Leiden, Nijhoff, 1991).

Schmitt, MN (ed), *Tallinn Manual 2.0 on the International Law Applicable to Cyber Operations* (Cambridge, Cambridge University Press, 2017).
Schulz, F, *Principles of Roman Law* (Oxford, Clarendon Press, 1936).
Shaw, M, *International Law*, 8th edn (Cambridge, Cambridge University Press, 2017).
Shiner, P and Williams, A (eds), *The Iraq War and International Law* (Oxford, Hart, 2008).
Sivakumaran, S, *The Law of Non international Armed Conflict* (Oxford, Oxford University Press, 2012).
Soldati, A, *La responsabilité des Etats dans le droit international* (Paris, Duchemin, 1934).
Stahn, C and Kleffner, JK (eds), *Jus Post Bellum: Towards a Law of Transition From Conflict to Peace* (The Hague, Asser, 2008).
Stephens, T, *International Courts and Environmental Protection* (Cambridge, Cambridge University Press, 2009).
Sunstein, CR, *On Freedom* (Princeton, NJ, Princeton University Press, 2019).
Sunstein, CR and Hastie, R, *Wiser: Getting Beyond Groupthink to Make Groups Smarter* (Boston, MA, Harvard Business Review Press, 2014).
Tams, CJ and Sloan, J (eds), *The Development of International Law by the International Court of Justice* (Oxford, Oxford University Press, 2013).
Tonkin, H, *State Control over Private Military and Security Companies in Armed Conflict* (Cambridge, Cambridge University Press, 2011).
Trapp, KN, *State Responsibility for International Terrorism* (Oxford, Oxford University Press, 2011).
UN (ed), *Seventy Years of the International Law Commission: Drawing a Balance for the Future* (Leiden, Brill, 2020).
VanSickle Ward, R, *The Devil Is in the Details: Understanding the Causes of Policy Specificity and Ambiguity* (New York, SUNY Press, 2014).
Vidmar, J. *Democratic Statehood in International Law: The Emergence of New States in Post Cold War Practice* (Oxford, Hart, 2013).
Watkins, D and Burton, M (eds), *Research Methods in Law* (Abingdon, Routledge, 2013).
Wolfrum, R (ed), *Max Planck Encyclopedia of Public International Law* (Oxford, Oxford University Press, 2010).
Wolfrum, R and Roeben, V (eds), *Developments of International Law in Treaty Making* (Berlin, Springer, 2005).
Xanthaki, H *Drafting Legislation: Art and Technology of Rules for Regulation* (Oxford, Hart, 2014).
Zidar, A and Bekou, O (eds), *Contemporary Challenges for the International Criminal Court* (London, British Institute of International and Comparative Law, 2014).
Zimmermann, A, Tomuschat, C, Oellers Frahm, K and Tams, CJ (eds), *The Statute of the International Court of Justice: A Commentary*, 2nd edn (Oxford, Oxford University Press, 2012).
Zuboff, S, *The Age of Surveillance Capitalism: The Fight for a Human Future at the New Frontier of Power* (London, Profile Books, 2019).

JOURNAL ARTICLES

Aaken, AV, 'Behavioral International Law and Economics' (2014) 55 *Harvard International Law Journal* 421.
Aaken, AV and Broude, T, 'The Psychology of International Law: An Introduction' (2019) 30 *European Journal of International Law* 1225.
Abass, A, 'Proving State Responsibility for Genocide: The ICJ in Bosnia v Serbia and the International Commission of Inquiry for Darfur' (2007) 31 *Fordham International Law Journal* 871.
Ackerman, B, 'The New Separation of Powers' (2000) 113 *Harvard Law Review* 633.
Akande, D and Tzanakopoulos, A, 'The Crime of Aggression in the ICC and State Responsibility' (2017) 58 *Harvard International Law Journal* 33.
Allott, P, 'State Responsibility and the Unmaking of International Law' (1988) 29 *Harvard International Law Journal* 1.
Amoroso, D, 'Moving towards Complicity as a Criterion of Attribution of Private Conducts: Imputation to States of Corporate Abuses in the US Case Law' (2011) 24 *Leiden Journal of International Law* 989.
Aust, HP, 'The UN Human Rights Due Diligence Policy: An Effective Mechanism against Complicity of Peacekeeping Forces?' (2015) 20 *Journal of Conflict and Security Law* 61.

Azaria, D, '"Codification by Interpretation": The International Law Commission as an Interpreter of International Law' (2020) 31 *European Journal of International Law* 171.
Baade, HW, 'Nullity and Avoidance in Public International Law: A Preliminary Survey and a Theoretical Orientation' (1964) 39 *Indiana Law Journal* 497.
Baker, RB 'Customary International Law in the 21st Century: Old Challenges and New Debates' (2010) 21 *European Journal of International Law* 173.
Bantekas, I, 'The Contemporary Law of Superior Responsibility' (1999) 93 *American Journal of International Law* 573.
Barnidge, RP, 'The Due Diligence Principle Under International Law' (2006) 8 *International Community Law Review* 81.
Bassett, TJ 'Cartography and Empire Building in Nineteenth Century West Africa' (1994) 84 *Geographical Review* 316.
Bassiouni, MC, 'A Functional Approach to "General Principles of International Law"' (1990) 11 *Michigan Journal of International Law* 768.
Baumann, R and Stengel, FA, 'Foreign Policy Analysis, Globalisation and Non state Actors: State Centric After All?' (2014) 17 *Journal of International Relations and Devlopment* 489.
Baxter, RR, 'Multilateral Treaties as Evidence of Customary International Law' (1965) 41 *BYIL* 275.
Bederman, DJ, 'Acquiescence, Objection and the Death of Customary International Law' (2010) 21 *Duke Journal of Comparative and International Law* 31.
Bellal, A, Giacca, G and Casey Maslen, S, 'International Law and Armed Non state Actors in Afghanistan' (2011) 93 *International Review of the Red Cross* 47.
Bethlehem, D, 'The Secret Life of International Law' (2012) 1 *Cambridge Journal of Interational and Comparative Law* 23.
Bianchi, A, 'Immunity versus Human Rights: The *Pinochet* case' (1999) 10 *European Journal of International Law* 237.
Bilkova, V, 'Armed Opposition Groups and Shared Responsibility' (2015) 62 *Netherlands International Law Review* 69.
Blatz, CV, 'Accountability and Answerability' (1972) 2 *Journal for the Theory of Social Behaviour* 101.
Bodansky, D and Crook, JR, 'Symposium: The ILC's State Responsibility Articles: Introduction and Overview' (2002) 96 *American Journal of International Law* 773.
Boivin, A, 'Complicity and Beyond: International Law and the Transfer of Small Arms and Light Weapons' (2005) 87 *International Review of the Red Cross* 467.
Bonnitcha, J and McCorquodale, R, 'The Concept of "Due Diligence" in the UN Guiding Principles on Business and Human Rights' (2017) 28 *European Journal of International Law* 899.
Boon, KE, 'Are Control Tests Fit for the Future? The Slippage Problem in Attribution Doctrines' (2014) 15 *Michigan Journal of International Law* 1.
Boutin, B, 'Responsibility of the Netherlands for the Acts of Dutchbat in Nuhanovic and Mustafic: The Continuous Quest for a Tangible Meaning for "Effective Control" in the Context of Peacekeeping' (2012) 25 *Leiden Journal of International Law* 521.
Broude T, 'Behavioral International Law' (2015) 163 *University of Pennsylvania Law Review* 1099.
Cannizzaro, E, 'The Role of Proportionality in the Law of International Countermeasures' (2001) 12 *European Journal of International Law* 889.
Caron, DD, 'The ILC Articles on State Responsibility: The Paradoxical Relationship between Form and Authority' (2002) 96 *American Journal of International Law* 857.
Carron, D, 'When Is a Conflict International? Time for New Control Tests in IHL' (2016) 98 *International Review of the Red Cross* 1019.
Cassese, A, 'The Nicaragua and Tadić Tests Revisited in Light of the ICJ Judgment on Genocide in Bosnia' (2007) 18 *European Journal of International Law* 649.
Charney, JI, 'Universal International Law' (1993) 87 *American Journal of International Law* 529.
Chase, AE, 'Legal Mechanisms of the International Community and the United States Concerning State Sponsorship of Terrorism' (2004) 45 *Virginia Journal of International Law* 41.
Chimni, BS, 'The Articles on State Responsibility and the Guiding Principles of Shared Responsibility: A TWAIL Perspective' (2020) 31 *European Journal of International Law* 1211.
Chinkin, C, 'A Critique of the Public/Private Dimension' (1999) 10 *European Journal of International Law* 387.
Chircop, L, 'A Due Diligence Standard of Attribution in Cyberspace' (2018) 67 *ICLQ* 643.

Chirwa, DM, 'The Doctrine of State Responsibility as a Potential Means of Holding Private Actors Accountable for Human Rights' (2004) 5 *Michigan Journal of International Law* 1.

Christenson, GA, 'Attributing Acts of Omission to the State' (1991) 12 *Michigan Journal of International Law* 312.

Clapham, A, 'Human rights obligations of non state actors in conflict situations' (2006) 88 *International Review of the Red Cross* 491.

Cohen, H and Dudai, R, 'Human Rights Dilemmas in Using Informers to Combat Terrorism: The Israeli–Palestinian Case' (2005) 17 *Terrorism and Political Violence* 229.

Côté Boucher, K, Infantino, F, and Salter, MB, 'Border Security as Practice: An Agenda for Research' (2014) 45 *Security Dialogue* 195.

Crawford, J, 'Revising the Draft Articles on State Responsibility' (1999) 10 *European Journal of International Law* 435.

Crawford, J, Peel, J and Olleson, S, 'The ILC's Articles on Responsibility of States for Internationally Wrongful Acts: Completion of Second Reading' (2001) 12 *European Journal of International Law* 963.

D'Aspremont, J, 'Rebellion and State Responsibility: Wrongdoing by Democratically Elected Insurgents' (2009) 58 *ICLQ* 427.

D'Aspremont, J, Nollkaemper, A, Plakokefalos, I and Ryngaert, C, 'Sharing Responsibility Between Non state Actors and States in International Law: Introduction' (2015) 62 *Netherlands International Law Review* 49.

Dana, JD, Jr 'General and Specific Legal Rules: A Mechanism Design Approach' (2005) 161 *Journal of Institutional and Theoretical Economics* 347.

Dannenbaum, T, 'Killings at Srebrenica, Effective Control, and the Power to Prevent Unlawful Conduct' (2012) 61 *ICLQ* 713.

Dannenbaum, T, 'Translating the Standard of Effective Control into a System of Effective Accountability: How Liability Should be Apportioned for Violations of Human Rights by Member State Troop Contingents Serving as United Nations Peacekeepers' (2010) 51 *Harvard International Law Journal* 113.

Davitti, D, 'On the Meanings of International Investment Law and International Human Rights Law: The Alternative Narrative of Due Diligence' (2012) 12 *Human Rights Law Review* 421.

Dawuni, JJ, 'To "Mother" or not to "Mother": The Representative Roles of Women Judges in Ghana' (2016) 60 *Journal of African Law* 419.

Degan, VD, 'Création et disparition de l'Etat (à la lumière du démembrement de trois fédérations multiethniques en Europe)' (1999) 279 *Recueil des cours* 195.

Dickinson, L, 'Public Law Values in a Privatized World' (2006) 31 *Yale Journal of International Law* 383.

Donnelly, J, 'Cultural Relativism and Universal Human Rights' (1984) 6 *Human Rights Quarterly* 400.

Dufresne, R, 'Reflections and Extrapolation on the ICJ's Approach to Illegal Resource Exploitation in the *Armed Activities* Case' (2008) 40 *International Law and Politics* 171.

Dumberry, P, 'New State Responsibility for Internationally Wrongful Acts by an Insurrectional Movement' (2006) 17 *European Journal of International Law* 605.

Dupuy, P M, 'The International Law of State Responsibility: Revolution or Evolution?' (1989) 11 *Michigan Journal of International Law* 105.

Dupuy, P M, 'Reviewing the Difficulties of Codification: On Ago's Classification of Obligations of Means and Obligations of Result in Relation to State Responsibility' (1999) 10 *European Journal of International Law* 371.

Duruigbo, E, 'Corporate Accountability and Liability for International Human Rights Abuses: Recent Changes and Recurring Challenges' (2008) 6 *Northwestern Journal of Human Rights* 222.

Eastwood, LS, Jr, 'Secession: State Practice and International Law after the Dissolution of the Soviet Union and Yugoslavia' (1993) 3 *Duke Journal of Comparative and International Law* 299.

Ellman, IM, 'Driven from the Tribunal: Judicial Resolution of Internal Church Disputes' (1981) 69 *California Law Review* 1378.

Engel, C, 'General and Specific Rules' (2005) 161 *Journal of Institutional and Theoretical Economics* 350.

Fairey, WF, 'The Helms–Burton Act: The Effect of International Law on Domestic Implementation' (1997) 46 *American University Law Review* 1289.

Feit, M, 'Responsibility of the State under International Law for the Breach of Contract Committed by a State Owned Entity' (2010) 28 *Berkeley Journal of International Law* 142.

Fisher, E, Lange, B, Scotford, E and Carlarne, C, 'Maturity and Methodology: Starting a Debate about Environmental Law Scholarship' (2009) 21 *Journal of Environmental Law* 213.

Fitzpatrick, J, 'Speaking Law to Power: The War Against Terrorism and Human Rights' (2003) 14 *European Journal of International Law* 241.

Foster, SR, 'Collective Action and the Urban Commons' (2011) 87 *Notre Dame Law Review* 57.

Franck, SD, 'Empirically Evaluating Claims about Investment Treaty Arbitration' (2007) 86 *North Carolina Law Review* 1.

Franck, TM, 'On Proportionality of Countermeasures in International Law' (2008) 102 *American Journal of International Law* 715.

Fried, G, 'The Collision of Church and State: A Primer to *Beth Din* Arbitration and the New York Secular Courts' (2004) 31 *Fordham Urban Law Journal* 633.

Fry, JD, 'Coercion, Causation, and the Fictional Elements of Indirect State Responsibility' (2007) 40 *Virginia Journal of International Law* 611.

Gaja, G, 'Interpreting Articles Adopted by the International Law Commission' (2015) 85 *British Yearbook of International Law* 10.

Garciandia, R, 'State Responsibility and Positive Obligations in the European Court of Human Rights: The Contribution of the ICJ in Advancing Towards More Judicial Integration' (2020) 33 *Leiden Journal of International Law* 177.

García Salmones Rovira, M, 'The Politics of Interest in International Law' (2014) 25 *European Journal of International Law* 765.

Gardner, J, 'The Mark of Responsibility' (2003) 23 *OJLS* 157.

Gaubatz, KT and MacArthur, M, 'How International Is "International" Law?' (2001) 22 *Michigan Journal of International Law* 239.

Gibney, M, 'The Downing of MH17: Russian Responsibility?' (2015) 15 *Human Rights Law Review* 169.

Gibney, M, Tomasevski, K and Vedsted Hansen, J, 'Transnational State Responsibility for Violations of Human Rights' (1999) 12 *Harvard Human Rights Journal* 267.

Graefrath, B, 'Complicity in the Law of International Responsibility' (1996) 2 *Revue Belge de Droit International* 371.

Green, L, 'Foreseeability in Negligence Law' (1961) 61 *California Law Review* 1401.

Griebel, J and Plucken, M, 'New Developments Regarding the Rules of Attribution? The International Court of Justice's Decision in *Bosnia* v *Serbia*' (2008) 21 *Leiden Journal of International Law* 601.

Hakimi, M, 'State Bystander Responsibility' (2010) 21 *European Journal of International Law* 341.

Hakimi, M, 'The Work of International Law' (2017) 58 *Harvard International Law Journal* 1.

Hakimi, M, 'Constructing an International Community' (2017) 111 *American Journal of International Law* 317.

Hakimi, M, 'Why Should We Care About International Law?' (2020) 118 *MLR* 1283.

Hakimi, M, 'Making Sense of Customary International Law' (2020) 118 *MLR* 1487.

Hart, HL A, 'The Ascription of Responsibility and Rights' (1949) 49 *Proceedings of the Aristotelian Society* 171.

Hassan, DS, 'The Role of Positivism in the Development of International Law' (2013) 87 *Philippine Law Journal* 778.

Hasselbacher, L, 'State Obligations Regarding Domestic Violence: The European Court of Human Rights, Due Diligence, And International Legal Minimums of Protection' (2010) 8 *Northwestern Journal of Human Rights* 190.

Held, V, 'Morality, care, and international law' (2011) 4 *Ethics and Global Politics* 173.

Helfer, LR and Wuerth, IB, 'Customary International Law: An Instrument Choice Perspective' (2016) 37 *Michigan Journal of International Law* 563.

Hessbreugge, JA, 'The Historical Development of the Doctrines of Attribution and Due Diligence in International Law' (2004) 36 *International Law and Politics* 265.

Heuston, RFV, 'Donoghue v Stevenson in Retrospect' (1957) 20 *MLR* 1.

Higashi, J, 'The Role of Resolutions of the United Nations General Assembly in the Formative Process of International Customary Law' (1982) 25 *Japanese Annual of International Law* 11.

Hmoud, M, 'Are New Principles Really Needed? The Potential of the Established Distinction Between Responsibility for Attacks by Nonstate Actors and the Law of Self defense' (2013) 107 *American Journal of International Law* 576.

Hohfeld, W, 'Some Fundamental Legal Conceptions as Applied in Judicial Reasoning' (1913) 23 *Yale Law Journal* 16.

Hollis, DB, 'Why State Consent Still Matters: Non state Actors, Treaties, and the Changing Sources of International Law' (2005) 23 *Berkeley Journal of International Law* 137.

Hoppe, C, 'Passing the Buck: State Responsibility for Private Military Companies' (2008) 19 *European Journal of International Law* 989.

Howard, J, 'Invoking State Responsibility for Aiding the Commission of International Crimes – Australia, the United States and the Question of East Timor' (2001) 2 *Michigan Journal of International Law* 1.

Hutchinson, T, 'Developing Legal Research Skills: Expanding the Paradigm' (2008) 32 *Melbourne University Law Review* 1065.

Hutchinson, T, 'The Doctrinal Method: Incorporating Interdisciplinary Methods in Reforming the Law' (2015) 3 *Erasmus Law Review* 130.

Jackson, M, 'State Instigation in International Law: A General Principle Transposed' (2019) 30 *European Journal of International Law* 391.

Jackson, M, 'Freeing *Soering*: The ECHR, State Complicity in Torture and Jurisdiction' (2016) 27 *European Journal of International Law* 817.

Jinks, D, 'State Responsibility for the Acts of Private Armed Groups' (2003) 4 *Chicago Journal of International Law* 83.

Jones, OR, 'Implausible Deniability: State Responsibility for the Actions of Private Military Firms' (2009) 24 *Chicago Journal of International Law* 239.

Kadish, SH, 'Complicity, Cause and Blame: A Study in the Interpretation of Doctrine' (1985) 73 *California Law Review* 323.

Kahraman, F, Kalyanpur, N and Newman, AL, 'Domestic Courts, Transnational Law, and International Order' (2020) 26 *European Journal of International Relations* 184.

Kälin, W. 'The Guiding Principles on Internal Displacement – Introduction' (1998) 10 *International Journal of Refugee Law* 557.

Kammerhofer, J, 'Uncertainty in the Formal Sources of International Law: Customary International Law and Some of Its Problems' (2004) 15 *European Journal of International Law* 523.

Kang, AJ, Kittilson, MC, Hoekstra, V and Escobar Lemmon, MC, 'Diverse and Inclusive High Courts: A Global and Intersectional Perspective' (2020) 8 *Politics, Groups, and Identities* 812.

Karavias, M, 'Shared Responsibility and Multinational Enterprises' (2015) 62 *Netherlands International Law Review* 91.

Kelsen, H, 'Recognition in International Law: Theoretical Observations' (1941) 35 *American Journal of International Law* 605.

Kelsen, H, 'The Principle of Sovereign Equality of States as a Basis for International Organization' (1944) 53 *Yale Law Journal* 207.

Koskenniemi, M, 'The Politics of International Law' (1990) 1 *European Journal of International Law* 4.

Lanovoy, V, 'The Use of Force by Non state Actors and the Limits of Attribution of Conduct' (2017) 28 *European Journal of International Law* 563.

Lanovoy, V, 'The Use of Force by Non state Actors and the Limits of Attribution of Conduct: A Rejoinder to Ilias Plakokefalos' (2017) 28 *European Journal of International Law* 595.

Larsen, KM, 'Attribution of Conduct in Peace Operations: The "Ultimate Authority and Control" Test' (2008) 19 *European Journal of International Law* 509.

Lauterpacht, H, 'Recognition of States in International Law' (1944) 53 *Yale Law Journal* 385.

Lillich, RB and Paxman, JM, 'State Responsibility for Injuries to Aliens Occasioned by Terrorist Activities' (1977) 26 *American University Law Review* 217.

Llamzon, AP, 'Jurisdiction and Compliance in Recent Decisions of the International Court of Justice' (2007) 18 *European Journal of International Law* 815.

Lobo De Souza, IM, 'Revisiting the Right of Self defence against Non state Armed Entities' (2015) 53 *Canadian Yearbook of International Law* 202.

Lockwood, C, 'Defining Indefiniteness: Suggested Revisions to the Void for Vagueness Doctrine' (2009) 8 *Cardozo Public Law, Policy and Ethics Journal* 255.

Lowe, V, 'Responsibility for the Conduct of Other States' (2002) 101 *Journal of International Law and Diplomacy* 1.

Macak, K, 'Decoding Article 8 of the International Law Commission's Articles on State Responsibility: Attribution of Cyber Operations by Non state Actors' (2016) 21 *Journal of Conflict and Security Law* 405.

MacCormick, N, 'Sovereignty: Myth and Reality' (1995) 11 *Scottish Affairs* 1.
Mackenzie-Gray Scott, R, 'Complicity and Its Limits in the Law of International Responsibility' (2017) 66 *ICLQ* 1009.
Mackenzie-Gray Scott, R, 'State Responsibility for Complicity in the Internationally Wrongful Acts of Non state Armed Groups' (2019) 24 *Journal of Conflict and Security Law* 373.
Mackenzie-Gray Scott, R, 'Due Diligence as a Secondary Rule of General International Law' (2021) 34 *Leiden Journal of International Law* 343.
Macleod, S, 'Private Security Companies and Shared Responsibility: The Turn to Multistakeholder Standard Setting and Monitoring through Self Regulation "Plus"' (2015) 62 *Netherlands International Law Review* 119.
Mazzeschi, RP, 'The Marginal Role of the Individual in the ILC's Articles on State Responsibility' (2004) 15 *Italian Yearbook of International Law* 39.
McCorquodale, R, 'An Inclusive International Legal System' (2004) 17 *Leiden Journal of International Law* 477.
McCorquodale, R, 'Defining the International Rule of Law: Defying Gravity?' (2016) 65 *ICLQ* 277.
McCorquodale, R and Simons, P, 'Responsibility Beyond Borders: State Responsibility for Extraterritorial Violations by Corporations of International Human Rights Law' (2007) 70 *MLR* 598.
McNair, A, 'The General Principles of Law Recognized by Civilized Nations' (1957) 33 *British Yearbook of International Law* 1.
Meron, T, 'Classification of Armed Conflict in the Former Yugoslavia: Nicaragua's Fallout' (1998) 92 *American Journal of International Law* 236.
Milanovic, M, 'State Responsibility for Genocide' (2006) 17 *European Journal of International Law* 553.
Milanovic, M, 'State Responsibility for Genocide: A Follow up' (2007) 18 *European Journal of International Law* 669.
Milanovic, M, 'State Responsibility for Acts of Non state Actors: A Comment on Griebel and Plucken' (2009) 22 *Leiden Journal of International Law* 307.
Milanovic, M, 'Human Rights Treaties and Foreign Surveillance: Privacy in the Digital Age' (2015) 56 *Harvard International Law Journal* 81.
Milanovic, M, 'The Impact of the ICTY on the Former Yugoslavia: An Anticipatory Post mortem' (2016) 110 *American Journal of International Law* 233.
Milanovic, M, 'Establishing the Facts About Mass Atrocities: Accounting for the Failure of the ICTY to Persuade Target Audiences' (2016) 47 *Georgetown Journal of International Law* 1321.
Milanovic, M, 'Special Rules of Attribution of Conduct in International Law' (2020) 96 *International Law Studies* 295.
Milanovic, M, 'Intelligence Sharing in Multinational Military Operations and Complicity under International Law' (2021) 97 *International Law Studies* 1269.
Milanovic, M and Papic, T, 'As Bad as it Gets: The European Court of Human Rights Behrami and Saramati Decision and General International Law' (2009) 58 *ICLQ* 267.
Milanovic, M and Papic, T, 'Makuchyan and Minasyan v Azerbaijan and Hungary' (2021) 115 *American Journal of International Law* 294.
Morgenthau, HJ, 'Positivism, Functionalism, and International Law' (1940) 34 *American Journal of International Law* 260.
Moynihan, H, 'Aiding and Assisting: The Mental Element Under Article 16 of the International Law Commission's Articles on State Responsibility' (2018) 67 *ICLQ* 455.
Murray, D, 'How International Humanitarian Law Treaties Bind Non state Armed Groups' (2015) 20 *Journal of Conflict and Security Law* 101.
Mylonopoulos, C, 'Contemporary Problems of International Criminal Law' (2015) 3 *Peking University Law Journal* 285.
Nabulsi, J, 'Risky Business: A Model of Sufficient Risk for Anticipatory Self Defence' (2020) 19 *Journal of Military Ethics* 292.
Nickel, JW, 'How Human Rights Generate Duties to Protect and Provide' (1993) 15 *Human Rights Quarterly* 77.
Nielsen, E, 'State Responsibility for Terrorist Groups' (2010) 17 *University of California Davis Journal of International Law and Policy* 151.

Nolan, A, 'Addressing Economic and Social Rights Violations by Non state Actors through the Role of the State: A Comparison of Regional Approaches to the "Obligation to Protect"' (2009) 9 *Human Rights Law Review* 225.

Nollkaemper, A, 'Liability of the Netherlands for Conduct of Dutchbat in Srebrenica' (2011) 9 *Journal of International Criminal Justice* 1143.

Nollkaemper, A and Jacobs, D, 'Shared Responsibility in International Law: A Conceptual Framework' (2013) 34 *Michigan Journal of International Law* 359.

Nolte, G and Aust, HP, 'Equivocal Helpers – Complicit States, Mixed Messages and International Law' (2009) 58 *ICLQ* 1.

Obama, B, 'The President's Role in Advancing Criminal Justice Reform' (2017) 123 *Harvard Law Review* 811.

O'Connor, N, 'Three Connections between Rising Economic Inequality and the Rise of Populism' (2017) 28 *Irish Studies in International Affairs* 29.

Paddeu, FI, 'Use of Force against Non state Actors and the Circumstance Precluding Wrongfulness of Self Defence' (2017) 30 *Leiden Journal of International Law* 93.

Paparinskis, M, 'Investment Treaty Arbitration and the (New) Law of State Responsibility' (2013) 24 *European Journal of International Law* 617.

Paparinskis, M, 'A Case Against Crippling Compensation in International Law of State Responsibility' (2020) 83 *MLR* 1246.

Paparinskis, M, 'The Once and Future Law of State Responsibility' (2020) 114 *American Journal of International Law* 618.

Paparinskis, M, 'Covid 19 Claims and the Law of International Responsibility' (2020) 11 *Journal of International Humanitarian Legal Studies* 311.

Piotrowski, G, 'Où en sommes nous sur le problème de l'agression' (1957) 35 *Revue de droit international* (Sottile) 415.

Pirjola, J, 'Shadows in Paradise – Exploring *Non Refoulement* as an Open Concept' (2008) 19 *International Journal of Refugee Law* 639.

Pisillo Mazzeschi, R, 'The Due Diligence Rule and the Nature of the International Responsibility of States' (1992) 35 *German Yearbook of International Law* 9.

Plakokefalos, I, 'Causation in the Law of State Responsibility and the Problem of Overdetermination: In Search of Clarity' (2015) 26 *European Journal of International Law* 471.

Plakokefalos, I, 'The Use of Force by Non state Actors and the Limits of Attribution of Conduct: A Reply to Vladyslav Lanovoy' (2017) 28 *European Journal of International Law* 587.

Pogge, T, 'Recognized and Violated by International Law: The Human Rights of the Global Poor' (2005) 19 *Leiden Journal of International Law* 717.

Posner, EA, 'Do States Have a Moral Obligation to Obey International Law?' (2003) 55 *Stanford Law Review* 1901.

Quigley, J, 'Complicity in International Law: A New Direction in the Law of State Responsibility' (1987) 57 *British Yearbook of International Law* 77.

Quigley, J, 'The United States Withdrawal from International Court of Justice Jurisdiction in Consular Cases: Reasons and Consequences' (2009) 19 *Duke Journal of Comparative and International Law* 263.

Roberts, A, 'Comparative International Law? The Role of National Courts in Creating and Enforcing International Law' (2011) 60 *ICLQ* 57.

Robinson, I and Nohle, E, 'Proportionality and Precautions in Attack: The Reverberating Effects of Using Explosive Weapons in Populated Areas' (2016) 98 *International Review of the Red Cross* 107.

Robinson, PH and Haque, AA, 'Advantaging Aggressors: Justice & Deterrence in International Law' (2011) 3 *Harvard National Security Journal* 143.

Rosand, E, 'Security Council Resolution 1373, the Counter terrorism Committee, and the Fight against Terrorism' (2003) 97 *American Journal of International Law* 333.

Rosenstock, R, 'The ILC and State Responsibility' (2002) 96 *American Journal of International Law* 792.

Ruys, T, 'Of Arms, Funding and "Non lethal Assistance" – Issues Surrounding Third State Intervention in the Syrian Civil War' (2014) 13 *Chicago Journal of International Law* 13.

Sadat, LN, 'Terrorism and the Rule of Law' (2004) 3 *Washington University Global Studies Law Review* 135.

Sari, A, 'Jurisdiction and International Responsibility in Peace Support Operations: The *Behrami* and *Saramati* Cases' (2008) 8 *Human Rights Law Review* 151.
Schabas, WA, 'State Policy as an Element of International Crimes' (2008) 98 *Journal of Criminal Law and Criminology* 953.
Schachter, O, 'Self help in International Law: US Action in the Iranian Hostages Crisis' (1984) 37 *Journal of International Affairds* 231.
Schauer, F, 'The Political Risks (if any) of Breaking the Law' (2012) 4 *Journal of Legal Analysis* 83.
Schmitt, MN and Watts, S, 'Beyond State Centrism: International Law and Non state Actors in Cyberspace' (2016) 21 *Journal of Conflict and Security Law* 595.
Schwebel, SM, 'The Effect of Resolutions of the UN General Assembly on Customary International Law' (1979) 73 *Proceedings of the ASIL Annual Meeting* 301.
Schwebel, SM, 'The Influence of Bilateral Investment Treaties on Customary International Law' (2004) 98 *Proceedings of the ASIL Annual Meeting* 27.
Schweiger, E, 'The Risks of Remaining Silent: International Law Formation and the EU Silence on Drone Killings' (2015) 1 *Global Affairs* 269.
Scott, GL and Carr, CL, 'Are States Moral Agents?' (1986) 12 *Social Theory and Practice* 75.
Shoemaker, D, 'Attributability, Answerability, and Accountability: Toward a Wider Theory of Moral Responsibility' (2011) 121 *Ethics* 602.
Singer, PW, 'War, Profits, and the Vacuum of Law: Private Military Firms and International Law' (2003) 42 *Columbia Journal of Transnational Law* 521.
Sivakumaran, S, 'Application of the Convention on the Prevention and Punishment of the Crime of Genocide' (2007) 56 *ICLQ* 695.
Sivakumaran, S, 'Command Responsibility in Irregular Groups' (2012) 10 *Journal of International Criminal Justice* 1129.
Sivakumaran, S, 'Beyond States and Non state Actors: The Role of State Empowered Entities in the Making and Shaping of International Law' (2017) 55 *Columbia Journal of Transnational Law* 343.
Sivakumaran, S, 'Techniques in International Law Making: Extrapolation, Analogy, Form and the Emergence of an International Law of Disaster Relief' (2017) 28 *European Journal of International Law* 1097.
Sloane, RD, 'On the Use and Abuse of Necessity in the Law of State Responsibility' (2012) 106 *American Journal of International Law* 447.
Smith, AM, 'Responsibility as Answerability' (2015) 58 *Inquiry* 99.
Smith, JC and Burns, P, 'Donoghue v Stevenson: The Not So Golden Anniversary' (1983) 46 *MLR* 147.
Snyder, DL, 'Civilian Military Contractors on Trial: The Case for Upholding the Amended Exceptional Jurisdiction Clause of the Uniform Code of Military Justice' (2008) 44 *Texas International Law Journal* 65.
Stephan, PB, 'Privatizing International Law' (2011) 97 *Virginia Law Review* 1573.
Tallberg, J and Verhaegen, S, 'The Legitimacy of International Institutions among Rising and Established Powers' (2020) 11 *Gobal Policy* 115.
Talmon, S, 'The Responsibility of Outside Powers for Acts of Secessionist Entities' (2009) 58 *ICLQ* 493.
Talmon, S, 'Determining Customary International Law: The ICJ's Methodology between Induction, Deduction and Assertion' (2015) 26 *European Journal of International Law* 417.
Tams, CJ, 'The Use of Force against Terrorists: A Rejoinder to Federico Sperotto and Kimberley N Trapp' (2010) 20 *European Journal of International Law* 1057.
Tams, CJ, 'The Use of Force against Terrorists' (2009) 20 *European Journal of International Law* 359.
Tarzwell, A, 'In Search of Accountability: Attributing the Conduct of Private Security Contractors to the United States Under the Doctrine of State Responsibility' (2009) 11 *Oregon Review of International Law* 179.
Taylor, S, 'Australian Funded Care and Maintenance of Asylum Seekers in Indonesia and Papua New Guinea: All Care but No Responsibility' (2010) 33 *NSW Law Journal* 337.
Thürer, D, 'The "failed State" and international law' (1999) 81 *International Review of the Red Cross* 731.
Timmermann, WK, 'Incitement in international criminal law' (2006) 88 *International Review of the Red Cross* 823.
Tourme Jouannet, E, 'The International Law of Recognition' (2013) 24 *European Journal of International Law* 667.

Trapp, KN, 'Back to Basics: Necessity, Proportionality, and the Right of Self defence against Non state Terrorist Actors' (2007) 56 *ICLQ* 141.

Trapp, KN, 'The Use of Force against Terrorists: A Reply to Christian J. Tams' (2010) 20 *European Journal of International Law* 1049.

Tsagourias, N, 'Self Defence against Non state Actors: The Interaction between Self Defence as a Primary Rule and Self Defence as a Secondary Rule' (2016) 29 *Leiden Journal of International Law* 801.

Tsagourias, N and Farrell, M, 'Cyber Attribution: Technical and Legal Approaches and Challenges' (2020) 31 *European Journal of International Law* 941.

Tversky, A and Kahneman, D, 'Availability: A Heuristic for Judging Frequency and Probability' (1973) 5 *Cognitive Psychology* 207.

Tzanakopoulos, A, 'The Right to be Free from Economic Coercion' (2015) 4 *Cambridge Journal of International and Comparative Law* 616.

Tzanakopoulos, A and Tams, CJ, 'Introduction: Domestic Courts as Agents of Development of International Law' (2013) 26 *Leiden Journal of International Law* 531.

Tzevelekos, VP, 'Reconstructing the Effective Control Criterion in Extraterritorial Human Rights Breaches: Direct Attribution of Wrongfulness, Due Diligence, and Concurrent Responsibility' (2014) 36 *Michigan Journal of International Law* 129.

Versteeg, R, 'Perspectives on Foreseeability in the Law of Contracts and Torts: The Relationship Between "Intervening Causes" and "Impossibility"' (2011) *Michigan State Law Review* 1497.

Vicuna, FO, 'Francisco V Garcia Amador' (1993) 25 *University of Miami Inter American Law Review* 5.

Vidmar, J, 'Remedial Secession in International Law: Theory and (Lack of) Practice' (2010) 6 *St Anthony's International Review* 37.

Vidmar, J, 'South Sudan and the International Legal Framework Governing the Emergence and Delimitation of New States' (2012) 47 *Texas International Law Journal* 541.

Vidmar, J, 'Territorial Integrity and the Law of Statehood' (2012) 44 *George Washington International Law Review* 101.

Vidmar, J, 'Some Observations on Wrongfulness, Responsibility and Defences in International Law' (2016) 63 *Netherlands International Law Review* 335.

Voigt, C, 'The Role of General Principles in International Law and their Relationship to Treaty Law (2008) 31 *Nordic Journal of Law and Justice* 3.

Webb, P and Garciandia, R, 'State Responsibility for Modern Slavery: Uncovering and Bridging the Gap' (2019) 68 *ICLQ* 539.

Weiss, EB, 'Invoking State Responsibility in the Twenty First Century' (2002) 96 *American Journal of International Law* 799.

Wet, ED, 'The Prohibition of Torture as an International Norm of *jus cogens* and Its Implications for National and Customary Law' (2004) 15 *European Journal of International Law* 97.

Wet, ED, 'Complicity in Violations of Human Rights and Humanitarian Law by Incumbent Governments Through Direct Military Assistance on Request' (2018) 67 *ICLQ* 287.

Wet, ED, 'The Invocation of the Right to Self defence in Response to Armed Attacks Conducted by Armed Groups: Implications for Attribution' (2019) 32 *Leiden Journal of International Law* 91.

White, ND, 'Due Diligence Obligations of Conduct: Developing a Responsibility Regime for PMSCs' (2012) 31 *Criminal Justice Ethics* 233.

Williams, B, 'State Morality in International Relations' (1923) 17 *American Political Science Review* 17.

Wither, JK, 'Outsourcing Warfare: Proxy Forces in Contemporary Armed Conflicts' (2020) 31 *Security and Defence Quarterly* 17.

Yotova, R, 'The Principles of Due Diligence and Prevention in International Environmental Law' (2016) 75 *Cambridge Law Journal* 445.

LEGAL INSTRUMENTS AND DOCUMENTS

African Charter on Human and Peoples' Rights (adopted 27 June 1981, entered into force 21 October 1986) 1520 UNTS 217.

African Union Convention for the Protection and Assistance of Internally Displaced Persons in Africa, Adopted by the Special Summit of the Union Held in Kampala, Uganda, 23 October 2009.

American Convention on Human Rights (adopted 21 November 1969, entered into force 18 July 1978) 1144 UNTS 123.
Articles on Responsibility of States for Internationally Wrongful Acts, adopted by the International Law Commission at its Fifty Third Session (2001), UN Doc A/56/10, 43, UN Doc A/RES/56/83, Annex, UN Doc A/CN.4/L.602/Rev.1, GAOR 56th Session Supp 10, 43.
Articles on the Responsibility of International Organizations, adopted by the International Law Commission at its Sixty Third Session (2011), UN GAOR, 66th session Supp No 10, UN Doc A/66/10.
Belgian Letter to UNSC, UN Doc S/2016/523 (7 June 2016).
Charter of the United Nations (adopted 26 June 1945, entered into force 24 October 1945) 1 UNTS XVI.
Comments and observations of Governments on part one of the draft articles on State responsibility for internationally wrongful acts, A/CN.4/414, YBILC (1988) vol II(1).
Comments and observations of Governments on part one of the draft articles on State responsibility for internationally wrongful acts, A/CN.4/351, Add 1–2 & Add 2/Corr 1, Add 3 & Corr 1, YBILC (1982) vol II(1).
Comments and observations received by Governments, A/CN.4/488 and Add 1–3 (1998).
Comments and observations received from Governments, A/CN.4/492 (1999).
Comments and observations received from Governments, A/CN.4/515 and Add 1–3 (2001).
Comments of Governments on part one of the draft articles on State responsibility for internationally wrongful acts, A/CN.4/342 and Add 1–4, YBILC (1981) vol II(1).
Consolidated Version of the Treaty on European Union [2008] OJ C115/13.
Convention (I) for the Amelioration of the Condition of the Wounded and Sick in Armed Forces in the Field. Geneva, 12 August 1949, Commentary (2016).
Convention Against Torture and Other Cruel, Inhuman or Degrading Treatment or Punishment (adopted 10 December 1984, entered into force 26 June 1987) 1465 UNTS 85.
Convention on the Prevention and Punishment of the Crime of Genocide (adopted 9 December 1948, entered into force 12 January 1951) 78 UNTS 277.
Convention on the Prohibition of the Use, Stockpiling, Production and Transfer or Anti Personnel Mines and on their Destruction (adopted 18 September 1997, entered into force 1 March 1999) 2056 UNTS 211.
Declaration on Principles of International Law Concerning Friendly Relations and Co operation Among States in Accordance with the Charter of the United Nations, UNGA Res 2625 (XXV), UN Doc A/RES/2625 (24 October 1970).
Draft articles on State responsibility: Text adopted by the Drafting Committee: articles 23 27 and title of chapter IV of the draft – reproduced in A/CN.4/SR.1513 and SR.1524, A/CN.4/L.271 and Add 1, YBILC (1978) vol I.
Draft Code of Crimes against the Peace and Security of Mankind, adopted by the International Law Commission at its Forty Eighth Session (1996), A/51/10, YBILC, vol II(2).
Draft Code of Offences Against the Peace and Security of Mankind (1954) UN Doc A/2693.
Drafting Committee: articles 1, 3, 4 (Part One, chapter I), 5, 7, 8, 8 bis, 9, 10, 15, 15 bis and A (chapter II), A/CN.4/L.569, YBILC (1998) vol I.
Eighth Report, State Responsibility, Roberto Ago, A/CN.4/318 and Add 1–4, YBILC (1979) vol II(1).
EU Council Decision 2013/109/CFSP amending Decision 2012/739/CFSP concerning restrictive measures against Syria (28 February 2013).
European Convention on Human Rights (adopted 4 November 1950, entered into force 3 September 1953) 213 UNTS 221.
Federal Securities Act (1933) US.
Fifth Report, International Responsibility, FV Garcia Amador, A/CN.4/125 and Corr 1, YBILC (1960) vol II.
Fifth Report, State Responsibility, Roberto Ago, A/CN.4/291 and Add 1 & 2 and Corr 1, YBILC (1976) vol II(1).
First Report, State Responsibility, James Crawford, A/CN.4/490 and Add 1–7 (1998).
Fourth Report on the Content, Forms and Degrees of International Responsibility, Willem Riphagen, A/CN.4/366 and Add 1 & Add 1/Corr 1, YBILC (1983) vol II(1).
Fourth Report, State Responsibility, FV Garcia Amador, A/CN.4/119, YBILC (1959) vol II.
Fourth Report, State Responsibility, Roberto Ago, A/CN.4/264 and Add 1, YBILC (1972) vol II.
General Comment No 36 (2018) on article 6 of the International Covenant on Civil and Political Rights, on the right to life, CCPR/C/GC/36 (30 October 2018).

German Letter to UNSC, UN Doc S/2015/946 (10 December 2015).
Human Rights Act 1998.
Human Rights Committee, Concluding Observations: Algeria, UN Doc CCPR/C/79/Add.95 (1998).
ILC, First Report, Responsibility of international organizations, UN Doc A/CN.4/532 (26 March 2003).
Interim Report of the Special Representative of the Secretary General on the Issue of Human Rights and Transnational Corporations and Other Business Enterprises (2006) UN Doc E/CN.4/2006/97.
International Convention on the Elimination of All Forms of Racial Discrimination (adopted 21 December 1965, entered into force 4 January 1969) 660 UNTS 195.
International Covenant on Economic, Social and Cultural Rights (adopted 16 December 1966, entered into force 3 January 1976) 993 UNTS 3.
International Covenant on Civil and Political Rights (adopted 16 December 1966, entered into force 23 March 1976) 999 UNTS 171.
International Convention against the Recruitment, Use, Financing and Training of Mercenaries (adopted 4 December 1989, entered into force 20 October 2011), 2163 UNTS 75.
International Law Commission, 1519th Meeting, A/CN.4/307 and Add l and 2 and Add 2/Corr l, YBILC (1978) vol I.
Montevideo Convention on the Rights and Duties of States (signed 26 December 1933, entered into force 26 December 1934) 165 LNTS 19.
Norms on the Responsibilities of Transnational Corporations and Other Business Enterprises with Regard to Human Rights (2003) UN Doc E/CN.4/Sub.2/2003/12/Rev.2.
Observations and comments of Governments on chapters I, II and III of Part I of the draft articles on State responsibility for internationally wrongful acts, A/CN.4/328 and Add 1–4, YBILC (1980) vol II(1).
Optional Protocol to the Convention on the Rights of the Child on the involvement of children in armed conflict (adopted 25 May 2000, entered into force 12 February 2002) A/RES/54/263, 2173 UNTS 222.
Preliminary report on the content, forms and degrees of international responsibility (Part 2 of the draft articles on State responsibility), Willem Riphagen, A/CN.4/330 and Corr 1, 2 (French only) and 3, YBILC (1980) vol II(1).
Report of the ILC to the UNGA on the Work of its Forty Eighth Session (1996), Art 18, 5, UN Doc A/51/10.
Report of the ILC, Seventh Session, 2 May–8 July 1955, UNGA, Tenth Session, Supp 9 (A/2934), YBILC (1955) vol II.
Report of the ILC, Fourteenth Session, 24 April–29 June 1962, UNGA, Seventeenth session, Supp 9 (A/5209), YBILC (1962) vol II.
Report of the ILC, Twenty First Session, 2 June–8 August 1969, UNGA, Twenty Fourth session, Supp 10 (A/7610/Rev.1), YBILC (1969) vol II.
Report of the ILC, Twenty Second Session, 4 May–10 July 1970, UNGA, Twenty Fifth Session, Supp 10 (A/8010/Rev.1), YBILC (1970) vol II.
Report of the ILC, Twenty Fifth Session, 7 May–13 July 1973, UNGA, Twenty Eighth Session, Supp 10 (A/9010/Rev.1), YBILC (1973) vol II.
Report of the ILC, Twenty Sixth Session, 6 May–26 July 1974, UNGA, Twenty Ninth Session, Supp 10 (A/9610/Rev.1), YBILC (1974) vol II(1).
Report of the ILC, Twenty Seventh session, 5 May–25 July 1975, UNGA, Thirtieth Session, Supp 10 (A/10010/Rev.1), YBILC (1975) vol II.
Report of the ILC, Thirtieth Session, 8 May–28 July 1978, UNGA, Thirty Third Session, Supp 10 (A/33/10), YBILC (1978) vol II(2).
Report of the ILC, Thirty First Session, 14 May–3 August 1979, UNGA, Thirty Fourth Session, Supp 10, A/34/10, YBILC (1979) vol II(2).
Report of the ILC, Forty Eighth Session, 6 May–26 July 1996, UNGA, Fifty First Session, Supp 10, A/51/10, YBILC (1996) vol II(2).
Report of the ILC, Forty Ninth session, 12 May–18 July 1997, UNGA, Fifty Second Session, Supp 10 (A/52/10), YBILC (1997) vol II(1).
Report of the ILC, Fiftieth Session, 20 April–12 June 1998 and 27 July–14 August 1998, UNGA, Fifty Third Session, Supp 10 (A/53/10), YBILC (1998) vol II(2).
Report of the ILC, Fifty First Session, 3 May–23 July 1999, UNGA, Fifty Fourth session, Supp 10 (A/54/10), YBILC (1999) vol II(2).

Report of the ILC, Fifty Second Session, 1 May–9 June 2000 and 10 July–18 August 2000, UNGA, Fifty Fifth Session, Supp 10 (A/55/10), YBILC (2000) vol II(2).
Report of the ILC, Fifty Third Session, 23 April–1 June 2001 and 2 July–10 August 2001, UNGA, Fifty Sixth Session, Supp 10 (A56/10), YBILC (2001) vol II(2).
Report on International Responsibility, FV Garcia Amador, A/CN.4/96, YBILC (1956) vol II.
Restatement (Third), *Foreign Relations Law of the United States* (1987) s 711 n 2B.
Rome Statute of the International Criminal Court (adopted 17 July 1998, entered into force 1 July 2002) 2187 UNTS 3.
Second Report, International Responsibility, FV Garcia Amador, A/CN.4/106 (1957).
Second Report, State responsibility, Gaetano Arangio Ruiz, A/CN.4/425 & Corr 1 and Add 1 & Corr 1, YBILC (1989) vol II(1).
Second Report, State Responsibility, James Crawford, A/CN.4/498 and Add.1–4 (1999).
Second Report, State Responsibility, Roberto Ago, A/CN.4/233, YBILC (1970) vol II.
Seventh Report, State Responsibility, Gaetano Arangio Ruiz, A/CN.4/469 and Add 1–2, YBILC (1995) vol II(1).
Seventh Report, State Responsibility, Roberto Ago, A/CN.4/307 and Add 1 & 2 and Corr 1 & 2, YBILC (1978) vol I(1).
Seventh Report, State Responsibility, Willem Riphagen, (A/CN.4/397 and Corr 1 & 2 and Add 1 & Corr 1), YBILC (1986) vol II(1).
Sixth Committee of the UNGA, Eighty Fourth Meeting, UN Doc A/C.6/SR.84 (26 October 1948).
Sixth Report, International Responsibility, FV Garcia Amador, A/CN.4/134 and Add 1, YBILC (1961) vol II.
State Responsibility, 50th Session of the ILC (1998), Agenda Item 2, Comments and observations received by Governments, A/CN.4/488 and Add 1–3.
State Responsibility, 53rd Session of the ILC (2001), Comments and Observations received from Governments, A/CN.4/515 and Add 1–3.
State Responsibility: Titles and texts of draft articles adopted by the Drafting Committee: articles 16 to 26 bis (chapter III), 27 to 28 bis (chapter IV) and 29 to 35 (chapter V) – reproduced in document A/CN.4/SR.2605, para 4, A/CN.4/L.574 [and Corr 1 and 3], YBILC (1999) vol I.
Statement of John Dugard, 2577th Meeting of the ILC, YBILC (1999) vol I.
Statute of the International Court of Justice (adopted 26 June 1945, entered into force 24 October 1945), 59 UNTS 993.
The OECD Guidelines for Multinational Enterprises, *OECD Declaration and Decisions on International Investment and Multinational Enterprises: Basis Texts* (DAFFE/IME, 2000).
Third Report, International Responsibility, FV Garcia Amador, A/CN.4/111, YBILC (1958) vol II.
Third Report, State Responsibility, James Crawford, A/CN.4/507 (2000).
Third Report, State Responsibility, Roberto Ago, A/CN.4/246 and Add 1–3, YBILC (1971) vol II(1).
Treaty on the Non Proliferation of Nuclear Weapons (adopted 1 July 1968, entered into force 5 March 1970) 729 UNTS 161.
UK Ministry of Defence, 'Military Interaction with Private Military and Security Companies', Joint Doctrine Note 1/08 (Development, Concepts and Doctrine Centre).
UK Ministry of Justice, 'Diversity of the judiciary: Legal professions, new appointments and current post holders' (2020 statistics).
UNGA Res 2625 (XXV), UN Doc A/RES/25/2625 (24 October 1970).
UNGA Res 56/83, UN Doc A/RES/56/83 (12 December 2001).
UNGA Res A/RES/21/2222, Treaty on Principles Governing the Activities of States in the Exploration and Use of Outer Space, including the Moon and Other Celestial Bodies.
UNGA, 'Use of mercenaries as a means of violating human rights and impeding the exercise of the right of peoples to self determination' (24 August 2007), Report of the Working Group on the use of mercenaries as a means of violating human rights and impeding the exercise of the right of peoples to self determination, UN Doc A/62/301.
UNGA, 'Use of mercenaries as a means of violating human rights and impeding the exercise of the right of peoples to self determination' (13 September 2006), Report of the Working Group on the use of mercenaries as a means of violating human rights and impeding the exercise of the right of peoples to self determination, UN Doc A/61/341.

UNGA, 74th session, Compilation of decisions of international courts, tribunals and other bodies, A/74/83 (23 April 2019).
UNGA, 71st session, Compilation of decisions of international courts, tribunals and other bodies, A/71/80 (21 April 2016).
UNGA, 68th session, Compilation of decisions of international courts, tribunals and other bodies, A/68/72 (30 April 2013).
UNGA, 62nd session, Compilation of decisions of international courts, tribunals and other bodies, A/62/62 (1 February 2007).
United Nations Convention on the Law of the Sea (signed 10 December 1982, entered into force 16 November 1994) 1833 UNTS 3.
United Nations, Reports of International Arbitral Awards, vol VI (United Nations publication, Sales No 1955.V.3) 160.
United Nations, Reports of International Arbitral Awards, vol VI (United Nations publications, Sales No 1951.V.1), p. 267.
UNSC Res 138 (23 June 1960), UN Doc S/4349.
UNSC Res 681 (20 December 1990), UN Doc S/RES/681.
UNSC Res 1373 (28 September 2001), UN Doc S/RES/1373.
UNYB (2000) vol 54.
Venice Commission, *The Rule of Law Checklist* (Council of Europe, 2016).
Vienna Convention on the Law of Treaties (adopted 23 May 1969, entered into force 27 January 1980) 1155 UNTS 331.

WEBPAGES

Akande, D, 'Outcome of 2016 Elections to the International Law Commission + Trivia Questions' *EJIL: Talk!* (5 November 2016) www.ejiltalk.org/outcome of 2016 elections to the international law commission/.
Akande, D, 'The Importance of Legal Criteria for Statehood: A Response to Jure Vidmar' *EJIL: Talk!* (7 August 2013) www.ejiltalk.org/the importance of legal criteria for statehood a response to jure vidmar/.
Akande, D, 'UK Case on Complicity by UK Intelligence Agencies in Torture Abroad' *EJIL: Talk!* (5 July 2011) www.ejiltalk.org/uk case on complicity by uk intelligence agencies in torture abroad/.
Askin, E, 'Due Diligence Obligation in Times of Crisis: A Reflection by the Example of International Arms Transfers' *EJIL: Talk!* (1 March 2017) www.ejiltalk.org/due diligence obligation in times of crisis a reflection by the example of international arms transfers/.
Associated Press, 'Victims of Colombian Conflict Sue Chiquita Brands' *New York Times* (15 November 2007) www.nytimes.com/2007/11/15/business/worldbusiness/15chiquita.html.
Asteriti, A, 'The Use of Cluster Munitions by Saudi Arabia in Yemen and the Responsibility of the United Kingdom' *EJIL: Talk!* (7 March 2017) www.ejiltalk.org/the use of cluster munitions by saudi arabia in yemen and the responsibility of the united kingdom/.
Badawi, Z, 'Reparations from Former Slave Owning Countries Are Long Overdue' *Financial Times* (28 July 2021) www.ft.com/content/d47cc0e1 4dab 4f35 ada5 a3e653b62131.
Banerjee, A, 'Indian Surgical Strikes: Accelerating the Emergence of Nascent Norms of Use of Force Against Non state Actors' *Cambridge International Law Journal* (6 September 2017) http://cilj.co.uk/2017/09/06/indian surgical strikes accelerating the emergence of nascent norms of use of force against non state actors/.
Borger, J, 'The Austrian Position on Arms Embargo in Syria – Official Document' *The Guardian* (15 May 2013) www.theguardian.com/world/julian borger global security blog/interactive/2013/may/15/austria eu syria arms embargo pdf.
Bremmer, I, 'Big Tech Can See a Future where the Nation State Is no Longer the Master' *The Times* (19 November 2021) www.thetimes.co.uk/article/big tech can see a future where the nation state is no longer the master ndt7cqzxf.
Council on Foreign Relations, Global Conflict Tracker, 'Civil War in Syria' (2 March 2018) www.cfr.org/interactives/global conflict tracker?marker=7#!/conflict/civil war in syria.

Council on Foreign Relations, Global Conflict Tracker, 'Conflict in Ukraine' (2 March 2018) www.cfr.org/interactives/global conflict tracker?marker=7#!/conflict/conflict in ukraine.

Dannenbaum, T, 'A Disappointing End of the Road for the Mothers of Srebrenica Litigation in the Netherlands' *EJIL: Talk!* (23 July 2019) www.ejiltalk.org/a disappointing end of the road for the mothers of srebrenica litigation in the netherlands/.

Dawuni, JJ, 'Disrupting Global Patriarchy: Why Gender Diversity at the International Court of Justice Matters for Africa and the World' *Opinio Juris* (17 November 2020) http://opiniojuris.org/2020/11/17/disrupting global patriarchy why gender diversity at the international court of justice matters for africa and the world/.

Erickson, AS, 'Understanding China's Third Sea Force: The Maritime Militia' Fairbank Center for Chinese Studies, Harvard University (8 September 2017) https://medium.com/fairbank center/understanding chinas third sea force the maritime militia 228a2bfbbedd.

Erickson, AS and Kennedy, CM, 'China's Maritime Militia: What It Is and How to Deal With It *Foreign Affairs* (23 June 2016) www.foreignaffairs.com/articles/china/2016 06 23/chinas maritime militia.

Finlay, L and Payne, C, 'Why International Law Is Failing to Keep Pace with Technology in Preventing Cyber Attacks' *The Conversation* (19 February 2019) https://theconversation.com/why international law is failing to keep pace with technology in preventing cyber attacks 111998.

Fisher, M and Sukumar, K, 'Syria's Tangled Proxy Wars: A Simple Visual Guide' *Vox* (3 November 2015) www.vox.com/world/2015/11/3/9664606/syria war visual guide.

Foer, F, 'What Big Tech Wants Out of the Pandemic' *The Atlantic* (July 2020) www.theatlantic.com/magazine/archive/2020/07/big tech pandemic power grab/612238/.

Goodman, R. 'Human Rights, Deprivation of Life and National Security: Q&A with Christof Heyns and Yuval Shany on General Comment 36' *Just Security* (4 February 2019) www.justsecurity.org/62467/human life national security qa christof heyns yuval shany general comment 36/.

Goodman, R and Lanovoy, V, 'State Responsibility for Assisting Armed Groups: A Legal Risk Analysis' *Just Security* (22 December 2016) www.justsecurity.org/35790/state responsibility aiding assisting armed groups legal risk analysis/.

Gottlieb, P, 'Aristotle on Non contradiction' in EN Zalta (ed), *The Stanford Encyclopedia of Philosophy* (2019) https://plato.stanford.edu/entries/aristotle noncontradiction/.

Green, L and Hamer, D, 'The Legality of the UK/Saudi Arabia Arms Trade: A Case Study' *EJIL: Talk!* (20 July 2017) www.ejiltalk.org/the legality of the uk saudi arabia arms trade a case study/.

Greenman, K, 'The Secret History of Successful Rebellions in the Law of State Responsibility' 6(9) *ESIL Reflection* (25 September 2017) www.esil sedi.eu/sites/default/files/ESIL%20Reflection%20Greenman.pdf.

Guntrip, E, '*Urbaser v Argentina*: The Origins of a Host State Human Rights Counterclaim in ICSID Arbitration?' *EJIL: Talk!* (10 February 2016) www.ejiltalk.org/urbaser v argentina the origins of a host state human rights counterclaim in icsid arbitration/.

Hart, E, 'We're Teaching Robots to Evolve Autonomously – So They Can Adapt to Life Alone on Distant Planets' *The Conversation* (1 February 2021) https://theconversation.com/were teaching robots to evolve autonomously so they can adapt to life alone on distant planets 153159.

Harvard Human Rights Journal, Forum on the International Law Commission's 'Draft Articles on the Expulsion of Aliens', Introduction, http://harvardhrj.com/forum essays/.

Heller, KJ, 'The Seemingly Inexorable March of "Unwilling or Unable" Through the Academy' *Opinio Juris* (6 March 2015) http://opiniojuris.org/2015/03/06/the seemingly inexorable march of unwilling or unable through the academy/.

Hesson, T, '15 Companies that Profit from Border Security' *ABC News* (15 April 2013) http://abcnews.go.com/ABC_Univision/Politics/15 companies profit border security/story?id=18957304.

Human Rights Watch, 'Coercion and Intimidation of Child Soldiers to Participate in Violence' (16 April 2008) https://www.hrw.org/news/2008/04/16/coercion and intimidation child soldiers participate violence.

Hyde, D. and Raffman, D 'Sorites Paradox' in EN Zalta (ed), *The Stanford Encyclopedia of Philosophy* (2018) https://plato.stanford.edu/archives/sum2018/entries/sorites paradox/.

ICJ, Members of the Court past and present (2021) www.icj cij.org/en/all members.

ICRC, Customary IHL Database, Rule 14, https://ihl databases.icrc.org/customary ihl/eng/docs/v1_cha_chapter4_rule14.

ICRC, Customary IHL Database, Rule 15, https://ihl databases.icrc.org/customary ihl/eng/docs/v1_rul_rule15.

Jorritsma, R, 'Emerging Voices: The Role of Attribution Rules Under the Law of State Responsibility in Classifying Situations of Armed Conflict' *Opinio Juris* (17 August 2015) http://opiniojuris.org/2015/08/17/emerging voices the role of attribution rules under the law of state responsibility in classifying situations of armed conflict/.

Kurzweil, R, 'The Accelerating Power of Technology' *TED Talks* (February 2005) www.ted.com/talks/ray_kurzweil_on_how_technology_will_transform_us.

Lane, L, 'The Horizontal Effect of International Human Rights Law' *GroJIL blog* (1 August 2018) https://grojil.org/2018/08/01/the horizontal effect of international human rights law/.

Mackenzie-Gray Scott, R, 'Torture in Libya and Questions of EU Member State Complicity' *EJIL: Talk!* (11 January 2018) www.ejiltalk.org/torture in libya and questions of eu member state complicity/.

McGregor, L, 'Why We Need to Stop Talking About "Killer Robots" and Address the AI Backlash' *EJIL: Talk!* (9 July 2018) www.ejiltalk.org/why we need to stop talking about killer robots and address the ai backlash/.

Milanovic, M. 'Self Defense and Non state Actors: Indeterminacy and the Jus ad Bellum' *EJIL: Talk!* (21 February 2010) www.ejiltalk.org/self defense and non state actors indeterminacy and the jus ad bellum/.

Milanovic, M. 'A Footnote on Secession' *EJIL: Talk!* (26 October 2017) www.ejiltalk.org/a footnote on secession/.

Milanovic, M, 'Attribution, Jurisdiction, Discrimination, Decapitation: A Comment on Makuchyan and Minasyan v Azerbaijan and Hungary' *EJIL: Talk!* (10 July 2020) www.ejiltalk.org/attribution jurisdiction discrimination decapitation a comment on makuchyan and minasyan v azerbaijan and hungary/.

Milanovic, M, 'European Court Finds Russia Assassinated Alexander Litvinenko' *EJIL: Talk!* (23 September 2021) www.ejiltalk.org/european court finds russia assassinated alexander litvinenko/.

Nollkaemper, A, 'The ECtHR Finds Macedonia Responsible in Connection with Torture by the CIA, but on What Basis?' *EJIL: Talk!* (24 December 2012) www.ejiltalk.org/the ecthr finds macedonia responsible in connection with torture by the cia but on what basis/.

Office of the Inspector General, US Department of Justice, 'Review of the Federal Bureau of Prison's Monitoring of Contract Prisons' (August 2016) https://oig.justice.gov/reports/2016/e1606.pdf.

Oltermann, P, 'Germany Agrees to pay Namibia €1.1bn over Historical Herero Nama Genocide' *The Guardian* (28 May 2021) www.theguardian.com/world/2021/may/28/germany agrees to pay namibia 11bn over historical herero nama genocide.

Paddeu, F and Pavlopoulos, N, 'Between Legitimacy and Control: The Taliban's Pursuit of Governmental Status' *Just Security* (7 September 2021) www.justsecurity.org/78051/between legitimacy and control the talibans pursuit of governmental status/.

Pillai, P, 'Representation of Women at the International Law Commission' *Opinio Juris* (7 October 2021) http://opiniojuris.org/2021/10/07/symposium on gender representation representation of women at the international law commission/.

Pillai, P, Women in International Law: A Vanishing Act? *Opinio Juris* (3 December 2018) http://opiniojuris.org/2018/12/03/women in international law a vanishing act/.

Sabbagh, D and Hern, A, 'UK Abandons Contact Tracing App for Apple and Google Model' *The Guardian* (18 June 2020) www.theguardian.com/world/2020/jun/18/uk poised to abandon coronavirus app in favour of apple and google models.

Simone, B, 'Strong States' Noncompliance, Absence, and Self Interest: How Effective Are Treaties Really? *Michigan Journal of International Law Blog* (July 2020) www.mjilonline.org/strong states noncompliance absence and self interest how effective are treaties really/.

Simons, N, 'The Legality Surrounding the US Strikes in Syria' *Opinio Juris* (25 April 2017) http://opiniojuris.org/2017/04/25/the legality surrounding the us strikes in syria/.

Sousa, RD, 'Forget Morality: Five Reasons Why Moral Philosophy is Distracting and Harmful' *Aeon Magazine* (23 July 2021) https://aeon.co/essays/five reasons why moral philosophy is distracting and harmful.

Tinkler, K, 'Rogue Satellites Launched into Outer Space: Legal and Policy Implications' *Just Security* (7 June 2018) www.justsecurity.org/57496/rogue satellites launched outer space legal policy implications/.

Vidmar, J., 'Catalonia: The Way Forward Is Comparative Constitutional Rather than International Legal Argument' *EJIL: Talk!* (24 October 2017) www.ejiltalk.org/catalonia the way forward is comparative constitutional rather than international legal argument/.

Warrell, H and Fildes, N, 'Amazon Strikes Deal with UK Spy Agencies to Host Top secret Material' *Financial Times* (25 October 2021) www.ft.com/content/74782def 1046 4ea5 b796 0802cfb90260.

Webb, P, 'The Weakest Link of the Troika? The Immunity of Heads of Government in Customary International Law' *EJIL: Talk!* (27 October 2021) www.ejiltalk.org/the weakest link of the troika the immunity of heads of government in customary international law/.

Weller, M, 'Secession and Self determination in Western Europe: The Case of Catalonia' *EJIL: Talk!* (18 October 2017) www.ejiltalk.org/secession and self determination in western europe the case of catalonia/.

Yates, SQ, 'Phasing Out Our Use of Private Prisons', US Department of Justice (18 August 2016) www.justice.gov/archives/opa/blog/phasing out our use private prisons.

WORKING PAPERS AND REPORTS

Amnesty International, *Libya's Dark Web of Collusion: Abuses Against Europe Bound Refugees and Migrants* (2017) www.amnesty.org/en/documents/mde19/7561/2017/en/.

Can, O and Seck, SL, 'The Legal Obligations with Respect to Human Rights and Export Credit Agencies' ECA Watch, Halifax Initiative Coalition and ESCR Net, Final Discussion Paper (4 June 2006).

Gómez del Prado, JL, UN Working Group on the Use of Mercenaries, 'Private Military and Security Companies and Challenges to the UN Working Group on the Use of Mercenaries' (2008).

ILA, Study Group on Due Diligence in International Law, First Report (7 March 2014).

ILA, Study Group on Due Diligence in International Law, Second Report (July 2016).

ILA, The Hague Conference, *Non State Actors* (2010), First Report of the Committee – 'Non state Actors in International Law: Aims, Approach and Scope of the Project and Legal Issues'.

Kryvoi, Y, 'Counterclaims in Investor–State Arbitration', LSE Law, Society and Economy Working Papers 8/2011, http://eprints.lse.ac.uk/38469/1/WPS2011 08_Kryvoi.pdf.

Moynihan, H, 'Aiding and Assisting: Challenges in Armed Conflict and Counterterrorism', Chatham House Research Paper (2016).

OECD, '"Indirect Expropriation" and the "Right to Regulate" in International Investment Law', OECD Working Papers on International Investment (OECD Publishing, 2004/04) www.oecd.org/daf/inv/investment policy/WP 2004_4.pdf.

Peters, A and Marxsen, C (eds), *Self defence Against Non state Actors: Impulses from the Max Planck Trialogues on the Law of Peace and War* (MPIL Research Paper Series No 2017 07).

Van Gestel, R, Micklitz, HW and Maduro, MP, 'Methodology in the New Legal World' EUI Working Papers (2012/13) 14, http://cadmus.eui.eu/bitstream/handle/1814/22016/LAW_2012_13_VanGestelMicklitzMaduro.pdf?sequence=1.

Yimer, B, Cisneros, N, Bisiani, L and Donde, R, 'Application of International Investment Agreements by Domestic Courts', Trade Law Clinic (E780), Geneva (10 June 2011).

Index

Introductory Note

References such as '168–69' indicate (not necessarily continuous) discussion of a topic across a range of pages. Wherever possible in the case of topics with many references, these have either been divided into sub-topics or only the most significant discussions of the topic are listed. As the work concerns the overall topic of state responsibility for non-state actors, the use of this term (and certain others which occur constantly throughout the book) as an entry point has been restricted. Information will be found under the corresponding detailed topics.

Milton Keynes UK
Ingram Content Group UK Ltd.
UKHW022310230823
427312UK00006B/145

9 781509 951543